Touring Virginia's and West Virginia's Civil War Sites

ALSO BY CLINT JOHNSON

Touring the Carolinas' Civil War Sites
Civil War Blunders
From Rails to Roads: A History of Perley A. Thomas Car Works and Thomas-Built Buses
Service—None Better: A History of Southern National Bank
7 Days in Winston-Salem (principal writer)
Richmond: A Renaissance City (contributing writer)

OTHER TITLES IN JOHN F. BLAIR'S *TOURING THE BACKROADS™* SERIES

Touring the Shenandoah Valley Backroads by Andrea Sutcliffe
Touring the Backroads of North and South Georgia by Victoria and Frank Logue
Touring the Coastal Georgia Backroads by Nancy Rhyne
Touring the Coastal South Carolina Backroads by Nancy Rhyne
Touring the Middle Tennessee Backroads by Robert Brandt
Touring the East Tennessee Backroads by Carolyn Sakowski
Touring the Western North Carolina Backroads by Carolyn Sakowski
Touring South Carolina's Revolutionary War Sites by Daniel W. Barefoot
Touring North Carolina's Revolutionary War Sites by Daniel W. Barefoot
Touring the Backroads of North Carolina's Upper Coast by Daniel W. Barefoot
Touring the Backroads of North Carolina's Lower Coast by Daniel W. Barefoot

Touring Virginia's and West Virginia's Civil War Sites

Clint Johnson

John F. Blair
Publisher
Winston-Salem,
North Carolina

BOOK DESIGN BY DEBRA LONG HAMPTON
PHOTOGRAPHS BY THE AUTHOR UNLESS OTHERWISE NOTED

The paper in this book meets the guidelines
for permanence and durability of the
Committee on Production Guidelines for
Book Longevity of the Council on Library Resources.

Photographs on front cover clockwise from top left—
Spring House at White Sulphur Springs
Confederate Monument in Arlington National Cemetery
Site of the firing of the last shot at Appomattox
Staunton River Bridge
Belle Grove Plantation
Statue of Stonewall Jackson

Library of Congress Cataloging-in-Publication Data

Johnson, Clint, 1953–
Touring Virginia's and West Virginia's Civil War Sites
p.   cm.
Includes bibliographical references (p.   ) and index.
ISBN 0-89587-184-X (alk. paper)
1. Virginia—History—Civil War, 1861–1865—Battlefields Guidebooks.
2. Virginia—History—Civil War, 1861–1865—Monuments Guidebooks.
3. West Virginia—History—Civil War, 1861–1865—Battlefields Guidebooks.
4. West Virginia—History—Civil War, 1861–1865—Monuments Guidebooks.
5. Historic sites—Virginia Guidebooks.
6. Historic sites—West Virginia Guidebooks.
7. Virginia tours.
8. West Virginia Tours.
E534.J64   1999
973.7'3'09754—dc21   99–41811

To my wife, Barbara,
who has put up with 16 years' worth
of listening to me talk about the war

Contents

Preface   ix
Acknowledgments   xiii

Preface

FOR MANY PEOPLE, Virginia *is* the American Civil War. It is the state where Confederate heroes like Robert E. Lee, Thomas J. "Stonewall" Jackson, and James Ewell Brown Stuart were born, lived, fought, and died. It is where Union generals like U. S. Grant, George McClellan, and Phil Sheridan made, polished, or tarnished their reputations. It is where the first sizable battles (Big Bethel and First Manassas) and the most strategic battles (Fredericksburg, Chancellorsville, and Seven Days) were fought. It is where the first soldiers for both North and South fell dead—the first of more than 620,000 Americans who would die in war between 1861 and 1865. It is where the capital of the Confederacy—the object of four years of Union campaigns—was located. The Old Dominion saw it all—incredible cruelty, amazing bravery, crushing sadness.

Virginia was literally torn apart by the war. Virginians west of the Shenandoah Valley, most of whom did not own slaves, saw no reason why they should leave the Union. So, almost immediately after the Virginia General Assembly voted the state out of the Union, western Virginians voted themselves out of Virginia. Still, they were Virginians, consumed with pride for their home state. When it came time to name the newest Union state, they chose the obvious—West Virginia.

The object of this book is to show travelers in Virginia and West

Virginia how to find places they've read about in history books or, even better, places they've never heard of. The tours visit large and small battlefields, historic houses and buildings, cemeteries, monuments and statues, rivers, and mountains. If something significant happened at a particular site during the war, I have tried to include it.

Of course, I could not include everyone and everything that made the war interesting. There are simply too many generals' graves scattered too widely around Virginia to include all of them, and there were too many skirmishes in both states to track down everything. I've missed some museums, and I mention others without details on their displays because they were not open when I visited. And there is simply a limit on how many words can be printed in one volume.

The book moves counterclockwise around Virginia and West Virginia, starting in Alexandria and ending at Appomattox Court House. The tours should be enjoyed at one's own pace. Though they can be taken independently of one another, they are arranged so that as one ends, the next one starts not too far away.

About the only thing you need to know is that C.R. is an abbreviation for County Road. I suggest always keeping at least half a tank of gas, as some of these tours go to rural areas where gas stations are few and far between. Be careful in these rural areas, as the roads curve often and do not always have yellow lines to keep everyone on their proper side. Be aware that construction can sometimes invalidate the directions in this book. And note that some of the streets you'll be traveling are one-way.

As you take these tours, you'll be struck by how "progress" is swallowing up battlefields and historic houses. Some important homes—like the one where J. E. B. Stuart died—are long gone. Fast-food joints lap at the edge of Manassas. Chantilly, where two generals and hundreds of men died in a violent thunderstorm, has been reduced to an embarrassing little park surrounded by apartments, strip malls, and office buildings. One of the forts that defended Williamsburg is now a curiosity beside a motel swimming pool. The battlefields of the Wilderness, Williamsburg, and Yellow Tavern and the spot where A. P. Hill were killed are now neighborhoods of single-family homes.

Yet in other spots, you expect to see regiments forming in the woods.

You get a sense of what Civil War combat must have been like when you walk the trench lines at North Anna and in Pamplin Park. You can still hear the clang of sabers at Brandy Station, where more than 10,000 men engaged in the war's largest cavalry battle. You'll get chills staring up the slight rise at Malvern Hill, knowing how Confederates were slaughtered as they rushed into the Federal cannons that can still be seen just below the crest. You'll see the difficulties faced by fighting men when visiting battlefields like those at Carnifax Ferry, West Virginia, where a cliff was at the back of the Confederates, and at Droop Mountain, West Virginia, and McDowell, Virginia, where a 10-minute walk over the same ground run by soldiers will leave you gasping for breath.

A person can read about the war, learning the tactics and the names of the regiments and generals, but it is visiting the places where the men and women of the Civil War lived that makes the action come alive. Walk these battlefields softly and quietly. People fought and died here. Both sides are to be honored for that. Explore the military cemeteries and look at the names and ages of the deceased; you'll find boys as young as 16 who died in a war they did not start, but one they felt compelled to fight.

It is the men and boys and women and girls of the war I hope people will think about when they read this book.

Acknowledgments

THE FIRST PEOPLE I MUST THANK are the same ones I thanked in *Touring the Carolinas' Civil War Sites*, the companion volume to this book. Without the local historians who found and transcribed original letters and documents, bought and preserved old books, combed real-estate records, tracked down old maps, and then tramped over battlefields, cemeteries, and other properties, books of this type would not be possible. It is those local historians, some of whom have been dead since right after the war, who put in all the legwork digging up the true history of what happened between 1861 and 1865.

I owe thanks to numerous living historians, people like Martin and Monika Fleming of Tarboro, North Carolina, who helped me on my Carolinas' book and volunteered sources and contacts for this one; Art and Carol Bergeron of Chester, Virginia, who offered tips and contacts; Joe Ferrell of St. Albans, West Virginia, who sent me tips on how to find generals' graves and accompanied me on a West Virginia tour; and Scott Mauger of Hopewell, Virginia, who sent me to graves and corrected some misinformation I had before I published it, and Gerald Fauth for help with finding graves.

Other historians who provided me valuable information include Mary P. Coulling, author of *The Lee Girls* and *Margaret Junkin Preston: A Biography*, who took me and my wife, Barbara, on a personal tour of Lexington; Megan Haley of the Stonewall Jackson House, who shared her extensive research on black people in Rockbridge County before and during the war; Melinda Day, David Lawson, John King, Catherine Bragaw, and Charles Snell, all of Harpers Ferry National Historical Park, who shared the National Park Service's research on the people of the town in 1859; and L. C. Angle of Abingdon, who told me about incidents of that region he has researched for decades.

Barbara Blakey and Keith Gibson of the museum at V.M.I. shared detailed information about artifacts and historic sites on the campus; Don Wood of the Belle Boyd House in Martinsburg, West Virginia, gave a personal tour of the museum; Linda Curtis of the McMechan House in Moorefield, West Virginia, gave a tour of her bed-and-breakfast and discussed its political significance; Phyllis J. Baxter and Don Coleman of the Rich Mountain Foundation in Beverly, West Virginia, gave detailed directions to battlefield points, while Lars Bryne of Philippi, West Virginia, filled in the details; and Robert Conte described The Old White Hotel, now The Greenbriar, at White Sulphur Springs, West Virginia.

Dale Clark, the unofficial mayor of Burning Springs, West Virginia, demonstrated why that lonely little spot was the object of a Confederate raid in 1864; Kitty Futrell of Courtland described the houses still standing after Nat Turner's revolt; Charlie Bill Totten of Saltville, Virginia, gave an overview of that area's importance to both North and South; Shirley Belkowitz of Richmond dug into her archives to find interesting stories about the city's Jews during the war; Chris Calkins of Petersburg, a National Park Service ranger and the author of several books about the final days of the war, told me how to find the unmarked spot where a Confederate general led a suicide charge into the face of the Federals.

Joe Matheson of Camden, South Carolina, alerted me to the location of some interesting graves, just as he did with the Carolinas' book; Angela Ruley, Robert Driver, and Martha Watkins offered some facts about the death of Union general Wesley Merritt at Natural Bridge, Virginia; Ralph Haines of Romney, West Virginia, opened his private museum to show the incredible war-era artifacts he has collected over the years; Lynne C. Lochen of the Norfolk Visitors Bureau filled me in on where to explore in the Hampton Roads area; and Mary Gillam of Rockbridge Baths told me that a house in which Mrs. Lee stayed was still preserved in the town.

There were also librarians in Matthews, Virginia, tourism officials in Norfolk, museum curators in Plymouth, North Carolina—people too numerous to mention who contributed something to this book.

I also want to thank my traveling companions, navigators, and photographers: my wife, Barbara, and my buddies from my Civil War reenactment unit (the 26th North Carolina Regiment), Bill Boyd and Randy Price. A special thanks also goes to Colonel Jeff Stepp of the 26th North Carolina for reading my initial list of sites to include in this book; he added several of which I was unaware.

I want to thank the staff of John F. Blair, Publisher, for continuing to have faith in me and for suggesting that there was room for another Civil War touring book on the shelves.

Finally, I want to thank the National Park Service, the park services of Virginia and West Virginia, the Virginia Civil War Trails organization, the Association for the Preservation of Civil War Sites, the Museum of the Confederacy, the Blue-Gray Educational Foundation, and all the local, state, and national nonprofit associations that work to preserve battlefields, historic buildings, and artifacts. Without the efforts of the dedicated professional and amateur historians who labor in conjunction with such organizations, we would have lost much Civil War history to residential, commercial, and industrial development.

Touring
Virginia's and
West Virginia's
Civil War Sites

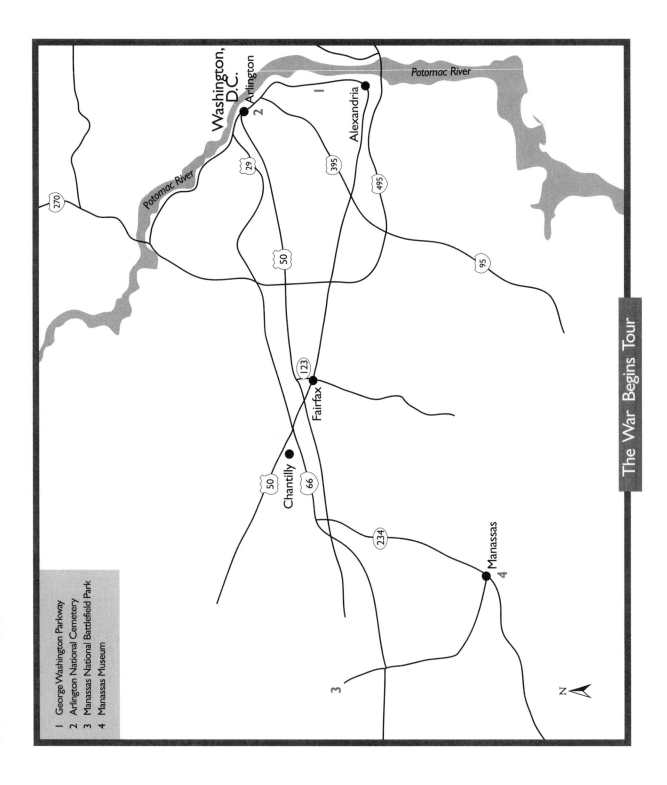

Potomac River

Washington, D.C.
Arlington
Alexandria

Potomac River

270

29

395

495

50

95

123

Fairfax

50

66

Chantilly

234

Manassas

3

4

1

2

N

1   George Washington Parkway
2   Arlington National Cemetery
3   Manassas National Battlefield Park
4   Manassas Museum

The War Begins Tour

The War Begins Tour

THIS TOUR BEGINS with a brief walk in downtown Alexandria. Leave your car at the Ramsay House Visitors Center, located at 221 King Street. Walk west on King for two blocks to South Pitt Street to visit the site of the Marshall House, the hotel where Union colonel Ephraim Elmer Ellsworth was killed after tearing down a Confederate flag. A Holiday Inn now stands here. A marker dedicated to James Jackson, the owner of the Marshall House, is on the wall of the hotel. The marker says that Jackson was "killed by Union soldiers defending his property. History will show he laid down his life in defense of his home and his native soil, his native state, Virginia."

More than any other Southern state, Virginia was caught in the middle of the secession crisis that swept the nation in 1860 and 1861. Both sides needed Virginia. It was the largest state in land area, stretching from the Atlantic Ocean to the Ohio River. It had 1.6 million people, making it the fifth-largest state in the Union. About a third of its population was black; most blacks were slaves, but about 11 percent were free, the highest percentage in the South. While Northern abolitionists propagated the image of the state as one of huge plantations, more than three-fourths of the population owned no slaves, and only a tiny percentage owned more than a few. The state raised tremendous amounts of food in its breadbasket, the Shenandoah Valley. Virginia was a vibrant, growing, progressive state that was proud of being the "mother of presidents."

Though South Carolina's fire-eaters had left the Union after the election of President Abraham Lincoln, Virginia politicians were convinced

This tour starts in downtown Alexandria, the site of one of the first acts of aggression and two of the first deaths of the war, then moves to the boyhood home and church of Robert E. Lee before going to a Union fort. It visits the graves of dozens of famous men in Alexandria cemeteries and Arlington National Cemetery, then proceeds to Fairfax Court House, where partisan ranger John S. Mosby captured a Union general in his bedroom. Next, the tour goes to Chantilly, a deadly battlefield now little more than a postage-stamp-size park surrounded by buildings. It then moves to Manassas National Battlefield, where Stonewall Jackson won his name, before ending in downtown Manassas near the railroad junction that was the Union army's objective at First Manassas in July 1861.

The tour includes walks in Alexandria, Arlington, and Fairfax and approximately 40 miles of driving, most of it in heavy, urban traffic. Count on a full day.

that a solution to the growing sectional conflict could be found. Of course, they had their own self-interest at heart. The North started just north of Virginia. If the newly elected Republican government carried through with its thinly veiled threat to forcibly return the Southern states to the Union, the way to get to those Southerners would be directly through the Old Dominion.

By the end of January 1861, there were already seven states in the Confederacy. Yet when Virginia held a secession convention, the delegates voted overwhelmingly to stay in the Union. In February, the state sponsored a peace conference of Northern and Southern states. Among the issues decided was a compromise aimed at appeasing the states of the Deep South; the compromise would allow slavery in the southern half of the nation all the way to the Pacific Ocean. The United States Congress rejected that idea.

On April 4, 1861, another convention was held, at which Virginia again rejected secession. Then, on April 12, Fort Sumter was fired on by Southern troops, and President Lincoln declared war. He sent a demand for eight regiments of Virginia troops to join the Northern states in invading the rebellious South, to which the governor of Virginia replied, "You have chosen to inaugurate civil war." He refused the demand.

On April 17, livid at Lincoln's call for a Southern state to fight its sisters, Virginia held its third secession vote. This time, the majority of delegates voted to leave the Union.

Within days, warlike actions started in Virginia, just as citizens had feared. The United States arsenal at Harpers Ferry and the United States Naval Yard at Gosport were seized by Virginia militia. Most Virginia-born officers—among them some of the most capable men in the United States Army—resigned, choosing love of state over orders from their nation.

War came early to Alexandria, as might be expected for a Southern city within sight of the White House in Washington. The first bloodshed came on May 24, 1861, just five weeks after Virginia had seceded. On that day, one of the nation's most famous militiamen marched into town.

Colonel Ephraim Elmer Ellsworth was a self-assured 24-year-old who had single-handedly created nationwide enthusiasm for militia drill teams in the years before the war. He had revived a marching club in Chicago, dressed the men in gaudy red-and-blue uniforms patterned after French Algerian troops called Zouaves, and then brought them on a national tour, on which they wowed young men across the North with their precision. In the summer of 1860, he went to Springfield, Illinois, where he studied law under Abraham Lincoln, who was in the midst of a national political campaign.

When the war started, Ellsworth went back to his native New York to recruit a unit of real fighting men who would do more than march in precision formation. He reasoned that the toughest men in New York City were firefighters, since they often battled each other over the honor of fighting fires. He dressed them up in modified Zouave uniforms but retained the red shirts that marked them as firemen.

They may have been good firefighters, but they were terrible soldiers. They prided themselves on being undisciplined and resented Ellsworth's attempts to tame them. And they were not about to let the fact that they were soldiers stand in the way of being firemen. When they heard fire bells in Washington, they rushed out of camp to find the fire.

When the firefighters marched into Alexandria on the morning of May 24, Ellsworth spotted the newly created Confederate flag flying from the Marshall House. He hastened to the roof and tore it down. As Ellsworth was headed back down the stairs, James Jackson shot him at point-blank range with a shotgun. A soldier with Ellsworth then bayoneted Jackson.

Both sides thus had their first martyr before any battle was fought.

Walk one more block on King Street, then turn right on North Asaph Street. Go four blocks and turn left on Oronoco Street. At 607 Oronoco is the home where Robert E. Lee lived as a child and as a teenager, before leaving to attend West Point. The house is now a museum.

Walk one block on Oronoco to Washington Street, turn left, and go four blocks to Christ Church. This simple brick structure, completed in 1773, was the home church of both George Washington and Robert E. Lee.

In the front yard facing Washington Street is a mound with a marker that describes how 34 Confederate soldiers who had died in Union hospitals were disinterred from a nearby Federal cemetery and reinterred in the churchyard.

On the left inside the church is the pew where Lee worshiped. He attended church here from the time he was four until he left for war. He was

Home where Robert E. Lee lived as a child

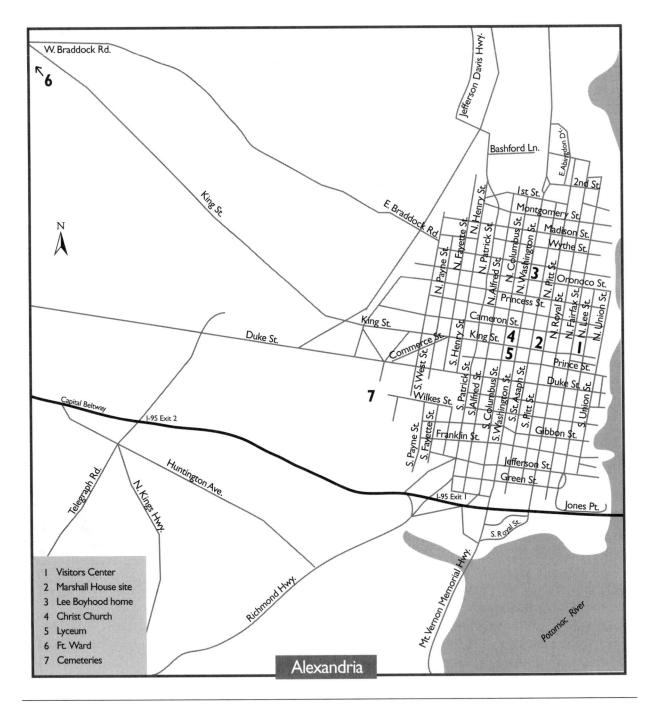

W. Braddock Rd.

↖ 6

Jefferson Davis Hwy.

Bashford Ln.

E. Abingdon D.

2nd St

King St.

E. Braddock Rd.

1st St.

Montgomery St.

Madison St.

Wythe St.

N

N. Henry St.

N. Fayette St.

N. Patrick St.

N. Alfred St.

N. Columbus St.

N. Washington St.

3

Oronoco St.

N. Pitt St.

N. Royal St.

N. Fairfax St.

N. Lee St.

N. Union St.

N. Payne St.

Princess St.

Cameron St.

King St.

Duke St.

King St.

Commerce St.

S. West St.

S. Henry St.

4

5

2

1

Prince St.

Duke St.

S. Union St.

7

Wilkes St.

S. Patrick St.

S. Alfred St.

S. Columbus St.

S. Washington St.

S. St. Asaph St.

S. Pitt St.

Gibbon St.

Capital Beltway

I-95 Exit 2

S. Payne St.

S. Fayette St.

Franklin St.

Jefferson St.

Telegraph Rd.

N. Kings Hwy.

Huntington Ave.

Green St.

I-95 Exit 1

Jones Pt.

S. Royal St.

Richmond Hwy.

Mt. Vernon Memorial Hwy.

Potomac River

1 Visitors Center
2 Marshall House site
3 Lee Boyhood home
4 Christ Church
5 Lyceum
6 Ft. Ward
7 Cemeteries

Alexandria

Christ Church, the home church of both George Washington and Robert E. Lee

married in the church and was confirmed here in 1853, along with two of his daughters. After resigning from the Federal army in April 1861, he came here to pray.

The museum attached to the church has a display that describes how Federal soldiers broke tombstones in the graveyard and stole the original brass marker for the pew where Washington worshiped. The display says that the church is interested in hearing from any descendants of Union soldiers who might have the stolen property.

Continue two blocks to the Lyceum, at 201 South Washington. Outside the building is a statue of a bareheaded Confederate without musket, cap, or cartridge box looking down as if in sorrow. His canteen and haversack are on the wrong side of his body. During the war, the Lyceum served as a Union hospital. Today, it is a museum that offers a good display on the deadly encounter between Jackson and Ellsworth, including a small piece of the flag Ellsworth tore down.

When you leave the museum, walk east on Prince Street for four blocks to Fairfax Street. Turn left. At 107 Fairfax is the Leadbeater Pharmacy, where local legend has Lee picking up some medicine for his wife when he learned of John Brown's raid on Harpers Ferry in 1859. Other sources have

Lee at Arlington when a young army lieutenant named James Ewell Brown Stuart brought orders for him to rush to Harpers Ferry.

Continue north on Fairfax to return to your vehicle at the Ramsay House Visitors Center. Head west on King Street (Va. 7). After about 2.7 miles, turn right on Kenwood Street, following the signs for Fort Ward. Go one block, then turn left on West Braddock Road. The entrance to Fort Ward is about 1 mile west.

Fort Ward was one of the 162 forts and batteries the Federal army threw up to defend Washington from Confederate attack. By the end of the war, more than 1,400 cannons would ring the city. Only once did Confederates attack Washington, and that was at Fort Stevens, a few miles north of the White House.

Today, Fort Ward has a fine museum interpreting the war and the placement of forts around the city.

Retrace your route to King Street, heading back toward Alexandria. After passing the George Washington Masonic Memorial, turn right on South Henry (U.S. 1). Drive four blocks to Wilkes Street and turn right, following the signs for Alexandria National Cemetery.

Before entering the national cemetery, look for the sign for Christ Church Cemetery, located on the right. Park inside the gate and walk back to the cemetery. At the far northern end of the cemetery is the grave of General Samuel Cooper. Already 63 when the war started, Cooper never set foot in the field, though he ranked higher than any other Confederate general, including Lee. Cooper was adjutant general, an administrative post that involved such matters as making sure orders were followed in the field. Historians love him because once the war was over, he turned over all his Confederate records to the United States Army. They can now be researched in the National Archives.

Grave of Samuel Cooper

Cooper was the only Confederate general born in Hackensack, New Jersey.

At the far eastern end of the cemetery, about 30 yards in from the intersection of Wilkes and Hamilton Streets, is the grave of James Murray Mason, the man who almost brought England into the war on the side of the South.

Mason was a 63-year-old United States senator from Virginia when the war started. A firm believer in both slavery and states' rights, he had drafted the Fugitive Slave Act of 1850, which required states to return runaway slaves.

At the outbreak of war, Mason and John Slidell, a former senator from Louisiana, boarded a British ship called the *Trent*, which was to take them, respectively, to England and France. Their mission was to convince those countries to come into the war on the side of the South. On the high seas, a Union captain, supposedly acting without higher orders, stopped the *Trent* and captured Mason and Slidell.

England threatened war over the stopping of a British ship on the Atlantic Ocean. Secretary of State William Seward defused the situation with a clever ploy. While claiming that the United States had the right to capture Confederates, he said the country was actually pleased that England was angry about the boarding of the *Trent*. In Seward's view, that proved that England was now ready to recognize the neutrality of ships on the ocean. It had been England's boarding of American ships on the high seas to impress sailors that had started the War of 1812.

Mason and Slidell were freed, but neither one succeeded in his mission. What they had not counted on was that England and France had stored up huge quantities of cotton in anticipation of a civil war in the United States. Neither country felt the need to deal with the South. Slidell never even came home from France. Mason returned in 1868 after being assured he would not be arrested. He died in 1871.

To the west and nearer Wilkes Street is an obelisk marking the grave of Sydney Lee, Robert's brother and the father of Fitzhugh Lee, the cavalry leader. Sydney served in the Confederate navy but never achieved the fame of his younger brother. He died just a few months before Robert.

After you have visited Christ Church Cemetery, begin your tour of Alexandria National Cemetery.

Just behind the office is an interesting monument, a boulder that lies among the graves of several United States marshals who drowned while pursuing Lincoln assassin John Wilkes Booth.

Also buried in Alexandria National Cemetery are 230 United States Colored Troops. For a while, black soldiers who died in nearby hospitals were buried in the Freedman's Cemetery. That changed when 440 soldiers in a single hospital signed a petition reading, "We are now sharing equally the dangers and hardships in this mighty contest, and should share the same privileges and rights of burial in every way with our fellow soldiers, who only differ from us in color." Soon, black soldiers were allowed to be buried in the military cemetery.

When you are ready to leave the national cemetery, drive out and turn right onto Hamilton Street. Follow the signs to St. Paul's Cemetery, located on the left. Turn in to enjoy a brief walking tour.

The grave of Confederate general Montgomery Dent Corse is along the western back edge of the cemetery. Corse fought the entire war. He was wounded four times, but never seriously.

From Corse's grave, walk toward the other side of the cemetery. Look for a brick-lined mausoleum. To the right of the mausoleum is the grave of Wilmer McLean.

McLean was a farmer and merchant who owned land near Manassas Junction. When the first major battle of the war raged near his property, he decided to move to Appomattox Court House in southwestern Virginia, far from what he considered any strategic targets. But on April 9, 1865, the war caught up to McLean again, when Lee's top aide asked if the two warring armies could use McLean's house as a place to make their peace. A quiet person who wanted to be left alone, McLean thus became famous as the man who owned property near the first major battle and the first of the Confederate surrenders.

In his prize-winning book, *Confederates in the Attic*, Tony Horowitz points out that rangers at Appomattox offer a different perspective of Wilmer McLean. They point out that McLean wasn't a farmer. He was more of an entrepreneur who rented his in-laws' plantation house to the Confederates during First Manassas. Instead of fleeing immediately after the battle, McLean stayed for two years until he realized that he could make more money in Southside Virginia.

McLean speculated in sugar, which he acquired through a brother in Cuba and then sold at inflated prices to the Confederate government. After the war, he went so far as to sell the furniture from the parlor where Lee and Grant met at Appomattox and even charged soldiers a gold coin to visit the room.

From McLean's grave, walk east toward the plot surrounded by an iron fence where a stone angel looks down on the grave of Colonel Julius Adolph de Lagnel, another Confederate born in New Jersey. De Lagnel holds the embarrassing distinction of being one of the first Confederate officers wounded and captured during the war; his position on top of Rich Mountain (now in West Virginia) was overrun on July 11, 1861. He was later exchanged. Though approved as a general by the Confederate Congress, de Lagnel refused the appointment, apparently recognizing that his best contributions would come from behind a desk, rather than in the field. He remained a colonel and served as an ordnance inspector.

Walk to the wall of the cemetery and turn left. After about 50 yards, you will reach the grave of Abraham Myers, the Confederacy's first quartermaster.

A career army officer cited for bravery in Mexico, Myers did his best to feed and clothe the Confederate army, though it was an impossible task. His wife was no help. Mrs. Myers got into a tiff with the pregnant Mrs. Jefferson Davis, calling the first lady "an old squaw"—a reference to Mrs. Davis's dark complexion. Davis stuck up for his wife, refusing to carry through with Myers's nomination for general, as had been suggested by the Confederate Congress. Had Davis proceeded with the nomination, Myers would have been the war's only Jewish general. Instead, he was relieved of command and resigned from the army.

Return to your vehicle and retrace your route to U.S. 1; head north on U.S. 1. Turn right on Prince Street, then go left on Washington, which becomes George Washington Parkway. It is about 7 miles to Arlington National Cemetery; brown signs mark the route.

On the same day that Alexandria was occupied, another Federal force took possession of one of Virginia's most famous houses. The home known as Arlington—located high on a hill looking across the Potomac at the city of Washington—was completed in 1818 by George Washington Parke Custis, the step-grandson of George Washington and a man who felt it his duty to preserve the relics of his famous step-grandfather. Custis was also the father of Mary Anna Randolph Custis Lee, the wife of Robert E. Lee.

The house and the surrounding lands were in poor shape when Lee returned to Arlington upon the death of his father-in-law in 1857. He took a leave of absence from the army for nearly three years to put the house back in good repair and his wife's plantation on firm financial footing. Though

Arlington House

Lee could have sold some of the estate's 200 slaves to pay off its debts, he refused to do so because his father-in-law wished them to be freed within five years of his death. Lee freed all the estate's slaves in 1862, before Lincoln issued the Emancipation Proclamation.

On April 23, 1861, Lee accepted command of Virginia's forces, a fact that did not escape the invading Federals the following month. The Union men felt justified in confiscating the property of a newly minted Confederate general. They moved in on May 24, nine days after Mrs. Lee had vacated Arlington.

Mrs. Lee made a grave mistake before leaving—she did not send the George Washington relics south for safekeeping. Like many people on both sides, she assumed it would be a short war and that the two sides would reach a political settlement. She never imagined that the occupying Federals would damage relics that once belonged to the father of our country.

She was wrong. As soon as the Federals moved into the house, Washington relics began disappearing. Even General Irvin McDowell, who made his headquarters in the house, could not stop the thievery. He finally collected the few remaining relics for safekeeping.

The Lees' slaves apparently bore the Lee and Washington families great respect. It was Selina Gray, one of the Lees' house slaves who stayed at the house after Mrs. Lee left, who badgered General McDowell into putting the remaining artifacts in safe storage.

Upon learning of the destruction of priceless history, Lee wrote his wife, "It is better to make up our minds to a general loss. They cannot take away the remembrance of the spot, and the memories of those that to us rendered it sacred. That will remain to us as long as life will last, and that we can preserve."

For the first three years of the war, the house served as a military headquarters. Then, in the summer of 1864, the estate captured the attention of the Union army's quartermaster, General Montgomery Meigs, a Georgia native who had stayed loyal to the United States. Meigs, who had served under Lee in the United States Army, considered all Southerners who joined the Confederacy to be traitors of the highest order. When he learned that Lincoln was looking for more national cemetery space, he knew just the place. Meigs wanted more than just a place to bury the growing number of Union dead. He wanted revenge on Lee for going against the Union.

When he visited Arlington in August 1864, Meigs became enraged upon learning that gravediggers were burying the soldiers on a distant part of the 1,100-acre estate. He immediately sent to Washington for 21 fresh bodies and personally oversaw their burial in Mrs. Lee's rose garden. He wanted to make sure that the Lee family would never try to reclaim its house.

Ironically, within months of creating what would become the nation's most famous national cemetery, General Meigs was forced to bury his own son in it.

A huge cemetery, Arlington holds the remains of 79 Civil War generals. Ask at the visitor center for the grid locations of those of interest to you; many are in the sections in front of and behind the Lee mansion, as those are the oldest in the cemetery. Some areas, particularly those on hillsides, are off-limits to visitors in order to keep the grass from being damaged. What follows is a bare summary of selected points of interest in this rich place.

The graves of Confederate general Joe Wheeler and Union general John Schofield lie within yards of each other on the hill just south of President John F. Kennedy's grave. Wheeler won the right to be buried among the

Union generals by rejoining the United States Army for the Spanish-American War. Legend says he kept forgetting who he was fighting in Cuba in 1898 and was heard to shout, "Charge those Yankees—I mean Spaniards!"

If you climb the steps to go to the Lee mansion and turn right, you'll see the grave of General George Crook just before the left turn toward the mansion. Crook's tombstone is decorated with a bas-relief of the capture of Geronimo.

Just left of Crook is General John Gibbon, the man who built the Army of the Potomac's only western brigade from Indiana and Wisconsin troops; that brigade came to be known as the "Iron Brigade."

Here, too, is Julius Stahel, a Hungarian who helped recruit immigrants into the Union army.

Not far away is Johnny Clem, the little drummer boy of Shiloh who stayed in the army for decades, long enough to make it to general.

Just in front of the Lee mansion underneath some trees and under an arrow-shaped tombstone lie the remains of Phil Sheridan.

The approach to the front of the house goes past the graves of the Federal soldiers Meigs ordered buried in Mrs. Lee's rose garden.

As for the Lee mansion itself, it is furnished with many of the family's possessions, accumulated over the years after being stored by relatives or returned by Federal soldiers or their descendants. Park rangers report that people occasionally contact them about items that have been in their families for years, such as the home's door knocker, which was returned decades after its theft. That door knocker was very likely the one that J. E. B. Stuart used to alert Lee of trouble at Harpers Ferry in 1859.

Among the home's treasures is a portrait of Mrs. Lee, painted just before she married Robert in the parlor of the house. The mansion also contains a red sofa purchased by Lee when he was superintendent of West Point.

Sad history was made on the second floor. Lee spent nearly 12 hours from midafternoon on April 19, 1861, until the next dawn pacing the master bedroom and pondering if he should end his career with the United States Army. The day before, he had been offered command of the Union army if he would stay loyal to the Federal government. But Lee was of Virginia. In those days, a person's first loyalty was to his or her state. It was that decision that troubled him all night—stay with the Union or go with the state he loved. In the wee hours on April 20, Lee wrote his letter of resignation on a writing desk still on display in the bedroom.

On April 22, he left Arlington for Richmond, where he accepted command of Virginia's forces. He would not see his wife again for more than a year. He would never return to Arlington.

Mrs. Lee left Arlington within three weeks. She returned only once, not long after the war. Her carriage pulled up in front of a house that was by then surrounded by freshly dug graves. Almost a total invalid, Mrs. Lee did not step down from the carriage, as she didn't want to see the inside of her house after four years of occupation.

Near the rose garden is a monument built over the bones of 2,111 unknown Civil War soldiers.

Just beyond that is the grave of Phil Kearny, marked by a large statue of the one-armed general.

Beyond Kearny between Humphreys Drive and Meigs Drive are the graves of a number of Civil War generals, including Abner Doubleday and Benjamin Kelley.

Under a raised tomb just past Kelley's gravesite are the remains of the

Grave of Benjamin Kelley

Grave of Phil Kearny

man who created the cemetery, Quartermaster General Montgomery Meigs.

In front of him is a curious—maybe bizarre—bronze statue. It is that of Lieutenant John Meigs lying dead on the ground.

Lieutenant Meigs was killed outside Dayton, Virginia, in October 1864 while on patrol with two other Union soldiers. The Federals met up with three Confederates, also on patrol. According to the Confederates, Meigs fired first, but a story got started that he was murdered, shot down without warning. In retaliation for his death, more than two dozen farms around Dayton were burned to the ground, a precursor to the burning of hundreds of Shenandoah Valley farms in the fall of 1864. Curiously, the statue shows Meigs's pistol lying at his side, which suggests that the statue maker felt that Meigs died in a fair fight.

Walk back to the Kearny statue and turn right onto Wilson Drive. Follow Wilson until it intersects with Farragut Drive. As you head west on Farragut Drive, you'll pass the graves of hundreds of black sailors and soldiers who were segregated from white Union soldiers even in death.

At the intersection of Farragut Drive and McPherson Drive is a fascinating monument to the Confederate dead.

For years after the war, the descendants of the dead Confederates (mostly

Graves of black troops in Arlington National Cemetery

Statue over the grave of Lt. John Meigs

hospital patients) buried in the cemetery were barred from decorating graves and sometimes even coming in the front gate. But during the Spanish-American War, many Southerners enlisted to help the United States, and the bad feelings started to fade. In 1900, Congress authorized a section of the cemetery to be set aside for the Confederate dead; nearly 500 men were reinterred at this site. In 1906, the United Daughters of the Confederacy (UDC) were granted permission to put up a Confederate monument; President Woodrow Wilson dedicated that monument in 1914.

It was crafted in Rome by Moses Ezekiel, a Virginia Military Institute graduate who had fought at New Market. The monument is a wealth of symbolism. It shows a woman representing the South leaning on a plow and holding a pruning hook to illustrate the Bible verse about beating swords into plowshares and spears into pruning hooks. Below her is the war goddess Minerva holding up a woman who has been wounded. Beside the wounded woman is a shield labeled "The Constitution," symbolizing the South's belief that it was defending the Constitution when it seceded. Numerous soldiers and sailors are depicted on the monument. One is a blacksmith leaving his forge to go off to fight. Another is a teenage boy leaving his clergyman father to do the same.

Two groups of figures show how clever Ezekiel and the UDC were in addressing racial issues. A black woman holds up a baby to be kissed by its father; a toddler clings to her dress, suggesting how trusting the white officer is of her. Nearby is a black dressed in uniform marching with white men; the black man does not appear to be carrying a weapon.

There is one odd thing about the statue—the rifles carried by the soldiers appear to be breechloading weapons, more modern by 50 years than the muskets Ezekiel knew on the battlefield.

Ezekiel is buried at the foot of the statue.

When you are ready to leave the cemetery, return to the congested George Washington Parkway traffic circle. Ease into the traffic and look for the signs for U.S. 50 West to Fairfax, which is located about 15 miles from the circle. Coming into Fairfax, turn left on Va. 123 (Chain Bridge Road), which leads to Old Fairfax Courthouse, the wartime center of the city. Turn left on Main Street, following the signs for 0.5 mile to the Fairfax Courthouse Museum and Visitors Center. The visitor center has a good display on the Battle of Chantilly. It also offers a walking-tour map of the downtown area.

Drive back toward Chain Bridge Road, following the one-way street to a parking lot off North Street. Park and walk west to Chain Bridge Road. Turn left to see the home of Antonia Ford, located at 3977 Chain Bridge. Antonia was one of the many Southern women who were good at being spies but poor at concealing their duties. Just 23 at the start of the war, she used her youth and charm to wheedle information out of Union officers who occupied the town. She also rode around the county mentally mapping Union placements, which she then turned over to partisan ranger John Singleton Mosby, who counted Fairfax County as part of "Mosby's Confederacy," thanks to insiders like Ford. Antonia was arrested and spent many months in prison before she figured out a way to get free—she charmed a Union officer and married him.

Turn around and head north on Chain Bridge to North Street. Located on the corner is the Moore House, at 3950 Chain Bridge. During his raid on the town in March 1863, Mosby came here looking for Sir Percy Wyndham, a British soldier of fortune who sported what must have been the largest mustache in existence, thrusting more than six inches from each side of his face. Wyndham spent most of the war talking about his exploits, rather than doing any of them, but he did threaten to burn nearby Middleburg to the ground if Mosby's raiding did not stop. That threat was bad enough, but he really angered Mosby by calling him a horse thief. Luckily for Wyndham, he was out of town when Mosby came calling.

Turn left and walk west on North Street to the Truro Church. Nestled behind some trees at 10520 Main Street is the Dr. William Gunnell House, now an office building for the church. It was here on the night of March 9, 1863, that Lieutenant John Mosby, the "Gray Ghost" of the Confederacy, woke up General Edwin Stoughton with a slap on his buttocks. The Union general awoke and asked if his men had captured Mosby. Mosby replied, "No, he has caught you." Mosby then slipped out of town with his tiny force of 29 men, who took with them the general, some other officers, and 58 horses. When Lincoln heard of the raid, he remarked that he could make a general with the stroke of a pen, but that he couldn't make new horses. Stoughton was later exchanged, but an embarrassed Union with-

House where John Mosby captured Edwin Stoughton

TOURING VIRGINIA'S AND WEST VIRGINIA'S CIVIL WAR SITES

drew his general's commission and kicked him out of the army for allowing himself to be captured in his own headquarters.

Return east on Main Street to Courthouse Square, where you'll see a marker dedicated to Captain John Quincy Marr of Warrenton, the first Southern soldier to die in the war. The distinction is *Southern*, rather than *Confederate*. Marr was technically a Virginia militiaman not yet sworn in as a Confederate soldier when Union cavalry rushed through town on June 1, 1861. Marr was shot down in a clover field 800 feet from where his monument now stands. Local stories say the ball that killed him did not pierce the skin, so he may have died a bloodless death.

The two cannons on the front lawn of the courthouse are boat howitzers, and the carriages on which they rest are not military issue.

Retrieve your vehicle and head west on North Street, which intersects with Main Street. Drive west for 0.3 mile from this intersection, watching for the walled entrance of the Fairfax Cemetery on the left. Turn into the cemetery.

Once inside, look to the left. In the second row of graves behind a hedge is the marker for Edward S. "Ned" Hurst, one of the original members of Mosby's Rangers. Hurst is credited by one historian with killing 18 Federals with his .44 revolver.

Drive to the cemetery's Confederate Monument and turn right to park. To the left under an arrow-shaped monument is the grave of James Jackson, the owner of the Marshall House in Alexandria and the South's first martyr.

In the rear of the cemetery to the right of the Confederate Monument is the grave of John Ballard, another of Mosby's Rangers. Ballard lost his leg in 1863 but was given an artificial one the following year after the death of its previous owner, Union colonel Ulric Dahlgren. Dahlgren was killed near Richmond. Found on his body were papers spelling out a mission to kill President Jefferson Davis and the Confederate cabinet. Ballard survived the war and raised money for the cemetery's Confederate Monument.

Return to Main Street and turn left. Main runs into U.S. 50; stay west on U.S. 50 for 3.1 miles. After crossing I-66, take the West Ox Road (C.R. 608) exit. Turn left at the light onto West Ox Road, drive 0.5 mile to Monument Drive, and turn right. The 4.5-acre wooded park to the

Monuments at Chantilly Battlefield to Phil Kearny and Isaac Stevens

left is all that has been preserved of the Ox Hill Battlefield, also known as the Chantilly Battlefield. Unfortunately, the demand for office buildings, apartments, and strip malls has all but obliterated the site of the bloody battle fought here on September 1, 1862. Park in the small, roadside lot.

On August 31, Lee trounced Pope at Second Manassas. Conscious that the Union army was demoralized, perhaps near panic, Lee sent Jackson rushing after Pope with the idea that Jackson might be able to cut the Federal army off from Washington, or at least slow it down so the rest of Lee's forces could come up and engage again. Jackson's tired corps found the Federals here and pressed the battle during a tremendous thunderstorm that confused the fighting.

Union general Isaac Stevens fell here, shot through the head. It was also here that the Union's most famous cavalryman, Phil Kearny, a one-armed general who rode with his reins in his teeth so he could grip a pistol, lost his sense of direction and rode into Confederate lines. The stunned Southerners grabbed his reins and begged him to surrender. Instead, he turned his horse and tried to flee. A dozen muskets cracked, and Kearny fell dead. Among those who lamented his death were Confederate generals who had fought with him in Mexico. They openly questioned why he had not just surrendered, since he would have been exchanged within weeks. Likely, Kearny's pride killed him. His body and all his belongings were returned to the Federals under a flag of truce ordered by Lee himself.

Pope, beaten in two battles in three days, was replaced by the smug George McClellan after Chantilly.

Return to your car. Retrace your route to I-66. Drive west on I-66 for 10.5 miles to Exit 47-B, then follow the signs to Manassas National Battlefield. Park at the visitor center.

Two major battles took place here. First Manassas was fought on land about one-quarter the size of Second Manassas, which came just 13 months later.

The tiny professional army that existed in early 1861 split down the middle at the outbreak of war, many of the most talented officers joining the Confederacy. The professional soldiers who stayed with the Union urged Lincoln to go slowly in building an army out of amateurs. But Lincoln was impatient. He appointed Irvin McDowell, a staff officer with little field experience, as commander of all Union forces, then told him to go into the field and whip the Confederates. When McDowell protested that his men were green, Lincoln replied, "So are the Confederates. You are all green together."

After training his troops for barely two months, McDowell took his 15,000-man army to Manassas Junction, a railhead 30 miles southwest of Washington that was protected by a Confederate force. McDowell's plan was simple—demonstrate on the Confederate right with a small force, then take the bulk of the army, splash across Bull Run farther to the west, and smash into whatever Confederates were around to fight. The Federals hoped to cross the creek and then turn east, their whole army facing the Confederate flank.

It didn't work that way. McDowell spent nearly four days on a march that should have taken no more than a single day, as his undisciplined men stopped all along the way to pick berries. Many of them were from urban New England and were unused to walking significant distances. By the time the Federals got to the battlefield, the Confederates were ready. Or at least they thought they were.

McDowell's plan actually worked for a while. On July 21, the Confederates were fighting a small skirmish at a bridge over Bull Run when Captain Porter Alexander noticed a glint of light to the west. Focusing his spyglass in that direction, he saw sunlight bouncing off the highly polished barrel of a Union cannon. Alexander, who had helped invent a system of signaling with flags, urgently used his new "wig-wag" system to warn his commander, General Pierre Gustave Toutant Beauregard, that their left flank was in danger.

Colonel Nathan "Shanks" Evans—whose nickname dated to his West Point days and referred to his thin legs—rushed part of his Confederate command to the trouble spot. Without waiting for orders, he sent a few hundred men on a charge against the entire 15,000-man Union army. The audacious attack so surprised the Federals that they slowed until realizing how few Rebels they faced.

Evans's attack bought time for Confederate general Barnard Bee to arrive with his force. Bee and Shanks then fought a withdrawing action up Henry House Hill.

Bee could see some Virginia regiments commanded by an officer of his acquaintance at the crest of the hill. He rode up to that officer and asked what he should do.

"Give them cold steel," came the reply.

Bee rushed back down the hill and pointed to the Virginians. "There stands Jackson like a stone wall! Rally round the Virginians!" he cried, giving his outnumbered men some comfort that reinforcements were at least in sight.

Some historians have questioned whether Bee was praising or cursing Thomas Jonathan Jackson for staying on top of the hill instead of rushing down to help. On one hand, Jackson could see that Bee needed assistance. On the other hand, the best place to defend an attack is from high ground. Bee never had a chance to explain his comment. He was mortally wounded not long after giving Jackson his famous nickname.

The overwhelming number of Federals soon pushed the troops of Evans and Bee to the base of Henry House Hill. For two hours, the battle lines surged up and down the hill. The Federals under heaviest attack were the New York Fire Zouaves, the thugs in red shirts who liked to fight fires and their fellow soldiers. To the satisfaction of the rest of the Yankees, many of

Manassas Bridge at Bull Run

TOURING VIRGINIA'S AND WEST VIRGINIA'S CIVIL WAR SITES

the New Yorkers turned and ran when faced with real combat.

Sometimes, the two sides could not tell each other apart. At this first battle, many Confederate troops wore blue uniforms, while many Union troops wore gray—whatever color they had worn in their militia days. And it was no help looking at flags. In a slight wind, the new Confederate flag, the Stars and Bars, could easily be mistaken for the United States flag.

It was a mistake in identifying sides that helped lose the battle for the Union. Late in the day, a Union artillery battery worked its way near the Confederate line. It was preparing to shoot up the line when its commander saw what he thought was a Confederate regiment coming out of the woods. Just as the cannons were turned to face the threat, a superior officer rode up to demand that the guns be turned back—the Federal gunners, he said, were about to fire on their artillery support! The battery's commander was sure the onrushing men were Confederates, but his commander refused to rescind his order. Glumly, the battery commander watched as the Confederate regiment fired, killing and wounding men and artillery horses. Thanks to the confusion over uniform colors, his superior officer had been dead wrong.

The Federal cannons are displayed in front of the visitor center today.

The end of the battle came when Confederate reinforcements from the Shenandoah Valley—the first men in military history to be moved by train to a battle site—arrived on the field to attack the Union flank. What had once been an orderly retreat turned into a scramble back to Washington.

Jefferson Davis, who always fancied himself more skilled as a battle leader than as a president, rode to the field and actually joined in the pursuit of the Federals.

Stonewall Jackson asked Davis's permission to attack Washington and end the war with this one battle. Davis refused, saying that the men were tired. The grumbling Jackson wondered if he would ever get such a chance again.

The visitor center offers a map of a 1-mile walking trail around the battlefield. Most sites are within easy view of the center.

The Henry House is about 300 yards north of the visitor center. It was here that Mrs. Henry refused to leave her sickbed—a fatal move on her part, as she was later killed by Union artillery.

Henry House

The high ground about 1 mile farther north is Matthews Hill, where the Confederates under Shanks Evans first tried to check the Federal advance across Bull Run. Evans's insistence on attacking the superior Federal force—which served to give the Confederates the time they needed to gather strength—was fueled in part by whiskey he had an aide carry around in a small cask.

A highly stylized statue of Jackson (which makes him look like a body-builder) gazes down on the valley about 100 yards east of the visitor center. It was Jackson's holding of Henry House Hill at this spot that gave the Confederate reinforcements from the Shenandoah Valley time to arrive.

Near Stonewall's statue lies what is left of the first Civil War battlefield monument ever erected. It was put up just six weeks after the battle in memory of Colonel Francis Bartow of Georgia. The men of Bartow's Confederate regiment chose a stone obelisk to mark the site of his mortal wounding, but it disappeared before the war was over. All that is left is the stone base. A more modern marker was erected in 1936; the original base lies a few feet away.

Virtually the same ground was contested just over a year later on August 29 and 30, 1862, when a new Union army under General John Pope formed lines near Henry House Hill. Pope, labeled a "miscreant" by Lee because of his orders encouraging his men to forage food from civilians and burn any houses suspected of harboring guerrillas, would not stay in command long. Lee and his army, enraged by Pope's casual cruelty to Virginia civilians, would crush him on this battlefield.

The stage was set when Stonewall Jackson stole a march around Pope's right flank just north of Culpeper. Jackson headed to Manassas Junction, where he captured the Federal food supply base. With Jackson's army now in his rear, Pope had to turn his army and rush to Manassas. The battle could have been a disaster for Jackson, since the rest of the Confederate army had not yet caught up with him. But the Federals sent only piecemeal assaults against Jackson. The two forces first met at Groveton, 2 miles northwest of the visitor center, in the late afternoon on August 28.

The next day, Second Manassas began in earnest when Pope started sending his troops westward against Jackson's Confederates, who were lying behind a conveniently located unfinished railroad embankment that made a perfect defensive earthworks. On the far Federal left, a force under General Fitz John Porter started to move westward under confusing orders from Pope. But Porter stopped in his tracks and did not attack when he realized that Confederate general James Longstreet had arrived on the field.

The next morning, Pope misinterpreted what he saw right in front of him when he ordered a frontal assault into a strong Confederate line. Porter drew the assignment. Union troops got so close to the Confederates that eyewitnesses reported that the battle flags of both sides seemed to be flapping together. When the Confederates started to run low on ammunition, Louisiana troops picked up rocks in the belief that if they couldn't shoot Yankees, they could at least bean them. Surprised Federals started throwing rocks back, creating a bizarre game of dodge rock.

Longstreet's men, whom Pope was convinced did not exist, poured into the Federal flank near the end of the day on August 30. Whole Union regiments seemed to melt away in the Confederate fire. The Federals fell back to Henry House Hill, where they put up a last-ditch defense that saved their army from total destruction.

The next day, the rear guard of the army would face Jackson one more time, at Chantilly.

The battle around Groveton on the Brawner Farm served as the baptism of fire for a brigade of Union soldiers from Wisconsin and Indiana, which were considered frontier states in 1861. These troops, dressed in long blue frock coats and tall black hats, would first carry the nickname "Black Hat Brigade" but would later become known as the "Iron Brigade."

How quickly the war became terrible can be illustrated by looking at the two battles here. At First Manassas, there were 5,000 casualties on both sides. One year later, there were 21,000 killed, wounded, and missing on both sides.

To see the sites associated with Second Manassas, leave the visitor center in your car and turn right on Va. 234. Drive 0.9 mile to the intersection with U.S. 29. Turn right and go about 1 mile to the replica of the Stone Bridge, a prominent landmark in both battles, which is located on the left side of the road. It was here that First Manassas started when Evans's men fought to hold the bridge. And it was here that Second Manassas ended when Pope's Union army crossed Bull Run on its retreat.

Return to Va. 234, turn right, and park at the Stone House at this corner. Pope made his headquarters just west of this home. The Stone House was used as a field hospital during both battles. Many people are said to have encountered the ghosts of wounded Federals here.

Continue north on Va. 234. You will soon pass Dogan Ridge; Federal units massed to attack Jackson's forces west of this position. Just east of here is Matthews Hill, where fighting flared during First Manassas.

At Sudley, just under 2 miles from U.S. 29, turn left off Va. 234 on to Featherbed Lane (C.R. 622). It was here at Sudley Ford that the Federals splashed across Bull Run during First Manassas.

Continue about 1.3 miles to the parking lot for the Unfinished Railroad. Walking paths beside the railroad show how well fortified the Confederate battle line was. The area where the rock throwing took place is marked.

Return to the parking lot and cross to the Deep Cut portion of the railroad embankment, the focal point of Porter's attack.

Continue down Featherbed Lane 0.8 mile to the intersection with U.S. 29 at Groveton. The Dogan House, where Mosby ate breakfast after capturing his Union general, is located here. On the opposite side of Featherbed Lane is the Groveton Cemetery, where 260 Confederates lay. The cemetery's entrance is off U.S. 29.

About 0.5 west of the cemetery is the Brawner Farm, where the Black Hats first came under fire. It was also in that general area that Confederate general Richard Ewell's kneecap was shattered by a Union bullet, requiring the amputation of his leg. Ewell later took command of Jackson's corps after Stonewall's death. But he would never be the general Jackson was.

At Groveton, turn left on the busy U.S. 29, then turn right almost immediately onto a National Park Service road that leads to monuments to the Fifth New York Regiment and the 10th New York Regiment. Some of the worst killing of Second Manassas took place here. Texans under Longstreet bore down on the New Yorkers, all of whom were Zouaves, dressed in red pantaloons, short blue coats, and white turbans. The two New York regiments had not even been warned that Longstreet was in their front and were not expecting an attack. The 10th's skirmishers encountered the Texans and fell back, right in front of the forming Fifth, whose men refused to fire until their friends were clear. That was a mistake, as the Confederates poured fire into both regiments. In 10 minutes, 120 of the 500 men of the Fifth New York were killed. Thirty minutes later, the regiment numbered about 60 men.

Continue east on U.S. 29 for 0.9 mile, then turn right on Va. 234. Drive 0.9 miles to the signs for a turnoff on the right leading to Chinn Ridge, where the Federals finally stopped Longstreet's attack. It was to Chinn Ridge that the survivors of the Fifth and 10th New York Regiments staggered.

Get back on Va. 234 and continue about 4 miles into Old Town Manassas, where the road becomes Grant Avenue. After passing under a railroad, turn left on Prince William Street. On the right is the Manassas Museum, where this tour ends. The museum offers displays about the battle and details on the city's resurrection after the war, which was mainly accomplished by a Union officer who moved to the town and became its greatest benefactor.

The Federal storehouses that Jackson captured in August 1862 were located along the railroad just across the street from the museum.

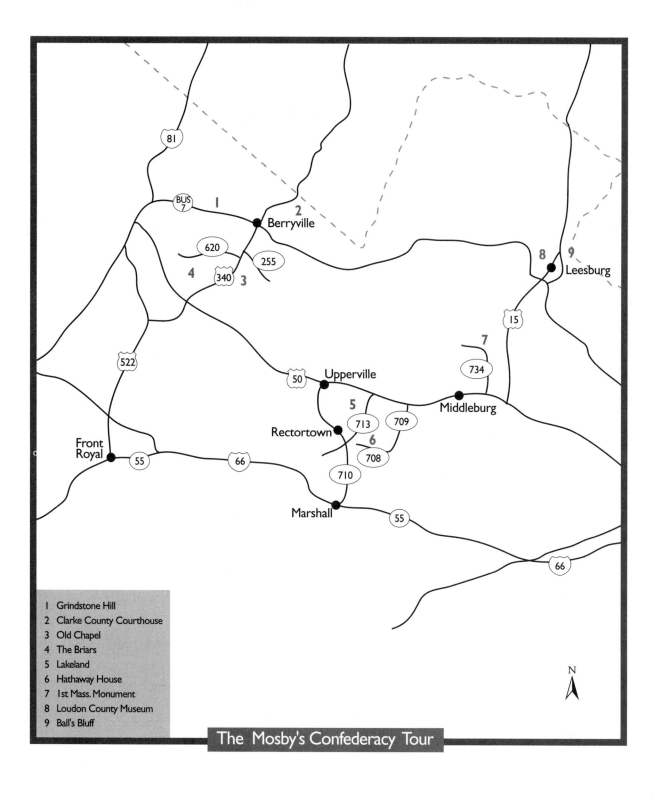

1 Grindstone Hill
2 Clarke County Courthouse
3 Old Chapel
4 The Briars
5 Lakeland
6 Hathaway House
7 1st Mass. Monument
8 Loudon County Museum
9 Ball's Bluff

The Mosby's Confederacy Tour

N

The Mosby's Confederacy Tour

This tour starts outside Berryville at the site where Union soldiers were hanged in revenge for the execution of seven of Mosby's men. It then proceeds to Front Royal, the town where Confederate spy Belle Boyd made a name for herself. The tour moves through the heart of Mosby's Confederacy, passing several houses where Mosby sought refuge and visiting a simple turn in a road where scores of Union soldiers met their maker. Next, it moves to the battlefield at Ball's Bluff, where a glory-seeking United States senator led his men into a deadly trap in November 1861.

The tour is approximately 90 miles long and includes stops at several museums. Count on a full day.

THIS TOUR COVERS many of the haunts of Colonel John Singleton Mosby, the "Gray Ghost," who won fame with his independent command, the 43rd Virginia Cavalry Battalion. Mosby was a partisan ranger, a soldier not attached to any army, whose job it was to operate behind Union lines to disrupt communications, steal supplies, and find out what the enemy intended to do. Mosby was so good at this kind of guerrilla fighting that Grant ordered his immediate execution, should he ever be captured. He never was.

The tour starts at the intersection of Va. 7 and Va. 7 Business west of Berryville. Go 0.9 mile east toward town on Va. 7 Business; drive slowly, looking for a rock-wall entrance to an unmarked dirt road. Pull to the shoulder.

To the left is Grindstone Hill, where in late 1864 Mosby ordered the execution of seven Federal soldiers—three by hanging and four by shooting—in retaliation for the execution of seven of his own men at Front Royal in September of that year. Before they reached this spot, two of the Federals escaped into a dark, driving rainstorm. Three Federals were hanged and two were shot here; the two who were shot survived their wounds. The hanging tree, which was located beside the road, was later cut up for souvenirs.

Continue 0.8 mile to downtown Berryville. Cross through a light at U.S. 340. At the second light, turn left on Church Street. Drive one block to the courthouse. A museum with its own entrance is located on the northern side of the courthouse.

The Clarke County Courthouse has a unique statue of a sad Confederate soldier with a handlebar mustache and his hat in his hand. He carries no musket, cartridge box, or cap box, and his haversack and canteen are on the wrong side of his body. Perhaps he represents a soldier who has surrendered and has just reached his home. The inscription reads, "Fortune denied them success, but they achieved imperishable fame."

Grave of Major John Esten Cooke

Retrace your route back to U.S. 340 and turn left or south on to U.S. 340. After 3.2 miles, turn left on Va. 255 and pull immediately into the parking lot of the Old Chapel. This chapel was established in 1790. In the rear of its cemetery under a large cross are the remains of Major John Esten Cooke, probably the South's most famous writer immediately before and after the war. Cooke had a regular column in the *Southern Illustrated News* and was the author of two novels and several nonfiction books, including biographies of Jackson and Lee. He popularized the phrase "wearing of the gray," which became the title of a favorite postwar song in the South. He served on the staff of J. E. B. Stuart, who was married to Cooke's cousin, Flora.

Get back on U.S. 340 and continue south about 1 mile to C.R. 620. Turn right. It is 3 miles to a large house on the left. This is The Briars, built in 1819. Cooke lived here from 1869 until his death in 1886 from typhoid fever.

The Briars

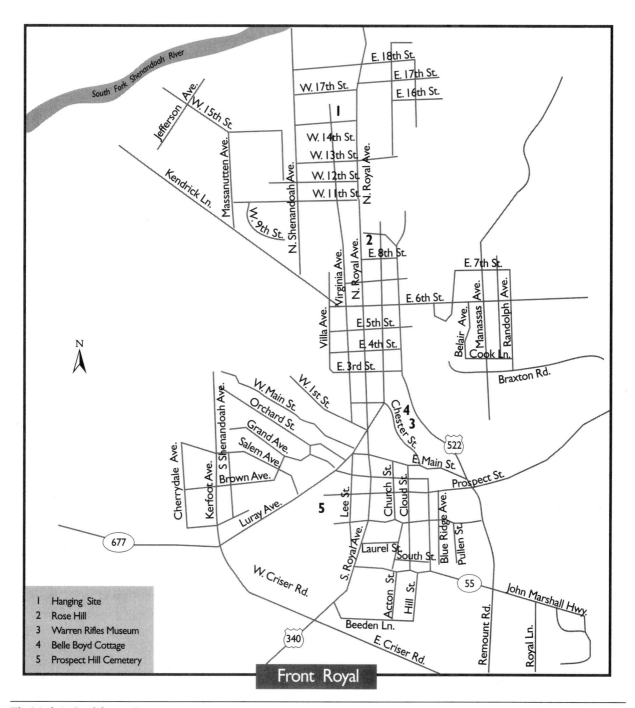

South Fork Shenandoah River

E. 18th St.
E. 17th St.
W. 17th St.
E. 16th St.

Jefferson Ave.
W. 15th St.
Massanutten Ave.
N. Shenandoah Ave.

W. 14th St.
W. 13th St.
N. Royal Ave.
W. 12th St.
W. 11th St.

Kendrick Ln.

W. 9th St.

1

Virginia Ave.
N. Royal Ave.
2
E. 8th St.

E. 7th St.
E. 6th St.
Belair Ave.
Manassas Ave.
Randolph Ave.

Villa Ave.
E. 5th St.
E. 4th St.
Cook Ln.

E. 3rd St.
Braxton Rd.

N

W. Main St.
W. 1st St.

Orchard St.
Chester St.
4
3

Cherrydale Ave.
Grand Ave.
522
Salem Ave.
E. Main St.
Kerfoot Ave.
S Shenandoah Ave.
Brown Ave.
Prospect St.
Church St.
Cloud St.

Luray Ave.
5
Lee St.
Blue Ridge Ave.
Pullen St.

677
S. Royal Ave.
Laurel St.
South St.

W. Criser Rd.
Acton St.
Hill St.
55
John Marshall Hwy.

340
Beeden Ln.
E. Criser Rd.
Remount Rd.
Royal Ln.

1   Hanging Site
2   Rose Hill
3   Warren Rifles Museum
4   Belle Boyd Cottage
5   Prospect Hill Cemetery

Front Royal

The Mosby's Confederacy Tour

31

Return to U.S. 340 and continue south; the road, which joins U.S. 522, leads to Front Royal in 16 miles. As you cross the Shenandoah River outside town, note that this is the area to which Union forces fled after Jackson drove them out in May 1862. You will also pass a historical marker describing the execution of some of Mosby's men in Front Royal.

Continue into town; the road you are traveling is now called North Shenandoah Avenue. Turn left at the light on to 14th Street. As the road curves to the right in two blocks, look to the left behind a motel. Here, on a hill now occupied by a bed-and-breakfast, was the hanging site of two of Mosby's men.

Continue south on the road now named Royal Avenue. Located on the right at Eighth Street is Rose Hill, a house from which a teenage girl watched the execution of a 17-year-old classmate by Federals.

Continue on Royal Avenue to Main Street. Turn left on Main and follow the signs to the town's visitor center. This is the best place to pick up information and ask questions about historic Front Royal.

Front Royal was one of those unfortunate towns that was often touched by the war because of its location; it sits at the northern end of the Shenandoah Valley not far from Thoroughfare Gap, an east-west passage.

This is also the town that gave birth to the legendary tactical skills of Stonewall Jackson. It was in Front Royal that Jackson launched his famous Shenandoah Valley Campaign on May 23, 1862. (Some historians contend that the campaign actually started on May 8 in the Allegheny Mountains with Jackson's victory at McDowell, Virginia.)

The little fight in Front Royal is interesting for two reasons. First, there is evidence (and some legend) that the fight went well for Jackson because he was operating with information given him by a teenage female spy. Second, it is interesting because the First Maryland Regiment did most of the fighting—on both sides! The First Maryland, U.S., held the town. The First Maryland, C.S.A., had been about to mutiny because its teenage troops wanted to join the cavalry. However, the young men rushed to the front of the column upon learning they would be fighting their neighbors who had stayed with the Union.

Belle Boyd was just 18 years old when she became a Confederate heroine. She had been sent to Front Royal from Martinsburg (now in West Virginia) to live with relatives after Federal officers in her hometown suspected she was spying on them. The change of scenery merely gave her a new cover.

Her uncle owned the hotel in Front Royal, which was frequented by Union officers. One night in mid-May 1862, she saw General James Shields and his staff go into the hotel parlor. Belle went to the second-floor room above the parlor and lay down in a closet, her ear pressed against either a knothole or a pre-drilled hole (the stories differ). She quickly learned that most of the Union garrison in town would be sent to help General George McClellan, who was then driving up the Peninsula toward Richmond.

That information was important. The town was suddenly wide-open to Confederate capture. Belle wrote down the information in a coded message and rode away on a 15-mile mission to find Jackson's cavalry chief, Colonel Turner Ashby. Ashby supposedly passed the information to Jackson, who used it to plan his lightning attack on Front Royal.

On the morning of May 23, Belle could hear the advancing Confederates. Concerned that Jackson might be slow in arriving, she ran across the no man's land between the Federals and the Confederates to reach his lines. Many Federals fired at her, but all of them missed. She got the message that the town was clear to one of Jackson's aides, Henry Kyd Douglas.

Jackson pushed the Federals right through town and over the Shenandoah River, finally capturing more than 700 of the 1,000-man garrison about 5 miles north. He lost only 100 of his own men. Some disputed sources claim he wrote a letter of thank you to Belle Boyd "for the immense service that you have rendered to your country."

Then, two years later, in September 1864, Front Royal experienced the worst the war had to offer. Just south of town near Chester Gap on what is now U.S. 522, a detachment of Mosby's Rangers discovered a Federal ambulance train. The rangers attacked, but the Federals reacted quickly, driving them off. One Federal lieutenant was shot and run down by the rangers in the melee. When recovered by the Federals, the mortally wounded man claimed he had surrendered, but that Mosby's men had then tried to murder him—a charge they would deny as long as they lived.

The accusation was enough for the Federals. They marched six captured rangers into downtown Front Royal. Two of them—one just 17 years old—were taken to a lot behind the Methodist church and shot to death. Another was taken to a nearby farm and shot. A fourth was 17-year-old Henry

Rhodes, an unlucky Front Royal resident who had joined the rangers just hours before the attack. Rhodes was dragged up Chester Street between two horses. When the boy's mother begged for his life, a Union soldier drew his saber and offered to behead both of them. Rhodes was dragged to a nearby field, where a Federal soldier emptied his pistol into him. The Federals let cows walk over the body before they would allow the boy's mother to retrieve it. A schoolgirl classmate watched everything from the second story of Rose Hill. The last two rangers were offered their lives if they would reveal where Mosby made his camp. Neither complied; one said Mosby would avenge their deaths. They were then hanged behind the present-day motel.

Historians are unsure who ordered the executions. It likely was General Alfred Torbert, but townspeople blamed General George Custer, who made a spectacle of himself by riding around town with his fancy uniform and red bandanna.

Mosby, who had not been part of the action because of a wound, settled on Custer as the object of his revenge. Two months later, on November 6, he and his men marched 27 captured Federals into the streets of Rectortown, about 15 miles east of Front Royal. The Federals drew seven slips of paper out of a hat—six for the rangers executed in Front Royal and one for a ranger left hanging by the side of a road in an earlier incident south of Front Royal. Mosby exempted two captured drummer boys from the drawing and allowed some prisoners to be swapped for others known to have been among Custer's men in Front Royal at the time of the executions there. One of Mosby's lieutenants used his Masonic connections to switch out a captured Federal Mason. Mosby, though allowing the swap, dryly commented, "My command is not a Masonic lodge."

The doomed Federals were tied and taken to Berryville, where their bodies were sure to be found by Federals then occupying Winchester. Mosby ordered four of them to be shot and three hanged—the same fate that had befallen his rangers. Mosby's men botched the job. Two Federals escaped in a rainstorm, and two others were wounded by pistol fire but recovered. Only the three scheduled to be hanged were successfully executed. The rangers put a note on one of the Federals saying that they had been executed in retaliation for what had happened at Front Royal. The note ended with the phrase "measure for measure."

Mosby did not order any other prisoners to take the place of those who had lived. Instead, he wrote a letter to Union general Phil Sheridan. "Hereafter any prisoners falling into my hands will be treated with kindness unless some new act of barbarity shall compel me reluctantly to adopt a course of policy repulsive to humanity," Mosby promised.

Sheridan wrote a letter back to Mosby promising that the executions would end. From then on, any captured rangers were treated as prisoners of war, and Mosby occasionally paroled Federals, since they were too much trouble to carry with him on raids.

From the visitor center, walk north on Chester Street—the same street up which the unfortunate Henry Rhodes was dragged before his execution.

The Warren Rifles Museum is located at 95 Chester Street. Inside this one-room museum is a wealth of war artifacts. One of the most unusual is a turtle shell into which a bored soldier from the 33rd Rhode Island carved his name and regiment. You'll also see a hip bone with a bullet embedded in it, as well as a piece of the thin rope that hanged John Brown at Harpers Ferry. Artillery historians will be pleased to discover the battle flag of the battalion commanded by 23-year-old Willie Pegram, an artillerist likely second in skill only to the fabled John Pelham. Pegram rose from private to colonel, only to be killed at Five Forks eight days before Lee surrendered. The museum also holds a handkerchief dipped in the blood of James Jackson, the hotel manager bayoneted in Alexandria in May 1861. In one display case are some spurs owned by Mosby; his horse must have been scarred, as the spurs look very sharp.

Behind the Warren Rifles Museum is the Belle Boyd Cottage, the home owned by Belle's uncle. It used to be located on Main Street but was moved about two blocks when the old hotel in which she did her spying was torn down. The cottage offers displays on her career. Belle once locked a New York newspaper reporter in the upper bedroom. He vowed he would ruin her reputation if she didn't let him out. She did not, and he subsequently wrote articles accusing her of being a loose woman—a rumor she never quite lived down.

Return to the visitors center and retrieve your vehicle. Turn east on Main and drive two blocks to Blue Ridge Avenue. Turn right, go three blocks to Short Street, turn left, and look for the Methodist church.

The shooting of the two rangers occurred in the backyard of this house of worship.

Continue on Short to Front Street and turn left. Turn left again at Prospect Street, cross Royal Avenue, and drive into Prospect Hill Cemetery. Stonewall Jackson watched the attack on Front Royal from this hill.

Look up the hill for two cannons flanking an obelisk. The obelisk was erected 35 years to the day after the men of Mosby's command were executed; some 150 former rangers came to the dedication. The two Parrott rifles, one of the best models of cannon used in the war, are of United States manufacture. At the top of the hill is the Confederate graveyard, where 186 men are buried in a circle. Air pollution has worn the tombstones so badly that no names can be read. Two of the executed rangers were also buried in the cemetery.

Retrace your route to Royal Avenue or U.S. 340 and turn right. After two blocks, turn left on Va. 55., which will merge with I-66 in a few miles. Drive approximately 19 miles to Exit 27 off I-66, where Va. 55 leaves the interstate at the town of Marshall (called Salem during the war). On the right at the edge of town is a historical marker that describes how Robert E. Lee was almost captured on August 27, 1862, just 6 miles southwest of town.

Lee and Longstreet spent the night of August 26 near the village of Orlean. The next morning, the two high-ranking generals and their staffs got up before dawn and started riding toward Manassas on their way to join Jackson. For some reason—likely negligence on some staff officer's part—the senior generals rode at the head of the column with few scouts in advance. In a good mood, the generals started pushing their horses farther and farther in front. Just as dawn broke, a Confederate scout came rushing up to Lee and Longstreet shouting, "The Federal cavalry is upon you!" Just then, the Ninth New York Cavalry—a full regiment of several hundred troops—rode into view. Lee had no more than 10 men with him.

The staff officers—likely armed with nothing more than pistols, which probably had not been fired in weeks or months or maybe not at all since the war started—formed in front of Lee, hiding him from the vision of the Yankees, who were no more than a few hundred yards away. The Federal column pulled up and looked at the Confederates, who were riding shoulder to shoulder in a tight formation. The Federals thought they were seeing an entire Confederate cavalry column, rather than the pencil-pushing clerks really in front of them. They wheeled around and rode as hard as they could back toward Manassas. It was thus that several hundred Federals were repelled by a dozen headquarters officers. Had the Federals attacked, Lee would have been captured or killed. This was one of his several close calls during the war.

In the town of Marshall, look for C.R. 710 (Rectortown Road) on the left. Just after turning on to this road, you'll see a historical marker for the field where Mosby disbanded his 43rd Virginia on April 21, 1865, rather than surrender his command. "The vision we cherished of a free and independent country has vanished and that country is now the spoil of the conqueror," Mosby said. "I disband your organization in preference to surrendering to our enemies."

Follow C.R. 710 for 4.5 miles through Rectortown, the place where Mosby selected the Federals he would execute. It was also in Rectortown that General McClellan learned that Lincoln was relieving him of command of the Army of the Potomac in November 1862. He turned over command to Burnside here.

It is about 8 miles on C.R. 710 from Marshall to the intersection with C.R. 712 (Delaplane Grade). Turn right on to C.R. 712 and follow it for 2.6 miles to U.S. 50 in Upperville, a town where one of the companies of Mosby's Rangers was formed. If traffic permits, linger a bit before turning right on U.S. 50, or pull to the side of the road at a convenient spot to learn a little about Upperville.

It was near here on June 19, 1863, that J. E. B. Stuart might have experienced a foreshadowing of his death. He and Heros Von Borcke, a Prussian adventurer who had come to fight for the South for his own amusement, were observing Federal movements near Middleburg (east of U.S. 50 from this spot) when a sharpshooter hit Von Borcke. The bullet tore through his throat and down into his lung. Stuart's aides loaded the 250-pound Prussian into an ambulance, which rushed off toward Upperville. At one point on the bumpy ride, Von Borcke rose from the back, put his pistol to the head of the driver, and ordered him to slow down.

A shaken, crying Stuart visited Von Borcke in Upperville on what he assumed would be his friend's deathbed. In a letter to his wife, Stuart theorized that the sharpshooters had really been targeting him; he and Von Borcke were both large men who dressed flamboyantly.

The strong-as-an-ox Von Borcke recovered and was at Stuart's deathbed just 11 months later.

Follow U.S. 50 East after its intersection with C.R. 712. On the left 0.4 mile later is a single-story stone house. It was to this house that Von Borcke was taken.

It is another 3.9 miles to a marker showing the area where Company A of Mosby's 43rd Virginia Battalion was formed. Near this marker, turn right on C.R. 713 (Rector's Lane/Atoka Road) and drive about 1 mile to the large stone house on the right; do not go up the private drive.

This is Lakeland. On the cold, snowy night of December 21, 1864, Mosby and one of his troopers stopped at this house to eat dinner. Hearing hoofbeats, they stood up from the table. Just then, a shot crashed through the dining-room window. Mosby was hit in the stomach. One of the daughters of the house took off her bonnet and gave it to Mosby to try to stop the bleeding. Mosby then wiped his mouth with the bonnet, spreading his own blood around and trying to make it froth. He then shoved his colonel's coat under a bureau.

When a Federal major came into the house and asked Mosby who he was, the Gray Ghost, one of the most famous Confederates, replied, "Lieutenant Johnson of the Sixth Virginia," which was a regular cavalry unit. The major (who Mosby said had been drinking) looked at the Gray Ghost's wound and the frothy blood around the mouth and declared him as good as dead. Without further questioning, the Federals abandoned Mosby to die, even leaving his horse tied up outside the house. Some of the soldiers did take the "lieutenant's" ostrich-plume hat and crimson-lined cape for souvenirs.

The ladies of the house bundled Mosby up, put him in the back of a cart, and assigned a six-year-old slave boy to take him to safety at a nearby house. The Federal major eventually sobered up and showed the hat to his friends, who identified it as Mosby's. But by the time the Federals returned to the house, the Gray Ghost had lived up to his name.

The bullet was extracted from Mosby. He was moved from house to house in the area until he could be safely transported to his home county. But by the time he recovered, it was obvious to him and his rangers that the war was winding down.

Return to U.S. 50 and turn right. This area was the heart of Mosby's Confederacy. The people of the rich farms of Fauquier and Loudoun Counties would allow themselves to be burned out rather than reveal the Gray Ghost's whereabouts. Many homes in these counties were indeed burned to the ground in a "lay waste" policy in November 1864 aimed at destroying Mosby's ability to operate. Hundreds of cattle, horses, and hogs were confiscated that month. But fewer than 30 men assumed to be guerrillas were killed or captured.

It was in this area that J. E. B. Stuart fought a cavalry battle on June 21, 1863, while on his way to Gettysburg. This all-day running battle started east of Upperville and then ran west of town. The action was really the culmination of four days of fighting in and around Upperville and the nearby towns of Middleburg and Aldie.

After 2.5 miles on U.S. 50, turn right on C.R. 709 (Zulla Road). Drive 3.7 miles, then turn right on the gravel C.R. 708. It is 0.5 mile to the Hathaway House.

In June 1863, Mosby's wife was staying at this house at the invitation of Mr. Hathaway when an informer told the Federals that the Gray Ghost himself would also spend the night here. The Federals raided the house after midnight and searched each room, finding nothing but a pair of spurs. Had they looked on the limb of the walnut tree that still stands outside the bedroom window, they would have discovered Mosby. After the Federals left, he climbed back into the bedroom, having lost his spurs and his horse but not his freedom.

Retrace your route to U.S. 50. After 1 mile, turn right to visit Middleburg, the unofficial capital of northern Virginia's wealthy "horse society." Downtown Middleburg is the home of the Red Fox Inn, one of Mosby's numerous safe houses during the war.

Continue through Middleburg. About 5 miles after leaving town, turn left just before reaching Aldie on to C.R. 734 (Snickersville Turnpike). Drive 1.2 miles and pull off to the right just before a hard left turn.

This was the scene of some hard fighting between Stuart's men and Union cavalry on June 17, 1863. The Confederates, supported by one cannon, fell back along Snickersville Turnpike and set up a skirmish line behind this stone wall facing Aldie. Men from the First Massachusetts Cavalry charged the position; they were virtually wiped out when they rounded a slight bend in the road and came face to face with the Confederates, protected by the stone wall. One Confederate said the fighting was so close that he could see "the dust fly from their jackets as the bullets from our pistols would strike them." Another said he had never seen so many dead Yankees in one spot.

The attractive monument on the site lists the names of all the men killed, wounded, and captured here.

Return to U.S. 50, turn left, and drive 1.6 miles to U.S. 15. Turn north on U.S. 15 and head to Leesburg, about 11 miles away.

When you reach downtown Leesburg, turn left at the light on to Loudon Street. On the right in the first block is the Loudoun County Museum. Inside this little museum are several war-related displays, including a bullet recovered from one of Mosby's men and an unusual photograph of twin Confederates.

Continue north on U.S. 15 (King Street) for about 1 mile to Battlefield Parkway, an oddly named road that leads through a middle-class neighborhood. Turn right on Battlefield, drive through the neighborhood, and con-

Monument to Union Cavalry at Aldie

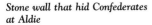

Stone wall that hid Confederates at Aldie

TOURING VIRGINIA'S AND WEST VIRGINIA'S CIVIL WAR SITES

tinue through the light at U.S. 15 Bypass. Take the first left, which is Ball's Bluff Road. Follow the brown signs through another neighborhood until the road ends at a gravel parking lot for the battlefield at Ball's Bluff. The tour ends here at the battlefield.

In some ways, the relatively small Battle of Ball's Bluff on October 21, 1861, was an even bigger Federal disaster than First Manassas, which had taken place exactly three months earlier and barely 20 miles away. At First Manassas, the Federals inflicted damage on the Confederates, and their officers performed fairly competently for a first battle. At Ball's Bluff, the officer in charge performed abominably, getting most of his command killed, wounded, or captured and being shot in the head himself.

October was a time when both sides were waiting for the enemy to make a move in northern Virginia. President Lincoln pushed his new commander, George McClellan, to do something. McClellan in turn pushed his commanders to try to force Shanks Evans's Confederates out of Leesburg. He ordered his general in Maryland, Charles Stone, to demonstrate on the Potomac River to see if that would force Evans to abandon the town, which would give Lincoln a small victory. Stone in turn ordered a subordinate—a man who had been forced on him—to make the demonstration. That subordinate was Colonel Edward Baker, a United States senator from the new state of Oregon who was a close personal friend of Lincoln. Indeed, Baker had sat beside Lincoln at the inauguration to hold the new president's hat. Stone, a West Pointer, knew that if he wanted his military career to continue, he better not anger the president's best buddy.

Baker was a skilled politician but an untrained officer. When the war started, Lincoln had offered to make him a general, but Baker had declined. He came to that decision not because he recognized his limitations, but because a general's commission would have forced him to give up his Senate seat. Baker relished striding into the Senate chamber, unbuckling his sword and pistol belt, and brushing off his dusty army uniform in front of his jealous colleagues.

The problem for Baker was that all that dust had accumulated by just riding around. He did not see action at First Manassas. If he wanted to play soldier much longer, he had to do some fighting. This demonstration on Leesburg would give him the chance.

Stone's orders to Baker stipulated that he should send a small force across the Potomac before committing a large number of troops. Baker ignored that order and committed all 1,700 men under his command, landing them on a narrow beach below the 100-foot-tall Ball's Bluff. The only way to the top of the bluff was to climb a one-man-wide path, hardly the best method to move so many men into what could be a battlefield. Baker told his men to follow the feather in his hat if they wanted to find the war.

When a West Point–trained officer got to the top of Ball's Bluff, a shiver went down his spine. The Federals were milling around in an open field surrounded by woods. If the Confederates were in those woods, his men were dead.

The Confederates were indeed in the woods. Astounded that the Federals would walk into such a trap, they opened up. The outcome was never in doubt. The two Union cannons that had been wrestled up the bluff were soon out of commission. One of them was fired, and the recoil sent it crashing over the bluff. The other lost its crew to Confederate fire.

Soon, the panicked Federals began to rush back down the path they had just climbed. Some leaped from the bluff, thinking it gave them a greater chance of reaching safety; what they did not count on was landing on the bayonets of the Federals already running down the path. And the panic did not stop at the water's edge. Men dove into the Potomac and swamped several boats loaded with wounded men being rowed toward the Maryland shore; the helpless wounded soldiers drowned. Bodies floated all the way down the river to Washington, where shocked citizens fished them out for days after the battle.

Of the 1,700 men who attacked Ball's Bluff, fewer than 700 made it to safety. The rest were killed, wounded, captured, or missing and presumed drowned. Baker himself died relatively early, shot in the head.

Angry senators needed someone to blame for the debacle. Since their friend Baker was dead, they settled on his commander, Charles Stone. The son of a prominent Massachusetts doctor and the seventh-ranking member of the West Point class of 1845, Stone was arrested at his home in February 1862 and imprisoned in solitary confinement for more than six months, while his accusers tried to find evidence that he was a Confederate spy who had intentionally killed Baker and his command. Finally released when no credible charges were brought against him, he served bitterly for another two years before resigning. He then went to Egypt and served its army for 13 years before returning to the United States. As a civilian, he designed the foundation for the Statue of Liberty. Though the army and the civilians who ran it had mistreated him, he chose to be buried at West Point upon his death, which came in 1887.

Part of the battlefield at Ball's Bluff has been developed into a neighborhood, but the portion on the river survives as a park with a walking path. Here, too, is the nation's smallest national cemetery, a walled enclosure holding 54 Union soldiers killed on the field. Only one of them is known— a man from the 15th Massachusetts. The walking path leads to the bluff, from which visitors can glimpse the Potomac. However, it is not possible to walk the same path the doomed Federals took.

The Confederate commander at Ball's Bluff was Shanks Evans, the same whiskey-swilling general who had saved the Confederates at First Manassas. Reports say he was drinking again at Ball's Bluff. Though the Confederate Congress gave Evans one of the first "Thanks of Congress" for his service in the war's first two battles, his commanders gave up on him because of his problems with the bottle.

Evans was shifted out of northern Virginia to less important commands. He died in 1868.

Federal cemetery at Ball's Bluff

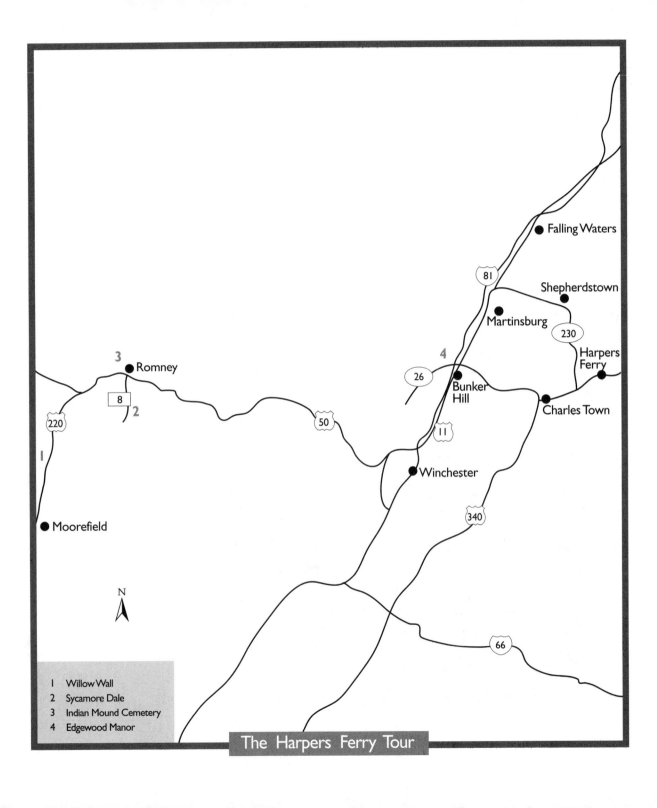

3 Romney

8

2

220

1

Moorefield

50

26

Martinsburg

81

Falling Waters

Shepherdstown

230

Harpers
Ferry

4

Bunker
Hill

Charles Town

11

Winchester

340

66

N

1   Willow Wall
2   Sycamore Dale
3   Indian Mound Cemetery
4   Edgewood Manor

The Harpers Ferry Tour

The Harpers Ferry Tour

This tour starts in the small town of Moorefield, West Virginia, the center of the territory controlled by partisan ranger John "Hanse" McNeill, a highly effective hit-and-run commander who tied up thousands of Federal soldiers in this area. It then moves to Romney, a town that changed hands more than 60 times and where a dispute nearly cost the Confederacy the services of Stonewall Jackson. It goes to a house near Bunker Hill where a Confederate general died after Gettysburg, then heads to Martinsburg and the childhood home of Confederate spy Belle Boyd. From there, the tour moves to Shepherdstown on the Potomac River, the site of skirmishing related to the nearby Battle of Sharpsburg in September 1862, and to Charles Town, the site of the trial of John Brown. It ends in Harpers Ferry, the river town where Brown hoped to launch a nationwide slave revolt.

The tour covers approximately 115 miles, much of it in rural areas. This is likely a two-day tour for those who wish to linger in Martinsburg or Harpers Ferry.

THE STATE OF WEST VIRGINIA did not exist when the Civil War started. But it was here that war between North and South first became a possibility.

The debate over slavery was an abstract concept to both Northerners and Southerners for most of the 19th century, since the majority of Northerners had never seen a slave and most Southerners did not own any. But over the course of a few weeks in 1859, a nervous nation heard all it cared to about slavery. The talk centered around John Brown and the events that occurred in Jefferson County.

When Virginia reluctantly left the Union on April 17, 1861, the politicians in Richmond knew they had trouble on their hands beyond just worrying about when the North would sweep into their state. They were more concerned about trouble erupting within their own borders.

The citizens of "western Virginia," roughly defined as the counties west of the Shenandoah Valley, had never really felt themselves a part of "Virginia." While the area from the Tidewater to the mountains was dotted with stately plantations, western Virginia—the land beyond those mountains—was a place of roughly made log cabins. While Virginians sincerely believed they led the nation in gentility, western Virginians sincerely believed they led the nation in pioneer spirit. While Virginia was the mother of presidents, western Virginia was the mother of mountaineers. While Virginia viewed slaves as necessary to tend cotton and tobacco and other cash crops, western Virginia had no need for slaves on its farms hacked out of mountainsides or located in creek bottoms, which produced only enough food to feed the farmers' immediate families. While Virginia viewed its poor western relations as close enough to be a source of tax revenue but too far to service with those taxes, western Virginia viewed its wealthy eastern relations as uncaring about what was happening in the mountains.

As talk of secession began to heat up in the late 1850s, the residents of western Virginia began to think of forming their own state. When Virginia seceded, that thinking turned to open talk, despite the fact that the United States Constitution specifically forbids any new state to be formed from an existing state. Within a month of the time Virginia joined the Confederacy, delegates from the 34 western counties elected their own governor and even sent their own congressmen to Washington, where they were welcomed.

Over the next two years, more meetings were held, five additional counties expressed interest in leaving Virginia, and a state government formed. The new state was officially welcomed into the Union on June 20, 1863. Initially, it looked like it would be called *Kanawha*, after its most important river, but *West Virginia*, an adaptation of what the region had always been called, won out.

Though West Virginia was not the scene of the major battles that would shock the world with their ferocity and bloodletting, it was in this mountainous, sparsely populated part of the Union that the Civil War really got its start with some small battles in May and June of 1861, more than a month before First Manassas. Philippi, Rich Mountain, and Corrick's Ford were all tiny skirmishes won by Union forces. These early examples of the supposed ability of Federal soldiers and the incompetence of the Confederates gave the Union confidence that all it had to do was show force and the Rebels would run away.

West Virginia was never truly important from a military point of view, but what happened here in October 1859, when John Brown brought the issue of slavery to a head, and in the spring of 1861, when the Federals came to believe the war could be won with little bloodshed, proved to be key events in the Civil War.

The tour begins in downtown Moorefield, West Virginia, at the McMechen House, a bed-and-breakfast located at 109 North Main Street

(U.S. 220). Built in 1853 by Samuel A. McMechen, a local merchant, the house was one of the finest in town and thus served as a headquarters for both sides. The most famous officer to occupy the house was Confederate general John McCausland, who stopped here in July 1864 on his return from burning Chambersburg, Pennsylvania, in retaliation for the Federal burning of the Virginia Military Institute earlier that summer.

On the second floor of the McMechen House is a rare political artifact—a wall painted with an American flag and the slogan "Buchanan & Breckinridge—The Union and States Rights." Note that whoever painted the sign had to start over when he or she discovered that more wall space was needed. Subdivided into sleeping rooms and closets years ago, this was the meeting room for Moorefield citizens interested in Democratic politics during the election of 1856. Presidential candidate James Buchanan and vice presidential candidate John C. Breckinridge ran on a platform that the Northern and Southern states could coexist, a political strategy that delayed the war for four years.

McMechen House

The street outside the McMechen House was the scene of fighting in the summer of 1864 after some Federals disguised as Confederates snuck up on Rebel forces about 4 miles away and chased them all the way into town. Legend says that a fleeing Union soldier was beheaded by a saber-swinging Confederate cavalryman trying to cover the escape of General McCausland.

From the McMechen House, drive south on Main Street for one block to East Winchester Street (W.V. 55), where you'll see a large, two-story building on the southwest corner, across from the Hardy County Library. This was once a prewar hotel owned by Charles Lee, the brother of Robert E. Lee. Family descendants have the hotel register where R. E. Lee signed in for the night.

Turn left on East Winchester. Pull over at 212 East Winchester and look to the right of the chimney. Until the summer of 1998, a Union cannonball fired from Cemetery Hill was lodged in the boards. The owner now keeps it as a paperweight.

Cross the railroad tracks on East Winchester. Approximately 0.1 mile after the tracks, turn right into Olivet Cemetery. Drive to the left around the cemetery and stop at the monument on the right. Buried in a semicircle around the monument are members of the 18th Virginia Cavalry, more commonly known as McNeill's Rangers. Just to the left of the monument is a small tombstone for J. H. McNeill.

Captain John Hanson "Hanse" McNeill never commanded more than 210 men, but that small force caused enough havoc in the valley of the South Branch of the Potomac River for Union general Benjamin F. Kelley to comment, "I want McNeill killed, captured, or driven out of this valley." McNeill was so respected by the government in Richmond that only his and Mosby's commands were exempted from a wartime order dissolving all partisan bands and folding the men into regular-army units.

Grave of J. H. McNeill

Partisan rangers were controversial. Much of the time, they went about their business as farmers or merchants, hiding any evidence that they were soldiers. When they put on uniforms and took up weapons, they never set up a permanent camp, never carried tents, and rarely carried more than a day's worth of food. Their preferred weapons were pistols and double-barreled shotguns, rather than the long-barreled rifled muskets carried by infantrymen and the sabers favored by cavalry.

When Federals like the Ringgold Cavalry came looking for McNeill's men, all they found were innocent-looking civilians. But when the rangers heard about Union wagon trains moving down the valley, they donned uniforms and attacked those trains. Because the rangers rarely operated in units larger than 50 men, the Union army considered them bushwhackers, subject to hanging, being shot on sight, or not being exchanged as prisoners of war. They got little more respect from Confederate generals, who had little use for cavalrymen who hit an enemy and then rode away, rather than slugging it out face to face in the Napoleonic tradition.

Moorefield was McNeill's hometown and the center of his unit's activities for most of the war, though it was occupied by Union forces on occasion. No matter how the war was going in other parts of Virginia, McNeill's men knew they could always find a hot meal and a warm bed with their friends in Moorefield.

Forty-five years old at the start of the war, McNeill looked like the devil himself. Descriptions and pictures show a stern-looking man with penetrating eyes and hair flowing over his ears and mingling with his beard, which stretched to the middle of his chest.

If McNeill had a problem, it was taking orders. On several occasions, military-school-trained generals like Tom Rosser and John McCausland tried to put him under their command and bend him to their will. He refused. In August 1864, when McCausland ignored McNeill's suggestion of a safe place to camp, McNeill pointedly moved his camp away from McCausland's. As usual, McNeill was right. McCausland was surprised by raiding Federals and lost several hundred men.

McNeill never lost a battle and never missed fulfilling his objective. But he met his fate on October 3, 1864, when he was mortally wounded near Mount Jackson in the Shenandoah Valley, two days from his beloved South Branch Valley. He was taken to a minister's home, where his hair and beard were shaved at the suggestion of the minister's wife in order to disguise him from raiding Federals. That worked until Union general Phil Sheridan, suspicious of the dying man, finally asked McNeill who he was. He admitted he was the famed raider. But the minister's wife was able to persuade Sheridan to leave McNeill, as he was too near death to be taken to a Union prison.

That night, McNeill was spirited to Harrisonburg. He died there on November 10 from a bullet that had entered his shoulder and then traveled downward to lodge near his spine; he endured intense pain for more than a month before expiring. It was in January 1865 that he was moved to Olivet Cemetery, which was called Cemetery Hill at that time.

About 200 yards east of the Confederate Monument, just past a large, open field, is a well-preserved trench line dug by Confederates. It was not far beyond these trenches that McNeill's Rangers raided a sleeping Union camp in September 1863, capturing 146 soldiers without firing a shot. The next year, raiding Federals set up cannons on this hill to shell the town—resulting in the cannonball damage still visible today.

McNeill's nonviolent capture of the 146 Federals was another strange turn in his war with his principal enemy, the Ringgold Cavalry. The two forces liked each other. Once, McNeill's Rangers came upon a party of Mosby's men well outside their normal territory. Mosby's men had captured one of the Ringgold Federals and were ready to hang him from a tree in retaliation for the hanging of a Confederate. McNeill's Confederates drew their pistols on Mosby's Confederates and demanded the release of the Federal into their care. Mosby's shocked men complied. After the war, the Ringgold men and McNeill's Rangers held reunions to talk about fighting each other.

Return to U.S. 220 and turn north. On the left about 4.1 miles out of

McNeill's house in Old Fields

Moorefield is the large brick house called Willow Wall. Built in 1818 by Daniel McNeill, Hanse's father, this house served as a base of operations for McNeill's Rangers. On August 7, 1864, it was the site of the Battle of Old Fields (also called the Battle of Moorefield), which came about when McCausland neglected to follow McNeill's advice about selecting secure grounds for his camp. Union general William Averell's cavalry, moving north to south down the valley road, surprised 3,000 sleeping Confederates and captured more than 400 of them before moving on to Moorefield, where McCausland himself was almost captured. Only McNeill's knowledge of how to lead the remaining forces into the mountains averted a total disaster.

Continue north on U.S. 220 for 14 miles to the junction with U.S. 50. U.S. 220 belonged to McNeill's Rangers from 1863 to 1865, judging from the reports of small skirmishes all along the route. His men captured a Union wagon train at Purgitsville and another one at the U.S. 50 junction.

Turn right on U.S. 50, heading toward Romney. After 5.6 miles, you will reach the South Branch of the Potomac River.

It was 6 miles north of this spot near the town of Springfield that McNeill's Rangers won their most amusing victory. McNeill's men were in the area gathering cattle on June 26, 1864, when they came upon the Sixth West Virginia Cavalry. Outnumbered at least two to one, McNeill's men might have quietly slipped away. Instead, they rushed the Federals, who could do little but throw up their hands—simply because they were skinny-dipping in the river. Without firing a shot, the rangers captured 60 Federals, more than 100 cavalry horses, and a good number of pants not in use at the time.

Just after crossing the bridge, make a hard right on C.R. 8. On the left 0.1 mile down the road is Sycamore Dale, a two-story house that was the scene of the formal surrender of McNeill's Rangers on May 8, 1865. Led by Jesse McNeill, Hanse's son, the rangers had made arrangements to surrender several days earlier.

Under the watchful eyes of several Federal officers, 36 rangers threw down their weapons in a pile in the front yard of the house. The only problem was that the weapons in question were broken and antiquated. Some of them were flintlocks that had not been used for decades before the war. According to one Federal officer, "The arms piled on the ground were not worth 10 cents a ton." When someone protested to McNeill that the weapons could not possibly be all that the rangers had, all he got in return was a cold stare. The Federals then noticed the bulges under the rangers' coats—the very pistols that had made this small band of Confederates feared throughout the valley.

Another Federal halfheartedly made the point that at Appomattox Court House, Lee had agreed to surrender all equipment but horses. Jesse McNeill replied that if his rangers had to surrender the Federal saddles, blankets, and other gear they now owned, they might as well keep fighting. Glancing behind them at their reinforcements, who were well out of range of helping, the Federals reluctantly agreed to let McNeill's Rangers go.

The war was over for the rangers. Most of them went on to lead productive lives. They even buried the hatchet with their enemies, particularly the 22nd Pennsylvania Cavalry, also called the Ringgold Cavalry. It was in 1895 that the survivors of the two forces gathered in Moorefield for a two-day reunion. The event was capped by a prayer service at Hanse McNeill's grave.

Return to U.S. 50, turn right, drive 0.3 mile, and make a hard left into Indian Mound Cemetery. Look to the left for a large white monument topped by what looks like an urn covered with a sheet. This is one of the oldest Confederate monuments in the nation, erected in 1867 by local ladies in honor of the dead from Hampshire County. The word *Confederate* does not appear, as it would not have been permitted by the victorious Union forces. The carving of an angel pouring water on a fallen Confederate officer is amazing in its detail. The man's closed eyelids, mustache, and fingers all are finely carved.

One of the oldest Confederate monuments in Romney

When you are ready to leave the cemetery, continue through Romney, a town that changed hands more than 60 times during the war—so often that citizens are said to have kept one Union and one Confederate flag handy, depending on who was in town that week.

On the right side of U.S. 50 about 0.2 mile past the intersection with W.V. 28 is Stonewall Jackson's headquarters, now a private house with a historical marker in front.

It was here during the winter of 1861–62 that Jackson's sensitivity to interference with his orders first surfaced. That winter, Jackson turned over command of the town to General W. W. Loring, a Floridian who acquired the nickname "Blizzards" for his oft-given command to give the Federals blizzards of bullets. Loring was nervous about having his command so far forward of the Confederate positions back in the Shenandoah Valley. Without asking Jackson, he wrote a letter to the Confederate secretary of war asking to move his men back to Winchester. The secretary agreed. When Jackson learned that his order had been countermanded, he wrote a furious letter of resignation and asked to be reassigned as a professor at the Virginia Military Institute. Only an apology from the governor of Virginia kept him in the army.

Jackson had it in for the officers who defied him at Romney. One example was General (then Colonel) William Taliaferro, who wrote the following about being stationed in Romney: "The best army I ever saw . . . has been destroyed by the bad marches and bad management. It is ridiculous to hold this place. For heaven's sake, withdraw the troops or we will not have a man in the army for the spring campaign." Jackson subsequently protested the decision to promote Taliaferro, accused him of being bad for the morale of his men, and tried to avoid him whenever possible.

One of the most successful adventures of the war moved through Romney. In February 1865, Jesse McNeill led a force of 50 men into Cumberland, Maryland, for the express purpose of capturing the Federal commander, General Benjamin F. Kelley, who had once arrested Jesse's mother and baby sister. While taking Kelley, McNeill also captured another Union general, George Crook. The generals were taken while sleeping in two different hotels; not a shot was fired. On the way back to safety, the Confederates rushed headlong through Romney puckishly flying Kelley's regimental headquarters flag. The townspeople were unsure which side was the victor, since the column included two Union generals and dozens of men in the uniforms of either side. The Union generals were taken to Winchester, more than 150 miles from Cumberland, where they were entertained at Confederate headquarters. Kelley admitted with a grin that "it was the most splendid exploit of the war." Mosby later ran into McNeill's men on a train heading to Richmond. He congratulated them, saying the only way he could top their raid would be to ride into Washington and capture Lincoln.

Continue through Romney on U.S. 50; it is approximately 37 miles to the outskirts of Winchester. Turn left on Va. 37/U.S. 11 North; continue on U.S. 11 North when the routes separate after passing under I-81. About 8.7 miles beyond I-81, look for a large monument on the left. Turn into the driveway for Edgewood Manor, a bed-and-breakfast built in 1839.

The monument honors General James Johnston Pettigrew, the North Carolinian who led the Tar Heels on the Pettigrew-Pickett-Trimble Assault on the third day at Gettysburg. Pettigrew was a brilliant man who graduated from college at age 17, spoke at least seven languages, including Hebrew, and was a lawyer and militia leader in Charleston, South Carolina, when the war started. It was Pettigrew's men who got the deepest into the Federal lines at Gettysburg. They later had the job of acting as the rear guard during Lee's retreat across the Potomac.

*Monument to
James Johnston Pettigrew*

At Falling Waters, Maryland, on July 14, 1863, Union cavalry rushed into Pettigrew's camp. A Union cavalryman recognized Pettigrew as a general and shot him at point-blank range. Enraged Confederates pulled the Yankee from his horse and killed him by crushing his chest with a large rock. Pettigrew was loaded into a wagon and taken to this house, where he died after pronouncing his last words: "It is time to be going."

Edgewood Manor was also the scene of several other historic events.

Confederate spy John Boyd was captured here when a slave girl betrayed him to searching Federals.

Stonewall Jackson camped in the front yard of Edgewood Manor for three weeks and used the house as a temporary headquarters. Robert E. Lee came to Jackson's tent to try to settle an acrimonious dispute between Jackson and A. P. Hill over command decisions, but he failed to extract a compromise from his hardheaded subordinates.

An amusing event involving J. E. B. Stuart also took place here. One night, Stuart arrived long after Jackson had gone to bed. As was the custom of the day, he stole into his commander's tent and lay down beside Jackson to snatch a few hours of sleep. The next morning, the usually serious Jackson cracked that Stuart, who had not bothered to remove his sword belt or spurs the night before, had ridden him "all night like a horse," meaning that Stuart's tossing and turning had disturbed Jackson's sleep. The embarrassed Stuart subsequently had a fine lieutenant general's uniform made for Jackson. Jackson, who was not much of a fashion plate, accepted the uniform and said

Christ Episcopal Church in Bunker Hill

he would wear it on special occasions. Stuart then demanded that Jackson model it for his staff, which he did.

When you are ready to leave Edgewood Manor, go left on U.S. 11, drive 0.2 mile into Bunker Hill, and turn left on Va. 26. After 0.2 mile, pull into the lot at Christ Episcopal Church. The aftereffects of artillery fire from the Battle of Bunker Hill are easily seen here. If the church is open, take a look inside to see the Civil War graffiti still found on the walls.

Return to U.S. 11 and continue 10 miles into the heart of Martinsburg; turn left off King Street on to Queen Street to remain on U.S. 11 North. Drive three blocks to East Race Street.

If you care to take a side trip to Falling Waters, continue 8.1 miles north on U.S. 11. Not long after passing a DuPont plant, make a right turn on Baldwin Camp Road. Immediately to the left is the Potomac River. This is the area where Lee's army recrossed the river after its defeat at Gettysburg. Pettigrew was mortally wounded on the far bank.

Those who do not care to take the side trip should turn right on East Race and drive one block to see the childhood home of famed Confederate spy Belle Boyd. Located at 126 East Race, the structure now houses the Berkeley County Historical Society and the Belle Boyd Museum. It was built in 1854 by Belle's father.

Stories about the young Belle abound. On one occasion, she was refused entrance into a party her father was hosting because she was too young to mingle with his political friends. In response, the preteen Belle brought her pony into the parlor and asked if it was old enough for the party. Another time, the headmistress of the local girls' school personally delivered Belle to her home and took the opportunity to tell her parents that the headstrong girl was a disruptive influence on the other students.

Belle Boyd House

When the war started, Belle became a Confederate spy. She took mental note of the comings and goings of Union forces and then passed encrypted messages to generals like Stonewall Jackson. She was arrested and sent to prison several times. (For more about Belle's war career, see The Mosby's Confederacy Tour, pages 32–33.)

Even after the war, Belle proved unusual. She married one of her Union captors, then divorced him and a later husband in an era when divorces were rare. She became an actress and was on tour when she died of a heart attack in Kilbourne, Wisconsin. Admirers still keep the Confederate flag flying over her grave.

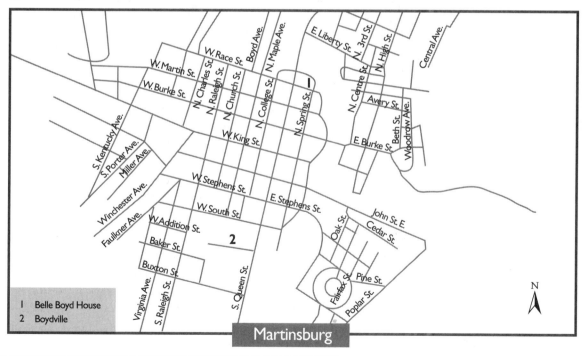

1 Belle Boyd House
2 Boydville

Martinsburg

The downstairs of the Belle Boyd House is a well-appointed Civil War museum of battles around Berkeley County. The upstairs offers a display of every known photograph of Belle, all of them showing her rather large nose, of which she was quite proud. You can also see an interesting letter from the teenage Belle to a male cousin, asking him if he knew any eligible bachelors who would like to meet his beautiful cousin. Indeed, Belle repeatedly used the word *beautiful* to describe herself.

Return to Queen Street and turn left. Drive to King Street, then continue two blocks on Queen to South Street. Located on the right at the intersection is a historical marker for another house once owned by the Boyd family. The home no longer stands. It was there that Belle shot and killed a Union soldier who had threatened her mother when Mrs. Boyd refused to hang a Union flag from the house. The Union soldiers were inclined to execute Belle, but their officers, impressed by her spunk, saved her. After that, Belle lived under constant surveillance.

Located well off the street at 601 South Queen is Boydville, a bed-and-breakfast. In 1864, this house was targeted for burning by Federal forces until the owner, a former minister to France, was able to get a desperate telegram to Lincoln. Lincoln then sent an order to the Federals specifically saving the home.

Turn around and proceed north on Queen. After passing under a railroad bridge, look for W.V. 45 on the right. Follow W.V. 45 approximately 8 miles to a four-way stop sign at W.V. 480 in Shepherdstown. Turn right on W.V. 480 and drive 0.2 mile to Elmwood Cemetery, on the right. Turn into the cemetery and bear to the right to the top of the hill, passing a small Confederate cemetery. Stop under the large tree on the left. Here is the grave of Alexander Boteler, the man who designed the Confederate seal; the seal shows the equestrian statue of George Washington that rests on the lawn at the Virginia Capitol.

On the opposite side of the road almost in front of Boteler's tombstone is the grave of Colonel Henry Kyd Douglas. A staff officer under Jackson, Douglas wrote a book called *I Rode with Stonewall*, considered one of the best first-person accounts of the Army of Northern Virginia.

About 20 yards from Douglas's grave is the simple tombstone of General William W. Kirkland, a North Carolinian who served ably during the war.

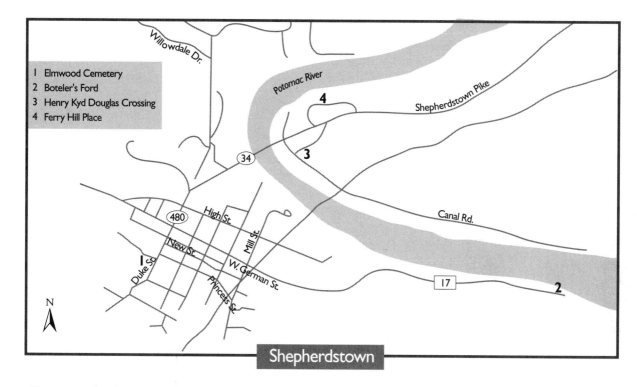

Shepherdstown

Legend:
1 Elmwood Cemetery
2 Boteler's Ford
3 Henry Kyd Douglas Crossing
4 Ferry Hill Place

Return to the four-way stop sign and turn right; you are now on German Street. Proceed straight through town; the road eventually runs along the Potomac. After about 2 miles, you will reach Boteler's Ford, also called Pack Horse Ford, where Lee's army crossed the river on the way to and from Sharpsburg, Maryland, in September 1862.

After reading the historic markers, turn around and begin retracing your route; after 0.1 mile, look to the right to see the remains of a cement mill that was the scene of fighting when the Federals tried to catch the Confederates after Sharpsburg.

Return to the four-way stop sign and turn right onto Va. 480, which soon becomes Va. 34. Drive over the Potomac River. Immediately after crossing, turn right onto Canal Road and proceed to the C & O Canal, which runs alongside the river.

In October 1862, a homesick Henry Kyd Douglas came to the Potomac to steal a glance at his home across the river, in an area then occupied by

Federals. A Union sergeant on the opposite shore motioned that he would meet Douglas in the middle of the river. The cautious Douglas found a rowboat. The sergeant invited Douglas to land and meet his parents, saying that all the officers were away and that the enlisted men would not stand in the way of a man visiting his mother.

A runner was sent to fetch Douglas's mother, who spent several minutes with her son on the canal's towpath. Douglas's father, who had been restricted to the yard of the house, watched from above; as much as he wanted to, he would not go back on his promise not to leave the property. After the tearful Douglas and his mother parted, he waved to his father from the rowboat. He never saw the thoughtful Union sergeant again.

Henry Kyd Douglas's childhood home

Drive back up Canal Road and carefully cross the highway to reach the headquarters of C & O Canal National Historic Park; note that this structure is not a museum, but just offices. Called Ferry Hill Place, it was Douglas's childhood home. Both Federal and Southern troops occupied the house during the war.

Cross the Potomac back into Shepherdstown and turn left on German Street at the now-familiar four-way stop sign. After three blocks, turn right on W.V. 230 and head out of town. After about 2 miles, you will reach a confusing intersection where the road splits to Charles Town (to the right) and Harpers Ferry (to the left). Bear right toward Charles Town, about 7.5 miles away; follow the signs to U.S. 340 heading west. Proceed to the intersection of U.S. 340 (Washington Street) and George Street in Charles Town, where you'll see the Jefferson County Courthouse.

Jefferson County Courthouse

John Brown was tried and sentenced in this courthouse, which has been modified through the years. A room displaying a window from the old courthouse and the railings from the courtroom is open to the public. An account of Brown's execution that appeared in *Frank Leslie's Illustrated Newspaper* hangs on the wall of the courthouse lobby. If it is accurate, this eyewitness version details some startling facts rarely mentioned in accounts of Brown's execution. It says that Brown hung for 35 minutes before his pulse faded. That means his neck was not broken by his fall from the gallows (the expected result of a well-planned hanging), but that he slowly strangled to death. The county's hangman either did a poor job of executing Brown or intentionally tortured him.

Walk south on George Street for four blocks to Hunter Street. Then walk one block east to Samuel Street. The lot at the corner of Hunter and Samuel, which is now the yard of a private home, was where Brown's gallows were erected. Before the hanging, he rode to this spot atop his own coffin. Among the crowd were a professor from the Virginia Military Institute named Thomas J. Jackson and an actor named John Wilkes Booth.

Walk back north on Samuels Street for three blocks to Congress and turn right on to Congress. Walk two blocks to the entrance to Zion Episcopal Church at East Congress and Church. To the left beyond the iron gates is the grave of Captain John Yates Beall.

Beall was a 29-year-old lawyer-turned-spy who came close to completing a fantastic mission in late 1864 to free the Confederate officers held prisoner at Johnson's Island, Ohio. Beall and some other Confederates captured a Union ship on Lake Erie. They planned to use it to capture

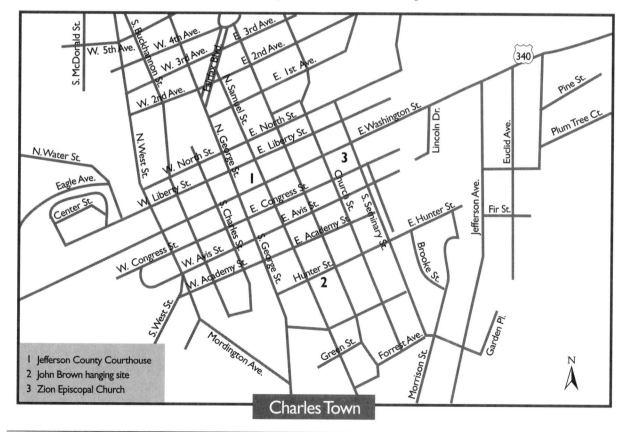

1 Jefferson County Courthouse
2 John Brown hanging site
3 Zion Episcopal Church

Charles Town

another, larger, armed Union ship, with which they would then attack the prison camp, free the men, and carry them to safety in Canada. Their plot was discovered before the raid could be made. Beall was later captured in New York State while trying to derail a train. He was hanged as a spy just six weeks before the war ended. In truth, he would not have lived long anyway. Beall was suffering from tuberculosis, which perhaps made him amenable to taking on suicide missions such as trying to capture Union ships hundreds of miles behind enemy lines.

Retrace your route to U.S. 340 and drive 6.5 miles to Harpers Ferry. Follow the signs to Harpers Ferry National Historical Park and leave your car at the visitor center. Take the shuttle into downtown Harpers Ferry. There is little space for public parking in the historic district, but most of the sites are within easy walking distance.

This town, perhaps more than any other in the South, demonstrates the complicated nature of slavery and the relationship between blacks and whites in those times. At the center of any discussion of Harpers Ferry and the issue of slavery, of course, is the controversial figure of John Brown.

Brown was a failure at everything he tried in his professional working life—except at motivating people to fight what he considered the greatest evil on the face of the earth, the existence of slavery in the South.

In the mid-1850s, Brown went on a spree of killing slave owners in Kansas. But he knew that his nighttime assaults on isolated farms would have little effect on the institution of slavery itself. Brown wanted to do something on a much grander scale. He wanted to strike at slavery not on its fringes, but at its heart. He chose Virginia because it was near the free states to the north, to which any freed slaves could be quickly escorted. Brown began to craft a plan that centered around attacking a mountain community, the theory being that mountains would act as a natural defense against any regular-army forces sent against him.

One of Brown's recruits told him about Harpers Ferry. The town was near Pennsylvania, a free state already part of the Underground Railroad, and it was also surrounded by mountains. Best of all, Harpers Ferry was home to a United States arsenal filled with muskets that could be issued to the slave army that would surely form after the coming revolts on the plantations to the south and east.

Brown set his sights on Harpers Ferry in the summer of 1858, more than a year in advance of the raid itself. He then concentrated on raising money from wealthy New England abolitionists and on recruiting followers, including his sons, his daughter, his daughter-in-law, and a mixed lot of blacks and whites whose only common interest was a hatred of slavery.

It did not surprise Brown that the wealthy men who bankrolled him did not have the stomach for the bloody battle he promised. But he didn't care that none of them volunteered for the dangerous mission. As long as they paid for the rental of the nearby Maryland farm from which he would stage his revolt and for the purchase of 200 Sharps carbines, 200 pistols, and 1,000 pikes, they could stay in the background.

The purchase of those weapons revealed much about Brown and what the 19th-century person—whether Northerner or Southerner—thought about blacks. Brown considered the slaves to be little more than children in search of a leader—himself. He imagined that the vast majority of blacks would not understand how to operate rifles and muskets. He wanted them

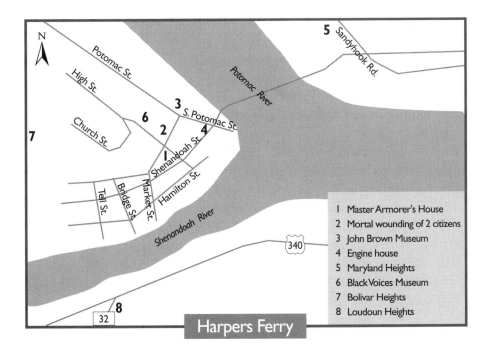

1 Master Armorer's House
2 Mortal wounding of 2 citizens
3 John Brown Museum
4 Engine house
5 Maryland Heights
6 Black Voices Museum
7 Bolivar Heights
8 Loudoun Heights

Harpers Ferry

to use pikes, which were similar to the simple spears they would have carried back in Africa—a continent that their grandfathers might have recalled, but of which most slaves had no direct memory.

On the night of October 16, 1859, everything was finally in place. Brown and 21 men, including his sons, crept into Harpers Ferry over the Baltimore & Ohio covered railroad bridge. They captured several night watchmen and gained access to the armory. Indeed, things were going so well that Brown sent several raiders 5 miles west of town on a totally unnecessary but symbolic mission. He had heard that Lewis Washington, a great-nephew of George Washington, lived between Charles Town and Harpers Ferry and that he had a sword given to General Washington by Frederick the Great. Brown was taken by the vision of leading an army of slaves with the sword of the father of the United States strapped to his side.

Brown's plan began to come apart at 1:25 A.M., when a baggagemaster named Hayward Shepherd discovered the raiders. Shepherd was running toward the station when he was shot in the back. Brown himself likely did not do the shooting, but the irony of the act could not be missed. Brown's holy war to free the slaves had claimed its first victim, a popular free black who held a respected position in the town. Shepherd died the next day despite the best efforts of his white doctor friend to save him.

Instead of seizing the thousands of weapons stored in the armory and escaping to try to incite a general slave revolt, Brown did something that puzzles historians to this day. He stayed put. He gathered more than 40 hostages in the local fire company's engine house, located over 100 yards from the railroad bridge he had crossed. Between the engine house and the bridge were several buildings he did not bother to seize, which were later occupied by townspeople. The engine house was a terrible place from which to fight a battle. Its windows were at the top of the walls, too high to be used as firing stands.

Late that night, Lieutenant Colonel Robert E. Lee of the United States Army and his aide, Lieutenant James Ewell Brown Stuart, arrived in town just behind a force of 90 United States Marines. Lee, who had rushed away from home so quickly that he was still in civilian dress, first offered to support the state militia in assaulting the engine house. The militia said it preferred that professional soldiers take on the task.

Lee then wrote out a surrender demand, which was delivered by Stuart.

Brown refused to surrender but offered to leave the engine house and go back to Maryland. Stuart, under orders not to listen to any counterproposals, dropped his hat as a signal for 12 handpicked marines to attack the engine house. The marines battered in the doors, after which the battle was over within three minutes. Two of Brown's raiders were killed by bayonet and sword. Brown himself was beaten to the ground with a sword.

Historians wonder about Brown's flawed tactics. He claimed he wanted to start a slave revolt, yet he made no effort before the raid to spread the word among slaves. He treated the slaves he captured from plantations more like prisoners than free men, so they were more afraid of him than they were of their masters. Once in Harpers Ferry, Brown let his presence be known to passing trains, assuring that the militia would rush to the scene. He also chose the worse defensive position from among dozens of possible buildings. If Brown's goal was to start a slave revolution, he failed miserably. But if his aim was to draw attention and set himself up for martyrdom, he succeeded wonderfully.

Less than 10 days after their capture, Brown and his followers went on trial in Charles Town for treason against Virginia, inciting slaves to riot, and murder. Brown's court-appointed attorneys initially tried to have him declared insane, since some members of his mother's family and some of his sons had been so declared. But Brown would have none of that defense. He wanted to be considered a hero, not a crazy man. The trial lasted less than four days, and the jury deliberated less than an hour before finding him guilty on all counts.

On December 2, 1859, Brown was taken to a field about four blocks from the Charles Town Jail and hanged. He left one of his jailers a note that read, "I am quite certain that the crimes of this guilty land will never be purged away, but with blood."

Within a year and a half, that prophecy came true. The Civil War officially started on April 12, 1861.

The National Park Service has tried to bring matters into focus with exhibits on slavery and the role Harpers Ferry played in the war. It offers displays in restored buildings on both sides of Shenandoah Street in the historic downtown area.

When you leave the shuttle, walk east on Shenandoah. The Master Armorer's House, which is marked by a sign located on the right, was the

Monument to Hayward Shepherd

home of J. P. Dangerfield, who was captured by Brown and held hostage in the engine house. Ironically, two years before the raid, Dangerfield had bought a slave girl from the Charles Town judge who later sentenced Brown to death. After the raid, Robert E. Lee was entertained at the Master Armorer's House.

Continue past the corner of Shenandoah and High Streets, where two Harpers Ferry citizens were mortally wounded by Brown's men.

Proceed to the John Brown Museum, located at the corner of Shenandoah and Potomac Streets. The museum tells the history of slavery and details the lives of the men who followed Brown. Among the interesting artifacts preserved here are a pike, a Sharps carbine, and pieces of the original engine house doors.

The museum is located in a home once owned by a white man named Philip Coons. John Douglass, a free black who lived in the house with Coons, discovered in 1856 that Coons was arranging to sell Douglass's wife and child to pay debts from his failed business. Douglass had only $400 of the $1,000 asking price, so he borrowed money from the white citizens of Harpers Ferry, using his wife and child as collateral. He raised the money, freed his wife and child, and later repaid the loan.

Near the museum on Potomac Street is a monument to Hayward Shepherd, the free black who was mortally wounded by Brown's raiders. His death likely made the slaves among the hostages suspect that Brown was a lunatic, rather than a savior come to set them free.

Continue east to the engine house, better known as John Brown's Fort, located about 100 yards from its original site. The smallness of the building and its high windows demonstrate how impossible it was to defend from attack. It was inside this building that Brown's two sons perished—deaths that Brown himself barely acknowledged and did not mourn.

Walk past the engine house to where the Potomac and Shenandoah Rivers meet. You'll see a footbridge that crosses the Potomac to Maryland; the footbridge parallels the old railroad bridge that Brown and his men took into Harpers Ferry. Just to the north are numerous rocks in the shallow Potomac. It was on such rocks that at least three of Brown's men were shot down while trying to wade back across the river after the raid went bad. According to some accounts, angry, bored, and drunken townspeople, upset that they could not get a clear shot at the raiders holed up in the engine house, used the bodies of these men for target practice.

It was also in the area north of the railroad bridge that more than 1,500 Union cavalrymen led by Colonel Benjamin Franklin "Grimes" Davis escaped Stonewall Jackson's three-sided capture of Harpers Ferry on September 14, 1862. Davis and his men proceeded silently over a pontoon bridge by muffling their horses' hooves. Once on the Maryland shore, they moved north until they could get out of the valley. Completely by accident, they then came upon a 91-wagon Confederate ammunition wagon train on its way to Sharpsburg. Davis, an Alabama native who had stayed loyal to the Union but kept his Southern accent, convinced the wagon drivers that the men in the darkness were a Confederate cavalry detachment. He led the wagon train into Pennsylvania before it got light enough for the Confederates to realize they had been captured. No shots were fired during the entire incident.

Hardy visitors can cross the footbridge and hike all the way up Maryland Heights, following steep trails to reach an excellent view of Harpers Ferry; some entrenchments left over from the Civil War are visible along the way. But be forewarned that this is a challenging hike for casual walkers. Even if you choose not to try the complete hike, crossing the footbridge and returning will be well worth your time.

Coming back to Harpers Ferry over the footbridge provides a good opportunity to contemplate how wily Stonewall Jackson could be. In May 1861, before he acquired his nickname, Jackson was assigned command of the city, which he used as a training base. Incredibly, it had not yet occurred to the Federal government to stop its trains from rolling through Harpers Ferry, which was Confederate territory. But the value of those trains to the South had indeed occurred to Jackson.

He sent a note to the president of the Baltimore & Ohio Railroad complaining that the coal trains passing through Harpers Ferry at all hours of the day and night disturbed his men's sleep. He asked that they be rescheduled to run between the hours of 11 A.M. and 1 P.M. only, so his men could get some needed rest from drilling. The railroad president complied.

Jackson then waited for a day when all the trains were bottled up along a short stretch of track, at which time he captured them without firing a shot. He subsequently transferred them south.

After getting off the footbridge, look straight ahead. The filled, empty land northwest of Potomac Street was the original armory site, where the engine house was located. Near the engine house was a water tower, the site where the mayor of Harpers Ferry was shot down by Brown's men.

Walk west along Shenandoah Street. Just off the intersection with High Street is the Black Voices Museum, which describes slavery and the struggle for freedom.

Hardy visitors might want to walk all the way up High Street to the Mountain House Cafe. In days gone by, Isaac Gilbert, a slave, lived here with his wife and three children. Gilbert was allowed to hire himself out and keep all the money he collected, so he used the opportunity to raise funds to buy his wife and children. Since a slave could not buy another slave, he asked the mayor of Harpers Ferry to make the purchase. Mayor Fountain Beckham agreed to do so; he even changed his will to read that the members of Gilbert's family should be set free if Beckham died before Gilbert made enough money to buy their freedom. In fact, Beckham died in October 1859, shot by John Brown's men. The members of Gilbert's family were thus the only slaves freed by Brown's raid—and they were freed by Virginia's strict laws regarding slavery, not by the revolt itself! Gilbert was later freed by the war, after which he and his family continued to live in Harpers Ferry.

Retrace your route to the shuttle area and return to your car. Leaving the parking lot, cross U.S. 340, after which the road becomes Washington Street. Within a quarter mile, turn left onto Whitman Avenue and drive 0.2 mile to Bolivar Heights, where the tour ends. This is another National Park Service site. It was here in 1861 that Jackson drilled his men into what would become the famous Stonewall Brigade of Virginia regiments, which could march 25 miles in a day and then go into battle.

A brief battle took place here in September 1862, before Sharpsburg. A Confederate artillery shell fired from Loudoun Heights across the valley exploded and mortally wounded the Federal commander, Colonel Dixon Miles. Within hours, the 12,500 Union soldiers on Bolivar Heights, surrounded on three sides by Confederates, surrendered, the largest mass surrender of American forces until Bataan in the South Pacific in 1942. When Jackson reviewed the captured troops, one Federal remarked that Stonewall was not much to look at, but that if he had not been in charge, the Union men would not have found themselves trapped the way they were.

Located down a long footpath is a Federal artillery battery aimed at School House Ridge, the ridge held by Jackson during the short siege.

President Lincoln visited this area after Sharpsburg to review the troops and to urge McClellan to be more aggressive in his pursuit of the Confederates. That effort failed.

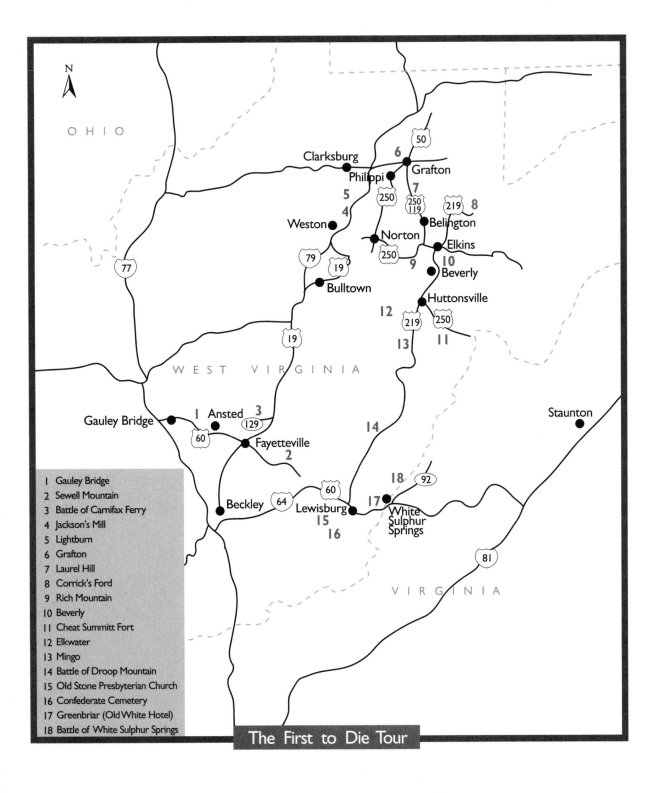

N

OHIO

Clarksburg
Philippi
5
Weston
4
79
19
Bulltown
19

WEST VIRGINIA

Gauley Bridge   1   Ansted   3
129
60
Fayetteville
2
Beckley
64
Lewisburg
15
16

6   50
Grafton
7
250
250
119
8
219
Belington
Norton
250
Elkins
9
10
Beverly
Huttonsville
12
219
13
11
250

14

18   92
17
White
Sulphur
Springs

81

Staunton

77

VIRGINIA

1 Gauley Bridge
2 Sewell Mountain
3 Battle of Carnifax Ferry
4 Jackson's Mill
5 Lightburn
6 Grafton
7 Laurel Hill
8 Corrick's Ford
9 Rich Mountain
10 Beverly
11 Cheat Summitt Fort
12 Elkwater
13 Mingo
14 Battle of Droop Mountain
15 Old Stone Presbyterian Church
16 Confederate Cemetery
17 Greenbriar (Old White Hotel)
18 Battle of White Sulphur Springs

The First to Die Tour

The First to Die Tour

This tour starts at the grave of a militia general in Beckley, West Virginia. It proceeds to the site where indirect artillery fire was first used and then goes to the grave of Stonewall Jackson's mother before backtracking to the spot where Robert E. Lee first saw his famed warhorse, Traveller. From there, the tour moves north to several battlefields and to the boyhood home of Stonewall Jackson before heading east to the spot in Grafton where the first soldier to die in the war fell. Next, it moves south to Philippi, Rich Mountain, Corrick's Ford, and Cheat Mountain—the sites of four Union victories that helped make the reputation of General George McClellan. It then visits Droop Mountain, the site of the largest battle in West Virginia, before moving to Lewisburg, the site of one of the war's shortest battles. It ends in White Sulphur Springs, a resort that attracted Lee after the war.

The tour covers 360 miles, mostly in rural areas. It will require more than one day.

THE TOUR STARTS IN THE BECKLEY CEMETERY, located at 1400 Kanawha Street just east of downtown Beckley, West Virginia. The grave of Alfred Beckley, a Confederate militia general, is within an iron fence to the right of the road leading into the cemetery just before it curves to the left. Beckley was one of the town's founders; he named the community after his father. The inscription on his gravestone reads, "Thou shalt here sweetly rest in the calmest repose undisturbed by life's cares, pierced by its woes."

Alfred Beckley's war career is a good example of how nothing seems to go right for some people. Early in the war, Beckley, a West Point graduate in the lackluster class of 1823, volunteered to raise a Confederate unit. He found very few volunteers, as most of the men in his county were Unionists. Still, he managed to wangle a commission as a general of militia, which was not the equal of a general's commission in the regular army. He raised a handful of militiamen and was put to work guarding river crossings. His work and his men were criticized as being useless to the war effort, so he resigned and went home to Beckley.

Almost as soon as he got there, Union forces came and arrested him as if he were a real Confederate general. He hastened to explain that he had only been trying to be loyal to Virginia, and that he was really a Union man. The Federals didn't buy it. They sent him to Camp Chase, a military prison in Columbus, Ohio, where he remained for several months before returning home in June 1862. Distrusted by both North and South, he sat out the rest of the war. His five sons all served the Confederacy.

To visit Wildwood, the former home of Alfred Beckley, turn left on to Kanawha, drive half a block, turn right on F Street, then go right on Laurel Terrace. Wildwood is now a house museum.

Wildwood, former home of Alfred Beckley

When you are ready to leave Wildwood, retrace your route to Kanawha Street and turn right. Drive 1 mile to U.S. 19, and turn left to head north. It is about 35 miles to Fayetteville. Turn right on W.V. 16 to reach the downtown area. Turn right on Maple Street at the second light and drive 1.3 miles to the historical marker on the left.

In May 1863, a Confederate battery at this location issued the first indirect artillery fire in military history. Until then, cannons were used as big muskets, throwing shells at distant, observable targets such as houses, bridges, and columns of troops, or as big shotguns, blasting away with canister at advancing enemy forces. But then Sergeant Milton Humphreys of King's Artillery got the idea of elevating his cannon's muzzle until it reached an angle he figured would lob shells into the Union soldiers occupying Fayetteville. Humphreys could not see downtown Fayetteville because of obstructing trees and hills, but he knew it was there. Knowing the range of his cannon and the distance to downtown Fayetteville, he used simple geometry to figure the angle he needed to elevate the muzzle. The Federals endured 69 artillery rounds dropping out of the clear blue sky before they managed to find the Confederate position. The sergeant's innovation is now a standard tactic for all artillery. Humphreys later became a college professor of Greek.

Turn around and go back to Fayetteville, retracing your route to U.S. 19. Turn right on to U.S. 19. Just north of town, you will pass over the second-tallest bridge in the United States. It stands more than 800 feet above the New River. Parachutists jump from it once a year.

Exit off U.S. 19 on to U.S. 60 West about 6.9 miles after leaving Fayetteville; head west toward Gauley Bridge and Ansted. In 5.6 miles, you will reach downtown Ansted. Look for a sign on the right that directs you down an unnamed street to Westlake Cemetery. Follow the signs to Westlake Cemetery. Park your car and walk diagonally toward the center of the cemetery until you reach a point directly in line with the road that came in from

U.S. 60. Here, you'll find the grave of Julia Beckwith Neale Jackson Woodson, the mother of Stonewall Jackson, who died at age 33, when Thomas was barely seven years old.

Sadly, Thomas was not with his mother when she died. He and his sister, both of whom had briefly lived on a farm near Ansted with their mother and stepfather, had been shipped off to Jackson's father's uncles after Blake Woodson determined he could not afford to raise two children who were not his own.

Jackson did not visit his former home until June 1855, when the lonely college professor, now a widower himself, felt the urge to track down his roots. He came to Ansted and found a man who claimed he had helped bury Julia in 1831, though he could not remember exactly where the unmarked grave was.

Grave of Julia Jackson Woodson, mother of Stonewall Jackson

Jackson never got a chance to return and erect a stone, as he had vowed to do. Years later, members of the Stonewall Brigade placed a marker over the presumed grave.

Return to U.S. 60 and head west. Just outside town is Contentment, the former home of Colonel George Imboden, commander of the 18th Virginia. It now serves as a museum.

It is 7.4 miles to Gauley Bridge; en route, the twisting road passes Hawks Nest, now a state park. This was the scene of a small battle in September 1861 when General Henry Wise and 1,000 Confederates tried to drive an equal-size force from the Hawks Nest, an overlook on the New River. Wise failed.

Cross the Gauley River and bear right on W.V. 16/W.V. 39 in the town of Gauley Bridge. The white two-story community center on the left was once a tavern used by two Union generals as a headquarters.

Gauley Bridge

Park along the street and walk toward the river. In the water are the original pilings for the wartime Gauley Bridge. Since this area is located at the confluence of two rivers, whoever controlled it controlled much of the state's commerce. The area was in Federal hands for most of the war.

Return to U.S. 60 and retrace your route east to U.S. 19 for 15.5 miles. Continue on U.S. 60 for 16 miles past U.S. 19, heading up Sewell Mountain. Slow down to look for a historical marker on the left side of the road. Just before the marker, turn left on Cavendish Road. Pull over at the top of

Spot where Robert E. Lee pitched his tent

the hill, where you'll see a big rock and a tree enclosed by an iron fence. The rock marks the spot where General Robert E. Lee pitched his tent while commanding forces in this area. The original tree here was cut down in the 1930s when it became diseased, at which time the current tree was planted.

It was at this campsite that Lee first observed a fine horse one of his soldiers was riding. Lee found out that the four-year-old, named Jeff Davis, had already been promised to an officer. Lee asked that officer about acquiring the horse, mentioning that he might need such a strong-looking animal himself.

A few months later, Lee was transferred to South Carolina to assess that state's ability to defend itself. One day while on duty, he saw Jeff Davis. The horse had by then been renamed Greenbriar, in honor of the county in western Virginia where it was born. The officer who owned the horse had also been transferred to South Carolina. Lee again asked about acquiring the horse, and the officer offered it to him as a gift, which Lee refused. Instead, he paid $200. Since Lee would be riding all over South Carolina looking at forts, he renamed the horse Traveller.

After the war, Lee described Traveller in a letter: "Fine proportions, muscular figure, deep chest, short back, strong haunches, flat legs, small head, broad forehead, delicate ears, quick eye, small feet and black mane and tail. Such a picture would inspire a poet, whose genius would then depict his worth and describe his endurance of toil, hunger, thirst, heat and cold and the dangers and sufferings through which he passed."

Finding Traveller was about the only good thing that happened to Lee on Sewell Mountain. Arriving in late September 1861, he found two generals under his command who were so paralyzed with hate for one another that they would not even unite to fight the Yankees, who were no more than a few miles in their front. No commander should have to deal with even a single general as incompetent as John Floyd or Henry Wise. But Lee was stuck with both.

Floyd, a 55-year-old lawyer elected Virginia's governor in 1848, had worked his way up the political ladder until he was made United States secretary of war by President James Buchanan in 1857. While in office, Floyd was accused of sending an excessive quantity of arms to the South.

Though he might have been preparing the South for eventual secession, he was not trained as a military man, as became evident when he was asked to perform in the field. President Jefferson Davis made Floyd a brigadier general in May 1861. The appointment came more out of a need to stroke a powerful Virginia politician than out of any recognition of his military skills.

Wise, also a 55-year-old lawyer, had been elected Virginia's governor in 1856 after serving 10 years in Congress, where he vocally defended his native region and the practice of slavery. Like Floyd, he had never served in the military. Davis also saw a need to appoint Wise as a general. Wise got his commission about two weeks after Floyd, which meant that Floyd was considered the senior officer of the two.

The two met for the first time as generals in August 1861 at White Sulphur Springs. Within minutes, they found themselves in a standoff that would never be resolved. Floyd ordered Wise's men into the field, but Wise, claiming his men had already been in the field, refused. He decided to write Lee—the new commanding general in western Virginia, who had not yet arrived on the scene—to separate his command from Floyd's.

On August 26, 1861, Floyd's little army surprised a resting regiment having its breakfast at a place called Kesler's Cross Lanes, capturing most of the Federals. Wise was following too far in the rear to take part in the short battle and therefore had to watch while Floyd accepted all the glory.

On September 10, Floyd's army was attacked at Carnifax Ferry on the Gauley River. Floyd beat off the Federals but left them the battlefield under cover of darkness. When he wrote his report, he said he could have defeated the Federals if Wise had cooperated and sent him some regiments he had previously requested.

It was at this battle that Floyd showed he was not exactly the brightest commander ever to strap on a sword belt. When the Federals attacked, he jumped on top of a stump to shout to his men, instantly offering himself as a target. On top of that, he wore an outsized white straw hat, which called even more attention to himself. The wound he suffered to his arm that day did not strike a bone.

After the battle, Wise referred to his rival as "that bullet-hit son of a bitch," perhaps implying that he wished the bullet had done more than pass through Floyd's arm.

Floyd and Wise retreated about 20 miles southwest to Sewell Mountain, but they could not even agree on combining their two little forces at one defendable spot. After seeming to agree on a course of action, Floyd marched his men right past Wise and pushed farther east, leaving Wise's 2,200 troops in the open.

It was at this point that Lee arrived at Floyd's camp. He urged the two men to unite their forces, but they ignored his pleas. Lee could not even get them into the same camp. He ended up shuttling back and forth between Wise and Floyd, a distance of 12 miles.

Then Jefferson Davis ordered Wise to turn over command of his troops to Floyd and return immediately to Richmond. Davis had finally realized his mistake in making both men generals and putting them in the same region. He swallowed his pride and brought Wise east, where he was sent to the Outer Banks of North Carolina to defend against an expected invasion.

Wise and Floyd never made much of themselves during the war, just as their performance in western Virginia predicted.

Wise botched the defense of the Outer Banks and even lost one of his sons in the process, one of the few Confederate casualties. He did little more for the rest of the war, though he was present at Appomattox.

Floyd was reassigned to Tennessee and was inexplicably put in charge of the strategically important Fort Donelson. When almost surrounded by Federals, Floyd turned over his command to a subordinate, then boarded a steamboat with just his Virginia regiments, leaving the rest of the Confederates to surrender. Had Floyd tried to break out of Fort Donelson as Nathan Bedford Forrest did with his cavalry, the whole command may have made it to safety. An exasperated Jefferson Davis subsequently removed Floyd from command. Floyd died in 1863.

For his part, Lee figured it would take time to get Floyd's and Wise's forces to work together. He waited nearly a month for the Federals to attack him on Sewell Mountain—a wait that earned him an unflattering nickname, "Granny" Lee. When asked why he did not attack, as was being demanded by the Richmond newspapers back east, Lee replied, "I could not afford to sacrifice the lives of five or six hundred of my people to silence public clamor."

When the Federals withdrew without attacking, Lee was ordered back to

Richmond in late October, having done little but look at the enemy. With winter coming on, there would be no more fighting in that part of Virginia in 1861. It could not even be called Virginia any longer. A few days after Lee left the area, the western counties started calling for the creation of a new state. West Virginia would formally join the Union in June 1863.

Retrace your route to U.S. 19. Drive north on U.S. 19 for 9.4 miles until you see the brown signs for the Carnifax Ferry Battlefield. Turn left on W.V. 129 and drive 5.1 miles to Carnifax Ferry Road or C.R. 23, then turn left and go 0.5 mile to the park entrance.

On September 10, 1861, just six weeks after the Confederate victory at Manassas, General William Rosecrans struck Floyd's 2,600 Confederates with three Ohio brigades. Floyd's men were well dug in and fought hard and well. In fact, they suffered no deaths and only 30 wounded, while the Federals had 130 casualties, including 27 killed.

All the same, Floyd's ineptness is obvious to anyone visiting the battlefield at Carnifax Ferry. If you walk to the back edge of the battlefield and look down, you'll note that the Gauley River lies several hundred feet below. If the Federals had ever gotten the Confederates retreating, there would have been nowhere for them to run except over a cliff. The first rules of warfare are to always have an escape route and to never fight a battle with a river at your back. Floyd left himself no escape route and had not only a river at his back, but a cliff to boot.

Rosecrans survived this early debacle of not crushing an inferior Confederate force. Two years and one week later, he would find himself crushed as the Union commander at the Battle of Chickamauga in Georgia.

The Patterson House was a focal point of the action at Carnifax Ferry. It served as a field hospital after the battle and is now a museum. Bullet holes are visible inside and outside the house.

The Patterson House

When you are ready to leave the park, return to W.V. 129, turn left, and proceed 0.9 mile to Kesler's Cross Lanes. A battle took place here on August 26, 1861, two weeks before Carnifax Ferry. It was a small affair; two men were killed on the Federal side and five on the Confederate side. The battle has an interesting alternate name—the Battle of Knives and Forks, so dubbed because the Confederates surprised the Federals while they were cooking breakfast.

Return on W.V. 129 to U.S. 19. Drive north on U.S. 19 for 40.5 miles, then take Exit 67 to continue on U.S. 19 toward Bulltown; the road narrows to a two-lane. After 12.1 miles on the two-lane, turn left on Millstone Run Road, following the signs for the United States Army Corps of Engineers–maintained park. Turn into the parking lot at the interpretive center. Do not go through the gate to the park itself.

This is Bulltown, a sleepy but strategically important spot where both the Little Kanawha River and the road could be protected by a single Federal fort on top of a hill. Walk up the trail behind the Catholic church to reach the well-preserved Federal entrenchments.

Trenches at Bulltown

Here, on October 12, 1863, a force of 750 Confederates crept up on 400 unsuspecting Federals in the predawn darkness. The Federal pickets were either asleep or not paying attention—at least until some dumb Confederate officer yelled "Charge!" and fired his pistol well below the crest of the hill. The Federals sprang into their trenches, where they proceeded to hold off the Confederate attackers. When asked to surrender, the Federal commander gave an excellent response: "I will fight until hell freezes over and then if forced to retreat, I will retreat on the ice." Though the fighting lasted all day, only seven Confederates and no Federals were killed.

The battle was more crucial than the light losses suggest. Had the Confederates won, they would have captured an important Union outpost and control of both the river and the land routes through the region. And had they been reinforced, they might have had a chance to start winning back lost territory in what was then officially West Virginia.

Walk back down the hill to the Cunningham House. Mr. Cunningham ran outside during the battle and shouted, "Hurrah for Jeff Davis!" A bullet whizzed past his head and took off part of his ear. He went back inside his house and did not cheer for the remainder of the day.

Return to U.S. 19 and continue 28.6 miles to Weston. About 2 miles north of town, turn left on C.R. 12, following the signs for Jackson's Mill. It is about 2.5 miles to a large white building on a stream.

Jackson's Mill is where seven-year-old Thomas Jonathan Jackson came to live with his uncle Cummins Jackson after his mother and stepfather gave him and his sister Laura up. Cummins was quite a character. Biographers describe him as greedy and not as loving as the two little children

probably needed. Nonetheless, he did provide them a home. Thomas grew up at the mill. Once, he taught a young slave friend how to write in exchange for a supply of pine knots that would burn bright enough for Jackson to read by at night. The slave used his newfound skills to forge himself a pass to escape to Canada.

While a teenager, Jackson met a newcomer to the area, Joseph Lightburn, a boy his own age. The two became fast friends, Jackson often walking from his home to borrow books from the Lightburns.

When Thomas was 18, he tried for an appointment to West Point but lost out to another boy. That boy went to West Point and took an immediate dislike to its discipline. He departed the next day, opening the appointment to Jackson. Thomas left Jackson's Mill in January 1842 for the military academy that would provide him the most stable existence he had yet known.

Grave of Jonathan Jackson, father of Stonewall Jackson

Today, the mill is a historical area. The house where Jackson lived no longer survives.

Continue on C.R. 12 to C.R. 1 and turn right. Follow C.R. 1 for 2.6 miles toward the community of Lightburn, then turn right on C.R. 8 (Broad Run Road). It is about 0.3 mile to Broad Run Baptist Church on the left.

Walk in back of the church, align yourself with the church bell, and walk away from the church about 200 feet to reach the tall obelisk marking the grave of Joseph Lightburn, Stonewall Jackson's boyhood friend—and later a Union general.

Four years after Lightburn was unable to get a West Point appointment, he joined the regular army as a private. That was about the same time that Jackson graduated from West Point with a second lieutenant's commission. Lightburn rose to sergeant, then resigned from the army, only to return 10 years later when the war started. At that time, he was appointed a colonel in charge of some western Virginia troops who had remained loyal to the Union. Good performance brought him a general's appointment.

Lightburn served credibly under Grant in Mississippi and Tennessee and under Sherman in Georgia until he was shot in the head near Atlanta. He was apparently a hardheaded man in a literal sense—the bullet traveled along his skull, rather than through it. Nonetheless, he suffered headaches for the rest of his life. After the war, he became pastor of this church.

His tombstone makes no mention of his service to his country or his faith. Likewise, biographers make no mention of whether Jackson and Lightburn, the two friends on opposite sides of the war, ever tried to communicate with each other during the conflict.

When you are ready to leave the church, go left on C.R. 8, heading toward the town of Jane Lew. It is about 3 miles from the church to I-79. Head north on I-79 toward Clarksburg. After 13.7 miles, take Exit 119 (the Clarksburg and Bridgeport exit) and get on U.S. 50 East.

Stonewall was born in Clarksburg in a house that no longer survives. The graves of his father and young sister are in a poorly maintained, hard-to-reach cemetery behind Jackson City Park off South Linden Street. The elder Jackson died when Thomas was barely two and so had little influence on the future general's upbringing.

Drive east on U.S. 50 about 15 miles toward Grafton. Just outside town is a sign announcing a historical marker; pull over to the right at the small stone monument.

If you consider that no one was killed during the bombardment of Fort Sumter, South Carolina, from April 12 to April 14, 1861, then the Civil War—the killing war, at least—started a couple of hundred yards northwest of this spot. It was along the nearby railroad track on May 22, 1861, that the first of more than 620,000 Americans died. The monument preserves the memory of Private Thornsberry Bailey Brown of the Grafton Guards, which became the Second West Virginia Infantry Volunteers.

The circumstances behind the death of Private Brown are both murky and interesting. The official story is that Brown's lieutenant wanted to test the vigilance and strength of Confederate pickets guarding the railroad bridge over the Tygart River. He ordered Brown forward and told him to fire on the Confederates to see what would happen. Brown let loose a shot, nicking the ear of one of the Confederates. They responded by sending three shots into his chest, killing him instantly. He was thus the first of more than 320,000 Union soldiers to die in combat during the war.

Other historians recount a story that before the war, Brown got into a scrap with a man named Daniel Knight. Having resisted arrest for stealing some bees, Knight moved to the Grafton area to escape the law. When the local sheriff found out Knight was nearby, he enlisted Brown's aid in bringing in the bee stealer. Knight swore vengeance, and it is said by some that it was he who shot Brown. If true, this means that the first man to die in the Civil War may have been the victim of a revenge murder, and that Brown's killing may not have been a true combat death resulting from an exchange of fire between pickets who were strangers to each other.

There is also some question whether Brown was even wearing a blue uniform, as his unit was not yet officially part of the Union army. He may have been in civilian clothes or a local militia uniform thrown together in the early days of the war.

Finally, some accounts say that Brown, Knight, and perhaps the other pickets were armed with pistols rather than military muskets. That would have made the first deadly exchange of the Civil War more like the gunfight at the O.K. Corral than a military battle.

Continue into Grafton on U.S. 50. After 0.6 mile, turn right on Main Street (which may not be marked with a street sign but is located beside the Grafton Animal Hospital). Go 1.2 miles to the first light and make a hard, downhill turn to the right on to U.S. 119. Cross the river, following the signs for Grafton National Cemetery; do not follow U.S. 119 where it turns right leaving town. Bear left, cross the railroad tracks, drive to Beech Street, and turn right to reach the cemetery.

You'll need to walk down two flights of steps to find Brown's obelisk, located in Section F on the right next to the sidewalk in the rear of the cemetery. The obelisk identifies Brown as the first soldier to die in the war and is unique in that it names the man who killed him, as well as the man's commanding officer. The naming of those two men may suggest the continuation of a local feud.

Retrace your route to U.S. 119 and head south out of Grafton. On the left less than 3 miles out of town is the former home of Anna Jarvis, the woman who created Mother's Day in honor of her own mother, who nursed wounded Union soldiers.

In another 10.3 miles, you will enter the outskirts of Philippi (pronounced FILL-a-pee), the site of the first true land action of the war. Watch on the right for Anderson-Broaddus College.

General Robert E. Lee, the provisional head of Virginia's forces in the spring of 1861, ordered the few volunteers in this area to recruit more men and to concentrate them at Philippi until they could be assigned. Federal forces under the command of Colonel Benjamin F. Kelley discovered the isolated Confederates and moved toward them in the dead of night on June 3.

A Union cannon position sits on the ridge now occupied by Anderson-Broaddus College. The signal for the Federals to fire the first land-cannon shot of the war was unwittingly given by a local woman who sympathized with the newly formed Confederacy. She had spotted the approaching Union soldiers and tried to send her son to warn the sleeping Confederates, but the boy was grabbed by Union soldiers as he tried to get out of the house. The woman then pulled a pistol and shot at the Federals in an attempt to free her son. Coincidentally, the Federal gunners had been waiting for a pistol shot as a signal to fire their cannon. They opened up at the sound of the woman's shot, several minutes sooner than they should have, since another Union column converging on Philippi was not yet in place.

The sleepy Confederates rushed from their tents at the sound of the Union cannons and rushed over the covered bridge out of town, retreating in a panic that the Federals dubbed the "Philippi Races." Indeed, the Confederates left town so quickly that the action can barely be called a battle. No one was killed on either side, though several men were wounded, including Colonel Kelley, who would fight mostly in West Virginia during his service.

Kelley was given a horse by his men in celebration of the battle. He named the animal Philippi.

Turn left off U.S. 119 on to U.S. 250 and cross the covered bridge—one of the few still located on a United States highway. Pull into the parking lot to get a better view of the bridge. A museum of the battle is located across the road.

One good thing came out of the action here. Wounded in the fighting, a Confederate named J. E. Hanger endured the amputation of his leg—probably the first of thousands of such battlefield operations performed during the war. While recovering, Hanger designed his own artificial leg. He later started a company to help other amputees. That company is still in business today.

Continue 11.2 miles to Belington on U.S. 250.

In July 1861, General Robert S. Garnett and his force of several thousand Confederates were just north of Belington at a place called Laurel Hill. General George McClellan, who had taken over command of the Union forces in this region just a few days earlier, sent a "feint" force to Laurel Hill on July 10, the purpose being to trick Garnett into thinking it was the Union's main attack. McClellan's target was really the Confederates at Rich Mountain, about 15 miles away; those Confederates sat astride the Parkersburg-Staunton Turnpike, a major east-west road over the mountains. McClellan knew that if he controlled that road, he could control the movement of troops of either side.

Garnett took the bait. He left Laurel Hill and moved toward the town of Beverly, where, from a distance, he could see men milling around. Thinking they were Union soldiers, he retreated north. What Garnett had actually seen were Confederates retreating from the Battle of Rich Mountain. In a comedy of errors that reflected how poorly organized the early armies were, the two Confederate forces marched right past each other. The Confederates retreating from Rich Mountain went to Laurel Hill, expecting to find Garnett and his 5,000 men, who were by then well on their way north toward Corrick's Ford. More than 500 demoralized and abandoned Confederates surrendered at Laurel Hill.

Continue through Belington for 6 miles to U.S. 33; turn left toward Elkins. It is about 1 mile to the junction with C.R. 151.

If you'd like to take a side trip to Corrick's Ford, continue 7.1 miles on U.S. 33 into Elkins, then turn north on U.S. 219 toward Parsons. Drive about 19 miles, then—if traffic allows—slow down on this narrow, twisting road. Just outside Parsons on the right side of the road is a historical marker at the site of the mortal wounding of General Robert S. Garnett on July 13, 1861. Do not stop on this blind corner; continue driving toward Parsons.

Garnett, the first general on either side to die in the war, was a West Point graduate, a Mexican War veteran, and a former superintendent of cadets at West Point. He was supervising his men's retreat from Laurel Hill when he heard firing at Corrick's Ford. He went to the rear of the column and was peering under some low-hanging vines when a Union sharpshooter hit him. Some histories say he died in a nearby house. Others say he died on the field. Garnett was buried in Brooklyn, New York. His more famous cousin, General Richard Garnett, was killed at Gettysburg on the third-day charge.

Retrace your route to the junction of U.S. 33 and C.R. 151, 6 miles west of Elkins, to complete the side trip. Turn left on to C.R. 151.

Head south on C.R. 151. After a short distance, turn left on C.R. 53 (Coaltown-Pumpkintown Road). Drive 4.2 miles, then turn left on C.R. 5 at Coaltown and cross Roaring Creek Flats, where the Union army camped before starting its attack. You are now on Rich Mountain Road.

The Battle of Rich Mountain, fought on July 11, 1861, was tiny as battles go. General George McClellan, the Union commander, ordered part of his forces to demonstrate on the western side of Rich Mountain, where most of the Confederates, under Lieutenant Colonel John Pegram, were camped. Meanwhile, the other half of the Federals, under General William Rosecrans, marched around the eastern side of the mountain and moved stealthily up the turnpike to attack the Confederates at the summit. It was not much of a fight. The Federals had six times as many men, and the Confederates had only one cannon. With little ado, the Federals charged and routed the Confederates. The Federals lost 12 killed and 62 wounded to the Confederates' 33 killed and 39 wounded.

McClellan was not even on the field at the Battle of Rich Mountain. He stayed on the western side to keep watch on the Confederate camp.

The plan was for him to attack the camp once he heard shooting on top of the mountain, but he never made that attack, much to the consternation of his officers, who wanted in on the fighting. This inaction on the battlefield was a habit throughout McClellan's career.

Though he had little to do with the victory, McClellan was given—and accepted—the credit for it. When General Irvin McDowell was defeated at First Manassas just 10 days later, Lincoln did not have far to search for his replacement. McClellan's absentee victory over 300 Confederates and one cannon, magnified well out of proportion, was enough for Lincoln to hand him the reins to all Union forces.

Follow Rich Mountain Road up the mountain for 3.75 miles (known as the Parkersburg-Staunton Turnpike during the war) as it climbs Rich Mountain. There is parking at Camp Pegram, the Confederate camp that McClellan kept watch on while Rosecrans did the real fighting. The road becomes gravel and has some steep switchbacks, but it should be passable except in inclement weather. Located at the summit of the mountain, the battlefield looks much like it did during the fight, except that the Hart House, which stood here in days gone by, burned down in the 1940s. If you have time, be sure to explore the markers and trails.

Continue over the mountain for another 3.75 miles and head carefully and slowly down to Beverly—the town where Garnett mistook milling Confederates for massing Federals. Turn right at the intersection with U.S. 250/U.S. 219 and drive one block to the Randolph County Historical Museum, formerly the Blackman-Bosworth Store, constructed in 1827. Park here. After visiting the museum, walk across the road to the wooden house facing the square. This is the Bushrod Crawford House, McClellan's headquarters while he was in Beverly. It is also the headquarters of the Rich Mountain Battlefield Association. It features good exhibits and maps of the battlefield.

Bushrod Crawford House

Walk north along U.S. 250 to view the house on the northwestern corner of the road that just brought you from Rich Mountain. This is the Jonathan Arnold House, built in the 1820s. It was purchased by the Arnolds in 1845 and was visited frequently by Thomas J. Jackson, since Mrs. Arnold was his baby sister, Laura.

Growing up, Laura and Thomas were inseparable. The death of their

Jonathan Arnold House, the house of Stonewall Jackson's sister, Laura

parents made them depend on each other for love and companionship. When separated by distance, such as when Thomas went to West Point, they wrote long letters to each other, offering advice and keeping away loneliness.

Nothing could drive the two siblings apart—except war. When the fighting started, Laura immediately expressed her love of the Union, despite the fact that her husband, Jonathan Arnold, was a Confederate sympathizer and her brother became a Southern hero. Brother and sister never wrote each other again. In fact, Laura turned mean, announcing to all who would listen that Thomas had cheated on his West Point entrance exams, though she never offered any proof. Other stories say she remarked that Jackson got what he deserved when he died in May 1863. Laura was so pro-Union that she openly invited Federal officers into her home, fueling local rumors that she was doing more than entertaining them socially. Such stories led to the Arnolds' postwar divorce. Laura moved away from Beverly after the war.

Beverly was captured for the last time on January 11, 1865, when 300 Confederate cavalrymen sneaked into town at three o'clock in the morning. All of the Federal pickets were asleep, thanks to a drinking party earlier that night.

When you are ready to leave Beverly, head south on U.S. 250/ U.S. 219 for 11 miles; stay to the left on U.S. 250 when the road splits at Huttonsville. It is 11.9 miles from the U.S. 250/U.S. 219 split to a gravel road called Cheat Summit Fort Road. Turn right and follow the gravel road to a **T** intersection; turn right to remain on Cheat Summit Fort Road, which can be a little rough. Follow the road to Cheat Summit Fort, an earthen fort built by Union forces.

Lee proposed to attack those forces on September 12, 1861, just before he left to try to mediate between Floyd and Wise. *Proposed* is the operative word. Lee laid out a detailed plan to attack the fort, which lay alongside the Parkersburg-Staunton Turnpike, but he left it to his commander in the field to carry out the orders. A colonel was to commence the attack at 10 A.M. Lee and everyone else waited to hear the sound of muskets. They did hear muskets—but from another direction. When Lee went to investigate, he found soldiers cleaning their weapons of mud and moisture by firing them. Lee was astounded. If he heard it, so did the Federals. The element of surprise was lost because of the laziness of those soldiers.

Viewed in another light, Lee was lucky that day. While he was on his way to find the source of the firing, a Federal cavalry detachment raced right past him twice, in opposite directions. Lee was just off the road in some woods within easy sight.

The 10 A.M. attack never came because the untrained Confederate officer in charge of it asked captured Federal pickets their opinion of the chance of the mission's success. The Federals replied that there were 4,000 soldiers in the fort, far more than would be necessary to hold it against the Confederates. The colonel listened to that advice and simply turned around and left, without orders from Lee. In fact, he didn't even inform Lee of his decision. He was later embarrassed to learn that the Yankees had lied to him—there were only 300 Federals in the fort. It could have been overrun with little loss of life.

Lee's first campaign thus ended before it started, simply because his inaugural wartime order was ignored. What made it worse was that word of the impending attack had leaked back to the Richmond press, which printed news of what it assumed would be an easy victory. After finding out that the Confederates had not even fired a shot other than to clean their muskets, the press began to grumble that Lee was a poor field commander. It would be eight months before the editors changed their minds.

From this debacle, Lee rode away to what he hoped would be a better opportunity—uniting Wise and Floyd. Little did he know how much worse things could get.

When you are ready to leave Cheat Summit Fort, return to U.S. 250.

If you wish to take a side trip to a Confederate fort where there was a real battle, turn right on U.S. 250 and drive about 15 miles through the town of Bartow. Watch for a historical marker for Camp Allegheny. Turn right near the marker on to a park service road, drive 0.6 mile, then turn right again on Old Pike Road. It is 1.3 miles to another marker, then 0.4 mile to a third marker; other markers may have been added by the United States Forest Service, which maintains this area. This was where Confederate troops went into winter quarters in December 1861.

On December 12, General Robert Milroy, the Union commander at Cheat Summit Fort, assembled a 2,000-man force and set out for Camp Allegheny, which was under the command of Colonel Edward Johnson.

The battle opened at 7:15 A.M. on December 13, when two wings of the Union force attacked both flanks of the fort. The attacks were uncoordinated and easily handled by Johnson's Confederates, who held the high ground and who had not been marching for a full day, as the Federals had. Both sides lost about 20 men killed, but the Federals left the field, so the Confederates were declared the winner. Johnson was promoted to general.

As it turned out, the Confederates might have wished that Camp Allegheny had been captured. They spent all winter out in the open. Disease swept through the camp, which was abandoned in April 1862.

Return on U.S. 250 to the turnoff to Cheat Summit Fort to complete the side trip.

Retrace U.S. 250 all the way to Huttonsville, then turn left on U.S. 219. It is 6.8 miles south on U.S. 219 to a marker on the right commemorating the death of Lieutenant Colonel John A. Washington, an aide to Lee and the last private owner of Mount Vernon, the home of George Washington, who was an ancestor of the colonel. Washington's death came about when he rode with Lee's son from their camp south of here to Elkwater, this site, to check the strength of the Federal picket line. Washington apparently rode too close.

Lee wrote a personal note to Washington's widow, the first of many such letters he would pen during the war.

It is another 10.9 miles to Mingo. Turn right on C.R. 51 (Mingo Flats Road). Drive about 1 mile until you see a Confederate statue on the left, seemingly in the middle of nowhere. This was the Confederate campsite where Lee planned the attack on Cheat Summit Fort that never came. Legend says that he started growing his beard in this camp because he had left his razor behind in a camp wagon. By the time the wagon caught up to him, the familiar gray beard was well under way. When Lee next saw his wife, she barely recognized him. He had worn a mustache for years but had never before grown a beard. He would wear it the last nine years of his life.

Continue on C.R. 51, making one left turn back toward U.S. 219; you will reach U.S. 219 about 2.5 miles after getting off it in Mingo.

Drive south on U.S. 219 for 37.6 miles to Droop Mountain State Park. Turn right into the park and follow the road to the top of the mountain, where you'll see two unusual battlefield markers with photographs of soldiers imbedded in them. Nearby is a small museum.

Confederate campsite where Lee started growing his beard

Closeup of the statue

The Battle of Droop Mountain, which took place on November 6, 1863, was the largest fight in West Virginia. The Federals made a two-part movement intended to sweep all the Confederates in the region into one spot, where they could be defeated by overwhelming numbers. General John Echols concentrated his 1,700 Confederates at Droop Mountain to await the 4,000 Federals. The Federals won by overwhelming numbers but did not kill or capture many Confederates.

The commanders at Droop Mountain were interesting figures.

One of the Union generals assigned to the pincer movement was Alfred Napoleon Alexander Duffié, a French soldier of fortune who went by the American nickname of "Nattie." Duffié never actually made it to the fight but participated in later battles.

The overall Federal commander was William Averell, who had been transferred from the main Union army after Chancellorsville because of his slowness in following up on advantages. After Averell made several long raids in West Virginia, he was brought back to the main army—before being fired when he proved slow again.

The Confederate commander was six-foot-four, 260-pound Harvard-educated

Droop Mountain battlefield marker

lawyer John Echols. A giant in a time when most men stood around five-foot-six and weighed about 150 pounds, Echols was apparently too big for his heart. Wounded once and often sick, he was relieved of command in 1864 due to constant illness.

Following their victory, the first body the Federals found on the battlefield was that of a black man in full Confederate uniform and accouterments.

One of the Federals assigned to a burial detail looked at the body of the Confederate he was dragging and noticed that one of his fingers was crooked. He looked again. The man was his brother.

Many of the soldiers on both sides at Droop Mountain were Virginians who had been faced with deciding for the Union or for Virginia.

The Confederates lost 33 killed, 100 wounded, and 12 captured, while the Federals lost 45 killed, 93 wounded, and two captured.

This battlefield is the site of some of the most bizarre ghost stories ever told.

After the battle, two little girls found some guns and brought them home to their cabin. As long as the muskets were in the house, rocks would be thrown at the girls by unseen hands. One day, a sheepskin rug in the cabin stood up and made a bawling sound. Bad things continued to happen until the girls returned the muskets to where they had found them.

There is also the story of a soldier who was beheaded by a cannon during the battle. For more than 130 years, people have reported seeing a headless man walking the battlefield, apparently looking for something.

When you are ready to leave Droop Mountain, continue 28 miles on U.S. 219 to Lewisburg. Turn right on Washington Street in the downtown area and go one block to Church Street. The North House Museum is located at this intersection. Built in 1820, it houses the collection of the Greenbriar Historical Society, including the saddle used in training Traveller.

Turn left on Church and go one block to Old Stone Presbyterian Church, erected in 1796.

After the Battle of Lewisburg, dead Confederates were buried in trenches beside this church. They were later dug up and reinterred in the Confederate Cemetery.

Behind the church is the Patton Vault, one chamber of which was re-

Old Stone Presbyterian Church

served for General A. W. Reynolds. Reynolds was an interesting man. He was fired from the United States Army while acting as a quartermaster when some discrepancies were found in his accounts. He officially remained in the army until October 1861, which was a neat trick because he had been made a captain in the Confederate army the preceding March and a colonel in July. After an undistinguished career in the Confederate army, he joined the Egyptian army in 1869. He died overseas in 1876. Records are unclear on whether his body was ever transferred to the United States.

Walk away from the church into the cemetery; when you are almost to the street, look for the grave of John Alfred Preston. Preston served with the Confederate cavalry and attended Washington College when Lee was president there. In 1897, Preston successfully prosecuted a man named Shue for the murder of his wife, Zona Heaster Shue, using the testimony of Mrs. Shue's ghost. It seems the ghost had told Mrs. Shue's mother that the death was not an accident, but murder. Furthermore, the ghost said that Mrs. Shue's neck had been broken by her husband. The body was exhumed, and just as the ghost said, the woman's neck was broken. Mrs. Shue's mother testified on the stand as to what her daughter's ghost had said, and the husband was convicted and sentenced to life in prison.

Also in this section of the cemetery is a monument to David S. Creigh, whose inscription describes him as a "martyr to his duty as husband and father." Creigh, a Confederate, came home after a battle to find a Union soldier looting his home and threatening his wife and daughter. He killed the soldier and hid the body. Seven months later, the Federals got wind of the story, arrested Creigh, and hanged him.

In the back corner of the cemetery near the intersection of Court and Foster Streets is the grave of William Rucker, a Unionist who guided the Federals during the attack on Lewisburg; Rucker pointed out the property of Confederates whose homes should be burned. After the war, he defended the man who murdered his ghostly wife.

When you are ready to leave Old Stone Presbyterian, continue 0.25 mile on Church Street to McElhenry Road and turn right. Drive up the hill to the Confederate Cemetery. This unique cemetery contains the graves of 95 unknown Confederates arranged in the shape of an 80-by-40-foot cross.

On May 23, 1862, during the Battle of Lewisburg, the Federals used this hill to fire on the Confederate positions to the east. This was one of the shortest battles on record, lasting less than an hour. The Confederates were so desperate for artillery that they used a Revolutionary War cannon that had been captured from the British. The Federals lost 13 killed and the Confederates 80 killed. The Confederates actually held a numerical advantage of 1,300 men, but they allowed a charge to sweep them away. The Confederate commander at Lewisburg, Henry Heth, a close friend of Lee and the only general Lee called by his first name, blamed the collapse of a militia unit for the defeat.

Return to Church Street. Turn left on Church, then go right on Foster Street and drive three blocks to the Methodist church. Note the artillery damage on the left front wall of the church.

Turn left on Lee Street and drive to U.S. 60. Turn right on U.S. 60 and head for White Sulphur Springs. In about 2.5 miles, you'll pass the turnoff to Organ Cave State Park. Saltpeter for making Confederate gunpowder was mined in the caves at the park.

It is another 5.8 miles to White Sulphur Springs, home of the Greenbriar Hotel. The Greenbriar dates to 1913, but the Old White Hotel stood on virtually the same site before, during, and after the war. The Old White

Spring house at Greenbriar

TOURING VIRGINIA'S AND WEST VIRGINIA'S CIVIL WAR SITES

was ordered to be burned by Union general David Hunter, but he was talked out of it. Park across the street from the entrance to the hotel.

The attraction for guests here was the sulphur springs, which were believed to have medicinal powers. For decades, the rich and famous gathered here. One letter on display in the President's Cottage is from a guest complaining about the $10-per-week board. He considered the fee outrageous. The board is considerably more than $10 a week now.

Walk on to the grounds of the Greenbriar. The Old White was located to the right of where the Greenbriar stands today and faced away at an angle.

Bear right along the street that the cottage awnings face. Many of the cottages are original to the site and served as auxiliary housing for the Old White. Walk down the row of cottages until you come to the one with a sign describing it as the Baltimore Cottage. Robert E. Lee and his family used this cottage, owned by the Harrison family, from 1867 through 1869. The cottage saw some remarkable political discussions. Many former Confederate generals and former vice president Alexander H. Stephens sometimes visited Lee.

Cottage at White Sulphur Springs where Lee stayed

Former Union general William Rosecrans, a Democrat, came to the cottage in 1868 to propose that Lee and other Southerners make some kind of public pronouncement that they realized the war was over and would treat blacks with fairness. Rosecrans was trying to counteract rumors from the Republicans that the South would attempt to return blacks to slavery if Reconstruction laws were slackened. Lee and other Confederate generals signed a letter that promised slavery was over, called the "White Sulphur Springs Letter." But Lee refused Rosecrans's requests that he go on the presidential campaign circuit for the Democrats. The letter did little to change anyone's mind about anything and fell far short of endorsing full political power for blacks.

There is no doubt that Lee was the most honored man at the Old White. The first time he entered the dining room, everyone in the room went silent, then stood and remained standing until he sat.

On one occasion, a Northern family came to the hotel, and Lee discovered that the Southerners were too resentful to extend a welcome. Lee stood up and asked if any of the young women in his party would accompany him to greet the family. One volunteered but asked if he did not feel bitterness toward Northerners. Lee replied, "When you go home, tell your friends it is unworthy of them as women, especially Christian women, to cherish feelings of resentment against the North. Tell them that it grieves me inexpressibly to know that such a state of things exists, and that I implore them to do their part to heal our country's wounds."

Once, a rumor swept the hotel that General Grant was coming to visit. A young woman asked Lee what he would do. Lee replied, "I shall welcome him into my home, show him all the courtesy which is due from one gentleman to another, and try to do everything in my power to make his stay agreeable." Grant did not show up.

In the summer of 1869, Lee sat for a group photograph that mixed former Confederate generals with politicians and benefactors. He looks uncomfortable in the photo, playing the role of a college president who has to stroke wealthy men to get money. Historians at the Greenbriar believe that the photo may have been taken near the tennis courts, as the background appears to show some open sky, which would indicate a ridge in the background.

Walk another 100 yards to the President's Cottage Museum, which details the history of the Old White and the Greenbriar. The walls are covered with murals depicting Civil War battles. A letter from Lee is on display.

When you are ready to leave the Greenbriar, continue east on U.S. 60 to W.V. 92. Turn left at the traffic light, then turn immediately right into the Hardee's parking lot, where the tour ends.

You are now on the battlefield at White Sulphur Springs, though the only evidence of the struggle here are two small markers in the front corner of the parking lot, which faces W.V. 92. The battle, known by a half-dozen names, was fought on August 26 and 27, 1863. Its objective was the most unusual of the war—law books. The Federals had been ordered to Lewisburg to confiscate the law library there and to transport the books to Beverly, where they were needed by the new court of appeals. The orders specified that great care be taken so the books would not be lost or damaged—certainly one of the few times that Confederate-owned property was to be protected, rather than destroyed. The battle between 1,300 Federals and 2,000 Confederates lasted until both sides simply ran out of ammunition, after which the Federals retreated without their law books. The wounded of both sides were cared for at the Old White.

It was thus that at least 50 men died in violent combat at what is now a hamburger joint.

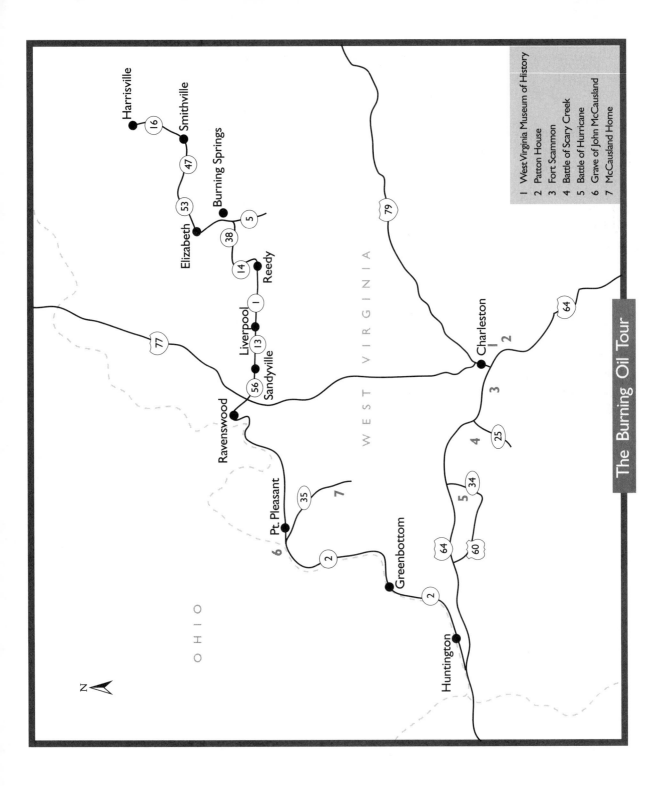

The Burning Oil Tour

N

OHIO

WEST VIRGINIA

Harrisville
Smithville
16
47
Burning Springs
53
Elizabeth
38
5
14
Reedy
1
Liverpool
13
Sandyville
56
Ravenswood
77
Pt. Pleasant
35
6
7
2
Greenbottom
2
34
5
64
60
Huntington
25
4
3
Charleston
1
2
64
79

1 West Virginia Museum of History
2 Patton House
3 Fort Scammon
4 Battle of Scary Creek
5 Battle of Hurricane
6 Grave of John McCausland
7 McCausland Home

The Burning Oil Tour

This tour starts on the West Virginia State Capitol grounds, where it visits statues and the West Virginia Museum of History. It moves to several small battlefields, then to the grave of a Harvard lawyer-general whose beard stretched to his waist. Next, it goes to the town on the Ohio River from which the first Confederate invasion of Union territory was launched. From there, the tour proceeds to Burning Springs, an almost-forgotten town today but a very important place in 1864; it was here that an oil field became a military target for the first time in world history. The tour then winds its way to Harrisville, the final resting place of the Union general who tried the Lincoln conspirators.

The tour measures approximately 220 miles, much of it on winding rural roads. Plan on a full day.

THE TOUR STARTS IN CHARLESTON on the grounds of the West Virginia State Capitol, a postwar structure. The visitors' parking lot is off Greenbrier Street, which runs along the western side of the State Capitol

Before the war, Charleston was a small town located near the dividing line between the counties to the east, which supported secession, and those to the west, which supported the Union. In 1861, western Virginia had 360,000 white people and 16,000 slaves. The whites thought of themselves as different from the Virginia planters far to the east in the flatlands. Their politics favored the Union.

When Virginia voted to secede on April 17, 1861, most of those representing the western counties voted to stay with the Union. Almost immediately, the western counties started thinking of seceding themselves—from Virginia. They held meetings in Wheeling, far north of Charleston, at which they quickly decided to stay with the Union. The State Capitol grounds here in Charleston reflect both Confederate and Union sentiments, demonstrating how divided the state was in its official and unofficial loyalties.

Walk to the northern end of California Avenue, on the far side of the State Capitol from the parking lot. There, you'll see a statue dedicated to the men and women who "saved West Virginia for the Union." The statue shows a mountaineer carrying a nonmilitary percussion rifle and a Union flag. The lower portion shows a wounded man being nursed by a woman.

Walk to the southern end of California Avenue to see a statue of the state's most famous soldier, Thomas J. "Stonewall" Jackson. The statue was erected in 1910 and has since been relocated twice on the grounds. It is unusual in that it depicts Jackson wearing a slouch hat, rather than his familiar forage cap. His frock coat is apparently being blown by the wind; presumably, the sculptor was trying to show Jackson standing up symbolically to a strong Northern wind. The piece also demonstrates the success of sculpture salesmen after the war. The very same statue stands in front of a barracks at the Virginia Military Institute. Duplicates of soldier statues were placed all over the South and the North until the 1920s, many of them mass-produced by Northern companies.

From the Jackson statue, follow Kanawha Boulevard west along the river to see another unusual statue, *Lincoln Walks at Midnight*. Erected in 1974, it depicts Lincoln in a robe.

Just to the west is a statue of a marching Union soldier. It honors the 32,000 men from western Virginia who joined the Union army. Erected in 1930, it shows that its sculptor did not know much about soldiering. The soldier's cartridge box is incorrect. He is wearing a blanket roll, though the vast majority of Union soldiers wore backpacks. And he is carrying his musket casually over his shoulder, which would have been greatly irritating to the man marching behind him because the muzzle could have hit him in the head.

Turn north off Kanawha Boulevard on to the capitol walkway to visit the West Virginia Museum of History, which is housed in The Cultural Center. In the basement of the museum is the first Confederate flag captured in battle, a huge adaptation of the first national flag of the Confederacy. It was not an official flag, as it has 15 stars, rather than the official seven stars in a circle, representing the first seven states to secede. Fifteen is an unusual number of stars, since the Confederacy had 11 charter states plus two unofficial states (Maryland and Kentucky). The flag maker must have hoped that Missouri would eventually join, but what would the 15th state have been? The flag looks like it was cut and stitched from a United States flag. It was captured on June 3, 1861, at the Battle of Philippi. It must have been flying from a staff, as it is too large to have been carried on the field.

One display at the museum addresses the legality of the creation of West Virginia from Virginia. The United States Constitution clearly says that no state may be created from another state without the consent of the original state's legislature. The Virginia legislature in Confederate Richmond was not about to agree to the creation of West Virginia, a state loyal to the Union. Lincoln's cabinet was divided over the issue. In the end, Lincoln, never one to strictly follow the Constitution when it didn't serve his purpose, said, "There is a difference between secession against the Constitution and in favor of the Constitution." The president sent the issue to what he considered the rightful government of Virginia, the Union loyalists who had set up a base in Wheeling. The Wheeling legislature approved the statehood measure—as well they might, since many of them had brought it up in the first place. West Virginia was admitted to the Union on June 20, 1863. After the war, some Virginians contemplated arguing the issue before the United States Supreme Court, but Reconstruction politics and Federal occupying forces made the issue moot.

The section of the museum covering West Virginia history contains a display on John Brown. Included are the leather collar Brown was forced to wear in confinement, the handcuffs used to restrain him, and one of the pikes he intended to issue to freed slaves. You'll also see the thin rope used to hang him. Efficient hangings were really neck breakings. When the prisoner dropped from the scaffold with a thick rope around his neck, the fall to the end of the noose was supposed to snap his neck, killing him instantly. Newspaper reports from 1859 indicate that it took more than 30 minutes for Brown to die, meaning he strangled to death—a slow, torturous process that his executioner must have intended as revenge for his attempt to start a slave revolt. The thinness of the rope would seem to support the idea that Brown's executioner wanted him to die slowly.

When you are ready to leave the museum, turn left from the parking lot and drive one block south on Greenbrier to Kanawha Boulevard. Turn left and go 1.7 miles to the Craik-Patton House at the Daniel Boone Park, which is located at 2809 East Kanawha Boulevard.

Built in 1834, this home was owned by Colonel George S. Patton. Patton graduated from the Virginia Military Institute in 1852, the same year Jackson went there to teach. When the war started, Patton formed the 22nd Virginia (otherwise known as the Kanawha Riflemen), a Confederate regiment raised from this area. He also designed the regiment's gaudy uniforms—light blue jackets, gray trousers with yellow trim, white gloves, and hats with ostrich feathers. Patton saw action at just about every major battle in western Virginia. He was the grandfather of a more famous Patton, Major General George S. Patton of World War II fame. A lack of fashion sense must have been in the genes, as Major General Patton designed a uniform for his tank corps that was just as gaudy as the Kanawha Riflemen's.

Retrace your route past the parking lot at the State Capitol; continue north on Greenbrier Street and get on I-64 West. Head west across the Kanawha River, then take Exit 58-A. Bear right on Oakwood Avenue, then turn right immediately on to Fort Hill Drive. You'll soon reach the neighborhood that was once the site of Fort Scammon, a Union fortification. In September 1862, before it was developed into a fort, the Confederates used this hill as an artillery position to bombard Charleston.

Get back on I-64 and continue west for 13 miles to Exit 44 (the St. Albans exit at U.S. 35). Drive south on U.S. 35 for 0.3 mile, and pull over at the historical marker. Just ahead is Scary Creek, the scene of a skirmish between Confederates under Captain George Patton and Federals under General Jacob Cox of Ohio on July 17, 1861. When Patton was wounded, Captain Albert Jenkins, a Harvard-educated lawyer, took command. The Federals lost 20 killed and the Confederates five. Both sides eventually retreated from the bridge over Scary Creek. Though the Confederates technically won the skirmish, General Henry Wise decided to retreat to Sewell Mountain to meet with Lee. That left this part of western Virginia in Federal hands.

Cox went on to serve the Union army well, rising to major general, though he had no military education. He was later elected governor of Ohio and served in Grant's cabinet.

Patton would be killed at the Third Battle of Winchester in 1864.

Jenkins, a United States congressman before the war, went on to become a general. He suffered a mortal wound at Cloyd's Mountain in May 1864.

The name of one soldier at Scary Creek later entered popular culture and became more familiar than that of any of the officers. That soldier was "Devil Anse" Hatfield, a Confederate and the leader of the clan that feuded with the McCoys.

In the 1920s, the graves of Union soldiers were discovered during an excavation beside the road.

Get back on I-64 and continue west to Exit 34. Follow W.V. 34 through the town of Hurricane to U.S. 60 (James River Pike). Turn right on U.S. 60.

The Hurricane Bridge, the object of a fight on March 28, 1863, between a force under Jenkins and Union troops under Captain Johnson, was located a few hundred yards to the right. Before firing a shot, Jenkins sent a message to Johnson under a flag of truce saying that the Confederates had superior forces and that the Federals should surrender the bridge. Not knowing how many troops Jenkins truly had, Johnson refused to surrender "unless forced to do so by an exhibition of your boasted strength."

Jenkins fought for more than five hours before pulling back. Only a handful of men were killed on either side. The Federals held their position. Jenkins has been criticized by historians for not showing his force, which was four times larger than the Federals', in order to force a surrender. Jenkins was not a trained soldier. His actions in other battles have also been questioned.

Follow U.S. 60 for 6.1 miles. Turn right onto C.R. 13 to pick up I-64 West at Exit 28. Leave I-64 at Exit 11 (Hal Greer Boulevard). Drive toward Huntington. Take a right on Ninth Avenue, then turn right on 20th Street. Get into the left lane and veer left on to Norway Avenue. Drive past the first entrance to Spring Hill Cemetery, then take the second entrance. The Confederate burial ground is on the right. General Jenkins's grave is located behind the Confederate Monument. This is actually his third burial site. The first was near the battlefield at Cloyd's Mountain and the second in a family cemetery. He was moved here in 1891.

Jenkins, one of several Ivy Leaguers to fight for the South, was one of the most prominent men in Huntington to side with the Confederacy. He was a well-known lawyer when he was elected to the United States House of Representatives in 1857. He resigned in 1861.

Jenkins's main contribution to Southern history was that he led the first invasion of the North. This came in the summer of 1862, when he rode into Ohio for a short raid before returning to his side of the Ohio River. Though it was common for Union commanders to burn Southern homes, Jenkins made it a point to tell Ohioans that he would not burn their property. In one town, more than 400 Federal soldiers surrendered en masse to his 350 cavalrymen without a shot being fired. "It was a curious thing to

Grave of Albert Jenkins

hear shouts for Jefferson Davis in Ohio," Jenkins said.

Jenkins's force was one of the first into Pennsylvania before the Battle of Gettysburg, occupying Chambersburg on June 20, 1863, some 10 days before the battle was fought.

Jenkins died nearly two weeks after his arm was amputated by Union surgeons after the Battle of Cloyd's Mountain in May 1864. The surgeons believed that a ligature they used to stop the flow of blood may have accidentally been knocked off the stump of Jenkins's arm by an orderly. Already sick with pneumonia, Jenkins may not have known that he was bleeding to death.

Colonel Rutherford Hayes of the 23rd Ohio took Jenkins's spurs as a souvenir. Hayes went on to be elected president in 1876. A deal to trade Southern electoral votes for the withdrawal of Union occupation forces helped seal his election.

Return to 20th Street and continue in your original direction to Fifth Avenue. Turn right and follow Fifth until it intersects with Main Street. Turn left and go one block to Third Avenue. Turn right to get on W.V. 2. This is Guyandotte, which was once a separate town. Guyandotte was burned by Union forces on November 11, 1861, in retaliation for an attack on a Union camp the previous day. This was one of the first instances of Union forces burning Southern property. The town's businesses, homes (including those belonging to Unionists), and churches were all leveled. One newspaper in Wheeling said that Guyandotte was the "orneriest" town on the Ohio and should have been burned three years earlier—that is, three years before there was a Confederacy.

Continue north on W.V. 2 for about 12 miles to the community of Greenbottom. About 3 miles after passing the Greenbottom sign, you will reach the prewar home of General Albert Jenkins, which was also called Greenbottom. It is now a house museum. Both Confederate and Union soldiers frequently camped on the grounds here. For unknown reasons, the Federals never burned the house, even though they knew it belonged to Jenkins and even though Mrs. Jenkins would throw water on them from an upstairs window if they got too close. The portrait of Jenkins over the mantel shows a man with a beard stretching almost to his waist—perhaps the longest beard of any Confederate or Union general. Notice the door on the second floor with a tiny door cut into it for the Jenkinses' cat to use when

mousing in the attic. A ghost story about the house says that Jenkins returned from the dead to bowl in the attic. Investigations have discovered no ghostly bowling alley, though squirrels sometimes roll nuts from one end of the attic to the other.

Continue north for 20.8 miles, then pull to the right shoulder; you should see a bridge over the Ohio River to the left and a bridge over the Kanawha River straight ahead. Located to the right under a canopy of trees high on a hill is the grave of General John A. McCausland, who lived until 1927, making him the next-to-last Confederate general to die. This is as close to the grave as you should get, as the walk is steep and on private land. Grave hunters who have made the trek report that there is nothing remarkable about McCausland's tombstone. Pictures show it to be rather small, in fact.

Get back on the highway. Within 0.2 mile, turn right on U.S. 35, heading south. After 15.6 miles on U.S. 35, you will reach McCausland's house, located on the right. Old stories say that McCausland used to sit in the cupola to keep watch over farm hands in the fields in front of the house. If he saw one malingering, he would take a shot at the ground nearby to let him know the boss was watching.

McCausland was an 1857 graduate of the Virginia Military Institute who returned to the school to teach math. He joined the war effort early, creating the 36th Virginia Infantry. He refused to surrender at Fort Donelson, Tennessee, and escaped with his men. Colonel McCausland took over command for Jenkins at Cloyd's Mountain; he was named a general later that month. He is best remembered for a raid into Pennsylvania in July 1864, when he burned the business district of Chambersburg in retaliation for the burning of Southern homes by Union general David Hunter. Few private homes were touched by the Southerners.

Rather than surrender with Lee at Appomattox, McCausland took his cavalry and rode through the Federal lines. Concerned that he would be accused of war crimes for burning the Northern town, he fled to Europe for two years. He returned in 1867 and lived to be 90 years old.

Retrace your route to W.V. 2, turn right, and cross the Kanawha River into Point Pleasant. It would be a good idea to check your fuel here, as much of the rest of the tour is in rural areas.

It was just below Point Pleasant that Jenkins reentered West Virginia after his Ohio raid. This town also claims to be the starting point of the American Revolution, as there was a large battle between British-incited Indians and Virginia militia here long before the battles at Concord and Lexington in Massachusetts.

McCausland's house

Continue on W.V. 2 for approximately 33 miles to Ravenswood. Turn left on W.V. 68 just outside Ravenswood, then head left (or west) on Sycamore Street to reach the Ohio River. It was here that Jenkins and 350 troopers crossed the river to begin their two-day raid into the state of Ohio, where they captured the town of Racine.

The Ohio River at Ravenswood

Just north of Ravenswood on the Ohio shore is where General John Hunt Morgan and his Confederate cavalry fought the Battle of Buffington Island on July 19, 1863. This was the largest engagement Morgan's men fought during their month-long raid through Indiana and Ohio. Morgan lost nearly half of his 2,500-man command to death, wounding, and capture in the battle, while the Federals lost fewer than 60 troops.

When Union forces occupied Ravenswood, they discovered a woman in their ranks dressed as a man. Records say she was discharged in the town.

Retrace your route to W.V. 2 and head east from Ravenswood. Continue under I-77, where the road becomes C.R. 56 heading toward Sandyville. From this point, the roads become narrow and include many hills and blind curves. After about 5 miles, turn north on C.R. 21 toward Sandyville, then look to the right for C.R. 13 (Liverpool Road) after you cross a bridge. Stay on C.R. 13 for 9.2 miles to the town of Reedy, then turn north on C.R. 14. After about 3 miles, turn right on C.R. 38 immediately after crossing a green bridge. Stay on C.R. 38 for 9.6 miles, then turn left on W.V. 5, about 0.5 mile before the community of Burning Springs.

In Burning Springs, park at the convenience store, buy some snacks, and ask the owner to take you across the road to show you where natural gas still seeps from the ground. The gas is so close to the surface that a match held to the end of a hose at the site will light it; *don't try this yourself!*

This tiny community was once home to more than 6,000 people. Some of the oil-drilling equipment that made it a boom town is still in evidence. On display are two wooden barrels like those used for holding oil in the 1860s.

Anyone who studies the history of American commerce or warfare should be interested in Burning Springs, nicknamed "Oiltown." This was the site of the first oil well in West Virginia, drilled in 1860, just one year after the nation's first well was opened in Pennsylvania. Though the various processes of refining oil were still being developed, and though no one had

Oil tank at Burning Springs

Oil well at Burning Springs

even dreamed of an internal-combustion engine that ran on gasoline, the value of oil was beginning to dawn on Americans. In those early days, it was used primarily for lubricating moving parts. By the start of the war, Burning Springs was sending oil down the Little Kanawha River in barges for refinement.

The town was first visited by Confederate troops in July 1863, when the survivors of Morgan's ill-fated raid into Indiana and Ohio camped here for one night.

A visit of a different sort came the following year. The growing commerce in Burning Springs did not escape the Confederates' attention. On May 6, 1864, Southern troops under General William E. "Grumble" Jones rode into Burning Springs. Jones described what followed in his official report:

> All the oil, the tanks, barrels, engines for pumping, engine-houses, and wagons—in a word, everything used for raising, holding, or sending it off was burned. The smoke is very dense and jet black. The boats, filled with oil in bulk, burst with a report almost equaling artillery, and spread the burning fuel down the river. Before night huge columns of ebony smoke marked the meanderings of the stream as far as the eye could see. By dark the oil from the tanks on the burning creek had reached the river and the whole stream was a sheet of fire. A burning river, carrying destruction to our merciless enemy, was a scene of magnificence that might well carry joy to every patriotic heart.

Jones estimated that 150,000 barrels of oil were destroyed. It was the first time in military history that an oil field served as a military target.

Drive another 7.5 miles on W.V. 5, then turn right on W.V. 53 on the southern outskirts of Elizabeth. Drive 9.5 miles, turn right on W.V. 47, and go 11.3 miles to Smithville. Turn north on W.V. 16 and proceed 11.5 miles to Harrisville. Turn left on Main Street, drive one block, and turn left on W.V. 31. After 0.3 mile, look to the left for the stone entrance to Odd Fellows Cemetery, where the tour ends.

Inside the cemetery, take the first paved road to the left, then turn right on the next paved road. The fourth large marker on the left stands at the resting place of General Thomas Harris. In the same plot are Harris's two wives, one facing in either direction.

Harris was a solid performer for the Federals. A native of western Virginia, he left his medical practice to raise a regiment for the Union. He fought in many actions and led one of the brigades that crushed the Confederate line at Petersburg.

Immediately after the war, Harris served as one of the judges who tried the Lincoln assassins. He was strongly in favor of pushing the execution of Mary Surratt, though there was little evidence against her beyond that fact that she owned the boardinghouse where John Wilkes Booth and his men sometimes met.

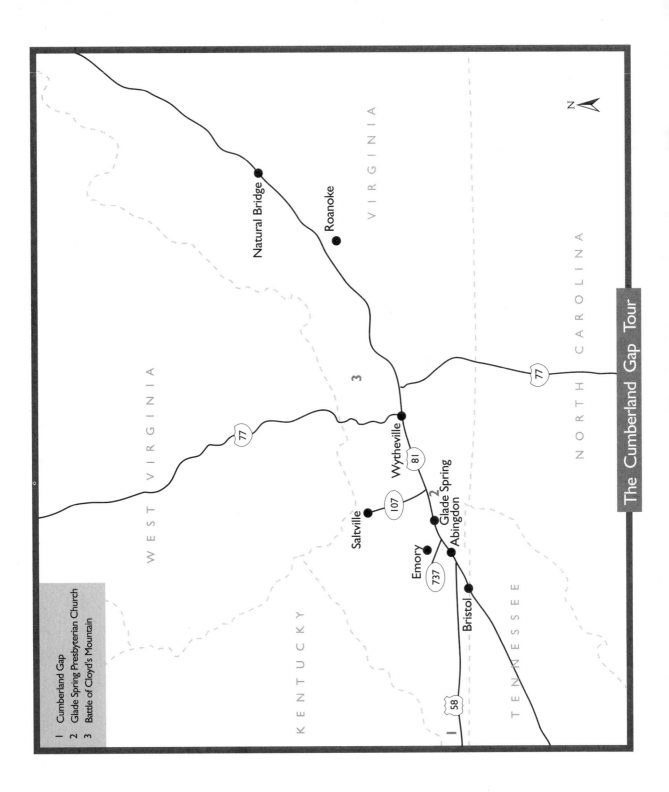

The Cumberland Gap Tour

1   Cumberland Gap
2   Glade Spring Presbyterian Church
3   Battle of Cloyd's Mountain

WEST VIRGINIA

VIRGINIA

VIRGINIA

KENTUCKY

TENNESSEE

NORTH CAROLINA

Natural Bridge

Roanoke

Wytheville

Saltville

Glade Spring

Abingdon

Emory

Bristol

3

2

77

77

81

107

737

58

N

The Cumberland Gap Tour

THE TOUR STARTS at the visitor center at Cumberland Gap National Historical Park, located on U.S. 25E near where Virginia, Kentucky, and Tennessee meet at the far western tip of the Old Dominion.

How embarrassing the loss of Cumberland Gap was to the Confederacy is demonstrated by a letter from Jefferson Davis on display in the visitor center. "Cumberland Gap was easily defensible," Davis wrote. "I am unable to express any explanation to this disaster which laid open Eastern Tennessee and Southwestern Virginia to hostile actions. This easy success for the enemy was followed by Rosecrans' entry into Georgia."

The Confederates took Cumberland Gap without a fight in September 1861. They had the next nine months to fortify the heights, which looked down on the main turnpike between Kentucky and Tennessee. Then, in June 1862, Federal forces using two other nearby gaps threatened to surround the Confederates, who pulled out without a fight. The Federals themselves left two months later when Confederates invaded Kentucky.

The Confederates, under General John W. Frazer, moved back in and stayed until September 1863, when the Federals came again. Union forces surrounded the gap and sent repeated messages to Frazer to surrender. Finally, he answered General Ambrose Burnside's demand for surrender and gave up his 2,300-man command, eight cannons, 160 head of cattle, 12,000 pounds of bacon, 1,800 bushels of wheat, and 15 days' rations of flour—all without firing a shot in defense. This listing of the food on hand is important because one of the reasons Frazer gave for surrendering was that the

This tour starts where Virginia, Kentucky, and Tennessee meet and even takes a short detour into the Volunteer State. From there, it winds north up the mountain valley to Abingdon, Virginia, a pretty little town where a poor Confederate general rests, then to Glade Spring, where a very good Confederate general rests. It then moves to Saltville, a town that found itself a Union target because it supplied the Confederacy with tons of preserving salt. Next, the tour goes to Wytheville, the final resting place of two generals, then to Cloyd's Mountain, where a Confederate general fell. It ends at Natural Bridge, where a once-amazing Union cavalry general died a lonely, befuddled, sick old man.

The tour covers approximately 320 miles, some of it on twisting mountain roads but most of it along an interstate. Abingdon makes a nice layover stop.

Federals were going to starve him out by capturing his gristmill.

Frazer, an 1849 graduate of West Point, was immediately condemned as a coward by the Confederates. Cumberland Gap was considered so important that he had been ordered to hold it at all costs. Instead, he gave it up without any cost.

Frazer was taken to Fort Warren, a stone fortification in the middle of Boston Harbor. It was on November 27, 1864, that he finally filed his after-action report to his Confederate superiors from a Union prison cell. This came more than a year after he had given up Cumberland Gap and been made a prisoner.

Reacting to Jefferson Davis's criticism of him before the Confederate Congress, Frazer wrote the report "as an act of self-defense and protection of my fair name." Frazer made some fair excuses—that there were other gaps that the Federals used to surround him; that he had only 100 rounds of cannon ammunition; that both his water spring and his flour mill were close to Federal lines; even that it was foggy. "An assaulting force equal to the garrison could carry it as easy as in the open field, if guided or informed of its weak points by disaffected persons in the vicinity, especially during the prevalence of fogs, which greatly demoralized the men, who were unaccustomed to service and had never been in action," he wrote. Frazer then knocked the quality of his regiments, saying he had no hope of defending against the enemy. "I might have made some reputation for desperate courage, but so selfish a consideration at so great a sacrifice of life forbade me to entertain so rash a design," he noted. The general ended his report by noting that, although President Davis had blamed him for opening up eastern Tennessee for capture, several cities (Knoxville and Chattanooga among them) had actually fallen before Cumberland Gap.

The Confederate high command was not impressed. It apparently never even asked the Federals to exchange Frazer, as was commonly done when one side captured a general. Frazer stayed in Fort Warren for the rest of the war. Perhaps disgusted with the way his fellow Southerners treated him after Cumberland Gap, he moved to New York State after the war. He is buried there.

When you are ready to leave the museum, drive up the park service road to Pinnacle Overlook; en route, watch for a sign for Fort McCook, where you'll see a cannon overlooking the road below. At the top is evidence of both the Confederate and Union occupations, including a cannon pointed down the mountain in case of attack.

Return down the mountain and go south on U.S. 25E for a quick trip through the tunnel into Tennessee to the Lincoln Museum at Lincoln Memorial University, located 0.7 mile after the tunnel in the town of Harrogate. The college was founded as a memorial to Lincoln. The museum has on display a copy of every single photograph for which Lincoln ever sat, in addition to other artifacts belonging to the 16th president.

Return through the tunnel on U.S. 25E North, then head into Virginia on U.S. 58 North, which later merges with U.S. 421 North. Stay on this road for 93 miles to I-81. Get on I-81 North near Bristol, Virginia, and drive about 17 miles to Exit 14 (Old Jonesboro Road), then proceed north to Main Street in the town of Abingdon. Drive 2 miles on Main to the Martha Washington Inn in downtown Abingdon.

Cannon pointed down the mountain at Cumberland Gap

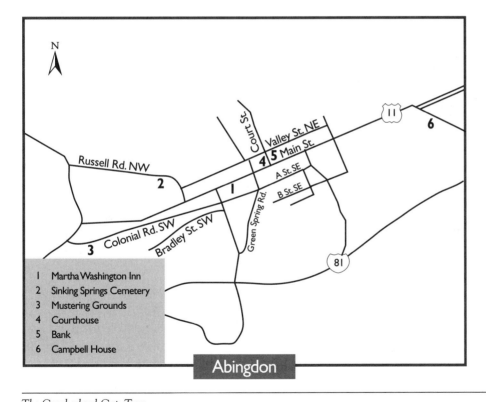

N

Russell Rd. NW

Court St.

Valley St. NE

Main St.

A St. SE

B St. SE

Green Spring Rd.

Colonial Rd. SW

Bradley St. SW

2

4 5

1

3

11

6

81

1 Martha Washington Inn
2 Sinking Springs Cemetery
3 Mustering Grounds
4 Courthouse
5 Bank
6 Campbell House

Abingdon

Built as a private home by the Preston family, whose members would later include John Preston, who ran the Confederacy's draft system, the house was expanded with wings on either side and turned into Martha Washington College just before the war. General W. E. "Grumble" Jones and his men trained on the lawn. The college remained in operation during the war and was occasionally used as a hospital.

On one occasion, a student at the college was pressed into service nursing a captured Union spy who was seriously wounded. Over the course of his stay, she fell in love with him. To comfort him, she played her violin. The soldier never recovered. For years, hotel guests have reported hearing mournful violin music coming from the halls. Some have seen a sad-looking woman ascending the stairs and going into one of the rooms—without opening the door.

Another story is told of a Union soldier who lingered too long in town during a raid. Confederates chased him down and killed him. His horse kept walking around the grounds of the college, waiting for the master who would never return. On moonlit nights, hotel guests have reported seeing a horse still looking for a master who has been gone for 135 years.

From the Martha Washington Inn, drive south on Main Street. Turn right (or west) on U.S. 58 Alternate, then left into Sinking Springs Cemetery. Follow the gravel road to the right until you reach the Confederate burial ground.

Located on the left inside an iron fence is the grave of John B. Floyd, one of the Confederacy's worst generals. (For more information about Floyd, see The First to Die Tour, page 72.) Floyd's tombstone is fascinating. It makes no mention of his status as a former United States secretary of war, a former Virginia governor, or a Confederate general. Instead, it refers to a Bible verse in the third chapter of Job; unfortunately, the deterioration of the stone has left it unclear whether it is verse 12 or verse 17. That whole chapter of Job has him cursing the day he was born. Verse 12 asks why the midwife let him live. Verse 17 begins, "There the wicked cease from troubling." In either case, it is not the usual stuff of epitaphs.

The mausoleum at the front of Sinking Springs Cemetery was the temporary crypt of General John Hunt Morgan, killed by Union soldiers in September 1864 at Greeneville, Tennessee. Most reports say that Morgan

was murdered by his captors, as he was unarmed and had his hands up when he was shot. His body was possibly mutilated and was at least stripped of its uniform down to the underwear. Morgan frequently visited Abingdon and had many friends in town, so his first funeral was conducted here before his body was shipped to Richmond. Two years after the war, he was moved to Lexington, Kentucky.

When you are ready to leave the cemetery, retrace your route to South Main Street and turn right. Drive 0.3 mile on Main, then turn left on Preston Street, a narrow street between two brick buildings across from the bus station. Cross the railroad tracks, then turn right on Colonial Road. After 0.4 mile, pull off to the right as far as you can.

The glade on the left was the Revolutionary War mustering ground where the Overmountain Men gathered before heading to Kings Mountain, where they defeated the Tories in a bloody battle that helped decide the fate of the English in the colonies.

To the left beside the mustering ground is the brick house where General George Stoneman spent the night of December 14, 1864, on his first raid into western Virginia. Eight thousand of Stoneman's Federals camped on the mustering ground and throughout the town.

There was to be a wedding on the premises the following day, so the house was filled with presents and food, all of which was eaten by the Federals. One of Stoneman's officers put on the bride's wedding bonnet and paraded around the house. The wedding cake was smashed. A borrowed wedding ring, which had been baked into the cake, was taken.

Years after the wedding was ruined, a local merchant was visiting Philadelphia to buy goods for his store when he casually mentioned that he was from Abingdon. The man he was buying from said he had something from Abingdon that he wished to return. It was the wedding ring. The man had been one of Stoneman's Raiders.

Retrace your route to Main Street. Turn right and drive north for 1.3 miles. The Episcopal church at the intersection marked "Traffic Signal 3" stands on the site of the church where Morgan's funeral was held.

On the northern side of this same corner is a small house. On the night the Federals raided, they threatened to burn this home, which was owned by the local clerk of court. He begged them not to do so, as his wife was inside giving birth. They relented. From that time on, the girl born that night was called the "Yankee Baby."

Continue on Main to Court Street. Pull to one side at the courthouse. On the lawn is a bronze statue of a Confederate soldier with holes in his pants, torn sleeves, holes in his shoes, and no coat—but a very determined look on his face. His finger is on the trigger of his cocked musket.

Across the street from the courthouse is a brick office building. During the war, this structure was protected by a black night watchman, who tried to keep it from being burned. When it was set afire, the Federals refused to let the night watchman out. He died inside his building.

The house on the left at 225 East Main was once the town's bank. The Federals came here looking for money, but it had been reburied and was not captured. The bank's original bars are still on the windows.

Continue driving north for 1.2 miles. Bear right at the light on to Old 11 Drive southeast, across the bridge, and pull to the shoulder. The home to the right is the Campbell House, built in 1825. Morgan used this home as a headquarters whenever he was in town. After his death, his body was embalmed here before being taken to his temporary resting place at the cemetery.

Continue on Old 11 for 0.8 mile to I-81. Drive north on I-81 for 6.7

miles to Exit 26, then take Va. 737 for 0.5 mile to the town of Emory and turn into Emory and Henry College, located on the right.

J. E. B. Stuart attended Emory and Henry for two years, from the age of 15 until he was accepted into West Point. Stuart became a Methodist at this Methodist-founded school, but that did not stop him from getting into a few scrapes. Once, he was late for an exam because he was trying to get his nose to stop bleeding after a fistfight. In one letter home, he promised his parents that he would put his Bible on his desk to ward off evil spirits and that he would try not to complain about the college food.

Located on the left as you pass through campus is Wyley Hall, rebuilt in 1912. The original Wyley Hall was used as a hospital during the war. After the Battle of Saltville, feared Confederate guerrilla Champ Ferguson came here and murdered some Union soldiers who were being treated for their wounds.

Get back on Va. 737. After passing under the railroad tracks, the road turns to the right. Drive 0.5 mile and turn left onto Linden Avenue or C.R. 866. Drive one block, then turn left into Emory Cemetery. Buried here are more than 100 Confederate soldiers who died in nearby hospitals. Their names are listed on an obelisk and matched to numbers on the tombstones.

Retrace your route to I-81 and continue north on the interstate. After 3 miles, take Exit 29 (the Glade Spring exit). Turn right on U.S. 11 South and drive 0.2 mile to Glade Spring Presbyterian Church.

Located behind the church are the two tombstones of General William E. Jones and his wife, Eliza. Her sad story is told on the stone. She married United States Army lieutenant W. E. Jones on January 5, 1852, and drowned in March while attempting to land in Texas from a wrecked steamship. She was apparently en route to join Jones at his military outpost. The stone says that Eliza was "personally beautiful, with a sweet disposition and intellect and was uncommonly brilliant. The early death of so hopeful a sister, child and wife left her friends, parents and husband an unspeakable sorrow."

His wife's tombstone inscription likely answers the question of how General Jones got his nickname—"Grumble." It was said that he never again found happiness after his wife's death.

Jones's much simpler tombstone doesn't even mention that he was a

Graves of "Grumble" Jones and his wife

Confederate general, noting only that he was killed at the Battle of Piedmont, Virginia, on June 5, 1864.

Before leaving, walk around the church and look out over the valley and the distant hills. This is truly a beautiful location for a place of worship.

Return to I-81 and continue north for about 14 miles to Exit 35. Head north on Va. 107 for about 6.8 miles to the scenic overlook for Saltville. Though you cannot see the battlefield from here, the overlook does give a good view of the salt ponds that attracted the attention of both Federal and Confederate troops during the war.

In those days, salt was much more than just a food enhancer. It was a preservative. Meats dried and coated with salt could be preserved for months and shipped to distant battlefields far more easily than livestock could be driven on the same journey. This area of the Virginia mountains was rich with salt beds. The saline waters of the springs had been used commercially for decades before the war.

As the conflict progressed, this salt became even more important, as other salt mines around the South were captured. Though salt-refining operations along the coast (such as in Florida) continued, they were easily spotted by the fires under their kettles. Inland production at a place like Saltville was more easily protected.

Or that was the theory, at least. As Union forces slowly worked their way deeper into the South from Ohio, Tennessee, and Kentucky, Saltville's refining operations grew more imperiled. Finally, on October 1, 1864, a 3,600-man force under General Stephen Burbridge, a Kentucky lawyer, came calling on a thrown-together force of 2,800 Confederates. The Confederates had the advantage of holding the high ground. After several Union attacks petered out, the Federals waited for nightfall. Having built fires to suggest that they intended to stay and fight the next day, they then departed under cover of darkness. Burbridge himself seems to have left before the battle on October 1 even ended, as he saw that the fight was going against the Federals and had reason to fear capture.

He feared capture mainly because more than 300 soldiers of the Fifth Colored Cavalry Regiment were fighting under his command. After experiencing several slave rebellions early in the 19th century, during which some white citizens were murdered by their slaves, the Southern soldiers were

Salt well

Salt kettles

enraged to see armed black men in their midst and did not figure to be easy on their commander, should they capture him.

On the morning following the battle, the Confederate troops went on to the field to see how many Union soldiers had survived. What happened next has been a subject of controversy since 1864. Northern newspapers and even some Southerners who were on the battlefield reported that upwards of 150 black soldiers were murdered by the vengeful Confederates. The Battle of Saltville was soon labeled the "Massacre at Saltville." Modern historians have tracked down records of the Fifth Colored and all the other regiments involved and have concluded that at least five, and perhaps as many as 12, black soldiers were murdered at Saltville. The discrepancy between 150 and 12 is probably due to three factors: early tallies that were never corrected for desertions and soldiers who were slow to return to their commands; Southerners who wanted to warn blacks what would happen to them if they took up arms; and Northerners who wanted to paint the Confederates as evil. For its part, the Confederacy started an investigation into the conduct of Southern troops at Saltville, but the war was winding down and the army found it had more important things to do. The investigation was never completed.

Elizabeth Cemetery

When you are ready to leave the overlook, continue on Va. 107 for 1.3 miles into Saltville. Turn right on Va. 91, drive north for 0.4 mile to Buckeye Street Extension, and turn right again. Turn left on Buckeye Hollow and drive another 0.4 mile to a small park located on some of the high ground held by the Confederates; you can still see some of their trenches and rifle pits. Looking north from here toward the modern bridge, you'll see the bottom land over which the Federals came against the Confederates. To the right on your same level is Sanders Hill, down which the Fifth Colored charged.

Retrace your route to Va. 91 and turn right. After a short distance, turn left into Elizabeth Cemetery. Walk to the twin obelisks behind the cannon to see the grave of William Alexander Stuart, J. E. B. Stuart's brother, who ran one of the local saltworks during the war. Also buried here are Archibald and Mary Stuart, J. E. B.'s parents. This cemetery was part of the battlefield. Men fought and died among the stones, using them for cover.

Turn around and head south on Va. 91. Drive about 2 miles south of town to Salt Park, located on the right. Here, you'll see several of the more than 2,000 salt kettles that were once used to boil water so the salt could be extracted. Behind the kettle display is a walking-beam pump, used to pump salty water to the surface. Behind the pump are the remains of one of the original salt furnaces.

Continue 0.2 mile on Va. 91, then turn left on Stuart Drive, where you'll see a log cabin built in 1795. This was the home of Flora Stuart after the death of her husband, J. E. B., in May 1864. She lived in half the house and started a grammar school in the other half. The timbers that make up the cabin are huge, indicating the size of the trees that existed in this area in the late 18th century.

Flora Stuart house

Retrace your route to I-81 and drive north for 36 miles. Take Exit 70 and follow North Fourth Street into downtown Wytheville. Turn left on U.S. 11 (West Main Street), then go left on South 11th Street, then right on East Goodwin Lane to reach East End Cemetery. Follow the gravel road into the cemetery and look on the right for the obelisk marking the resting place of General William A. Terry, the last commander of the Stonewall Brigade, the unit made famous at First Manassas by its first commander, Thomas J. "Stonewall" Jackson.

Terry was a lawyer and newspaper editor when the war started. He joined as a lieutenant with the Fourth Virginia, one of the original regiments of the Stonewall Brigade, the only brigade in the Southern army that acquired a nickname. He eventually rose to command the regiment through most of the famous actions of the war and took command of the whole brigade after Spotsylvania.

Terry led a charmed life during the war years. He was wounded in the elbow and side at Groveton, then was hit slightly in two other battles. He was more seriously wounded at Third Winchester in September 1864 but returned to duty in February 1865. He was slightly wounded again the following month. Terry was trying to return to his command when he heard that Lee had surrendered.

He became a United States congressman after the war. The officer the Yankees couldn't kill drowned while trying to ford a creek near his house at the age of 64.

Walk 30 yards to the right of Terry's grave to find that of James Alexander

Walker, a general who led the Stonewall Brigade before Terry.

Walker met Jackson, the man who would be his mentor, under less-than-ideal circumstances. In 1852, Walker was a self-assured cadet at V.M.I. when he ran into self-assured professor Thomas J. Jackson. One day, Jackson ordered Walker to the blackboard to work out a physics problem. Walker tried but did not perform to Jackson's expectations. Jackson ordered him to the board again the next day, at which time Walker became loud and abusive and refused to return to his seat. Jackson had the young man arrested and brought before a student court, which convicted and expelled him. Walker challenged Jackson to a duel. Jackson ignored him. The boy's father was then summoned to V.M.I. to pick up his son before further trouble ensued.

Walker must have matured by the time he served under Jackson in the field a decade later, as Stonewall himself apparently suggested that V.M.I. send the younger man a diploma—10 years after he had been thrown out because of the dispute at the blackboard. Jackson also suggested that Walker be promoted to general.

Grave of General Walker

Wounded in the left arm at Spotsylvania Court House, Walker underwent surgery that took several inches of bone from his arm. After the war, the arm was almost useless.

When Walker returned to his law practice, it became obvious that he had not completely lost the temper he displayed at V.M.I. Once, he got into a fistfight with another lawyer in the courtroom. In 1899, just after finishing two terms in the United States House of Representatives, he got into a pistol battle with another lawyer and was shot twice. His right arm became paralyzed, but by sheer will—maybe meanness—he forced it back into usefulness. He died at the age of 69.

When you are ready to leave the cemetery, retrace your route to Main Street and follow the signs for 1.5 miles to I-81. Head north on I-81 for about 7.7 miles to the I-77 junction.

If you wish to make a side trip to the birth site of J. E. B. Stuart, take I-77 South to Mount Airy, North Carolina. Drive 37 miles to Exit 101 (N.C. 89). Drive east for 6.5 miles to N.C. 104. Turn north or left and drive 6.5 miles to the J.E.B. Stuart Birthplace on the left. The house no longer stands, but future plans include a statue of the general. Retrace your route to I-81 to complete the side trip.

It is about 17 miles north on I-81 from the I-77 interchange to Exit 98. Go north on Va. 100 to the town of Dublin. Continue 7 miles to the historical marker on the left at the base of Cloyd's Mountain.

The Battle of Cloyd's Mountain, fought on May 9, 1864, was as vicious a fight as either side ever experienced, when measured by the firepower expended and the men killed and wounded. This often-overlooked fight at the southern end of the Shenandoah Valley was part of Grant's grand strategy to weaken the Confederacy by attacking it on several fronts. While Grant was busy going after Lee around the Wilderness, Sherman was moving toward Atlanta, and other forces were beginning to destroy the northern end of the Shenandoah Valley. To take care of the southern end of Virginia, Grant ordered an attack to destroy the Virginia & Tennessee Railroad.

Union general George A. Crook started moving from Gauley Bridge in West Virginia toward the railroad bridge over the New River at Dublin on April 29, 1864. Drenching rain slowed him down, giving the Confederates time to set up a defense on Cloyd's Mountain. Outnumbered three to one, General Albert Jenkins's 2,400 men dug in on the slopes and waited for the Yankees to cross the mountain. The Federals first tried the Confederate right flank, but that attack was turned back. Next, they tried the center. Counterattacks pushed the Federals back, but when the Confederates left their breastworks, they were exposed to the Union reserves.

Eventually, the superior numbers proved too much, and the Confederates were crushed. Crook marched into Dublin and burned the railroad bridge. But he failed to follow up on his advantage. When he heard that Grant had been beaten at the Wilderness, Crook retreated to his base of operations.

It had been a costly battle to defend and burn a bridge. Jenkins lost 23 percent of his men and Crook 10 percent.

Jenkins himself was wounded in the arm and captured near the end of the battle. His arm was amputated two days later. He seemed to improve, but on May 21, a ligature on his arm was apparently knocked loose, and he bled to death in his sickbed.

Retrace Va. 100 to I-81, but pass under the interstate and follow the signs to the Wilderness Road Museum, which offers displays on the fighting in this area.

Get back on I-81 and drive north to Exit 175. Go north on U.S. 11, following the signs to the Natural Bridge Hotel, where the tour ends. The present-day hotel stands on the same site as one that existed after the war. Then as now, the hotel's purpose was to give tourists a place to stay while visiting the Natural Bridge, a large stone arch first surveyed by George Washington and once owned by Thomas Jefferson.

Union general Wesley Merritt died in the old hotel in 1910. Once one of the best Union cavalry leaders, he was left senile by hardening of the arteries by the age of 76.

There is a reason why everyone has heard of George Custer but few except war historians recognize the name of Wesley Merritt. Custer (and later his wife) knew how to play the publicity game to keep his exploits— true or not—in the public eye. Merritt, a contemporary of Custer, never tried to do that.

A native of New York City, Merritt graduated from West Point in 1860 and served as a lieutenant in the dragoons before the war started. Assigned to desk duty early in the conflict, he wangled a field position just in time to fight at Brandy Station, the June 9, 1863, battle that marked the point when the quality of the Union cavalry finally caught up with the Confederate cavalry. Merritt was lucky that day. A Confederate took a good swipe at him with a saber, but Merritt's thick hat and the bandanna he used as a sweatband took the blade.

After a cavalry fight at Middleburg, Virginia, later that month, Merritt went from captain to general in one leap. From that time on, he fought in most of the cavalry actions of the war, becoming a favorite of Sheridan, even if he was always in the shadow of the more flamboyant and younger Custer.

Merritt stayed in the army after the war, becoming a major general and fighting Indians. He served as superintendent of West Point and commanded an expedition to the Philippines in 1898 during the Spanish-American War.

Before you leave the area, take time to see the Natural Bridge, one of Robert E. Lee's favorite places for picnics with his children.

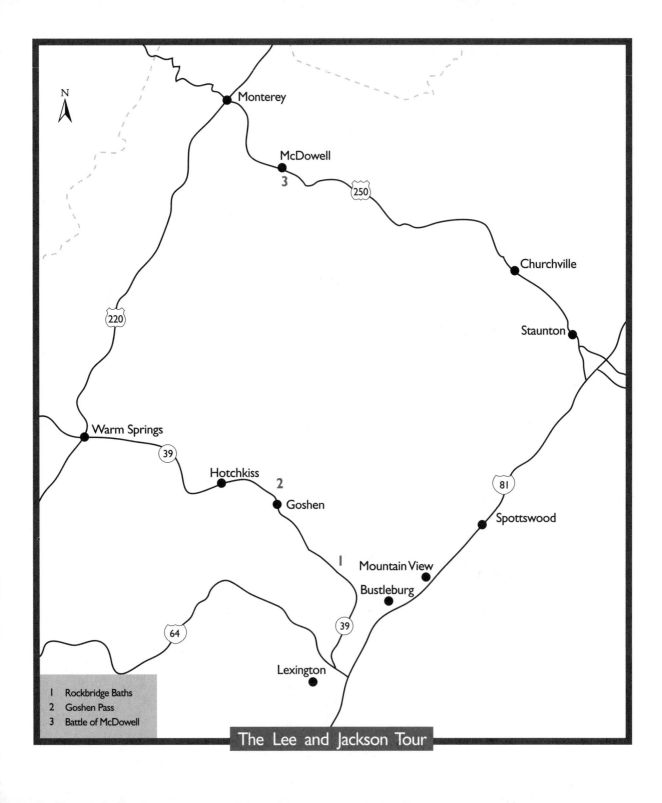

N

Monterey

McDowell
3

250

Churchville

Staunton

220

Warm Springs

39

Hotchkiss

2

Goshen

81

Spottswood

1

Mountain View

Bustleburg

64

39

Lexington

1 Rockbridge Baths
2 Goshen Pass
3 Battle of McDowell

The Lee and Jackson Tour

The Lee and Jackson Tour

This tour starts in Lexington, the final resting place of two of the South's favorite heroes, Robert E. Lee and Stonewall Jackson. There, it visits two museums and one house museum. It then moves through the mountains to Rockbridge Baths and Warm Springs, two spots where the Lee family liked to relax. Next, the tour visits McDowell, a mountain battlefield that must have been exhausting for the soldiers, since it is so steep. It ends in Staunton at the grave of a New York–born Confederate officer who became famous when Stonewall turned to him and said, "Make me a map of the Valley."

The tour covers approximately 100 miles and includes a walking tour of downtown Lexington. Many visitors will want to spend a whole day in Lexington, making this a two-day tour.

THE TOUR BEGINS with a brief driving loop before concentrating on a walking tour of downtown Lexington. Start at the Lexington Visitor Center, located on East Washington Street at the corner of Randolph Street. Turn left out of the parking lot on to East Washington. Follow Washington as it curves to the right; at the curve, look to the left. This residential neighborhood was once a cemetery for local blacks. At least two of Stonewall Jackson's slaves were buried here. After the war, the Colored Cemetery was moved to another area of Lexington, and a man was paid to relocate the graves. Present-day historians believe he may have taken the money but never moved the graves. At the very least, some blacks are believed to be buried in this neighborhood to this day.

Turn left at the light on to Nelson Street (U.S. 60 East). Drive 3.8 miles, then turn left across traffic to enter Ben Salem Wayside Park. Park your car and walk down to the Maury River to view the remains of the last lock on the river.

Before, during, and after the war, bateaux—shallow-draft wooden boats that were up to seven feet wide and 60 to 90 feet long—navigated the river to bring supplies to and from Lexington. The last stop was just northeast of Lexington at a place called Jordan's Point, where there was a short waterfall.

Look up the river toward Lexington. This is the same scene that the sad boatmen aboard the bateau *Marshall* had in May 1863 as they brought Stonewall Jackson's body back to his home in Lexington, after it had lain in state in Richmond. Robert E. Lee's wife, Mary, one of his daughters, Mildred, and one of his sons, Rob, saw the same landscape in December 1865 as they made their way by river to their new home in Lexington, where Lee had taken a job as president of Washington College.

Start heading back into Lexington on U.S. 60. After about 2.9 miles, turn right on Quarry Lane and drive to Sunny Hill Lane. Just ahead is a quarry. On the other side of Sunny Hill is what is left of Thomas J. Jackson's pride and joy while he was a professor at the Virginia Military Institute—the 18-acre farm he loved. The tract includes the quarry itself.

Purchased in 1859 for $500, the farm was a larger version of the vegetable garden Jackson maintained in the backyard of his house. He grew wheat and vegetables here. Jackson, who loved digging in the dirt, would ride out with his slaves to tend the crops. His correspondence often mentioned what was coming up or flowering.

Return to U.S. 60 and head back to the visitor center on East Washington Street. The rest of the Lexington portion of the tour is on foot.

Before leaving the parking lot, look one block north and slightly west. This was the general area of a tannery in which Jackson invested. At the time, it was situated on the edge of the city—the only location for such a smelly business of slaughtering cows to make leather from their hides.

Walk west on Washington to the Stonewall Jackson House, on the right at 8 East Washington. The home was built in 1801 and expanded in 1848. Professor Jackson and his second wife, Mary Anna Morrison Jackson, lived here from 1859 to 1861, when he left for war just before First Manassas. Jackson never again returned to the house. It served as a hospital from 1906 to 1954, when it was converted into a museum. In 1979, the Historic Lexington Foundation acquired it and restored it to the way it looked when Jackson lived here. This is the only home Jackson ever owned.

The rear grounds of the house are filled with a vegetable garden, just as Jackson liked. Jackson suffered all his life from what he called dyspepsia—chronic indigestion. His method of treating his problem was to eat bland food without much seasoning. He did eat meat, but most of his diet consisted of stale bread and unseasoned vegetables, which he grew himself.

Stonewall Jackson House

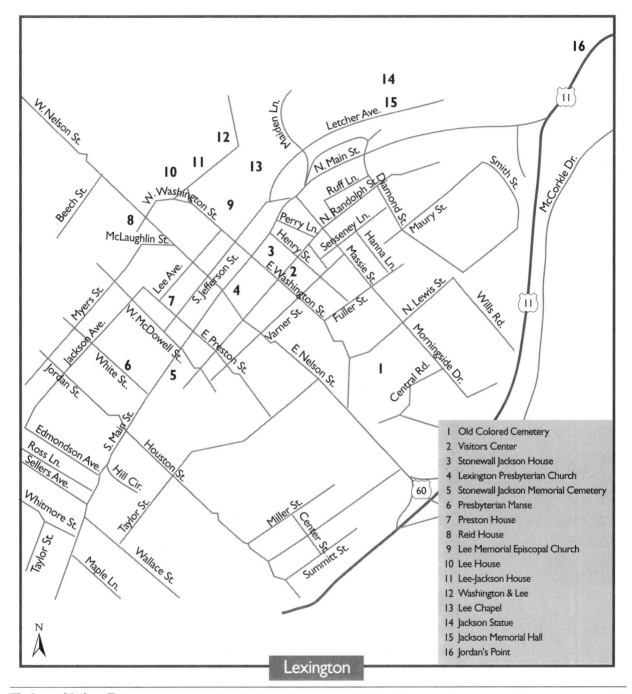

1 Old Colored Cemetery
2 Visitors Center
3 Stonewall Jackson House
4 Lexington Presbyterian Church
5 Stonewall Jackson Memorial Cemetery
6 Presbyterian Manse
7 Preston House
8 Reid House
9 Lee Memorial Episcopal Church
10 Lee House
11 Lee-Jackson House
12 Washington & Lee
13 Lee Chapel
14 Jackson Statue
15 Jackson Memorial Hall
16 Jordan's Point

Lexington

When you enter the house, take time to read the extensive displays on Jackson's early days in Lexington, including the newspaper clippings describing his lackluster attempts at humor and how he would immediately fall asleep upon sitting down in church. One newspaper story tells how he flustered a V.M.I. cadet by asking him to figure out how long it would take a train to go from one city to another. Jackson then pointed out that no train ran between those two cities.

In 1851, Jackson was serving at Fort Meade, Florida. He hated post life in peacetime. At Fort Meade, he occasionally led patrols that lasted days and covered hundreds of miles, the object being to report on the presence of Seminole Indians. Since most of the Seminoles had long since retreated to the safety of the Everglades, more than 100 miles south of Fort Meade, Jackson had no luck finding any in the region he was supposed to patrol. That angered his commander, who insisted there must be some Indians somewhere for the army to fight. When he questioned Jackson's ability as an officer, the two began to clash over everything, including how and where to put up new buildings on the post.

When Jackson discovered a rumor that the post commander was carrying on with a servant girl, he reported it to his commander at army headquarters. To Jackson's surprise, his veracity was doubted because he was questioning the integrity of a superior officer. About that same time, Jackson got a letter from the commander of the Virginia Military Institute asking if he was interested in joining the 11-year-old military college as a professor of artillery and natural and experimental philosophy (physics). Jackson, disgusted with how the army was treating him, wrote back that he would indeed like his name put before the college's board. Daniel Harvey Hill, a friend of Jackson's from the Mexican War, pushed the superintendent of the military school, Colonel Francis Smith, to hire Jackson, based on Jackson's bravery and skill with artillery during the war.

Within months, Jackson resigned from the army and traveled to Lexington, which he had never before visited. His Florida commander, William Henry French, was not severely disciplined. In fact, he later rose to the rank of general and faced his former subordinate during the Seven Days battles.

Jackson lived in Lexington for eight years before buying this house for

$3,000, a good deal for what real-estate agents today would call a "fixer-upper." He immediately poured himself into preparing it for his second wife, Mary Anna, and his hoped-for family. The orphan boy who had never known a permanent home, the soldier who had served from New York to Mexico to Florida, the widower who had lost his first wife during the birth of their first child, was now a 35-year-old professor who was ready to settle down.

Jackson furnished the home with fine couches shipped south from New York City. He had a special desk made so he could study the Bible and memorize his lessons standing up. He often faced the wall so his mind would not be distracted until he had memorized everything he would teach the cadets the next day.

There were about 4,000 slaves in Rockbridge County in 1860. Six of them belonged to Jackson. Period photos of the back of the home show outbuildings that could have housed slaves, and there was room inside the house for at least one slave. Jackson did not talk or write extensively about slavery, but he had experienced it from an early age, having grown up with slaves as playmates on his uncle's farm. Despite laws forbidding it, he had taught at least one of his black friends to read. Jackson grew up trusting blacks from the time as a seven-year-old when an older slave had taken him and his sister to their mother's deathbed.

Whatever Jackson thought about one man owning another, he believed everyone needed a relationship with God. When he moved to Lexington, he started a black Sunday school, though the evidence is unclear if that included teaching slaves to read in defiance of the law. For a while, the Sunday school was controversial with townspeople, but most people eventually came to believe that Jackson was teaching the slaves worthwhile habits.

Lexington's slave community must have watched Jackson closely to see if his Sunday-school face was the same one he wore in private. One day, a slave named Albert stopped Jackson on the street and asked Jackson to purchase him from his owner. As the deal developed, Albert did not actually work for Jackson, but was hired out as a hotel waiter. Another slave, Amy, may have been acquired the same way. Amy cooked for the family until Jackson left for war. Her death in November 1861 "brought tears to my eyes," Jackson wrote in a letter to his wife. Records indicate that he sent money to a Lexington cabinetmaker to pay for her coffin.

Three other Jackson family slaves were Hetty and her two sons, Cyrus and George, who had belonged to the Morrison family in North Carolina; Hetty had been with Mary Anna since Jackson's wife was a baby. Described as a headstrong woman not inclined to like the discipline Jackson expected of everyone, Hetty nevertheless became close to the Jacksons. She particularly liked working on the farm with her two sons.

Jackson's last slave was a four-year-old orphan named Emma who may have been retarded, as Mary Anna's description of her was that she was "not a treasure." There is some indication that Jackson bought the little girl out of pity, since her owner was an elderly woman. The girl would surely have been sold away from Lexington had Jackson not purchased her. Mary Anna noted how Jackson "persevered in drilling [Emma] into memorizing a child's catechism, and it was a most amusing picture to see her standing before him with fixed attention."

When Jackson went to war, he occasionally wrote home asking about the slaves. He also sent them gifts during the holidays. He trusted his slaves without question, and they seem to have trusted him. None of them apparently ever tried to run away, and they joined in the mourning of his death in May 1863.

One black closely associated with Jackson was apparently not his slave. Jim Lewis seems to have belonged to the Lewis family, from whom Jackson hired his services as a servant in the field. Why he did not simply take Cyrus or George has never been determined. Jackson, a very logical man, might have thought that the two brothers and their mother made a good team at home and that splitting them up might have damaged the relationship.

Jim Lewis cooked for Jackson, took care of his horses, and acted as a gatekeeper, trying to control the general's schedule so he could get some sleep. He apparently knew Jackson well enough that he could defy him when necessary. One story says that Jackson ordered one of his horses saddled just before a battle. When he came out of the tent, he found that Lewis had saddled a different horse. Jackson demanded to know why Lewis had defied him. Lewis calmly informed him that the other horse had been ridden all day the previous day and was much too tired to be saddled again. The general, he said, would have to ride this fresh horse. Jackson did not argue with his servant.

Lewis survived Jackson and attended his funeral. He later became a servant of Sandie Pendleton, a young Jackson staffer. When Pendleton was killed in 1864, Lewis returned home to mourn the two men he had served so ably. Lewis died later in 1864 of unknown causes. Several years later, newspapers began trying to raise money for a proper tombstone for the most famous servant of the war, but it apparently never came to pass. Lewis's unmarked grave lies in either the old Colored Cemetery or the new. It has never been determined if his body was moved.

Get back on Washington Street and continue to Main Street. Turn right and walk one block to the McCampbell Inn, which now serves as a bed-and-breakfast. In 1865, it was the Central Hotel, one of the hotels where Lee lived while waiting for the president's home to be finished.

Turn around and head south on Main. It is two blocks to the intersection with Nelson Street, the site of Lexington Presbyterian Church. The church was organized in 1819; the present building was finished in 1845. Jackson was a deacon of the church. Up by the communion rail is where his coffin rested on May 13, 1863, for his funeral.

On the far left side in the second pew is where Jackson sat—and slept. Try as he might, there was simply something about preaching that put him to sleep almost from the opening line of the sermon. It was not a comfortable sleep, since the precise Jackson insisted on sitting at a 90-degree angle. Later, during the war, he probably looked on those lazy Sunday mornings with envy. Many of the battlefield mistakes attributed to Jackson came at times when he was deprived of sleep. There are recorded instances when Jackson slept so deeply that his aides could not wake him even by shaking him and shouting in his ear.

Look back north up Main Street toward the Virginia Military Institute. Jackson's funeral parade came down this street after his body had lain in state in a lecture room at the school.

Walk south for one more block on Main, then turn into the Stonewall Jackson Memorial Cemetery. Located on the right are the graves of General William Nelson Pendleton and his son, Lieutenant Colonel Alexander Swift "Sandie" Pendleton, Jackson's staffer who was killed in 1864.

The elder Pendleton was an 1830 graduate of West Point who resigned from the army after three years of service to become an Episcopal minister. Already 51 when the war started, he joined the Confederate army as a captain

*Grave of General
William Nelson Pendleton*

of artillery. He served at First Manassas, where legend says he named his cannons Matthew, Mark, Luke, and John. After firing on the Federals, he would look skyward and ask God to have mercy on the souls of the enemies he had just slain. Pendleton proved to be a good organizer, but his performance in the field showed that the fighting was better left to younger men.

It is young men like 21-year-old Sandie Pendleton who fight most wars. A graduate of Washington College and a member of a literary society with Professor Jackson, Pendleton joined Jackson at the start of the war as his ordnance officer. Pendleton was one of the few men Jackson implicitly trusted to carry out his orders. Pendleton believed it his duty to stand between Jackson and his commanders, who often had no clue what Jackson expected of them from one hour to the next. Pendleton was with Jackson right through his death and served as one of the general's pallbearers. Pendleton himself was mortally wounded in September 1864 at Fisher's Hill, a Shenandoah Valley battlefield outside Winchester. He died six days short of his 24th birthday.

Beside Sandie Pendleton is General Edwin Gray Lee, who married General Pendleton's daughter. Diagnosed with tuberculosis in 1860 at age 24, he served as an aide to Jackson when he was not on sick leave. He was promoted during the war despite those frequent leaves. He made it to general, though the Confederate Senate rejected his nomination. He died after the war at the age of 34.

Continue into the cemetery toward the statue of Jackson. On the left in the first fenced area is the Junkin family plot. Here rests Ellinor Junkin Jackson, the 29-year-old daughter of the president of Washington College and Jackson's first wife. Jackson met Ellie when he first came to town. He started calling on her after they became friends while teaching Sunday school. One day, the puzzled professor went to his friend Daniel Harvey Hill to inquire about a strange illness he was experiencing. He simply could not stop thinking about Ellie. The diagnosis offered by Hill was *love*. That stunned Jackson. He had never before been in love.

The two were secretly engaged. They married in August 1853. Ellie's sister Margaret, who opposed the marriage, went with them on their honeymoon trip to New York State and Canada. When they returned, the couple moved into a new wing of the president's home.

Statue of Jackson at Stonewall Jackson Memorial Cemetery

The marriage was a short one. Ellie soon became pregnant, a joyous event for Jackson, who always melted in the presence of young children. The pregnancy seemed to go well right up to the day of birth, October 22, 1854, when Ellie produced a stillborn son and then quickly faded herself. The baby was placed in Ellie's arms before the coffin was closed.

The deaths of his son and wife stunned Jackson. The orphan boy who had looked forward to starting his own family was now alone again. He had to be led away from the grave long after the funeral was over. He remarked to several people that he wished God would take him, too.

Only time healed Jackson's wounds. It helped that Margaret, Ellie's sister who had opposed the marriage, became close to him now that both had lost their best friend. The two grew into such good friends that Jackson may have contemplated marrying her, but Presbyterians did not allow a widower to marry the sister of his wife. Margaret later married another V.M.I. professor, John Preston. Her grave lies nearby.

Continue walking toward the Jackson statue. Just east of the Junkin plot is the spot where Jackson was first buried; the original tombstone is still in place. He was moved when the statue was created by Edward Valentine in 1891. It shows a very lifelike Jackson clutching a pair of binoculars and staring into the distance. Here are buried Jackson, his second wife, and his daughter.

The lemons sometimes left at the base of the statue are intended as a gesture of respect, but they are based on a legend started decades ago that Jackson went into battle sucking on a lemon half. Lemons are a tropical fruit that do not grow in the Shenandoah Valley. It is true that Jackson sometimes enjoyed lemons, but there is greater evidence of his eating peaches and apples, which are native to the Valley. If you want to leave something in honor of Jackson, leave an apple or a peach.

Just in front of Jackson is the grave of Elisha "Bull" Paxton, a Harvard-educated lawyer who served on Jackson's staff before being promoted to general and being given command of the Stonewall Brigade. That appointment was not popular among the colonels serving in the field with the regiments Paxton would command. One resigned in protest. Paxton never got a chance to prove himself. He was shot dead the morning after Jackson was wounded at Chancellorsville.

Also in front of Jackson is the grave of William D. Washington. Washington was not a general, but rather an artist. In 1864, he painted a scene called *The Burial of Latané*, which depicted the burial of Captain William Latané, the only man killed on Stuart's "Ride around McClellan" in the summer of 1862. The painting shows a slave and several women mourning the death of the young captain. It was reproduced as prints and sold around the Confederacy as a way to raise money for humanitarian efforts.

When you are ready to leave the cemetery, return to Main Street, turn left, cross the street, walk to the next street and turn right on to White Street. The Presbyterian manse is on the left three houses from the corner, at 6 White Street. Built in 1848, it was the home of Dr. William S. White, a clergyman who frequently met here with Jackson to discuss religion and God's ways. White preached the burial service for Ellie Jackson and then, nearly 10 years later, did the same for Stonewall. He apparently never took offense that Jackson slept through his sermons. One story goes that a hypnotist came to Lexington and asked for volunteers to be put under his spell. Jackson volunteered, but the frustrated hypnotist never could put him to sleep. A spectator yelled that this was because the Reverend White was not preaching.

Walk one more block on White Street, turn right on Jackson Avenue. Walk two blocks to Preston Street and turn right. Located at 110 West Preston Street is a gray house built in 1821 for the president of Washington College. In 1844, it was purchased and renovated by J. T. L. Preston, the V.M.I. professor who later married Margaret Junkin, the sister of Jackson's first wife. It was from this house that Margaret watched Union general David Hunter's burning of V.M.I. in June 1864. Fearful that the Federals would burn her home if they believed her to be harboring war material, she cut up some Confederate uniforms she was hiding. When the soldiers came to her house, they stole all the food, leaving the family nothing. Margaret cooperated in every way—with one exception. Underneath the folds of her dress, she successfully hid a sword that Stonewall Jackson had sent to the family the previous year.

From the Preston house, turn left on Lee Avenue. At 111 Lee is the home where General William Pendleton lived after he retired as rector of the Episcopal church.

Two houses down, at 109 Lee, is the home where Pendleton lived while serving as rector. Robert E. Lee, a friend of Pendleton's, visited this house many times.

Once, Pendleton complained to Lee that too many of Washington College's Episcopal boys were ignoring their own church in favor of visiting the Presbyterian church to hear Dr. Pratt on Sundays. What Pendleton did not recognize was that the Presbyterian preacher had a very attractive daughter named Grace. When Pendleton persisted that something was dreadfully wrong with the backsliding young Episcopalians, Lee replied, "The attraction is not so much Dr. Pratt's eloquence as it is Dr. Pratt's Grace." Lee didn't care if the young men became Presbyterians. But he was indeed concerned about their faith. "I dread the thought of any student going away from the college without becoming a sincere Christian," he once said.

Turn left off Lee Avenue on to Nelson Street. Just behind the post office at 208 West Nelson is the house built in 1821 for Samuel Reid, Rockbridge County's clerk of court. It was here on September 19, 1865, that Lee spent his first night in Lexington. He tried to check into the Lexington Hotel, since the Reids did not expect him until the following day, but he was recognized as soon as he rode down Main Street, and the Reids insisted that he stay with them. Rather than impose on their hospitality until the president's residence was ready, he later moved to the Lexington and Central Hotels, where he stayed until his family joined him and the house was ready.

Return to Lee Avenue, turn left, and cross Washington Street to enter R. E. Lee Memorial Episcopal Church. This church was built in 1883, some 13 years after Lee's death. Grace Church, the church he attended, is no longer standing. The last church-council meeting that Lee attended was to discuss raising money for the church now named in his honor. Just before leaving for the meeting, he told his daughter that he didn't really care to go, as he did not want to listen "to that pow-wow." It was just after returning from that meeting that the general apparently suffered a stroke. After his death, Mrs. Lee took over his goal of raising money for the church, hand-tinting copies of Custis and Lee portraits herself.

R. E. Lee Memorial Episcopal Church

From the church, walk west on Washington to the Lee House, located at the junction with the walking path for Washington and Lee University.

This home was built for Lee and his family and remains the residence of the president of Washington and Lee. Lee helped design the house, insisting on a wide wraparound porch so Mrs. Lee, who had been in a wheelchair for several years, could maneuver. The garage on the southern side was once a stable built for Traveller and Lucy Long. Lee insisted that it be attached to the house so he could say that he and his faithful horses were living under the same roof. It is tradition for the garage door to remain open so visitors can see where Traveller lived. Don't trespass, though, as the house is private.

The handsome home has a bay window built into the northern side of the dining room. It was to the dining room that Lee returned after leaving the church meeting. He sat down at the dinner table and started to say grace. His lips moved, but no words came out. Mrs. Lee poured him a cup of tea, but the general could not muster any thanks. Instead, his eyes showed a look of resignation that his long-recognized heart problems had caught up to him. Mrs. Lee later commented that when she saw that look, "I knew that he had taken leave of earth."

A bed was brought down from the second floor and put in the place of the dining-room table in the bay window. For the next week, Lee lay there

The Lee House

TOURING VIRGINIA'S AND WEST VIRGINIA'S CIVIL WAR SITES

taking his meals and his medicine, but he seemed to know that he would not leave the bed. Once, when his daughter insisted that he take his medicine, he whispered, "It is no use." Another time, a doctor teased him by saying that Traveller had been standing in his stall too long and needed the regular exercise Lee gave him. Lee shook his head and pointed skyward.

On the night of October 11, there was a rare celestial occurrence—an appearance of the aurora borealis, the dancing, shimmering lights that are frequently seen in northern latitudes but are almost unknown as far south as Lexington. Residents shuddered at the sight, for they knew the old Scottish verse, "All night long the northern streamers shot across the trembling sky; Fearful lights that never beckon save when kings or heroes die."

At 9:15 A.M. on October 12, 1870, Robert E. Lee passed away in the bed placed in the bay window of the president's house. He was 63 years old.

Tradition has it that Lee's last words were "Strike the tent." This is said to have come several hours after he said, "Tell [A.P.] Hill he must come up!" Modern readings of the doctors' reports and Lee's symptoms—he was able to move but could barely speak—suggest that he might have suffered a stroke in conjunction with pneumonia. Indeed, it was pneumonia that may have dealt Jackson his final blow. Many doctors now suggest that Lee could not have uttered his famous last words just before dying, but that he may have said them earlier in his last illness.

Almost three years to the day after Lee died, his daughter Agnes passed away in her bedroom in this house at the age of 32. The cause of death was gastroenteritis.

Just over three weeks later, Mrs. Lee, finally crushed by the deaths of her husband and two of her daughters (Annie had died 11 years earlier), passed away in the house at the age of 66. The official cause of death was rheumatism.

Fall was not a good season for the Lees. Annie died of fever in North Carolina on October 20, 1862. Mary Custis Lee, the last surviving daughter, died on November 22, 1918. Son William Henry Fitzhugh "Rooney" Lee died on October 15, 1891. Son Robert Jr. passed away on October 19, 1914. Mildred and Custis were the only family members to break the pattern. Custis died in February 1913; Mildred in March 1905.

Beside the Lee House is the Lee-Jackson House, built in 1842. This was the first residence of the president of Washington College. It was here that President George Junkin and his wife lived with their daughters, Ellie and Margaret.

Jackson married Ellie in 1853. They lived in the northern wing of the house. It was also here that Ellie died in childbirth. After Ellie's death, Jackson continued to live in their room. His father-in-law worried that Jackson was slipping into melancholy.

During that same period, Jackson spent time in his room here and in his classroom expanding the list of maxims for living he had started compiling at West Point. He apparently read the maxims over whenever he thought he was about to stray. The list includes many sayings that are familiar today. While Jackson might not have been the original author, he did popularize the sayings, which included "A man is known by the company he keeps" and "Sacrifice your life rather than your word." His most famous: "You may be whatever you resolve to be."

Behind and just north of the Lee-Jackson House is Washington Hall, built in 1824. The statue of George Washington over the entrance was used to shame the Federals who burned V.M.I. from doing the same to Washington College. In fact, a group of Lexington women pointed out the statue and told the Federals how the college had been named in honor of the first president. As a result, the college was left intact, even though four companies of its students left Lexington to form the Fourth Virginia Regiment.

Turn now to Lee Chapel, located 50 yards east of Washington Hall. The chapel was finished in 1868, two years after Lee came to the campus. The design was suggested by his son George Washington Custis Lee, who became president of Washington College upon the death of his father. Though called a chapel, the building was never consecrated as a church and was used for many student activities, such as lectures, concerts, and commencement ceremonies. Upon its completion, Lee moved into an office on the basement level.

Lee's foresight is evident in the chapel's construction. When he agreed to become president, the college had just 40 students, hardly enough to keep the doors open. By the end of his second year here, the enrollment was 90. Lee instructed that the chapel be designed to accommodate a whopping 600 students. The enrollment was 400 by 1870, the year he died.

Lee's funeral was scheduled to be held in the chapel on October 15, 1870, not long after Mrs. Lee had rejected the idea of burying him in Richmond's Hollywood Cemetery, as had been authorized by the Virginia legislature. At the same time that Mrs. Lee agreed to have the general buried at the college, the trustees voted unanimously to rename the school Washington and Lee.

Mrs. Lee had the general's body dressed in a plain black suit because she feared the federal government would try to stop the funeral if she buried him in his gray uniform. She did not want to be accused of treason. Partly for that reason and partly out of respect for the general's hatred of pageantry, none of the old soldiers who flooded the town to pay their respects wore their old Confederate uniforms. No Confederate flag covered the simple casket, which had been recovered following a flood that had washed the local undertaker's supply down the river. Though Lee's body was to be moved only a few hundred yards from his house to the chapel, there was a symbolic funeral procession through town. Traveller walked just behind the empty hearse.

Lee Chapel

The chapel service was read by General Pendleton. The Reverend White, the same man who had presided over Jackson's funeral, also made some remarks. Colonel Walter Taylor and Colonel Charles Venable, two of Lee's trusted staff members, were there, but few other famous men attended, mostly because it had been raining for days on end and the rivers all over Virginia had overflowed their banks, making travel almost impossible. Lee was attended by the men who had served him—thousands of soldiers, rather than their generals. As the service ended, one of the men started singing "How Firm a Foundation," Lee's favorite hymn. An impromptu choir joined the song.

Inside the chapel is Edward Valentine's famous statue of Lee sleeping on a cot on the battlefield, a pose that Mrs. Lee suggested before she died. Surrounding the statue are replicas of Confederate battle flags hanging from original flagstaffs, including two that were cut from tree branches; until the 1980s, the original flags were used. The portion of the building housing the statue and the flags was added in 1883. The statue itself was started in 1871 and finished in 1875.

Valentine's skill as a sculptor is amazing. He was able to cut away stone to simulate not only the folds of the blanket covering Lee, but the weave in that blanket as well. Lee's boots appear to have the texture of leather, in sharp contrast to the textures of the blanket and Lee's skin and uniform.

Walk downstairs. At the bottom of the stairs is the Lee Tomb, which houses all the members of Lee's immediate family, including the bodies of his three sons and three of his daughters and the ashes of a fourth daughter.

Lee's youngest daughter, Annie, was moved to Lexington from her original burial site in Warrenton, North Carolina, in 1994; Lee visited her grave only a few months before his own death. Daughter Mary asked to be cremated upon her death in November 1918. Mildred died in 1905 of a stroke while attending Mardi Gras in New Orleans. None of the Lee girls ever married.

Also here are sons George Washington Custis Lee, a general who spent most of his military career as an adviser to President Davis, and General William Henry Fitzhugh "Rooney" Lee, who forsook his Harvard education to join the United States Army, which he left after two years to become a farmer. He later joined the Confederate army and worked his way up the chain of command. Rooney Lee narrowly escaped death in September 1862 when he fell off his horse and was run over by his own men while crossing a bridge. He was subsequently wounded in the thigh at the Battle of Brandy Station. He was captured while recovering and was kept by the Federals for nine months. He later rejoined the army and was promoted to major general. Rooney Lee became a United States congressman. He died at his farm near Alexandria in 1891. His remains were moved to Lexington in 1922.

Lee's last son, Robert Jr., started the war as a common soldier. During the Battle of Sharpsburg in September 1862, young Robert watched his father ride up to his artillery battery, which had already been heavily engaged. Junior stood by expecting to hear a few words of affection from his father, but Lee did not recognize his own son, hidden by the grime of black powder on his face. When Junior finally spoke up to ask if they would be thrown back into the fight, the general recognized him by his voice.

"Yes, my son. You must do what you can to drive those people back," Lee said.

Young Robert frightened the family near the end of the war by disappearing for nearly a month. His horse was wounded on the retreat from Petersburg, and by the time he found another, the Federals were between him and his father's army. He turned south and was in the room in Greensboro, North Carolina, when Davis got confirmation that Lee had surrendered.

Robert became a farmer and a mining speculator after the war; his mining venture near Lexington went bust. In the 1890s, he wrote a book called *My Father, General Lee*. He died in 1914.

The bodies of Lee and his family were moved to this tomb when the building was finished. Previously, they had been buried under the floor of the chapel. A star now marks the spot of the original burials.

After viewing the tomb, walk to Lee's office. During his time as president of the college, the room was not as dark as it is today; the low light helps preserve the original artifacts. It was in this office that Lee conceived many of the innovations he brought to the school. He started the college of law and introduced courses in journalism (though he had often complained during the war that reporters gave the enemy valuable information by publishing news of his troop movements), languages, and modern agriculture. It was here that Lee wrote down everything that he felt students at Washington College needed to know to succeed: "We have but one rule here and that is that every student must be a gentleman." Changed slightly since the school has gone coed, Lee's basic rule is still the guiding principle here today.

Historians believe the office is much as Lee left it the day before suffering his stroke. He saw several students that day and answered some correspondence. Perhaps the last thing he did in his office was autograph a picture for a sophomore who was getting a gift for his girlfriend.

In the museum at the chapel are the Washington-Custis-Lee portraits, which demonstrate the connection between the Washington and Lee families and those families' connection with today's Washington and Lee University. It was George Washington who helped save the original Liberty Hall Academy, forerunner of the college, by giving it 100 shares of James River Canal stock. In 1865, Robert E. Lee saved the faltering school by agreeing to become its president. The most familiar portraits are of Washington, Mary Anna Randolph Custis Lee (Lee's wife), and Lee himself, painted when he was a young army lieutenant in 1838.

The Lee Chapel Museum looks at Lee's entire life, rather than just his war years or his years at Washington College. On display are the surveying instruments he used as an army engineer and his sketches of wildlife observed in his travels. You can also see such things as his binoculars and the only copy in Lee's own hand of General Orders Number 9, the order he wrote at Appomattox announcing to the Army of Northern Virginia that he had surrendered. It is a postwar copy by Lee, not the original order. Lee's ability as a fashion designer is also in evidence, in the form of a sketch of the feathered shako hat still worn by the cadets at West Point.

Lee's relationship with Traveller is not overlooked. One of the most famous photographs of Lee, taken somewhere around Lexington, shows him on Traveller. A watch fob made of Traveller's hair is on display—which likely would have irritated Lee, as he once complained that his favorite horse looked "like a plucked chicken," so many people having pulled a hair for a souvenir.

Traveller's grave

On the left outside the exit of the museum is Traveller's grave. Lee acquired the gray-and-black horse in 1862. For most of the war, he rode Traveller, a mare named Lucy Long, and several other horses on occasion. Only once did Traveller fail him. In August 1862, Lee was standing on the ground when a false alarm about approaching Federal cavalry spooked the horse. When Traveller reared, Lee grabbed for the reins. The general fell heavily to the ground, breaking a bone in one of his wrists and spraining the other wrist. His hands were in wooden splits for weeks, leaving him in constant pain and perhaps sometimes clouding his thinking.

Traveller and later Lucy Long and a lesser-known mount named Ajax accompanied Lee to Lexington. Traveller was allowed to roam the lawn of the college. Whenever Lee came out of the house and Traveller saw him, the horse gave the old general a nod of his head. Lee usually had a sugar lump for him. Observers often saw Lee just staring at his old war-horse, as if remembering all the times they had led the army into battle.

Traveller survived Lee by only seven months. He picked up a rusty nail while grazing on the lawn and developed lockjaw. Traveller was always worshiped as a Lee icon. His bones were displayed in the museum for many years before being buried outside Lee's tomb in 1971.

Lucy Long, a gift from J. E. B. Stuart in the fall of 1862, did not become nearly as famous as Traveller, though Lee rode the two alternately to give them rest. Lucy Long was stolen near the end of the war. After the conflict, Lee heard about a horse that looked like her and made the trip to discover that it was indeed his mare. He bought her again as a symbol of respect for the dead Stuart. Once, Lee accidentally choked Lucy Long by putting a buggy collar too tightly around her neck when he took Mrs. Lee for a ride down by the river. When Lucy Long fell from lack of air, Lee ripped the collar off and begged her forgiveness, saying aloud how ashamed he was for being so careless. Lucy Long survived another 20 years before being humanely put down. The location of her grave is not known.

Ajax died not long after coming to Lexington when he ran into an iron fence.

Though Lee used his horses as tools of war, he loved all animals. During one battle, his astonished staff watched him dismount to put a little bird back into its nest. Just a month before he died, he wrote one of his sons asking him to find a little dog that Lee could have as a pet, as he felt he was getting too old to ride Traveller. Lee even loved cows. He kept a milk cow at Lexington and was distressed when he had to leave her when she was sick. He penned a letter when she died. "Her troubles are over now and I am grateful to her for what she has done for us. I hope that we did our duty to her," Lee wrote.

From the Lee Chapel, turn right on to the campus path and walk north to the Virginia Miliary Institute, which lies adjacent to Washington and Lee.

Founded in 1839 on the grounds of an arsenal maintained by Virginia to defend the western part of the state, V.M.I. opened with 23 cadets, who pulled the double duty of learning a college curriculum while guarding the weapons kept in the arsenal. The first superintendent of the school was Professor Francis H. Smith.

Though West Point contributed its share of general officers to both sides in the Civil War, V.M.I.'s contribution may have been even greater. At the start of the war, 300 members of the cadet corps were ordered to Richmond to teach basic drills to the civilian soldiers gathered at the capital. Of the 1,800 V.M.I. alumni living at the start of the war, 94 percent joined the

Confederate army. Three major generals, 17 brigadier generals, and 92 colonels were graduates of the institute.

Once inside the grounds, stay on the sidewalk and bear to the right. Stop at the statue entitled *Virginia Mourning Her Dead*, designed by Moses Ezekiel, a V.M.I. graduate. Behind the statue are the remains of six of the V.M.I. students killed or mortally wounded at the Battle of New Market in 1864. The other four students killed at the battle are buried elsewhere in the state.

Walk across the yard to view the unusual statue of Jackson that seems to show the wind blowing up his frock coat. Most biographers describe Jackson as always wearing his army-issue fatigue cap. In this statue, he is wearing a wide-brimmed hat that is either pinned on one side or is being blown by the wind, like his coat. The same statue stands on the grounds of the West Virginia State Capitol.

At the base of the statue is the grave of Jackson's faithful war-horse, Little Sorrel. Little Sorrel's lineage is unknown. Jackson's men captured the horse at Harpers Ferry in May 1861 when they stopped a Federal train loaded with cows and horses. Jackson saw the little horse and bought him on the spot, intending to send him to his wife. But after riding Little Sorrel, Jackson kept him. The horse remained close to Jackson for the rest of the general's life. It was said that he seemed to know where Jackson wanted to go and could almost be given his head without control of the reins. When Jackson was wounded, Little Sorrel rushed toward the Federal lines but was recaptured within a few days. Like Traveller, he outlived his master. Little Sorrel resided for a time in Lexington before being moved to the Old Soldiers Home in Richmond, where he died in 1886. Reports say that he never forgot his service to the Confederacy. While living on the V.M.I. campus, Little Sorrel would dance and prance whenever he heard the martial music he had grown used to in Confederate camps.

The four cannons on display in front of the statue are unusual in that they are 320 pounds lighter than normal six-pounders. These special lightweight guns were ordered by Superintendent Smith because V.M.I. did not have horses to move equipment during gunnery practice. Rather than exhaust his cadets, Smith simply ordered lighter guns, figuring that the more important instruction came in loading and firing the pieces, rather than in

Statue of Jackson and the four cannons

TOURING VIRGINIA'S AND WEST VIRGINIA'S CIVIL WAR SITES

moving them by hand. Jackson used these same guns in his artillery drills. One of the cannons was used on July 2, 1861, at Falling Waters, Virginia. In fact, the guns took part in several battles. But war technology rapidly bypassed them, and they were returned to V.M.I. by 1863. Their most historic use came in firing salutes during the funeral for their old commander, Jackson, in May 1863. Two heavier howitzers were also located on the campus. Those guns were taken to John Brown's hanging in Harpers Ferry. They subsequently disappeared into Confederate service, and their current location is unknown.

Note how the cadets leaving their barracks behind Jackson's statue salute the general even though he is facing away from them. Carved into the arch they walk through is Jackson's most famous axiom: "You may be whatever you resolve to be."

When you are ready to leave the statue, walk into Jackson Memorial Hall, located about 30 yards east. Jackson Memorial Hall houses the campus museum.

One of the main attractions in the building is *The Battle of New Market*, an 18-by-23-foot painting by 1880 V.M.I. graduate Benjamin West Clinedinst. Clinedinst visited the battlefield and talked to many veterans to correctly depict his scene of the cadets slipping and sliding on the ground. His own son Wendell served as the model for the cadet shot in the head. The painting was unveiled in 1914 by the five-year-old granddaughter of the man who led the cadets. After the ceremony, a Yankee who had ridden on the raid that burned Lexington tried to shake her hand, but the little girl refused and put her hands behind her back. In those days, when burned-out farms marked only by scorched chimneys could still be seen in the Shenandoah Valley, even little girls had hard feelings for Yankees.

Walk down into the museum. You'll see a display detailing the life of Francis Smith, the first commandant. Smith stayed at the school for 22 years and died three months after his retirement. During his tenure, he got to know the cadets personally. At graduation, he gave each boy a Bible with an inscribed verse that he thought matched the cadet's personality. Smith and Jackson often butted heads, as both were strong-willed characters. But unknown to Jackson, Smith stuck up for the professor when he was accused of making his exams too difficult to pass.

Turn left after passing the Smith exhibit. Located on the left are some Jackson artifacts. The blackboard on which he wrote his dull lessons is there. In the same case is the uniform he wore while a professor—probably the same one he wore when he headed off to First Manassas. You'll also see the faded blue forage cap that Jackson favored over the more practical broad-brimmed hat. Though it seems tattered and worn, it was described as such even in 1861. Above it is the black rubber raincoat Jackson was wearing on the night he was shot. A bullet-hole patch is visible in the left shoulder.

It is puzzling that Jackson was wearing a raincoat that night. He put it on early in the morning on May 2, 1863, when the air was chilly, but there was no threat of rain that day. By midday, the temperature climbed to at least the mid-80s. It was probably still warm enough for just a uniform coat at 9 P.M., when Jackson was shot, but for some reason, he chose to wear this dark raincoat. It has not been recorded if he wore it all day or put it on after the sun fell.

The raincoat has an interesting history. It was picked up on the battle-field at Chancellorsville by a scavenger and traded to the overseer of Ellwood, the house where Jackson's amputated arm was buried, for a pack of meal. Having no idea whose coat he had acquired, that man tossed it into an outhouse. His wife retrieved it and patched the slit left sleeve and a bullet hole she found. The man used it for months, then sold it to one of Mosby's Rangers.

The ranger bought it strictly for its intended use. But as he examined his new purchase, he began to wonder. He finally surmised who the original owner was because the bullet hole and the slit sleeve fit the description of Jackson's wounding. When he looked at the coat more closely, he found "T. J. Jackson" written on the inside back, an identification that the overseer of Ellwood and his wife had both missed.

After the war, the young ranger sent the coat to Robert E. Lee, asking him to do what was right. Lee contacted Mary Anna Jackson, who told him that while it would be painful to see the coat again, she did want it. Mrs. Jackson then passed the raincoat along to a visiting Scotsman, who took it back to Scotland and displayed it next to the uniform coat of General O. O. Howard, whose Union flank Jackson had smashed at Chancellorsville.

Next, Mrs. Jackson wrote to the man in Scotland to request the coat. He initially refused, saying that it was a symbol for all Scotsmen. Later, feeling guilty for ignoring her wishes, he mailed her the coat. She kept it in Charlotte, North Carolina, until her death in 1915. Her granddaughter donated the coat to the museum at V.M.I. in 1926.

In a display case facing the raincoat is the stretched skin of Little Sorrel, one of only two fully mounted Civil War horses on public display anywhere. Union general Phil Sheridan's horse, Renzi, is on display at the Smithsonian Institution in Washington. The head of Old Baldy, Union general George Meade's horse, is on display in Philadelphia.

As was frequently noted by Jackson's men, Little Sorrel looks too small to have supported Jackson. One early description said he was 15 hands tall, making him a size more fit for a woman than a man. But Jackson always said that the horse had a gait that suited him. However great a soldier Jackson was, no one ever accused him of being a good rider. His staffers regarded his riding style as awkward. He had a peculiar habit of leaning far forward in the saddle. Observers said it sometimes looked as if his head was even with the horse's head.

Jackson's house at Washington and Lee University

When you are ready to leave the museum, return along the campus path to Washington Street, turn left, and walk east to the Lexington Visitor Center to retrieve your vehicle. Drive west on Washington, then turn right on Main Street. Follow the signs for U.S. 11 North, passing V.M.I. on the left.

Just before crossing the bridge over the Maury River, look to the left. This is Jordan's Point, the farthest spot up the river to which boats could navigate. It was here that the body of Stonewall Jackson was taken off the boat by V.M.I. cadets, and it was here that the Lee family first joined the general in Lexington. It was also here that Lee inaugurated a new sport for the students—rowing. His son George Washington Custis Lee had been a rower at Harvard, and Lee thought that the new sport would bring home the importance of teamwork.

The city of Lexington is planning to make Jordan's Point into a park.

Just after crossing over I-64, turn left on Va. 39. Follow this winding road for 8.9 miles to Rockbridge Baths. Just after crossing the bridge over Hayes Creek, pull to the right side of the road. The bright yellow house on the left is the last surviving cottage from what was once a resort built around the baths. The Lee family came to this cottage on occasion to soak in the baths. Mrs. Lee spent the summer of 1869 here, where she received a visit from Rooney's wife and grandson.

A famous photograph of Lee in civilian clothes and a wide-brimmed straw hat sitting astride Traveller was taken in the backyard of this house. Visible behind the house is the same mountain that can be seen in the photograph.

Lee cottage at Rockbridge Baths

The block wall of the house on the right now encloses the Rockbridge Baths.

Continue on Va. 39 through Goshen Pass after 2.5 miles. This used to be the stagecoach route through the mountains. The Lees often took this road.

Matthew Fontaine Maury, a V.M.I. professor and the man who had revolutionized naval navigation by charting the oceans, claimed that Goshen Pass was the most beautiful spot on earth. He said that when he died, he wanted to be carried through the pass when the rhododendrons were in bloom. At his death in 1873, the V.M.I. cadets did just that. A marker honoring Maury is located near the wayside park in the pass.

It is about 27.5 miles from Goshen Pass to U.S. 220 in Warm Springs. Turn left on U.S. 220 and drive a few hundred yards to the two round bathhouses on the right. These are not the same structures the Lees used when they visited here, but they look much the same. The women's bathhouse has the chair Mrs. Lee used for being lowered into the warm water, since her legs were almost useless in her later life.

Visitors can still take baths here; the cost is $12. True to its name, the water is warm to the touch.

Across the road from the bathhouses is a historical marker that tells the story of the Terrill brothers, both of whom were generals during the Civil War, but for different sides.

William Rufus Terrill was a 27-year-old West Point graduate when the war started. He decided to cast his lot with the Union but promised his father that he would never fight against his home state. At his own request, he was sent west to fight in Kentucky and Tennessee. On October 8, 1862, at the Battle of Perryville, Kentucky, he was mortally wounded by a shell fragment. He was buried at West Point.

William's younger brother, James, a graduate of V.M.I., was practicing law in Warm Springs when the war started. James joined the Confederacy and fought in many of its battles. On May 30, 1864, he was killed at Bethesda Church northeast of Richmond. Without knowing he was dead, the Confederate Congress approved his promotion to general the next day. Although Terrill was apparently buried on the battlefield by Federal troops, his body was later moved to a private cemetery in Mechanicsville.

After the brothers' deaths, a legend sprang up that their father, a former United States congressman and a well-known Virginia lawyer, erected a monument to his sons bearing the inscription "Only God Knows Which One Was Right." Modern-day historians have searched for this monument but have found it neither on the Terrill property nor in a nearby cemetery.

If you care to make a brief side trip to Hot Springs, the spring Lee visited just two months before his death, continue south for a few miles on U.S. 220. Lee's letters from that period seem to show a man who was slowing down, dying. The original building in which he stayed at Hot Springs has been replaced by a modern structure that is more suited to a golf resort than a healing spring. Return to Warm Springs to complete the side trip.

From Warm Springs, head north on U.S. 220. It is 28.2 miles to the town of Monterey. Turn right on U.S. 250 and head east for 9.3 miles. About 1 mile after passing through the small town of McDowell, you'll reach a historical marker for the Battle of McDowell, fought on May 8, 1862. It was here that Jackson started to earn a reputation for moving his men with impossible quickness in directions that confused the Federals.

After suffering a defeat at the First Battle of Kernstown on March 23, Jackson found himself slowly but steadily pursued by General Nathaniel Banks. At the same time, Lee needed Jackson's help in drawing off Union reinforcements that might otherwise be sent to McClellan, who was advancing up the Peninsula toward Richmond.

Jackson decided that the best course of action was to attack. His scouts told him that another Union army, under General John C. Frémont, was advancing eastward toward Staunton with the intention of catching the Confederates in a pincher movement. Jackson figured correctly that Frémont would never expect to be attacked, particularly in the middle of the mountains. He rushed his men westward, pushing them so hard that they nicknamed themselves "Jackson's Foot Cavalry." They made it to this high ground, Setlinger's Hill. The Federals tried for four hours to dislodge them, to no avail. Much of the fighting was in darkness. It was a battle between infantry forces, as the ground was too steep for cavalry and artillery. The Federals finally pulled back, leaving the Confederates in control of the field, although they had suffered more losses—about 400 killed and wounded, compared to 250 killed and wounded for the Union.

Jackson didn't actually direct the Battle of McDowell, unlike most other fights. He left it up to 45-year-old general Edward Johnson, who didn't mind it when his men called him "Old Allegheny," since his service to that point had been in the mountains of West Virginia. Johnson must have looked a sight. He was a large man with a full goatee and a receding hairline who had suffered a facial wound during the Mexican War that caused him to wink constantly. He carried neither a sword nor a pistol. Instead, he cheered and swore at his men while waving a club. He had to use that club as a crutch after McDowell, since he was shot in the ankle.

Johnson was captured at Spotsylvania Court House in 1864. An amused Union general who had been Johnson's prewar friend witnessed him clubbing the privates who were trying to capture him and take him to the rear.

One general at McDowell whom Jackson despised was William Booth Taliaferro, a 39-year-old Harvard Law–trained solder who had fought in the Mexican War and worked his way up to major before leaving the army for a political career. He had known Jackson back at V.M.I., when Taliaferro was on the board of visitors.

Taliaferro crossed Jackson by siding with General William Loring in a dispute against Jackson's order that Loring's men spend the winter of 1861–62 in Romney, Virginia (now West Virginia), in what Loring considered an exposed position. Taliaferro even went to Richmond and spoke to President Davis in an attempt to get Jackson replaced.

Jackson was a man to hold a grudge. As his star rose, he did all he could to put Taliaferro in his place, including trying to keep him from being promoted. Taliaferro was promoted anyway, which only made Jackson dislike him more.

After McDowell, where Taliaferro performed fairly well, Jackson wrote a short report giving credit for the victory to God, rather than to anything that Taliaferro or the other generals on the field did.

Continue east on U.S. 250. After about 3 miles, you'll reach a highway rest stop on top of a mountain. Located here are some breastworks dug by Confederates before the Battle of McDowell. The very steep trail to the site gives a feel for what both sides had to contend with in this area. From the top of the trail, visitors can look back toward the battlefield at McDowell.

It is about 30 more miles into Staunton, where U.S. 250 becomes Churchville Road (later it becomes Churchville Avenue). Go through three lights, watching for Gypsy Hill Park on the right. As Churchville makes a turn to the left, bear right on to Thornrose Avenue. Stay on Thornrose as it bears left at the ball field. At the next traffic light, turn left on to West Beverly Street and drive a half block to the entrance to Thornrose Cemetery. Drive through the arch, then pull over and park. The tour ends at this cemetery.

Tomb and monument of General John Echols

Straight ahead to the left of the entrance road is the large stone mausoleum of General John Echols, another Harvard-educated lawyer and state legislator who became a general. Echols started his career raising the 27th Virginia, one of the original regiments of the Stonewall Brigade. He was a huge man for his day, standing nearly six-foot-five and weighing nearly 250 pounds, yet he often reported himself sick. He was wounded once but fought the entire war. Echols was the losing field commander at the Battle of Droop Mountain in November 1863. He died of kidney disease at age 63. A Bible verse on his monument quotes the third chapter of Job, verse 26: "I was not fat and lazy, yet trouble struck me down."

Walk back down the entrance road, turn left, then walk to the next road leading into the cemetery. Turn left and head up the hill. Watch on the left for the tombstone of Major Jedediah Hotchkiss, one of Jackson's most trusted and valuable staff members. Hotchkiss was a New York State native who moved south while still a teenager to make his way in the world. He loved teaching and by age 21 had founded his own school. His favorite hobby was making maps.

Grave of Major Jedediah Hotchkiss

That hobby made Hotchkiss invaluable to the Confederate cause. He had an eye for drawing terrain and measuring distances. He often sketched his maps without even dismounting from his horse, changing colored pencils when the terrain changed. Jackson would send him and Keith Boswell, a civil engineer, to find roads and determine which ones were best for moving the army. During the Shenandoah Valley Campaign in the spring of 1862, all those marches where Jackson's army seemed to disappear, only to

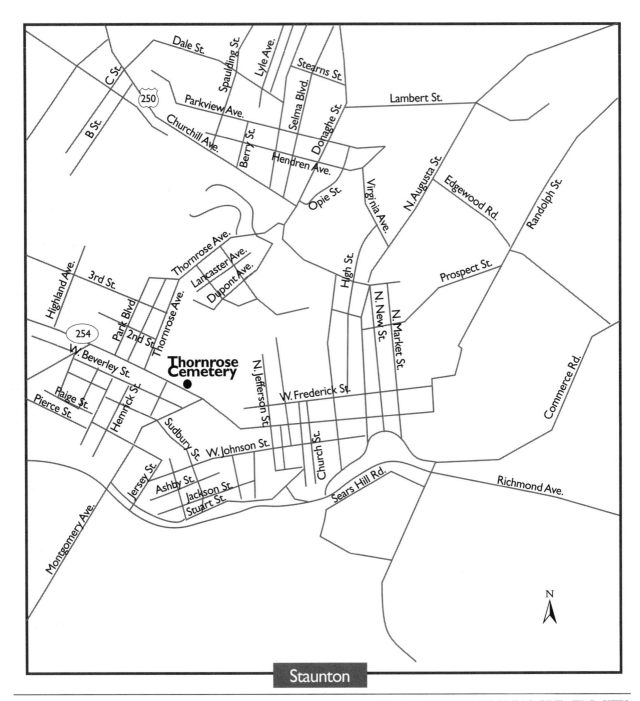

Staunton

pop up miles away, were the direct result of the efforts of Boswell and Hotchkiss in finding roads and quickly drawing maps so Jackson could make decisions about which way to go.

Following Jackson's death, Hotchkiss drew maps for General Richard Ewell and General Jubal Early.

After the war, Federal authorities tried to make Hotchkiss give up his maps, but he went all the way to President Grant, who agreed that the maps were his private property. Hotchkiss made copies for the government but kept the originals. More than 120 of his maps were printed in the *Atlas to Accompany the Official Records of the Union and Confederate Armies*, which is still in print today. Hotchkiss also wrote the Virginia volume of the *Confederate Military History* and became a well-received lecturer. He died in 1899 at the age of 71. Though he had never risen above the rank of major, he was one of the most valuable officers in the entire Confederate army.

Follow the next road as it curves to the right and back down the hill toward the entrance. As the road curves toward the street, look to the right for the grave of Robert Doak Lilley. Lilley was a competent, steady performer in the 25th Virginia Regiment who slowly rose in rank until being named a general in May 1864. He participated in Jubal Early's raid on Washington that summer.

Grave of Robert Doak Lilley

In July 1864, Lilley was scouting near Winchester when he was spotted by Federal troops. Actually, he was more than spotted. He was targeted. Within seconds, a fragment from a cannon shell pierced his thigh, a minie ball shattered his arm, and another minie ball went through the already-injured thigh. His horse ran away, and Lilley was captured on the field. Union surgeons subsequently amputated his arm and treated his thigh.

Four days after he was wounded, the Confederates retook Winchester. Lilley was recovered before he could be sent to a prison camp, where he surely would have died from his wounds.

He later commanded reserve forces in the Shenandoah Valley.

After the war, Lilley became the chief financial officer of his alma mater, Washington College. He was credited by the president of that institution, Robert E. Lee, with putting the school back on a firm financial foundation.

Lilley's wounds probably contributed to his early death at the age of 50 in 1886. The cause of death was listed as paralysis.

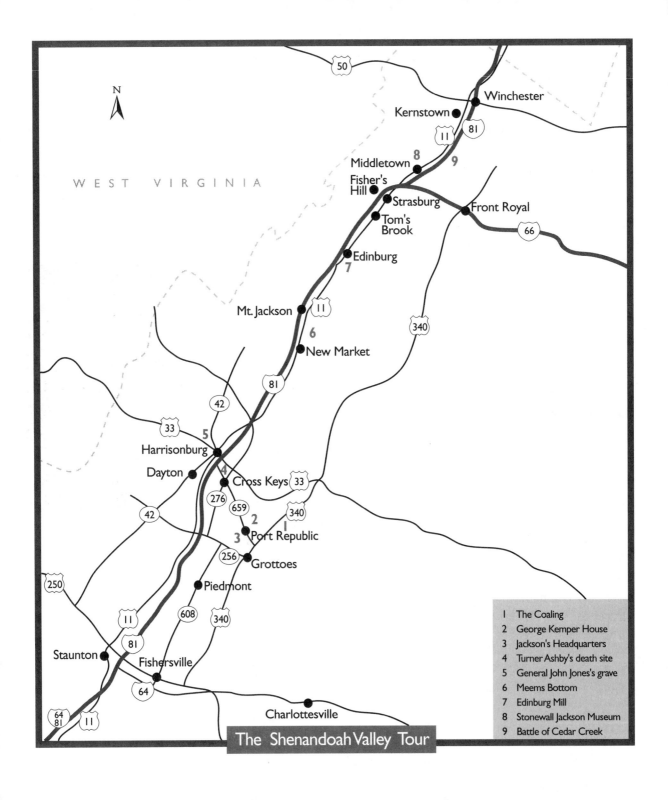

The Shenandoah Valley Tour

1 The Coaling
2 George Kemper House
3 Jackson's Headquarters
4 Turner Ashby's death site
5 General John Jones's grave
6 Meems Bottom
7 Edinburg Mill
8 Stonewall Jackson Museum
9 Battle of Cedar Creek

The Shenandoah Valley Tour

This tour starts outside Staunton at the little-visited site of the Battle of Piedmont, which still looks like it did in 1864 when Confederate general Grumble Jones fell dead here. It then moves to several battlefields of Stonewall Jackson's Shenandoah Valley Campaign and visits the site where General Turner Ashby was mortally wounded. Next, the tour visits New Market, the site of the battle that made the V.M.I. cadets famous, and Cedar Creek, the site of the only battle that was won and lost by two different sides on the same day. It ends in Winchester with a walking tour of the town where Stonewall had his headquarters.

The tour is approximately 100 miles long but may require two days, as it stops at several major battlefields.

THE TOUR STARTS at the junction of U.S. 250 and I-81 on the eastern outskirts of Staunton. Drive east on U.S. 250 for 4.4 miles to C.R. 608 in Fishersville. Turn left and head north on C.R. 608 for about 10 miles to the village of Piedmont. About 0.5 mile north of the village, look to the right to see the large marker overlooking the field where the Battle of Piedmont was fought on June 5, 1864.

Just three weeks earlier, on May 15, the Confederate victory at New Market had given Lee a false sense of security that the Shenandoah Valley was now safe from Union invasion. He put the victorious Confederate troops on the march to join him in the fight to save Richmond from the new Union commander, Grant.

What Lee did not count on was Grant's determination to fight the Confederates on every front in an attempt to wear them down, just as he had done in Mississippi and Tennessee. Within days of New Market, the defeated Union commander, Franz Sigel, was replaced by David Hunter, an avowed abolitionist who wanted to punish the South for slavery. Hunter started advancing south up the Valley toward Staunton, an important rail hub. The startled Confederates had to reach all the way down into southwestern Virginia to bring General William E. "Grumble" Jones into the action.

Jones came by his nickname in a sad way. In 1852, the young army lieutenant's new wife drowned off the coast of Texas while en route to joining him at his post. He would never smile again. Jones's sour attitude and profane manner must have instantly clashed with the jovial and deeply religious bearing of his superior officer early in the war, J. E. B. Stuart. Stuart never liked Jones and refused to promote him to major general despite Jones's fighting abilities, which were recognized even by Lee. After Gettysburg, Stuart and Jones had one major, final clash. Stuart had Jones arrested and court-martialed. Lee allowed the court-martial to go through and saw to it that Jones was sent as far from Stuart as possible.

Now, Jones's abilities were needed. He rushed his 6,000 troops to a point north of Piedmont and set up what he knew would be the only defensive line Staunton would get against Hunter's 10,000 advancing men.

Though the Confederates had some early success during the battle, their line collapsed in panic when it was pierced. While trying to rally his troops back into order, Jones was killed by a minie ball to the head. He was buried on the field by the Federals. After the war, his body was moved back to the yard of his home church near Abingdon.

More than 1,000 Confederates surrendered here, and another 600 were killed or wounded. Staunton was open to plunder. Hunter next pushed south in the Valley to Lynchburg, where Jubal Early defeated him.

Piedmont Battlefield where "Grumble" Jones was killed

Continue north on C.R. 608 for 3.8 miles to Va. 256. Turn right and head toward the town of Grottoes. After 2.3 miles on Va. 256, turn left on U.S. 340. Drive north on U.S. 340 for about 3 miles (ignoring, for now, the signs pointing to Port Republic). Watch on the right for a historical marker at Grace Episcopal Memorial Church. Park in the small church lot.

This is The Coaling, the major portion of the battlefield at Port Republic and the site of one of Jackson's famous victories during the 1862 Shenandoah Valley Campaign. After climbing the hill at The Coaling, stop and look out toward the plain.

On June 9, 1862, Jackson's men were marching north against General James Shields's Union troops, who held this high ground for their artillery. The place was known as "The Coaling" because it had been mined for years for charcoal. Two regiments—one from Virginia and the other from Louisiana—charged across the plain toward the Union cannons. The Federals were so intent on shooting that they didn't notice the charge of additional Louisiana troops who had sneaked through the woods to outflank the artillerymen.

Some of the most fierce hand-to-hand fighting of the entire war ensued. The Louisiana troops, nicknamed "Tigers" as much for their willingness to fight other Confederates as to do the same with Yankees, crashed into the Union guns and clubbed the Federals to the ground. The Tigers, one of the South's most international units, composed of men from a dozen countries, then jumped on the guns, laughing and slapping each other on the back. They didn't notice another Federal artillery battery just 350 yards away wheeling its guns in their direction. As the artillery shells began landing, Confederate officers ordered the men to start killing the artillery horses with guns and knives, to keep the guns from being retaken by the Federals.

"It was a sickening sight, men in gray and blue piled up in front of and around the guns and with the horses dying and the blood of men and beasts flowing almost in a stream," wrote one horrified Tiger after the battle.

A regiment of Ohio soldiers rushed the guns and drove the Confederates back. The Federals were dragging the cannons away when the same Tigers charged a second time. The Confederates were pushed back, and the Federals again started dragging the guns. Then the Tigers charged a third time. On this occasion, their commander, General Richard Taylor, son of former

United States president Zachary Taylor, threw in everyone he had, including his regimental band. The Federals had endured enough. They retreated from the field, having saved one cannon. They left the other five in the hands of the Louisiana Tigers, who dragged them off the field.

The carnage at The Coaling was frightening. More than 300 men from Ohio and Louisiana lay dead on this hill, all killed fighting for the same six cannons. All told, nearly 300 men from the Louisiana Brigade were killed at Port Republic—a third of Jackson's total losses during the battle. Jackson himself rode to the grisly scene and thanked the Tigers for their sacrifice. He said the future use of the captured cannons would be dedicated to the memory of the Tigers.

Retrace your route on U.S. 340 toward Grottoes. After 2 miles, turn right on C.R. 659 and head toward the village of Port Republic, located about 2 miles away. Just after crossing the bridge, turn to the right into the parking lot for the Port Republic Museum, the yellow frame house that was the home of Frank Kemper during the war. Though the museum is open only on Sundays, a look through the front window will prove both interesting and startling.

House where Turner Ashby's body was displayed

Here in an open wooden coffin is General Turner Ashby—or at least a picture of Ashby taken after his death, blown up to life size, and placed in the coffin. Ashby was killed on June 6, 1862, while leading a charge southeast of Harrisonburg. His remains were brought to this house the following day. Stonewall Jackson came into the room alone to pray over Ashby. Jackson had an unusual relationship with Ashby. He found him a great fighter but thought his men lacked the discipline to be great soldiers. Ashby was promoted to general over Jackson's protests. He was a general for only a few days before his death.

From the Port Republic Museum, turn left on The Point Street to view the river. Just before the battle, some Federals rushed into town over a ford near here.

After one block on The Point Street, turn left on Main Street. Carefully cross C.R. 659, drive 0.75 mile on Main, and turn right on to C.R. 605. The large two-story house on the left was built on the foundation of what was the George Kemper House during the war. The George Kemper House served as Jackson's headquarters in Port Republic. It was here on Sunday, June 8, 1862—the day after Jackson viewed Ashby's remains—that he was almost captured or killed due to a lack of preparation.

Port Republic is nestled between two rivers that meet just northeast of town. Jackson placed his army north of the rivers and made his headquarters in the village, meaning that he was separated from his men, something a general normally does not do. Jackson may have done so simply because he was too tired to think straight; one indication of this is that he ordered his wagon supply train to camp near headquarters, rather than near the army.

On the morning of June 8, Jackson and his staff were in the yard of the George Kemper House when they heard cannon fire. A Federal raiding party of more than 150 cavalrymen had split up and was attacking both of the fords on the South River, just a few hundred yards from Jackson's staff and the wagon train.

Port Republic Battlefield Civil War Site

Jackson and a handful of aides mounted and rode toward the valuable bridge over the North River. The Federals threw a few shots their way. Within minutes, Federal cavalry rode down the same street in the opposite direction, toward Jackson's headquarters. They arrived in time to capture two of his late-sleeping aides. The Confederates guarding the ford nearer to Jackson's headquarters fell back to the house and started fighting there. A few cannons were brought up, and the George Kemper House became the center of a hastily thrown-together battle line that halted the Union advance toward the wagon train.

Retrace your route on Main to C.R. 659 and turn left, heading north. You will cross the river at the same point Jackson did. Notice how the northern side of the river is much higher than the southern side. Jackson made it across the river to this point, then directed the first cannon crew he could find to start firing on the Federals milling in the village. The members of that gun crew were reluctant to fire, as they could see another gun crew organizing on the opposite side of the river and believed it to be Confederate, though its men were dressed in blue uniforms. Their uncertainty fueled Jackson's. He shouted to the suspect cannon crew to bring its gun to the northern side of the river. It replied by throwing a canister shot Jackson's way, which killed a nearby soldier. That was all it took to convince the Confederate crew. It fired on the men in blue, killing at least one of the gunners.

Later that morning, a force of Union infantry marching toward Port

Republic was shattered by Confederate cannons set up on this hill. Jackson sat on his horse beside one of the guns and watched the firing with a slight smile on his face. Even the religious Jackson was not above vengeful feelings.

Drive 3.6 miles on C.R. 659 to C.R. 679 (Battleground Road) and turn left. Drive 1.3 miles, turn right on Va. 276, go 0.2 mile, then pull over at the markers for the Battle of Cross Keys.

Cross Keys was fought on June 8, the day before Port Republic. Jackson recognized that it was the Federals' intention to catch him in a vise by moving in forces from the west and the east, so he split his army in two. He took his men toward Port Republic to meet Shields, and General Richard Ewell set up a defensive line along a ridge at Cross Keys to meet Union general John Frémont, the noted explorer and 1856 presidential candidate.

Frémont, advancing from west to east, made a major mistake by not throwing out a skirmish line to find the Confederates. His men stumbled into a 1,500-man force hiding behind a wooden fence and tall grass. From almost point-blank range, the Confederates blasted the leading Federal line. One regiment alone lost 200 men. The Confederates, led by General Isaac Trimble, a 60-year-old civil engineer, rushed forward and drove the Federals back. Believing he was outnumbered, Frémont broke off the attack on all fronts.

That night, many of the Confederates rushed eastward to reinforce Jackson's part of the army at Port Republic.

Though the victory at Cross Keys was part of Jackson's Valley Campaign, he was never actually on the battlefield.

Turn around on Va. 276 and head south for 0.3 mile. Turn right on to C.R. 679. Drive for 3.6 miles to Pleasant Valley, where C.R. 679 merges with C.R. 704. Follow C.R. 704 for 4.3 miles until it runs into Va. 42 in Bridgewater. Turn north and drive about 2 miles on Va. 42 into the town of Dayton. On the northern side of Dayton, follow the signs if you care to visit the Shenandoah Valley Museum, which offers a small but effective electric-light display explaining the Shenandoah Valley Campaign.

A battlefield death that occurred less than a mile north of here was the cause of millions of dollars' worth of destruction in the Shenandoah Valley.

Lieutenant John R. Meigs was a promising young lieutenant when he graduated first in his West Point class of 1863. Beyond his skills, he likely would have gone far simply because his father was General Montgomery C. Meigs, quartermaster general of the Union army.

Young Meigs and two aides spent October 3, 1864, surveying the exact location of all of General Phil Sheridan's camps, in order to document where to send orders. Darkness grew and a light rain began to fall on Swift Run Gap Road as they headed toward Harrisonburg, their headquarters. They saw three riders coming toward them. Those riders turned from the Federals and tried to get away, but Meigs called on them to halt. They did, spacing themselves out as they slowly wheeled their horses.

As Meigs and his two men drew closer, the riders—Confederates on a scouting assignment of their own—pulled their pistols from under their oil-cloths and demanded that the Federals surrender. Instead, Meigs, who had secretly drawn his own pistol, fired. Two of the Confederates fired back, both hitting Meigs. One of the Federals jumped off his horse and ran into the woods. The other surrendered.

When the Federal soldier got back to camp, he said that Meigs had surrendered and been murdered in cold blood. Hearing the story, Sheridan ordered that the town of Dayton and all houses within a 3-mile radius be burned. That task fell to General George Armstrong Custer, who promised Sheridan he would know when the plan was carried out by the smoke columns. This action took place just two weeks after Custer was involved in the execution of six of John Singleton Mosby's men in Front Royal. Perhaps believing he was fighting more guerrillas, he was happy to burn the area around Dayton.

The town itself was mostly spared burning, thanks to a regiment that ignored the order, but local houses were looted. More than two dozen farms around Dayton were burned to the ground. All of their stored crops were destroyed and their livestock slaughtered. The women living in the farmhouses were sometimes given only a few minutes to gather personal belongings. When they piled those items in the yard, the Federals often picked through them and took what they wanted.

For years after the war, mapmakers dubbed the area around Dayton the "Burnt District." Sheridan subsequently widened his action against the farmers of the Valley into a three-week campaign that came to be known simply as "The Burning."

He never bothered to investigate whether the soldier's story was true.

After the war, the leader of the three Confederates wrote articles defending himself and describing how Meigs had fired the first shot. An examination of the Federal's revolver showed that it had been fired once, just as the Confederates claimed. Since they were far behind Federal lines, it is doubtful that the Confederates would have risked their mission and their lives by firing their pistols unless they had no other choice. Perhaps that is the best evidence that they were telling the truth. Sheridan may have suspected that the incident did not constitute a murder. Regardless, the killing of Meigs gave him an excuse to carry the war right to the civilians, which was in keeping with Grant's plan to demoralize the population and destroy its means of supplying the Confederate armies with food.

When you are ready to leave Dayton, head south on Va. 42 to Bridgeport. Look for the signs for I-81 North. Follow the interstate to the outskirts of Harrisonburg, then take Exit 245 and head southeast on Va. 659 (Port Republic Road). After 1.1 miles on Va. 659, turn left on Turner Ashby Lane, which dead-ends at a small park with a monument to the general killed here on June 6, 1862.

Ashby was one of those Confederate leaders who died too early in the war for it to be determined what his lasting contribution might have been. In his early thirties at the start of the conflict, he had never had a day of official military training. He apparently did have a sense of how to lead men, however, as he organized his own militia unit to protect his neighborhood. Having stood guard as a militiaman at the trial of John Brown in 1859, Ashby helped capture Harpers Ferry when the war started.

Early on, Ashby's charisma drew men to him in droves—so many that his cavalry unit became almost unmanageable. Ashby cared little for discipline or drill, two things that his commander, Stonewall Jackson, loved. Jackson tried to keep Ashby from being promoted because he felt the higher up the chain Ashby went, the worse officer he would become. The general was not without his reasons—Ashby had earlier given Jackson faulty information that led to Jackson's attack on, and defeat by, a superior force at Kernstown.

Ashby found himself at this spot while acting as a rear guard during Jackson's march toward Port Republic. This came just two weeks after he had received a promotion to general over Jackson's objections. Ironically, it was while running, rather than riding his customary horse, that Ashby met his end. The shot that ripped through his heart came just after he shouted, "Charge, for God's sake, boys, charge!" The deadly shot came from a rifleman with the 79th Pennsylvania Bucktails, a unit whose men decorated their caps with the tails of the white-tailed deer they had shot to prove their marksmanship.

Retrace your route to I-81 and continue north on the interstate for about 2 miles to the exit for Va. 33. Turn left on Va. 33 and drive 1.2 miles to Woodbine Cemetery, which is surrounded by a rock fence. Turn left into the cemetery, then turn left on to the road within the cemetery. The remains of General John R. Jones are on the left beneath a tall tree and a tall obelisk.

Grave of John R. Jones

A lackluster general, Jones was charged with hiding behind a tree during one battle early in the war. He was relieved of command after Chancellorsville. When he was later captured, the Confederacy never bothered to ask for him back.

Jones's fame has grown lately, thanks to *Freedom's Child: The Life of a Confederate General's Black Daughter* by his granddaughter, Carrie Allen McCray. After his first wife died, Jones took up with a young black servant. He apparently never denied fathering his black children. It is the perseverance of those children that is the subject of the book.

Return to I-81 and drive 17 miles north to Exit 264 (the New Market Battlefield exit). Drive under the interstate, then turn right on Va. 305. If you have time, visit all three of the museums located within a mile on this road. The first is a cavalry museum; the second is a general military museum that covers all wars; and the third is Virginia's Hall of Valor, owned and maintained by V.M.I. in memory of the 10 cadets who fell on the New Market Battlefield, which is located behind the hall.

In May 1864, when Grant was moving against Lee around Richmond, he ordered an army under General Franz Sigel into the Shenandoah Valley in an attempt to draw troops away from Richmond. Grant did not have much choice of whom to send. Sigel, a leader in the German immigrant community and a man who had been in the country only 10 years, was a political favorite of Lincoln's because he could deliver votes in the presidential election that fall. Sigel had done some fighting out west earlier in the war, so Grant held his breath and sent him into the Valley with 6,500 men.

Opposing Sigel was General John C. Breckinridge, a Kentucky native and former vice president of the United States and 1860 presidential candidate. Breckinridge had no military training, but Jefferson Davis appointed him a general anyway, figuring that the spectacle of a United States vice president fighting for the South would help draw attention to the cause. Breckinridge turned out to be a pretty fair leader and a popular man with the Kentucky "Orphan Brigade," so named because its men knew they could never go home again, since their native state had remained in the Union.

Breckinridge was transferred east away from the Orphan Brigade and given the task of fighting Sigel with whatever men he could scrape together. Reluctantly, he called on the cadet corps at V.M.I. to join his little army of 5,000 men. Some 229 teenagers rushed from their classrooms and into their uniforms and started marching north to meet their foe.

On Sunday, May 15, 1864, Sigel's march south, up the Valley, and Breckinridge's march north, down the Valley, intersected at the village of New Market. Sigel set up his 28 cannons and began firing on the Confederates. The battle was already under way when the cadets, dressed in fine gray uniforms with the same distinctive crossed black stitching and gold buttons that today's cadets wear, arrived on the scene. Nicknamed "Katydids" by the grizzled veteran soldiers, the cadets stayed in the rear until Breckinridge reluctantly issued the order to "send the boys in."

They first came under fire near a hill south of where the museum is today. When they reached the farmhouse belonging to the Bushong family, they had to split to either side. They stopped in the orchard on the far side of the house, very close to six Union guns that delivered a steady fire into their ranks. Finally, the boys broke into a run through an open, muddy field that sucked their shoes right off of them; ever since, that ground has been known as the "Field of Lost Shoes." They made their way to a fence, lay down, and began to return fire into the Federal lines.

With the boys holding their part of the line and occupying the attention of the Union gunners, the other Confederates were able to flank the Federals. Seeing that, the Federals started retreating. The cadet corps was then given the command to charge. Not waiting to form themselves into companies, they rushed the Federals and didn't stop until specifically ordered by Breckinridge. Ten cadets were killed or mortally wounded and another 45 were wounded, a 23 percent loss ratio, which shows just how heavily engaged they were.

The next month, the Federals took their revenge on the cadets by burning V.M.I.

When you are ready to leave the battlefield, retrace your route toward I-81, but pass under the interstate and turn left on U.S. 11 North. About 3.8 miles north of town, you will reach a marker for Rude's Hill. The Federals used this hill as an artillery position at New Market. Five months later, Confederate artillery used it to repulse some of Sheridan's cavalry marching up the Valley.

Federal cannon pointing toward "Field of Lost Shoes"

Located on the left 600 yards past the marker is the old house where Confederate partisan ranger John Hanson "Hanse" McNeill was taken after his wounding on October 3, 1864, at nearby Meems Bottom. McNeill, who was authorized to operate behind Federal lines much like John Singleton Mosby, had attacked a Union camp of 100 men with 30 of his rangers. He was shot down in the melee. His men brought him to this house, which was owned by a Methodist minister and his wife.

The 48-year-old McNeill ordered his men—mostly teenagers and young men in their early twenties—to "leave me to my fate. I can do no more for

House where McNeill was taken after his wounding

my country." The rangers then escaped over the mountains toward their home base at Moorefield.

The minister's wife nursed McNeill as best she could. She was also savvy enough to cut his waist-length beard and shoulder-length hair, trademarks that the Federals would recognize.

The haircut worked for a while. At least two search parties took a glance at "Mr. Hanson"—as the minister's wife called him—but did not recognize him as the feared ranger. Once, the Federals brought a captured ranger with them and asked him if the man in the bed was McNeill. The minister's wife touched the captured ranger lightly on his arm and looked into his eyes when the question was asked. He got the hint and denied knowing his old leader.

Finally, General Phil Sheridan himself came to the house and did something the other Federals had not. He asked the wounded man if he was McNeill. "I am" came the reply. A Union surgeon then stepped forward and said he had been captured by the rangers several months earlier and had been treated kindly. For some reason—perhaps this acknowledgment of McNeill's past kindness—Sheridan allowed the ranger to stay in the house and did not order it burned, as he had dozens of others in the Valley.

McNeill would finally be moved south to Harrisonburg by his men, where he died five weeks after his wounding.

Continue north on U.S. 11. Located below Rude's Hill is Meems Bottom, the site of the attack in which McNeill was wounded.

Drive 2 miles into Mount Jackson. On the left on the northern side of town is a Confederate cemetery filled with the graves of men who died at a hospital located across the road. Note the sad statue of the soldier with his hat removed; he is looking downward and has his musket at rest.

It is about 7 miles to the small town of Edinburg. Located on the left in the downtown area is the Edinburg Mill. After Sheridan ordered this mill burned (along with all the others in the area), two young girls burst into his headquarters begging him to spare it, as they would need it for meal and grain during the coming winter. One story says that they had a puppy with them. Sheridan asked if they would rename the dog Phil if he granted their request. The outraged girls said no. Sheridan, amused at their spunk, wrote out an order stopping the mill from being burned. The little girls had to join a bucket brigade from the river to save the structure.

Continue north from Edinburg on U.S. 11. After about 9 miles, you'll see a marker for the action at Tom's Brook. This small cavalry battle on October 9, 1864, showed how broken-down the Confederate cavalry had become and how strong the Federal cavalry had grown. Confederate general Tom Rosser's men had camped at Tom's Brook, apparently unaware of how close Custer's men were. When the Federals attacked, the panicked Confederates retreated so quickly down the Valley Pike (what is now U.S. 11) that the Federals nicknamed the battle the "Woodstock Races," after the nearby town of Woodstock.

About 2.3 miles farther north is a historical marker for the Battle of Fisher's Hill. The marker describes the death of Colonel A. S. "Sandie" Pendleton near this spot. Pendleton served as Jackson's aide and was the son of General William Pendleton.

Continue 1.7 miles north, then turn left on C.R. 601 and follow the brown signs to the battlefield at Fisher's Hill, which is owned by The Association for the Preservation of Civil War Sites, Inc. The battlefield walk goes up Fisher's Hill. One of the several stops along the way is the Signal Tree, a tree that looks oddly flat on top because Confederate observers cut its branches so they could see the action and signal distant parts of the battlefield.

The Signal Tree at Fisher's Hill

The Battle of Fisher's Hill, fought on September 22, 1864, was a continuation of Sheridan's campaign against Jubal Early, who had been defeated at the Third Battle of Winchester on September 19. Early fell back to what was supposedly a strong position here, but Sheridan outmaneuvered him and pushed him off the high ground.

After this battle, Sheridan felt the way was clear for him to burn the Valley. He believed the Confederates were no longer a threat. He would learn differently about a month after Fisher's Hill.

Retrace your route to U.S. 11 and continue north through Strasburg. On the northern side of the city is the Stonewall Jackson Museum at Hupp's Hill, the site of a skirmish in mid-October 1864 that told Sheridan there were indeed still Confederates in the area. The museum offers displays and artifacts focusing on the action in the Valley.

Continue north on U.S. 11. You'll soon cross a bridge over Cedar Creek.

On the western side of the road are the remains of a mill burned by Sheridan. Turn left on C.R. 727 about 5 miles after the museum. Follow this road until you reach Belle Grove Plantation. This was where the Battle of Cedar Creek was most fiercely fought. It was here that the Confederates fell upon the sleeping Federals camped around the house.

The Battle of Cedar Creek surprised the Federals. After soundly defeating Early at Fisher's Hill, the overconfident Sheridan assured his commanders, his subordinates, and himself that he had rid the Valley of Confederates, paying little attention to the sharp fight at Hupp's Hill on October 13.

His men settled in for some rest around Belle Grove Plantation, satisfied that Cedar Creek was all the protection they needed. What they did not count on was a New York–born topographer with a keen eye for terrain. Once Confederate major Jed Hotchkiss climbed an outcropping on Massanutten Mountain, he could see all of the Federal camps and some approaches where the Confederates could reach them. Hotchkiss laid out a battle plan for Early organized around a night march that would put the Confederates right on top of the Federals at first light.

One of Early's commanders was General Stephen Dodson Ramseur, a 27-year-old who had graduated from West Point in 1860 and quickly risen from regimental command to division command. A year earlier, Ramseur had married his distant cousin after a year of courtship by long, loving letters. On the day before he was to lead his men into battle at Cedar Creek, he got a signal message relayed all the way from North Carolina. His wife had delivered a child.

On the morning of October 19, 1864, Ramseur put a yellow flower in his lapel in honor of his new child and laughingly shouted to his men that they would have to drive the Yankees hard, since he had to get leave to go see his new baby. They promised they would.

Early's men smashed into the Federals in the predawn darkness. The attack was such a surprise that most of the Federals were still asleep and had little warning from pickets. Thousands of men quickly grabbed their muskets and ran to the rear, hoping their officers would find some way to organize them once it was light enough to see.

As the Confederates entered the Union camps around Belle Grove, they made the same mistake that their compatriots had made in the predawn attack at Shiloh, Tennessee, in April 1862—they stopped fighting to eat. Early knew his men were tired from their all-night march. They were also hungry, since Sheridan's men had destroyed virtually all the food in the Valley. He allowed them to stay a few hours in the Federal camp to eat what food they could find.

While Early's men were eating, Sheridan's were reorganizing, or at least slowing their retreat.

Sheridan himself was not on the battlefield when the attack came. So confident was he that he had gone to a conference in Washington the day before. He was at his headquarters in Winchester when he heard cannon fire to the south. Sheridan jumped on his horse and started for Cedar Creek. The closer he got, the greater the number of frightened, beaten men he encountered. He neither berated nor threatened them, but simply told them that he was going to the front to fight, and that if they wanted to come along, he would love to have them. The courage of a commander who would head straight toward an enemy without taking an organized force with him inspired the men. They stopped running and began to re-form themselves into an army.

By 4 P.M., the badly smashed Federals had regained their courage. Their counterattack proved too much for the outnumbered Confederates, whose turn it was to retreat. This was perhaps the only time in the war that an army was completely defeated, then managed to reorganize, then counterattacked and completely defeated the formerly victorious enemy—all in the same day! Sheridan suffered twice as many casualties as Early, but by the end of the day, he had retaken the battlefield.

The greatest Confederate loss was that of Ramseur. He was trying to hold back the Federal counterattack northwest of Middletown when his second horse of the day was killed underneath him. The major general, one of the youngest to hold that rank in either army, was mounting another horse when he was shot through the lungs.

Captured by the Federals, Ramseur was taken to Belle Grove Plantation, where litter bearers put him in the library. The surgeons knew that he would die from his wounds, so they put out the word for his West Point friends to come see him. They did just that. Union generals George Custer and Wesley

Merritt and Captain Henry DuPont all spent the night helping their West Point classmate die among friends. During moments of consciousness, Ramseur murmured that he would die happy, since he knew he would see his wife and new child in the afterlife.

Ramseur's widow wore a black dress or a mourning pin every day for the rest of her life. His daughter, the baby born just before his death, never married, saying she did not want to lose the Ramseur name. All three are buried side by side in Lincolnton, North Carolina.

Return to U.S. 11 and turn north once more. On the north side of town, you will pass a historical marker describing how Sheridan rode from Winchester to Middletown to rally his broken troops.

Continue on U.S. 11 for about 9 miles to Va. 706 on the outskirts of Winchester. Just before reaching Va. 706, turn left to visit Ocquon Presbyterian Church, the site of the First Battle of Kernstown, fought on March 23, 1862. It was the only battle that Stonewall Jackson truly lost.

It was not his fault. Colonel Turner Ashby, Jackson's scout, had been ordered to scout Winchester. He reported back to Jackson that the town was virtually abandoned. Ashby's mistake was in talking to local residents, rather than taking a look himself. Residents said that just a few hundred troops remained in town, a number that Jackson's 4,500 men could easily handle. In reality, a whole division was still in town—more than 10,000 Federals. Trusting Ashby, Jackson did not check out the situation himself.

When the fighting started and it was obvious that a great force of Yankees was present, Jackson sent an aide to estimate the true number of enemy. When that aide reluctantly told him there was a division in front of him, Jackson replied with one of his best understatements: "We are in for it."

The Confederates fought mostly from behind a stone wall, which helped make up for their small numbers. After a while, General Richard Garnett's brigade began to run out of ammunition. He ordered his men—who included Jackson's old command, the Stonewall Brigade—to the rear. This action caused the whole Confederate line to start back in a broken retreat. An enraged Jackson, who had been in the rear trying to organize men to move to the front, discovered his old command in full retreat. He immediately put Garnett under arrest and challenged his leadership abilities.

Garnett would never recover from the embarrassment of being charged with cowardice by Jackson, though he was never formally tried. And he never got satisfaction from Jackson himself, who was killed 10 months later. Two months after that, Garnett was killed at Gettysburg. He had been kicked by his horse just before the battle, so he chose to ride toward the Federal line, which made him a target. Some historians believe he did it to demonstrate that he was indeed a brave man, despite what Jackson and others believed.

Oddly, though Jackson lost the First Battle of Kernstown, he won the Valley Campaign, which started with Kernstown. The two Union divisions that had been moved out of the Valley returned to chase Jackson, and another division was placed on alert. These tens of thousands of Union soldiers had been scheduled to be sent to McClellan, who was then planning his invasion of the Peninsula. When he did not get these forces, he complained that his army was undermanned and that he might be unable to take Richmond. Though Jackson lost nearly 500 killed and wounded at Kernstown, as well as part of the shine from his early reputation, the coming Union chase of him around the Valley would make him a legend.

This general area was also the site of the Second Battle of Kernstown, fought in July 1864. The Confederates under Jubal Early retreated through the area on their way back from their raid on Washington on July 13. The Federals, determined to destroy Early, chased him until July 24, when he turned around and smashed back, much to the Federals' surprise. The counterattack came so suddenly that a large number of Union supply wagons had to be burned by the Federals to keep them out of the hands of the attacking Confederates.

In the end, however, Early's victory may have hastened the Valley's destruction. Frustrated Federal authorities, tired of losing to generals like Jackson, Breckinridge, and Early, brought in General Phil Sheridan. Sheridan would change tactics from attacking armies to attacking civilians.

When you are ready to leave the church, return to U.S. 11 and continue north. After 3 miles, you'll pass a fenced cemetery on the right. Somewhere within it in an unmarked grave is the body of Hayward Shepherd, the free black station manager at Harpers Ferry who was the first man killed by John Brown's raiders in 1859 in their effort to start a slave rebellion. Shepherd, a man popular with both blacks and whites, rode the train to Winchester every day to work.

Continue north on U.S. 11 into downtown Winchester. Turn right on Millwood Avenue, then left on Cameron Street. Drive north for seven blocks to the Downtown Welcome Center, also known as the Kurtz Cultural Center, located at the corner of Cameron and Boscawen Streets. The center maintains exhibits on the fighting in the Valley. Park nearby to enjoy a brief walking tour of the downtown area.

Walk one block west on Boscawen to Loudoun Street. On the southwestern corner is a restaurant located in a house where a young woman defiantly fired a pistol at Federals during their occupation of Winchester. That young woman was later forced to leave the city because of her anti-Union sentiments.

Turn right and proceed north on the downtown mall, which runs along Loudoun Street. In the first block, you will pass the Old Courthouse, which is being converted into a museum. On the lawn is a statue of a Confederate soldier; the statue was manufactured in Chicago.

The Old Courthouse

Continue one block to see the old Taylor Hotel, located on the left. Built in 1830, the hotel was the temporary home of the photographer who took the now-famous full-face shot of Stonewall Jackson that Mrs. Jackson considered her favorite. Jackson had his photograph taken only four times—twice during the war. The picture taken at the hotel shows Jackson's casual concern for his appearance. His uniform coat is wrinkled, and a button has been sewn on the coat so that it doesn't line up with the others.

Walk down the alleyway beside the hotel and then through the parking deck behind it to reach the corner of Braddock and Amherst Streets.

On the southwestern corner is Powell Female Academy, where Mildred Lee, one of Robert E. Lee's daughters, attended school.

On the northwestern corner is the former home of Dr. Hugh Holmes McGuire, whose son Hunter McGuire was Jackson's personal physician. It was Dr. Hunter McGuire who amputated Jackson's arm, who told the general on May 10, 1863, that he would die that same day, and who recorded Jackson's famous last words: "Let us go over the river and rest in the shade of the trees."

Walk one block north on Braddock to Piccadilly Street. The large white home with the columns on the southwestern corner is the Logan House. One of the finest homes in Winchester during the war, the Logan House

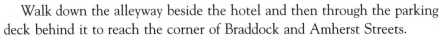

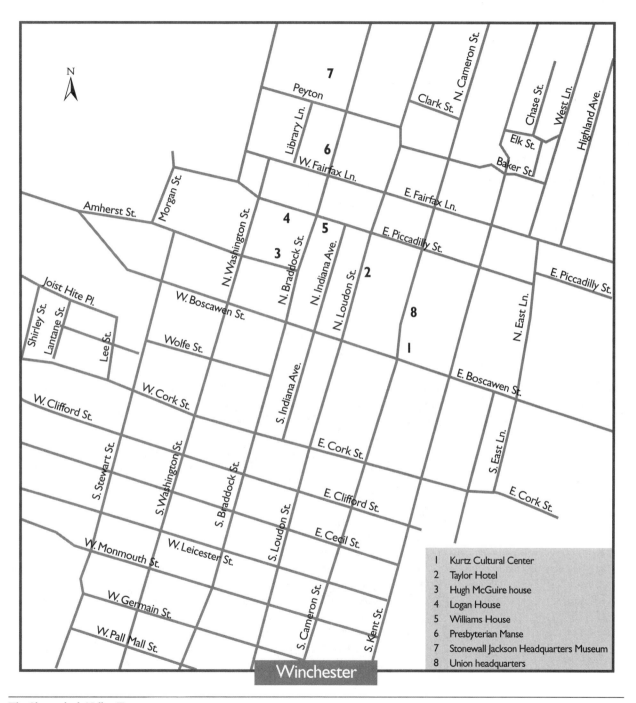

N

7

Peyton

Library Ln.

Clark St.

N. Cameron St.

Chase St.

West Ln.

Highland Ave.

6

Elk St.

W. Fairfax Ln.

Baker St.

E. Fairfax Ln.

Morgan St.

Amherst St.

4

5

E. Piccadilly St.

3

N. Washington St.

N. Braddock St.

N. Indiana Ave.

N. Loudon St.

2

E. Piccadilly St.

W. Boscawen St.

8

N. East Ln.

Joist Hite Pl.

Shirley St.

Lantane St.

Lee St.

Wolfe St.

1

S. Indiana Ave.

E. Boscawen St.

W. Cork St.

W. Clifford St.

E. Cork St.

S. East Ln.

E. Cork St.

S. Stewart St.

S. Washington St.

S. Braddock St.

E. Clifford St.

W. Monmouth St.

W. Leicester St.

S. Loudon St.

E. Cecil St.

W. Germain St.

S. Cameron St.

S. Kent St.

W. Pall Mall St.

Winchester

1	Kurtz Cultural Center
2	Taylor Hotel
3	Hugh McGuire house
4	Logan House
5	Williams House
6	Presbyterian Manse
7	Stonewall Jackson Headquarters Museum
8	Union headquarters

was confiscated and used as a headquarters by several Union generals, including Milroy, Banks, and Sheridan. It was from this house that Sheridan began his ride to Cedar Creek after hearing cannons booming to his south.

Turn right and walk east on Piccadilly for half a block. On the southern side of the street behind an iron fence is the Williams Home. It was here that Colonel George S. Patton of the 22nd Virginia was taken in September 1864 after being wounded in the Third Battle of Winchester. Patton, who had fought in dozens of battles, mostly in western Virginia, died in this house on September 25. His grandson, George S. Patton III, would win larger fame as the man who revolutionized tank warfare before World War II and as a controversial Allied army commander.

House where George S. Patton died

Return to Braddock and head north again. On the left at 319 Braddock is the Presbyterian manse. Jackson and his wife lived in this house with the pastor and his family for several weeks during the winter of 1861–62 while Jackson's army was operating in the Valley. Jackson never used this house for military matters. He wanted to separate his work from his home life. His daughter was likely conceived here.

Continue several houses farther north to the Stonewall Jackson Headquarters Museum at 415 North Braddock Street. Jackson used this house as

Jackson's headquarters in Winchester

TOURING VIRGINIA'S AND WEST VIRGINIA'S CIVIL WAR SITES

his headquarters during his time in Winchester. The home belonged to an officer in the Stonewall Brigade, who offered it to his commanding officer. The most famous action that took place in this house was Jackson's resignation from the Confederate army.

On January 31, 1862, Jackson was stunned to find a letter addressed to him from Judah P. Benjamin, the Confederate secretary of war. The short letter instructed Jackson to order General William Loring back toward Winchester from his post at Romney (now in West Virginia). Loring had circumvented Jackson and directly lobbied the secretary of war for the order in the belief that his command was in an advanced position vulnerable to attack by the Federals.

Jackson, a man who believed in military discipline, was stunned. One of his subordinates had gone over his head without his knowledge and had been successful in obtaining an order that was in direct opposition to what he, Jackson, believed to be correct. Loring was in no immediate danger from Federal attack, and his men's presence in Romney was important.

Jackson immediately wrote a reply to Benjamin acknowledging that he would order Loring to vacate Romney. Then, in his second paragraph, he stated that "with such interference in my command I cannot expect to be much service in the field." He asked to be ordered back to V.M.I., where he would return to his job as a professor. If that order was not forthcoming, he would submit his resignation to the governor of Virginia.

What Jackson did not know was that Loring and a few other officers had taken their complaints all the way to President Davis. Benjamin's letter was actually Davis's opinion.

Prominent Virginia citizens immediately lobbied the Confederate president to keep Jackson, and the governor went into a tirade in the secretary of war's office. Benjamin finally admitted that he had overstepped his bounds, and the governor sent a letter to Jackson imploring him to keep his command, since Virginia needed him more than ever. Jackson finally relented and wrote the governor a letter saying that he would not resign.

Jackson then filed charges of insubordination against Loring, a man who had lost his arm in Mexico and who answered to the nickname "Blizzards" because he ordered his men to give the enemy blizzards of fire. Loring was transferred to Mississippi, far from Jackson. The two never met again.

Return to Piccadilly Street, turn left, and walk east for two blocks to Cameron Street. Turn right on Cameron and start heading back toward the welcome center. At 114 North Cameron is a home that was used as a Union headquarters. Unionist citizens of Winchester were invited to parties here.

Nearby was the home of Mrs. Hugh Holmes Lee, who wrote a thick diary of the happenings in Winchester during the war. Indeed, she was such an ardent Confederate that General Sheridan threw her and several other women out of town early in 1865. Sheridan used the excuse of the kidnapping of Union generals Crook and Kelley by Confederate partisans that February to rid himself of the vocal women, who openly mocked the Union invaders. One of those women once asked a Union officer how the biblical Lazarus and the Confederacy were alike. The puzzled man shook his head. "Both were licked by dogs" came the answer.

Retrieve your vehicle, head east on Boscawen Street for two blocks, and pass through the stone entrance to Hebron Cemetery, where the tour ends.

On the right about 150 yards into the cemetery is the grave of Mrs. Hugh Lee; the grave is surrounded by boxwoods. Mrs. Lee was dubbed the leader of the "devilish diarists" who criticized the Union occupation of the town. When she died in 1906, her body was returned to Winchester for burial beside her husband.

Continue through the cemetery to Confederate Lane, turn left, and park your vehicle.

Much of the Third Battle of Winchester was fought in Hebron Cemetery, which was established in 1844. Many men of both sides died within yards of where they would be buried. The remains of more than 3,000 Confederates are located here.

The cemetery has a large and interesting Confederate section dominated by a unique statue of a sad, long-haired, mustachioed soldier resting on arms, his musket's muzzle on his foot and his forehead and arms resting across the stock. This arms command is used for mourning or praying for fellow soldiers. Behind the statue are the dead of all the Confederate states. Most of the states have their own monuments. The one for Maryland reads, "Unheard, unorganized, unarmed, they came for conscience's sake and died for right." This refers to how the Confederates from Maryland, a border state, knew that they could never return home, since their state officially stayed in the Union.

Statue of mourning soldier in Hebron Cemetery

TOURING VIRGINIA'S AND WEST VIRGINIA'S CIVIL WAR SITES

Located on the right side of Confederate Avenue is the grave of General Archibald Campbell Godwin, who was killed in the cemetery on September 19, 1864. Godwin was an interesting man who ran for and almost won the governorship of California in 1860, immediately before he returned to his native Virginia to fight against the Union. Godwin might have become known as the man who won the Battle of Gettysburg, as it was his command that came close to capturing the high ground around Culp's Hill before being ordered to stop fighting for the night. Back in Virginia a year later, he was struck down and killed instantly by a Union shell fragment not far from where he is now buried.

Next to Godwin is General Robert Daniel Johnston, a North Carolinian who was in the thick of many battles. Wounded seven times during the war, he died as a banker in 1919. On his tombstone are these words: "I have fought the good fight. I have kept the faith."

Also next to Godwin is a touching monument to Colonel Charles Christopher that says, "Southern independence had never a braver or truer defender than he."

Next to Christopher is the common tombstone for two brothers, Captain Richard Ashby, who died at Gettysburg, and General Turner Ashby, killed near Harrisonburg.

Two stones down is the common stone for two Patton brothers: Tazwell, who was killed in the third-day charge at Gettysburg and George S., who was mortally wounded in the Third Battle of Winchester. The stone says that George's last words were "In Christ alone, perfectly content."

Across from the North Carolina Monument in the civilian section of the cemetery is the grave of General John George Walker, who was so proud of his service in the Mexican War that the flag of that nation is carved into his tombstone. His Civil War career was unremarkable, much of it being spent in out-of-the-way commands in Louisiana and Texas. After the war, Walker embarked upon a bureaucratic career that took him to the nation of Colombia in South America.

Tombstone of the Ashby brothers

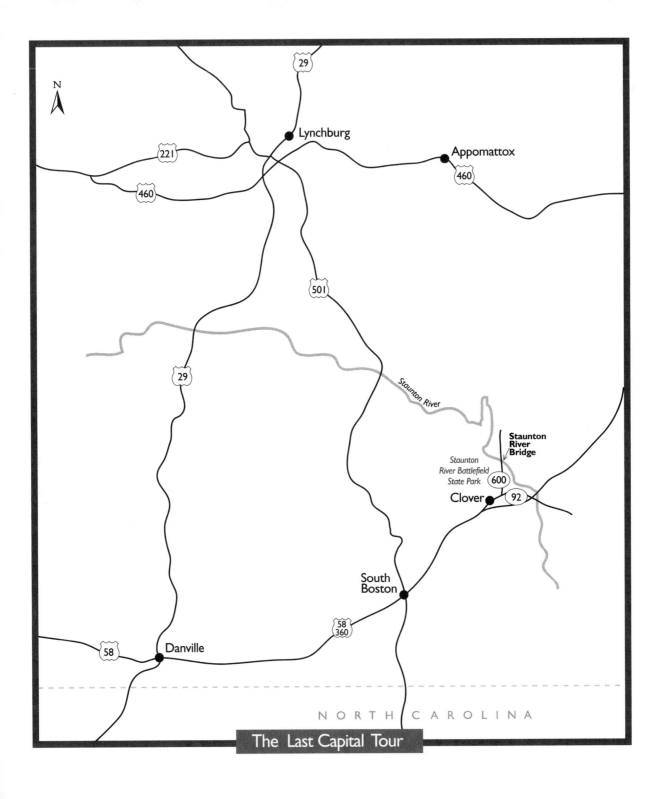

The Last Capital Tour

The Last Capital Tour

This tour starts at a battlefield once thought by the Confederates to be too far distant to be attacked. They were wrong. It then moves to Danville, where the last Confederate proclamation was issued from a home that is now a museum. Next, it heads to Lynchburg, where it visits two museums, the final resting spot of the boat that took Stonewall Jackson's body to Lexington, and two cemeteries.

The tour covers approximately 120 miles and will likely take a full day.

THE TOUR STARTS at a little-known battlefield in southern Virginia where a few hundred young boys and old men bolstered by a handful of regular troops prevented thousands of seasoned Federal cavalrymen from burning a vital railroad bridge over the Staunton River.

Staunton River Battlefield State Park is located off U.S. 360; head west on Va. 92 through the town of Clover, which is about 12 miles north of South Boston. Turn left on to C.R. 600 and drive 3 miles, following the brown park signs to the visitor center, which has a map and an audio program describing the battle, as well as some artifacts.

Follow the park's walking trail down to the preserved earth fort and the bridge over the Staunton River. This is not the original bridge, though it stands on the same site.

By June 1864, Lee had fought a long, slow, deadly retreat from the Wilderness to Petersburg. Grant, concentrating on encircling Lee, set his sights on the railroads that continued to provide the Army of Northern Virginia with supplies. By cutting those railroads, Grant could stop Lee's food supply.

At the head of the list was the Richmond & Danville Railroad and its bridge over the Staunton River. Untouched to date, the railroad seemed ripe for the picking. Lee's army was pinned down in Petersburg. Early's army was occupied in the Shenandoah Valley. The railroad bridge appeared to be open to attack.

What Grant did not count on was the tenacity of the local militia. Watching over the bridge on the southern side of the river were Captain Benjamin Fairnholt and a garrison of 296 reserves, who had spent most of the war building a dirt fort. On June 23, the lowly captain got a dispatch from the highest general in the army—Lee himself. A large detachment of Federal cavalry was on its way to destroy the bridge. The general had ordered cavalry under his nephew Fitzhugh Lee to try to stop the force, but the message was clear—Fairnholt and his tiny force would have to rise to the occasion.

At the head of the Federal column was General James Wilson, a 26-year-old who had graduated from West Point in 1860 near the top of his class. A protégé of Grant, Wilson had proven himself a good cavalry officer out west, and Grant had rewarded him with command of a division of cavalry and the mission of wrecking the railroads in this part of Virginia.

Fairnholt used Lee's early warning to put out the word to the surrounding counties to send him all their militia units. Within a few hours, his force grew to more than 900. But his 296 reserves were not front-line troops, and most of the other 600 militiamen had never seen combat in any form. The cavalry they would face numbered more than 3,300, men who had been in the field for years. Though they were not the Union's top-line cavalry, they were trained soldiers. More importantly, they had 16 cannons. All Fairnholt could muster were six.

Fairnholt did have a sense of guile about him. All that night and the next morning, he had a train run back and forth over the rail line stretching between the bridge and Clover Depot. The Union scouts on the other side of the river, unable to see that the train was empty, made the assumption that it was bringing reinforcements. That was the best ruse the Confederate captain could hope to achieve.

By 4 P.M. on June 25, the Federals, knowing that Confederate cavalry was pursuing them, opened up on the bridge, confident that they could destroy it before the pursuing Southern horsemen caught them with their backs to the river. One eyewitness among the reserves said that when the cannon fire started falling on the Confederate side of the river, the young boys in the militia broke into "outbursts of weeping."

The Federals were at a disadvantage in having to charge across an open field. Four times the dismounted Union men tried to charge from the cover

TOURING VIRGINIA'S AND WEST VIRGINIA'S CIVIL WAR SITES

of some drainage ditches, and four times the undermanned force at the bridge beat them back. For some reason, the Federal artillery never seemed to be able to zero in on the Confederate fort and entrenchments and so was unable to give any relief to the charging men.

At the end of the fourth charge, the Confederate cavalry finally arrived. Now, the Federals came under fire from two directions. Wilson broke off the attack and fled under cover of darkness back toward Petersburg. The Federals had to fight their way back to their own lines. Eventually, they lost their artillery and their supply wagons—even their wounded.

For a lesser man, it would have meant banishment, but Wilson was resilient. He was promoted and transferred west to reorganize the Union cavalry that had consistently failed to defeat General Nathan Bedford Forrest. He achieved that late in the war, capturing Selma, Alabama, before Forrest could react. On top of that, it was Wilson's troops who captured Jefferson Davis deep in Georgia in May 1865. That was just a year after a handful of old men, young boys, and wounded soldiers had thoroughly humiliated Wilson at the bridge over the Staunton River.

When you are ready to leave the park, return to U.S. 360 and drive west to where it merges with U.S. 58; continue west to Danville, about 50 miles from the park.

As you come into Danville on U.S. 58, look on the left close to downtown Danville for an iron railroad bridge over the Dan River. This structure was built on the original abutments that carried the 1860s bridge. In their flight from captured Richmond, Jefferson Davis and his cabinet rode over that bridge and into Danville on April 3, 1865.

A few hundred yards after the bridge, turn left and cross the Dan on to Main Street. Drive 1 mile to 975 Main Street and park behind the Sutherlin Mansion, which houses the Danville Museum of Fine Arts and History.

The Sutherlin home where Jefferson Davis stayed

This home belonged to Major William T. Sutherlin, the wartime quartermaster for Danville and a delegate to the convention that took Virginia out of the Union. When Davis made it to Danville, Sutherlin offered him the use of his home.

This house, like several others still standing in North Carolina, South Carolina, and Georgia, lays claim to being the last capital of the Confederacy. But the Sutherlin Mansion may have a greater right to the claim than the others, as Jefferson Davis did stay in the house for a full week, did

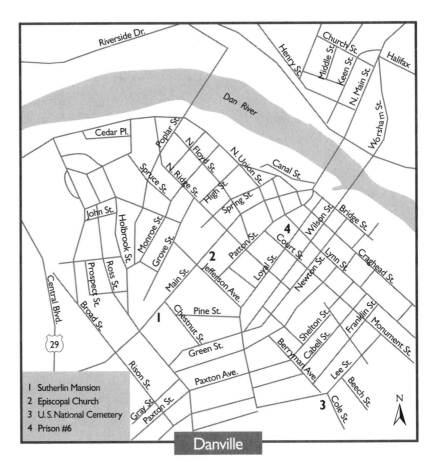

Episcopal Church of the Epiphany in Danville

Danville

1 Sutherlin Mansion
2 Episcopal Church
3 U.S. National Cemetery
4 Prison #6

issue his last official proclamation from here, and did meet here with his full cabinet several times. The other houses in question entertained Davis, his family, and varying members of the cabinet for only a night or so, and the government had thoroughly collapsed by the time he got to them. It was here at the Sutherlin Mansion that Davis still had some hope of keeping his country alive.

Davis stayed in the back bedroom of the two-story house. His room offered a commanding view to the east, so he might have some early warning in the event that Union forces approached. On the same floor is a meeting room used by the local chapter of the United Daughters of the Confederacy; the room contains the table on which Davis wrote the last proclamation.

That proclamation, a copy of which is on display, is a remarkable document. In it, Davis admits that Richmond has been captured but goes on to suggest that it might be a good thing, since the army was then "relieved from the necessity of guarding cities and particular points, important but not vital to our defense. . . . [The army is] free to move from point to point and strike in detail the detachments and garrisons of the enemy, operating on the interior of our own country, where supplies are more accessible and the foe will be far removed from his own base. Nothing is now needed to render our triumph certain but the exhibition of our own unquenchable resolve."

Davis went on to say that even if there were temporary setbacks, the Southern people would come back again and again "until the baffled and exhausted enemy shall abandon in despair his endless and impossible task of making slaves of a people resolved to be free."

Five days after Davis wrote that proclamation, Robert E. Lee surrendered the largest of the Confederate armies to U. S. Grant at Appomattox Court House, located about 60 miles away. Davis was trying to keep the fighting spirit alive in a people whose largest and best army was about to surrender.

Davis learned of Lee's surrender on April 10, 1865, the day after it happened. He left on a train that night for Greensboro, North Carolina, a man whose country was disintegrating before his eyes.

The house is preserved as it existed in 1865. On the first floor, you can examine a copy of Virginia's Ordinance of Secession and materials about the history of the regiments raised from the area. In the basement, you can learn about the history of the town's prisoner-of-war camps. You'll also see a newspaper on display that was published by Union occupying troops immediately after the war. It is interesting in that its front page contains advertisements offering rewards for runaway slaves. Apparently, the Union soldier-editors were unaware that Lincoln had freed the slaves in the rebelling states two years earlier. Another display case has an interesting item—blue sunglasses left behind by Jefferson Davis.

Get back on Main Street and drive two blocks toward the river. At 781 Main is the Episcopal Church of the Epiphany. Built in 1879, the current church is a copy of the wartime church where Davis and his cabinet (with the exception of the agnostic Judah P. Benjamin) heard a strong pro-Confederate sermon on April 9. They did not know that Lee would surrender his army the same day.

Turn right on Jefferson Avenue immediately before the church and follow it to Lee Street, making a slight jog to the right at Wilson Street to continue on Jefferson. Turn left on Lee. Located to the right are the town's cemeteries, including the United States National Cemetery, which contains the remains of more than 1,300 Union soldiers who died in the town's six prisons.

Retrace your route to Wilson Street and turn right. Drive two long blocks to Lynn Street and turn left. Look for a parking spot at the corner of Lynn and Loyal Streets. On the southwestern corner is what is left of Prison Number 6. This is the last surviving such building in the city. It is now a machine shop and bears little resemblance to a prison.

The first Union prisoners arrived in Danville in November 1863. They occupied six vacant tobacco and cotton warehouses. The buildings housed about 4,000 men, nearly 1,300 of whom died.

The Federals developed an ingenious method of hiding escapes at this prison, using a hole cut between the two floors. It was common practice for the sergeant of the guard to stand at the door of each floor and count heads. Once he counted one floor, he started for the next. If, say, two men from the upper floor had escaped while outside the walls on a work detail, the lower floor would send two men up the hole to be counted twice. The scam worked for weeks until a captured prisoner revealed that he had come from Danville. The camp commander, who believed he had a perfect no-escape record, then conducted a thorough search of the building and discovered the hole between the floors.

More than 70 men successfully escaped from Danville's prisons.

Drive one more block on Lynn Street before turning right on to Patton. Patton runs into Main Street, just before reaching the bridge. Cross back over the Dan River and return to U.S. 58. Turn left at the light and follow U.S. 58 until it intersects U.S. 29. Turn north on U.S. 29 and head for Lynchburg, located approximately 50 miles away.

Take U.S. 29 Business into town; U.S. 29 Business makes a right turn and becomes Fort Avenue on the outskirts of Lynchburg. After about a mile, watch on the left for an earthen fort with a brick building sitting in the middle of it. Look for a place to park in the surrounding neighborhood and walk back to examine the fort, which is now the home of the Fort Hill Woman's Club.

This is Fort Early, a key defensive position for the city when it came under attack by General David Hunter on June 17, 1864. Hunter, who had set fire to V.M.I. in Lexington just a few days earlier, believed his way was open to raid up the Shenandoah Valley as far as he liked. Alerted to the danger, Lee dispatched Jubal Early's corps from around Richmond to meet Hunter. Smaller Confederate units slowed Hunter's advance while Early's men pushed for Lynchburg.

Fort Early

When Early arrived, he placed most of his troops at Fort Early, an earth redoubt along what was then the Salem Turnpike. To convince Hunter that he was facing more troops that he actually was, Early borrowed a train. He ran it to the south, then brought it back toward town. He ordered bands to play and citizens to cheer each arrival of the empty train. The ruse worked; Union reports noted how Confederate reinforcements arrived all night long. It was a lie. Early had no more than 16,000 troops to face Hunter's 19,000. He also had only 10 cannons, most of which were mounted in Fort Early. The Federals had nearly three times as many.

The Confederates made a bold attack down the Salem Turnpike but were pushed back. The Federals then counterattacked, but they, too, were stopped. As the two sides faced each other after fighting to a stalemate, Hunter decided to retreat. Once that retreat started, the Confederates left their positions and began pressing hard—so hard that the Federal retreat almost turned into a rout.

Lynchburg was not a major battle, but it set the stage for a Confederate raid that had the potential to change the face of the war.

After putting the Federals on the run, Early looked north down the Valley. Seeing no Federals in his way, he launched a march that would end only 6 miles from the White House in Washington on July 12, 1864. Had Early not been stopped for 24 hours at the Battle of Monocracy, Maryland, on July 9, he might have completely surprised the Washington defenses, since almost all of the available Federal troops had been sent to Petersburg to help Grant.

When told that Early was on his way to Washington, Grant at first

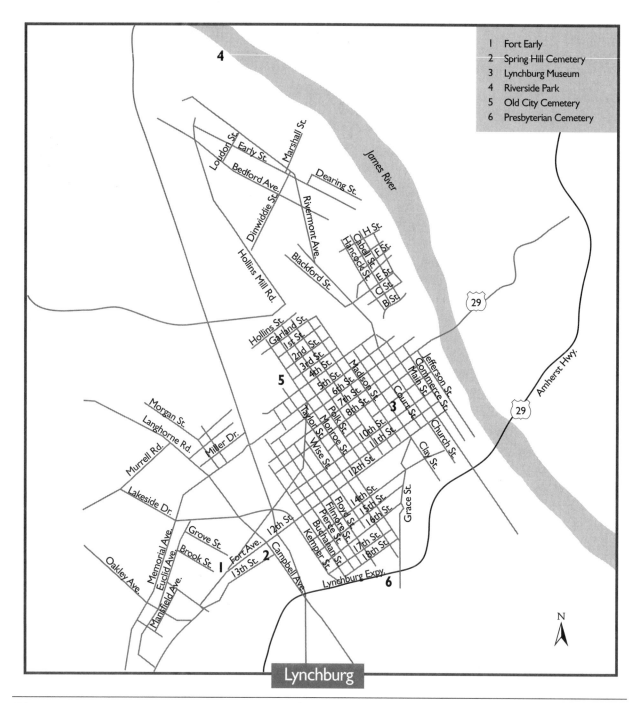

1	Fort Early
2	Spring Hill Cemetery
3	Lynchburg Museum
4	Riverside Park
5	Old City Cemetery
6	Presbyterian Cemetery

Lynchburg

N

refused to believe that any Confederates had broken through the lines. It was not until Monocracy that he finally understood that the capital city was open to attack. Had Early been able to get to Washington without fighting for a full day at Monocracy, he might have caught President Lincoln in his bed at the White House.

There is a push-button audio history of the Battle of Lynchburg outside the Fort Hill Woman's Club. If someone is available to open the building for you, you may enjoy visiting the small museum inside, which offers some wall panels describing the battle.

Drive another 1.2 miles on Fort Avenue to Spring Hill Cemetery, located on the right. Take the first entrance and drive all the way to the back; en route, you will have to bear right. In the rear corner of the cemetery is the grave of General Jubal Early, whom Lee playfully called "my mean old man."

It seems that Early developed that reputation early in life. While at West Point, he angered another cadet, Lewis Armistead, so much that Armistead broke a plate over Early's head. Armistead was thrown out of West Point for the act, though he later got his lieutenant's commission and fought in the same army as Early. Armistead even became a general. He became famous during the Pettigrew-Pickett-Trimble assault at Gettysburg.

Early got his commission in 1837, after which he was assigned to the Seminole War in Florida. Following that conflict, he became a lawyer. When Virginia was threatened by invasion, he put aside his Unionist leanings and strapped on his sword.

Forty-four years old when the war opened, Early never had the physical vigor of younger generals, but that did not stop him from fighting as hard as they. He was hurt at the Battle of Williamsburg on May 5, 1862, when a minie ball entered one shoulder, traveled across his back, and exited the other shoulder, a very painful wound that never really healed. Early rose in rank, eventually heading Jackson's old Second Corps after taking it over from General Richard Ewell. Jackson would have rolled over in his grave had he known that Early was following him in command. In contrast to the deeply religious Jackson, Early was highly profane in speech and manner.

It was after the war that Early made his greatest contribution to Southern legend. The first president of the Southern Historical Society, he took it upon himself to raise Robert E. Lee to the highest possible status in the minds of all Southerners. Early exerted control over the editing of papers presented to the society and made sure that those honoring Lee got prominent play. So much of the society's work was devoted to the war in the East and to Lee in particular that there was rarely room for material covering the West. Early was also largely responsible for launching the postwar verbal and literary attack on General James Longstreet, blaming his delays on the second day of Gettysburg for losing that battle.

The cause of Early's death at age 78 is something of a mystery. His problems began when he fell down the steps at the Lynchburg post office. Although the doctor could find no broken bones, Early did suffer damage to his speech, perhaps suggesting that he had hit his head. He died three weeks later, but no cause of death was established.

After viewing Early's tombstone, turn around and walk about 15 yards toward Fort Hill Drive. Located in the circle is the grave of General James Dearing, who has the unhappy distinction of being the last Confederate general killed in combat.

Only 20 in 1861, Dearing had to resign from his West Point appointment when the war began. The Virginian then somehow joined the prestigious Washington Artillery from New Orleans and worked his way up as an artillery commander. In 1864, he was transferred to the cavalry, where he was promoted to general.

Tombstone of James Dearing

During the march toward Appomattox, Dearing's brigade discovered that Federals were planning to burn the High Bridge over the Appomattox River on April 6, 1865. Dearing soon found himself engaged in a pistol duel with the Union commander, Brevet General Theodore Read, who had lost an arm earlier in the war. The two men rode beside each other shooting. Read finally dropped dead from his horse, the last Union general to fall in battle. Dearing was shot through the lungs, a wound that virtually assured him of an eventual death. The two opposing generals had engaged in personal combat, one of the few times such a thing has happened in history. This came just three days before Lee agreed to surrender.

Taken to a hospital in Winchester, Dearing lingered for nearly three weeks and died three days before his 25th birthday.

The grave of Colonel Thomas Munford is located outside the circle and a few yards closer to Fort Avenue underneath a dogwood tree. Some sources

TOURING VIRGINIA'S AND WEST VIRGINIA'S CIVIL WAR SITES

suggest that Munford was promoted to general very late in the war. Munford was a good cavalry commander who decided he would not surrender at Appomattox. Instead, he carefully avoided the Federal cavalry and took his men to Lynchburg, where he disbanded them, rather than officially giving up their weapons. His was one of the few Confederate commands that did not follow Lee's order to surrender arms peacefully. Munford lived until 1918.

Get back on Fort Avenue and head into town. Bear right on 12th Street (U.S. 460 Business). Turn left on Court Street, which is the next street after Clay Street near the downtown area. The Lynchburg Museum is located at 901 Court Street in the 1855 courthouse.

Across the street is a Confederate statue designed by someone who didn't know much about Confederate soldiers. The soldier's canteen is on the wrong side; he does not have a cartridge box; and he is wearing some type of lace-up gaiters over his shoes that were not in use during the war.

Continue four blocks on Court Street, then turn right on Fifth Street. After two short blocks, turn left on Rivermont Avenue. Go about 1.8 miles to Riverside Park, located at 2240 Rivermont. Drive to the rear of the park, which overlooks the James River. Keep your eye out for what remains of the keel of the canal boat *Marshall*, the vessel that took Stonewall Jackson's body to Lexington. It is surrounded by a chain-link fence.

On May 13, 1863, Jackson's remains were brought by train to Lynchburg, where a church service was held. The next morning, the general's body, Mrs. Jackson, and their daughter boarded the *Marshall* and began an all-day trip up the James to the North River (now the Maury River), ending in Lexington.

This may also be the canal boat that took the Lee family to Lexington in December 1865. In all the accounts of that trip, including one written by Robert E. Lee, Jr., the boat was never named but was said to be personally owned by the president of the canal-boat company. The *Marshall* was described as being the "queen" of local riverboats—as might suit the president of the company.

Retrace Rivermont to Fifth Street and turn right. After nine blocks, turn right on Taylor Street. Watch for the signs for Old City Cemetery and the Pest House Medical Museum.

Enter the cemetery and park your car as the road starts downhill. On the left is the Confederate section, where more than 2,200 men from 14 states are buried. Most of them died in the hospitals that were set up in Lynchburg. During the war, as many as 20,000 men were treated in town for disease and battle wounds. About 3,000 of them died despite the best efforts of more than 50 full-time military surgeons.

One of the hospitals was run by Mrs. Lucy Mina Otey, a 60-year-old widow who lost three sons in the war. Tired of just rolling bandages, Mrs. Otey went to a hospital one day to help but was rebuffed with these words: "No more women, no more flies." Enraged, she traveled to Richmond and got permission from President Davis himself to start the Ladies Relief Hospital. The hospital had room for only 100 patients, yet the ladies' loving care and concern for hygiene helped give it one of the best reputations in town. Though the worst cases seemed to be sent their way, the ladies had the lowest mortality rate.

Walk into the Confederate section. There is a sad, yet uplifting, feeling here. The city's undertaker kept very precise records of the deaths in local hospitals, so the grave of almost every person here is marked, which is rare among wartime burial grounds, where most graves are labeled *Unknown*. On the other hand, time and air pollution have ruined most of the tombstones, so the names are almost lost.

The burials here were by state. A pyramid of 14 stones, each of which is marked by a state's name, dominates the cemetery.

In early June 1864, some 200 members of the V.M.I. cadet corps and 700 ambulatory wounded camped here among the graves, banding together to form one of the oddest reserve units in history. For a while, they were the only troops available to protect Lynchburg from General David Hunter, who threatened to burn the city as he had V.M.I. The walking wounded and the boys from V.M.I. held off Hunter until Early's Second Corps arrived from near Richmond.

The leader of the "Crippled Corps" was General Francis T. Nicholls, who had lost his left arm at Winchester in May 1862 and his left leg at Chancellorsville in May 1863. Amazingly, Nicholls survived the war. In 1876, his party solemnly nominated "all that is left of General Nicholls" for the governorship of Louisiana. He won two terms. The general who Yankee artillery and Confederate surgeons couldn't kill lived to be 72.

Buried here are at least a dozen black men who fought for or otherwise served the Confederacy. Signs at the entrance describe the actions of men such as Samuel Bryce, who left with the Lynchburg Home Guard in April 1861 and didn't return until the end of the war. His funeral expenses were paid by the 11th Virginia Regiment. Also buried here is Silas Green, a slave who enrolled in the Confederate army. Green was subsequently forced out of the service by his owner, who had not given him permission. Green thus organized and trained his own company of white soldiers, who then went off to battle and left him on the farm. He applied for a Confederate pension in 1926 but was denied, as he had never actually served in the field.

It was at this cemetery immediately after the war that the Southern Memorial Association organized one of the first Decoration Days, during which the women of Lynchburg put flowers on the graves of Southern soldiers. Northerners saw the service and adopted it as their own. The result was the national celebration of Memorial Day, now observed the last weekend in May each year.

Walk to the right through the cemetery to reach the Pest House Medical Museum. Moved to its present site in 1987, the building was used in the 1840s as the office of Dr. John Jay Terrell, who worked outside Lynchburg at his family's farm.

The original Pest House, located a few blocks away but still near the cemetery, was the last stop for residents who developed highly contagious diseases like smallpox or measles. During the war, it served as a quarantine hospital for Confederates. When Dr. Terrell volunteered to run the Pest House, he undertook a series of reforms that reduced the mortality rate of sick soldiers from 50 percent to 5 percent. Dr. Terrell survived the war despite all his contact with disease and practiced for more than 40 years in this office.

The museum has a soundtrack describing the various instruments Dr. Terrell used in his practice; those instruments are visible through the windows. On display are an operating table, an amputation kit, and a hypodermic needle that looks very painful.

Retrieve your vehicle and drive through the cemetery and past the Pest House. En route toward the entrance, you'll see a historical marker for the Glanders Stable, an early landmark in the history of veterinary medicine.

Glanders is the name of a respiratory disease that swept through the Confederate herd of horses during the war. It was both highly contagious and fatal. Anxious to stop the disease before it immobilized the army, Confederate officials asked Dr. Terrell and Dr. James Page, who were experienced in treating smallpox in humans, to research glanders. Though they were not trained veterinarians, the two men undertook the task and performed experiments on 19 horses.

Their breakthrough came when they successfully infected a healthy horse by contact with a diseased horse, then autopsied the previously healthy horse to study the symptoms of the disease. What they found was that glanders was spread by horses sharing communal watering troughs and nuzzling each other in crowded stables. Though they did not discover a cure for the disease, they found that by keeping horses in the open or in well-ventilated, well-cleaned stables, they could stop it from spreading. In 1864, they wrote a booklet on how to stop the spread of glanders that was immediately distributed throughout the army.

The road through the cemetery will take you to Fourth Street. The traffic on Fourth can be heavy, so turn right on to Fourth and then left at the first opportunity to reach Fifth Street. Turn left on to Fifth and drive 8 blocks to turn right on to Clay Street. Follow Clay until it intersects Grace Street at 12th Street. Get on Grace Street and follow it over U.S. 29, then turn into Presbyterian Cemetery, at 2029 Grace. The tour ends here.

Located on the right about 30 yards from the entrance behind a small obelisk and underneath a large tree is the grave of General Robert Rodes. Rodes is not as famous as that other V.M.I. professor who became a Confederate general, but he did almost prevent Jackson from becoming a professor. When the faculty position came open in 1851, the search committee first voted to offer it to Rodes, who had graduated from V.M.I. in 1848 and briefly served as a professor there. The college president convinced the committee to hold the slot for a West Point graduate who could bring some variety and prestige to the school. Rodes would rejoin the faculty later.

Rodes was a fighting general who had Jackson's complete trust—something that was not easily earned. He always seemed to be in the thick of the fighting, from Seven Pines to South Mountain and Sharpsburg. It was Rodes whom Jackson chose to lead the crushing flank attack at

Chancellorsville. When the 28,000 men of Jackson's corps were in position, he turned and asked, "Are you ready, General Rodes?"

"Yes, sir," came the reply.

"You can go forward then," was Jackson's next order, launching what became one of the most famous attacks in the war. Rodes's attack surprised the Union's Eleventh Corps and sent most of its men running to the rear. After the battle, Rodes was promoted to major general.

At Gettysburg, Rodes did severe damage to his reputation when he sent his men straight toward the town from the north on the first day. Eager to get into the fight, he did not order skirmishers out in front of the march. As his men neared the town, Federals hidden behind a stone wall rose up as a unit and blasted the Confederate front ranks so severely that the men fell to the ground in a perfect line. Rodes's brigadier, Alfred Iverson, Jr., took the blame for not protecting his front lines, and Rodes kept his command. The Confederates killed in the debacle were buried where they fell in an area called "Iverson's Pits." That area generates ghost stories to this day.

Rodes was killed at Third Winchester on September 19, 1864, when a Federal shell fragment struck him in the head. He was 35.

Confederate general Samuel Garland, Jr., a native of Lynchburg who graduated from V.M.I. a year after Rodes, is buried just a few yards away, also along the right side of the road.

Tombstone of Samuel Garland, Jr.

A lawyer when the war started, Garland organized a militia company. After suffering a wound at Williamsburg, he was promoted to brigadier general. The next several months were a frenzy of battles during which Garland bravely, if sometimes needlessly, exposed himself to fire. Selected as one of the brigades to hold back McClellan's army at South Mountain, Maryland, while Lee set his defense at Sharpsburg, Garland's outnumbered men fought gallantly. Ignoring pleas from his men to take cover, Garland was shot and killed on the field. He was 31.

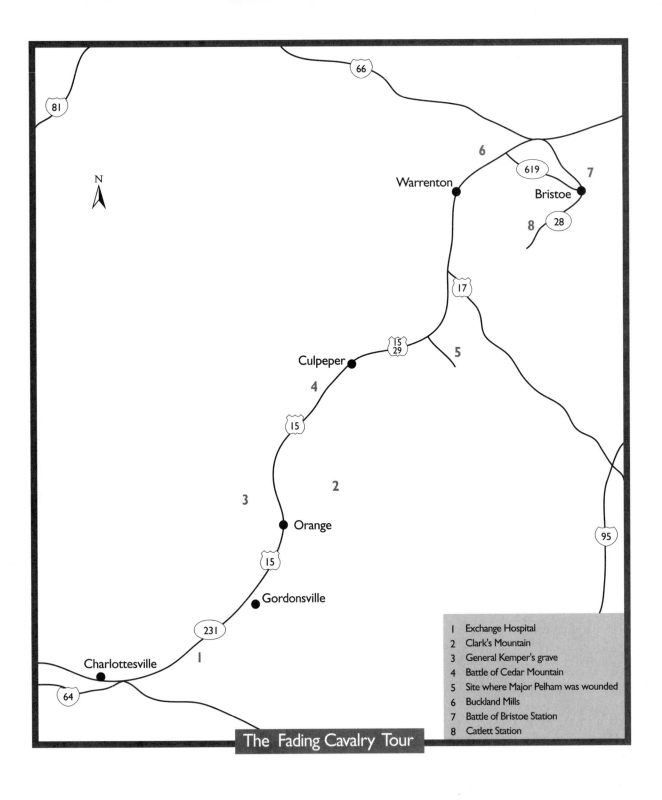

The Fading Cavalry Tour

1 Exchange Hospital
2 Clark's Mountain
3 General Kemper's grave
4 Battle of Cedar Mountain
5 Site where Major Pelham was wounded
6 Buckland Mills
7 Battle of Bristoe Station
8 Catlett Station

The Fading Cavalry Tour

THE TOUR BEGINS at the junction of U.S. 250 Business and U.S. 29 west of Charlottesville. Drive east on U.S. 250 Business (Ivy Road) for 0.8 mile toward the city, then turn right on Alderman Road; St. Mark's Lutheran Church is on the corner. Drive 0.7 mile; a walled cemetery is on the left. Turn left on McCormick Road and park at one of the meters.

Walk to the entrance nearest Alderman Road to view the Confederate monument, which stands over the graves of unknown soldiers. The inscription reads, "Fate denied them victory, but groomed them with glorious immortality." The buried are listed by state on the statue. The soldier has his hat removed to honor the dead, but his musket is cocked, as if ready for combat. More than 1,100 soldiers who died in Charlottesville hospitals are buried in this section.

Walk into the main part of the cemetery, toward the university. Follow the path. Look for an obelisk bearing the name Dabney; the remains of General Carnot Posey rest under a simple monument near the obelisk. Posey's tombstone offers no date of birth or death, perhaps because no one knew them.

Posey was a 43-year-old Mississippian who attended law school at the University of Virginia and served as the United States district attorney for part of Mississippi before the war. He organized his own regiment and brought it east in time to fight at First Manassas and all the other major battles early in the war. He was wounded at Cross Keys but recovered and returned to duty. It was at Bristoe Station in October 1863 that Posey was wounded a

This tour starts in Charlottesville at the University of Virginia's cemetery, then moves downtown to view three magnificent statues before going to another cemetery. Next, it visits Monticello, where visitors can take in the home of the third president of the United States, Thomas Jefferson, and see the grave of his grandson, a Confederate general. It then goes to Gordonsville, where a Confederate hospital still survives, and to Orange, the center of the winter quarters of the Army of Northern Virginia. From there, it moves to the top of Clark's Mountain, where Lee watched Grant enter the Wilderness, and then to the battlefield at Cedar Mountain. Next, it visits Brandy Station, the site of the largest cavalry battle of the war, and Warrenton, the home of John Singleton Mosby. The tour travels to Bristoe Station, the site of a Confederate disaster, before ending at Catlett Station, where Union general John Pope was embarrassed.

The tour is approximately 130 miles long. It will likely occupy two days, as it stops at several museums and battlefields.

second time, by a shell fragment to his thigh. Infection set in, and he died of blood poisoning. Posey's Charlottesville friends buried him in their personal plot. It remains a mystery why such a prominent Mississippian was not returned home. The bodies of general officers were almost always sent to their home states, even if they were killed hundreds of miles away.

Retrieve your vehicle and retrace your route to Ivy Road. Turn right and drive 1.75 miles. The road's name changes to University Avenue, then to Main Street as it passes through the University of Virginia. In the downtown area, turn left on Ridge Street, then immediately right on Water Street. Find a place to park near the junction of Water and First Streets.

Walk north on First Street for two blocks; you will pass the downtown mall on your way to Lee Park, which is bordered by Market, First, and Second Streets. The park features a large, impressive statue of Lee erected in 1924. Purists will notice that the horse looks nothing like Traveller.

Walk three blocks east on Market Street, then turn left on Fourth Street and go one block north to Jefferson Street to see a similar statue of Jackson, erected in 1921. Jackson's statue is much more warlike than Lee's benevolent-looking image. Jackson's horse is striding forward behind an angry, avenging angel using a Confederate flag as a shield. Another angel looks very sad, perhaps because it is mourning the war dead. Jackson, a terrible rider, looks right at home on this horse.

Statue of Jackson

Walk one block east on Jefferson Street to the county courthouse. It was here in 1852 that University of Virginia student John Singleton Mosby was tried for shooting a fellow student after an argument at a party at the farm of Mosby's family. Convicted of unlawful shooting and jailed for a short time, Mosby received a pardon after nearly 300 residents signed a petition to the governor asking for his freedom. Mosby had no hard feelings toward the prosecutor in the case. In fact, the two became friends, and Mosby later studied law in his office, which stands to the right of the courthouse.

An unusual Confederate soldier statue flanked by two bronze cannons stands in front of the courthouse. Erected in 1909, the statue is inscribed, "Warriors, your valor, your devotion to duty, your fortitude under deprivations teach us how to suffer and grow strong." The soldier appears to be in his forties, making him at least twice as old as the average. He has his musket ready to fight but is missing his cartridge box, his cap box, and his canteen.

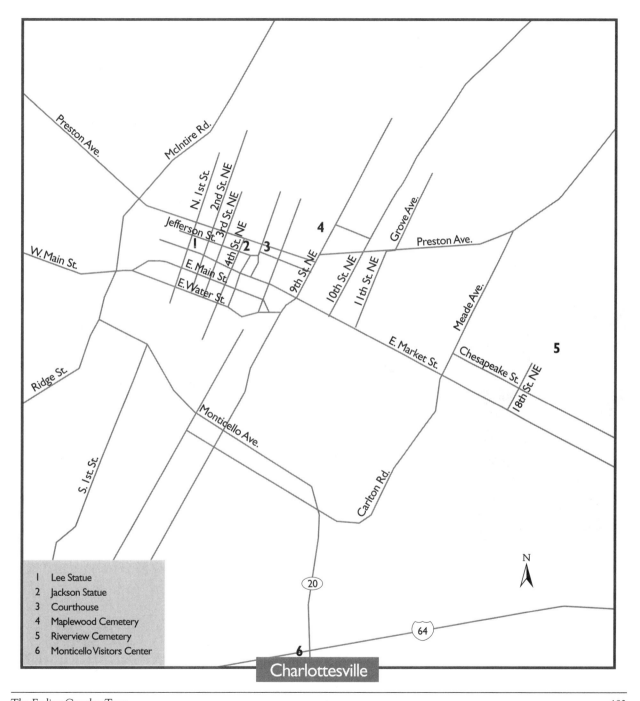

Legend

1 Lee Statue
2 Jackson Statue
3 Courthouse
4 Maplewood Cemetery
5 Riverview Cemetery
6 Monticello Visitors Center

Charlottesville

Retrace your route to your car. Drive east on Water Street to Ninth Street, where you turn left on to Ninth. Ninth becomes Lexington Avenue as you drive through the light. You'll see a hospital on the right. To the left is Maplewood Cemetery, where two Confederate generals are buried. Park nearby if you can find a spot.

The grave of General Armistead Lindsay Long is located in the rear of the cemetery to the right of the path. Long served as Robert E. Lee's secretary. He did very little fighting during the war but did assist Lee in suggesting where to place artillery batteries.

Though blindness overcame Long in 1870, he didn't let it stop him from contributing to the literature on the war. Using a slate designed for the blind, and assisted by former general Marcus Wright, Long wrote a biography of Lee that he called *The Memoirs of Robert E. Lee*. Published in 1891, the book is still in print, though its title is highly inaccurate. Lee intended to write his memoirs, but he died before he could collect all the material he needed.

Grave of General John M. Jones

Nearby is the grave of General John M. Jones, an 1841 graduate of West Point who was made a general in 1863. Seriously wounded on Culp's Hill at Gettysburg, he was back in the service by September 1863. He was then wounded in the head in November. Still, he returned to the field. Jones opened the Battle of the Wilderness, but a Federal counterattack crushed his lines. While attempting to rally his men, he was shot dead.

Nearby is a memorial marker for General Mosby M. Parsons, a Charlottesville native. Parsons moved to Missouri in the 1850s and served as that state's attorney general. He spent his military career in the West, fighting in Arkansas and Missouri. After the war, he fled to Mexico, where he planned to help lead the forces of Maximilian. Parsons was caught in an ambush by Mexican revolutionaries in August 1865. He is assumed to be buried somewhere near where he was killed.

When you are ready to leave the cemetery, retrace Lexington to Ninth Street to the intersection with Market Street two blocks from the light. Turn left on Market, drive 0.8 mile to 18th Street. Turn left on 18th Street and proceed to Chesapeake Street, where you will turn right. Turn left off Chesapeake into Riverview Cemetery. Drive to the fourth road to the left and stop. Twenty yards off the main road on the left is an obelisk honoring

Tom Rosser, a Confederate general who ran hot and cold. Rosser was personally brave, but as the number of troops under him grew, his ability to direct them on the field shrank.

Rosser resigned from West Point just before graduating. He joined the Washington Artillery from New Orleans, then transferred to the cavalry in June 1862. He became a favorite of J. E. B. Stuart, who increased Rosser's rank and often overlooked his inability or reluctance to do the preparation necessary to command thousands of men.

Obelisk honoring Tom Rosser

Rosser shone in leading small-scale raids behind Federal lines. On several occasions, he led his cavalry deep into Union-held territory to loot warehouses of food and supplies.

He suffered his worst defeat at Tom's Brook in the Shenandoah Valley in October 1864. His old classmate George Custer sent the Confederates retreating so quickly that the running battle came to be called the "Woodstock Races."

The last days of the war brought Rosser infamy. He was the man who invited fellow generals George Pickett and Fitz Lee to a shad bake near Five Forks, south of Petersburg. As the three generals were eating fish that Rosser had personally netted, their forces were being smashed less than 2 miles away. It is believed that an atmospheric condition called an acoustical shadow hid the sounds of battle from the lunch party, leaving the generals unaware that any fighting was happening until they saw Union soldiers coming their way.

Rosser's postwar career proved much more valuable. He used the engineering skills he had developed at West Point to become the chief civil engineer on the Northern Pacific Railroad. As his men laid out the railroad, they were protected by his old friend Custer, who was then fighting Indians.

More than 30 years after the Civil War, when Rosser was 62, he was appointed a general again, this time by the United States Army during the Spanish-American War. He died in 1910.

Retrace your route to Market Street, turn right, and drive to Ninth Street. Turn left on Ninth, which becomes Va. 20 South. Drive 1.6 miles, following the Va. 20 South signs. Located on the other side of the junction with I-64 is the visitor center for Monticello. Though Thomas Jefferson's home did not play a role during the war, the grounds were occupied by both Confederate and Union troops. Park at the visitor center, which has some Civil War—era displays.

Confederate general George W. Randolph, Jefferson's grandson, is buried in the same family cemetery at Monticello as the president. Though Randolph already had tuberculosis when the war started, he fought in one of the first battles, Big Bethel, where his skills as an artillery commander were noted. Hoping to capitalize on the fame of President Jefferson, Jefferson Davis appointed Randolph as the Confederate secretary of war in May 1862. While in that role, Randolph pushed through the hated Conscription Act, forcing men to serve in the Confederate army, which could no longer rely on the volunteers who had first rushed into service. He also set up the basic bureaucratic organization of the Confederate military, which made him more valuable than he ever would have been in the field.

But President Davis's belief in himself as a hands-on military man began to grate on Randolph, and he left his post just nine months after taking it. He then became active in the defense of Richmond, even taking a position as a city councilman.

But most of his energy was focused on trying to regain his health. Randolph ran the blockade to Europe to seek medical treatment. He returned to Virginia in 1866, after receiving promises that he would not be prosecuted. He died in 1867 at the age of 49 of the tuberculosis that had plagued him for years. One story goes that the deteriorating condition of his lungs left him almost speechless for the last years of his life, but that on the day he died, he regained his voice and renounced his long-held agnosticism.

Drive east on I-64. After 3.0 miles, get off at Exit 124 and turn right on to U.S. 250 East. Go a little less than 2 miles, then turn north on Va. 22. After 6 miles, Va. 22 runs into Va. 231. Drive north on Va. 231 for 9.3 miles to Gordonsville. As you come into town, turn right on Va. 33 at the traffic circle, following the brown signs for the Exchange Hotel Museum. After about 0.25 mile, you'll reach a Presbyterian church on the left.

This church hosted Jackson at its services when he was in town in July and August 1862, just before the Battle of Cedar Mountain. As he did at every town where he stopped, Jackson made friends with the local Presby-

Exchange Hotel Museum

terian pastor and spent hours with him discussing theological questions. He also kept up his habit of sleeping through church services.

Jackson's corps of 22,000 men camped, drilled, and rested in the fields around the town while he attended to paperwork and the distasteful business of court-martials and executions. Jackson started court-martial proceedings against General Richard Garnett for disobeying orders at Kernstown but never completed the trial, as the Union army started moving. The trial site was northwest of Gordonsville at a place called Victory Mills.

Follow the signs for another 0.5 mile to the Exchange Hotel Museum. Before the war, this was a brand-new railroad hotel that catered to well-to-do train passengers who were changing trains or resting from long journeys. During the conflict, it was used as a hospital by more than 70,000 wounded and sick soldiers. More than 700 of them did not make it out alive.

This was a receiving hospital, meaning that patients who came here had already been treated at a battlefield hospital. Brought here by train, they received additional care before being sent on to long-term military hospitals in Richmond, Charlottesville, and Danville.

Today, the rooms look much as they did when the building served as a receiving hospital. One is set up as an operating room. The medical reenactments that are occasionally held here are so realistic that people have been known to faint as the surgeon starts sawing through bone during a mock amputation.

Turn around and head back toward the traffic circle. Get on U.S. 15 heading north toward Orange. The land surrounding Gordonsville and Orange was used as a camp by the Confederates. Both towns were threatened by Federal raids at various times, but they never became battlegrounds.

It is about 9 miles from Gordonsville to Orange. Coming into Orange, slow down to watch for St. Thomas Episcopal Church on the right at 119 Caroline Street, which is also U.S. 15. Lee attended services here during the winter of 1863–64. His pew is marked. Lee's headquarters were about a mile east of downtown.

If you care to make a rewarding side trip to Clark's Mountain—used by the Confederates to keep track of the Federals north and east of Orange—pick up Main Street, a half block north of the church. Turn right. Drive 0.3 mile to Byrd Street, following the Business Va. 20 signs. Turn left on

Scene from Clark's Mountain

Va. 20 East. Drive about 5.0 miles from this point, then turn left onto C.R. 628 (Clifton Road). Drive 3.5 miles, then turn right on C.R. 627 (Clark Mountain Road). Go 1.1 miles and turn left on C.R. 697. Drive to the top of the mountain, but be sure to turn around without stopping, as the land at the top is private property.

It was from here that Lee and Longstreet watched the movement of Pope's army away from a trap they had hoped to spring on him in August 1862. The plan was to catch Pope's army between the Rapidan and Rappahannock Rivers.

It was also from here that Lee saw Grant moving across Germana Ford on the Rapidan River in May 1864. Lee then rushed his troops forward to catch Grant in the Wilderness.

Officers used to bring young women to the observation area on top of Clark's Mountain to impress them with the scenery.

Return to Va. 20. If you care to continue the side trip, drive east on Va. 20 for another 6.0 miles to the hamlet of Verdiersville. On August 18, 1862, J. E. B. Stuart lost his famous plumed hat and his red-lined cloak here. He almost lost his freedom or even his life. And it was here that Pope captured an order that saved his army. A historic marker is at the spot.

Stuart and several aides, including John Mosby and Heros Von Borcke, rode into the village after midnight thinking they would intercept the cavalry of Fitz Lee and pass along Robert E. Lee's plan to cut off Pope. Some members of Lee's corps should have been in the village, but all was quiet. On the assumption that Lee's men had not arrived, Stuart pulled into the yard of a house, dismounted, stretched out on the porch, and promptly went to sleep, using his haversack as a pillow. He had only a handful of men with him. Since everyone was tired, Stuart did not bother to post any pickets, a lapse in judgment that worried his aides, most of whom slept nervously, their hands on their pistols.

At about 4 A.M., the sleepy Confederates heard riders coming. At first, they assumed the tardy Lee had finally arrived. Stuart walked to a picket fence to watch the approaching riders as Mosby and an aide rode out to meet them. As the riders got closer, Mosby whirled his horse and dashed back to the farmhouse, shouting a warning that the men approaching were Yankees, not Confederates. Stuart leaped on his horse, leaving his hat, cloak, and haversack on the porch.

The Federals captured one of Stuart's aides but didn't try to pursue the fleeing men. Instead, they tossed the hat up in the air on their sabers. Finally, one of the Union officers asked the captured aide the identity of the man riding off into the night. The aide laughed when he said it was General Stuart. The stunned officer thought about going after Stuart, but he knew it was too late.

Stuart made it back to camp without further incident. He draped a handkerchief over his thin hair until a sutler gave him another hat the next day.

The story proved too comical to keep quiet. Whenever Stuart rode past a group of soldiers, someone would shout, "Where's your hat?" What made the loss even worse was that the hat had been a gift from a Yankee general whom Stuart had talked to during a flag of truce to bury the dead after the battle near Culpeper. The Union general had bet Stuart a new hat that the Northern press would call the fight a Union victory, instead of the defeat it actually was. Within a few days, the Union general sent Stuart a new hat and a newspaper account of the battle that indeed described a Union victory.

Captured with the aide near Verdiersville was the order Robert E. Lee had written to Stuart explaining the plan to trap Pope between the two rivers. This was a far more important loss than Stuart's hat and cloak. Stuart must have kept the order to pass along to Fitz Lee instead of destroying it and committing it to memory. It detailed plans for the cavalry to cross behind Pope and bottle him up with the rivers on either side of him, so the infantry could launch a major attack from which Pope could not escape. Had the plan been carried out, it might have meant nothing short of a slaughter or a mass surrender of an entire Union army.

When Pope got the captured order, he finally saw how vulnerable his army was. He pulled his men out and crossed the fords. Watching this lost opportunity gave Robert E. Lee another idea—splitting his army and sending Jackson toward Pope's rear to cut off his railroad supply line. Jackson would engage Pope in combat, and then Lee would come up and smash in from the other side. This plan gave birth to Second Manassas on August 30, 1862, a battle whose necessity can be traced to the night that J. E. B. Stuart stopped to sleep on a farmhouse porch.

Return west on Va. 20 to Orange to complete the side trip.

In downtown Orange, find U.S. 15 and drive north, heading toward

Culpeper. About 2.2 miles out of town, pull over if traffic permits to read the historical marker about General James Kemper, whose grave lies a few hundred yards away on private property.

Kemper, an 1842 graduate of Washington College, was 37 when the war started. One of Virginia's most prominent politicians, he had already served five terms in the Virginia legislature, including one stint as Speaker of the House.

He was named colonel of the Seventh Virginia and was present at First Manassas. After Williamsburg in May 1862, he was promoted to brigadier general. He won his greatest fame in July 1863 when he commanded one of the brigades in Pickett's division during the Pettigrew-Pickett-Trimble Assault on the third day at Gettysburg. Kemper took a minie ball to the leg that barely missed his femoral artery. The ball then traveled up his leg and lodged near his spine. Briefly captured by the Federals in the melee, he was recovered by his men and hustled to the rear. By chance, Kemper's men carried him near Lee, who was still watching the fighting. Lee asked how he was doing, and Kemper replied that he thought his wound was mortal, as it was bleeding profusely.

During the retreat toward Virginia, Kemper was captured again, and his life was saved by Union surgeons. He was exchanged later that year. But the ball remained in his back dangerously close to his spinal cord. He served in minor roles for the rest of the war.

In 1874, Kemper was elected governor of Virginia. He lived another 21 years with the pain from the bullet, dying in 1895 at the age of 71.

Within a hundred yards of the marker is the Rapidan River, the site of thousands of baptisms during the time Lee's army camped around Orange. Indeed, a religious revival swept through the army during the winter of 1863–64.

Soldiers have always sought God before going into battle, and Civil War soldiers were no different. Soldiers' diaries recount how they often saw playing cards blowing across fields and dice scattered along the road—the discarded vices of nervous men who didn't want the Lord to look unfavorably upon them as their spirits knocked on heaven's door.

But something else happened in 1863. Even the chaplains themselves never quite figured out what it was. Perhaps it was only what preachers always hope will happen during revivals—men infecting each other with the spirit of religion.

The Reverend William D. Jones, a chaplain in the Army of Northern Virginia, estimated in his 1887 book, *Christ in Camp*, that 15,000 men in Lee's army publicly dedicated their lives to Christian living. After quoting another chaplain who estimated that 150,000 Confederates in all the armies professed being saved during the war, and that up to a third of all the soldiers belonged to some church, Jones upped his figure to 50,000 in Lee's army. He admitted that tracking such a thing as religious conversion was difficult. But he did know that more than 40 chapels were constructed along the banks of the Rapidan that winter. In fact, the men built their churches before they built their own winter quarters.

Part of the reason for the revival might have been the public religiousness of the leaders of the army. Lee, Jackson, and even the rollicking Stuart—who professed to love God as much as he did singing, dancing, and flirting with the ladies—were all openly religious.

Once, during the Mine Run Campaign of November 1863, Lee was riding down his battle line when he stumbled upon a knot of soldiers who were praying just before being sent into the action. With cannons already booming and bullets whizzing nearby, Lee dismounted and knelt in prayer beside his surprised men. Before another battle, Lee spied a chaplain walking alone toward the front. Lee dismounted, knelt with the pastor, and asked him to pray that his judgment on the battle plan had been right.

Jackson was so religious that some of the first questions he asked officers assigned to him concerned their faith. If any made the mistake of not professing to believe or not having strong beliefs, Jackson mentally crossed him off his favored list. This explains why the dour, shy, moody Jackson took such a liking to the happy, joshing Stuart. Behind Stuart's fun-loving facade was a deep religious commitment that Jackson honored, even if he did not like all the partying that went on in Stuart's camp.

Jackson's religion leaned more toward the fiery Old Testament than the forgiving New Testament. When chaplains sometimes brought up forgiveness as a reason why Jackson should release men held for execution for desertion, Jackson would explode with anger and answer that any man who deserted his comrades deserved no mercy.

On one occasion, 82 soldiers were to be baptized on this riverbank. When the chaplain arrived, he found 5,000 men lining both banks to watch. That night, the same chaplain gave an impromptu church service attended by 5,000. When he asked for those who wanted special prayers to come forward, 600 did. Among those, 200 said they had not been Christians before that night.

Some men saw their faith affirmed during the war. Not far from here on the banks of the Rappahannock, a preacher had just finished leading a circle of men in a hymn when a Federal cannon shell slammed into the ground right between two captains. Neither of the officers was hurt beyond being showered with dirt, since the shell did not explode as it should have. A chaplain who witnessed the event said that the leader of the hymn did not even stop singing, though he did move the service a little farther out of range. The next day, many of the men at that service fought at Second Manassas.

The Federals were never far from this river. On one occasion, Union pickets heard activity along the river and moved silently to intercept what they thought was a Confederate patrol. Through the bushes, they saw a chaplain baptizing several men in the Rapidan. Signaling their presence, the Federals put down their muskets, walked to the river, and joined in a hymn to celebrate the men's conversion to Christianity. Once the prayers were finished, both sides went back to their lines without firing a shot.

About 1.3 miles after crossing the Rapidan, you will see a sign at Locus Dale describing how Jackson crossed at this ford on his way to the Battle of Cedar Mountain on August 9, 1862.

In another 7.9 miles, look to the right to see a big silver barn, silos, and a red-brick house. This home was Jackson's headquarters for the Battle of Cedar Mountain.

Look for C.R. 691 (Carver School Road) across from the brick house. Turn left on C.R. 691, drive to a stop sign, and turn right on C.R. 657 (General Winder Road), the old road that led into Culpeper. After 0.9 mile, you'll see a marker for General Charles Winder. Proceed to the road that turns back right (called Crittenden Lane during the war) and look toward Cedar Mountain. Park here to read the marker for Winder. Judging by the illustrations in Northern newspapers, the mountain looks almost as it did on the day of the battle.

The battle stretched from the lower slopes of Cedar Mountain (also known as Slaughter Mountain) across what is now U.S. 15 and up Crittenden Lane toward your present position. Jackson made the mistake of allowing the engagement to start before all of his 22,000 troops were in place. General Nathaniel Banks pushed his Federals through a cornfield toward the guns on the slopes and Jubal Early's infantry on the right. At the same time, other Federals attacked the Confederate left under the command of General Winder, who was heading Jackson's old outfit, the Stonewall Brigade. Winder's position was anchored on a farm gate at this bend in the road.

Jackson, who seemed disengaged from actively placing troops for much of the battle, suddenly realized that his left was about to be turned. It was thrown into disarray after a Union artillery shell passed right through Winder, tearing off his arm and mortally wounding him. Jackson rushed from the right side of the battlefield and across what is now U.S. 15, yelling for his men to hold firm. When he got to this point, he tried to draw his saber from its scabbard, but it had rusted from disuse. Instead, Jackson unhooked the scabbard from his belt and waved the whole thing over his head, shouting, "Jackson is with you, men. Hold your positions!" He then grabbed a

Cedar Mountain

battle flag with his free hand and waved both the sword and the flag, having dropped his reins in the hope that Little Sorrel would not run.

Finally, A. P. Hill's division appeared on the road. Jackson was able to rush Hill's men into position to save the day. Banks pulled back toward Culpeper, the town Jackson had intended to occupy. After a truce was called to bury the dead—during which several Union generals got their first good look at Jackson—Stonewall pulled his army back to Orange Court House. Though he left the field to the Federals, he had won the battle. The Confederates had suffered 1,400 casualties and the Federals 2,500.

Jackson also unexpectedly caused Pope to make a mistake after the battle. Pope, halfway believing he had won Cedar Mountain, since it was Jackson who had left the battlefield, started a cautious realignment of his army south toward Orange, which put his men between the Rapidan and the Rappahannock. Lee saw the potential for trapping the Federals, but his order for doing just that was captured at Verdiersville. At that point, Pope saw his mistake and quickly extricated himself before the Confederates could move.

Jackson called Cedar Mountain one of his greatest battles, but historians are not so sure. Had A. P. Hill not come up when he did, both Confederate wings might have fallen in on themselves. Jackson made a cardinal mistake in starting the battle before his army was fully in place. Many of his subordinate generals, coming along behind, had no idea where they were going or what they were supposed to do when they got there. Fighting a battle that day came as a big surprise to many of them. Had Jackson kept them informed, or even warned them that action might be possible, they might have moved up the road faster and averted the near-disaster.

On the other hand, the weather that day may have limited everyone from moving faster. The temperature hovered around 100 degrees, making this possibly the hottest day of any Civil War battle. Records and personal accounts indicate that many men, exhausted from the march and the heat, simply keeled over dead from heatstroke before any bullet reached them.

Jackson mourned the loss of Winder. A Maryland native, Winder had resigned from the United States Army just before the war. Because he was from a Union state, he had no constituency in the Confederate army. When Jackson appointed him to head the Stonewall Brigade, Virginians did not like it. They also did not like Winder's strict discipline for even the slightest infraction. Behind Winder's back, some men threatened to kill him in the heat of battle, thereby getting rid of him while sparing themselves the charge of murder. That turned out to be unnecessary, as a Federal artillery shell took care of their work for them.

Follow Crittenden Lane down to U.S. 15 and turn left. The ridge you'll see to the right after about 0.75 mile on U.S. 15 had Confederate guns on it after the battle. Those guns fired on the retreating Federals. Their commander was young Willie Pegram, who had about two more years to live before his death at Five Forks.

Continue 7 miles to downtown Culpeper. Settled in 1759 but not incorporated until 1834, Culpeper was a strategic location during the war because of the Orange & Alexandria Railroad, which ran through town. Culpeper became a Confederate supply depot, which also attracted Federal attention. Historians count more than 100 battles or skirmishes around the town.

U.S. 15 Business runs conjunctively with Main Street in the downtown area. Most of the downtown buildings date to the postwar period, thanks to a fire. One exception is the boyhood home of General A. P. Hill, an 1850s Italian villa–style house on the northwestern corner of Main and Davis Streets. Park near here.

A very good tour book describing all the historic structures around Culpeper is available from the local chamber of commerce, located on West Davis Street.

Walk one block north on Main to Cameron Street. This is the site of the Shackelford House, where the severely wounded John Pelham was brought after the fight at Kelly's Ford. The house, since replaced by a commercial building, was the home of a judge and his three attractive daughters, who no doubt drew the attention of the bachelor Pelham. Legend says that when the major's death was announced, at least three women around the South announced themselves as his grieving fiancées.

Retrieve your vehicle and continue on U.S. 15 Business for about 3.2 miles to where it intersects U.S. 29 northeast of town. Drive 2.6 miles north on U.S. 15/U.S. 29. Turn right on C.R. 663, then right on C.R. 762 at Brandy Station. It is about 2 miles to a parking lot at a state police facility.

Turn right into the parking lot to see the site of the grand cavalry review that the proud J. E. B. Stuart held on June 5, 1863. On the way you will pass a marker for a second review held on June 8.

The June 5 event followed a gala ball held the night before in Culpeper that attracted enough notables to fill the city's hotels and rooming houses. The next morning, Stuart assembled almost 10,000 cavalrymen so they could ride past him and his admirers. As the cavalrymen raced past and his horse artillery fired in the background, Stuart beamed with satisfaction. For their part, his men grumbled over the waste of powder and energy.

Then, three days later, they did it again for Lee, who had been unable to make the June 5 review. Lee, who may have heard about the ostentatiousness of the display three days earlier, ordered Stuart to tone it down. This time, there were no mock cavalry charges and no artillery rounds, but just a simple display of the cavalry.

Retrace your route to U.S. 15/U.S. 29. Carefully cross the highway and take the first right, which is C.R. 685. Drive 0.3 mile, then pull over. The ridge ahead and to the left is Fleetwood Hill and the house is the Barbour House, where Lee spent the night of June 8.

Brandy Station

The Battle of Brandy Station started before dawn on June 9, 1863, the day after the grand review. At 4:30 A.M., more than 8,000 Federal cavalrymen came riding down on the Confederate camp in a surprise attack. In fact, the attack was so sudden that the Confederate cavalrymen who were supposed to be picketing Beverly Ford found themselves riding bareback and fighting in their underwear. They got off a lucky shot that killed the commander of one of the Union wings, Colonel Benjamin F. "Grimes" Davis, the Southern-born cavalryman who had stayed with the Union and successfully led his troops away from Harpers Ferry just nine months earlier, before Sharpsburg (see The Harpers Ferry Tour, page 65).

Drive another 0.6 mile to a historical marker on the right at the top of a small flight of steps. Stuart made his headquarters at this site. Turn around and look toward Fleetwood Hill and the Barbour House. The hill changed hands several times during the course of the morning as the Confederate cavalry finally came to realize it was under attack. Watching from the house was Lee, probably forgotten by Stuart in all the excitement.

More fighting took place about 2 miles east of this site. Colonel Matthew Butler, a South Carolina aristocrat who was married to the daughter of his state's governor and whose uncle had been a United States senator, was holding back an overpowering Union column when a cannonball cut off his foot at the ankle. The same ball also cut off his aide's leg. As the aide was being carried away, he called for the men to hand him his leg. "It is an old friend, gentlemen and I do not wish to part with it," he said. The aide soon died from loss of blood. His body was taken to Culpeper, where he was laid out in a dress uniform. He had left the uniform in the care of a young woman with instructions that if anything happened to him, he was to be dressed in it and sent home to his mother.

Butler recovered to fight not only in this war, but also in the Spanish-American War. During that conflict, he wore the blue uniform of the United States Army.

Continue straight ahead for 0.8 mile, then turn left on C.R. 676. Drive 0.6 mile to where the road becomes C.R. 677. Do not turn; continue straight, passing the airport on the right. The road will turn to gravel. After 1.2 miles on C.R. 677, you'll reach a slight bend to the right. It was at this spot that Grimes Davis was killed after running into General W. E. "Grumble" Jones's half-clothed Confederate defenders. Without their commander, the Yankees stopped their attack, giving the Confederates time to mount a defense.

Find a spot to turn around. Retrace your route for 1.2 miles on C.R. 677, then turn right on C.R. 676 and drive 0.2 mile. During the war, this was the location of St. James Church, which no longer stands. The Confederates fell back to this position, re-formed while their cannons pounded the approaching Union cavalry, and then charged.

If you face north, toward Beverly Ford, you'll see what the Confederates saw. Fascinated cannoneers watched as thousands of cavalrymen slashed at each other with sabers, a weapon that had been out of date for decades, since the advent of the pistol.

By this point in the history of warfare, cavalry was used mainly to scout for the enemy, to screen your own troops, and to raid enemy supply bases and get out before the infantry reacted. The grand cavalry charge was nearly a thing of the past, yet here at Brandy Station, it happened again, though this time it was mixed with pistol shots and occasional shotgun blasts.

At one point, the Federal cavalrymen rode in among the cannons. The gunners responded by swinging at them with rammers. Some of the Federal cavalrymen were from the Sixth Pennsylvania, otherwise known as Rush's Lancers, a regiment that used the archaic lance as its primary weapon. It was not long after this battle that the men decided they might want to hang up the spears and equip themselves with carbines.

The Federals under General John Buford tried to slide around the strong Confederate line at St. James Church, but they were stopped by Confederates fighting dismounted from behind a stone wall in the woods. Though Buford failed here, he won fame just a month later, when his stubborn command held back the first Confederates attacking Gettysburg. His cavalry's defense at Gettysburg bought time for the Federal infantry to move up to defend the high ground behind the town. Buford did not survive the war, dying of typhoid fever.

By the end of the day at Brandy Station, the frustrated Federals finally withdrew across the Rappahannock, unaware that they rode within pistol-shooting range of Robert E. Lee.

By the numbers, Brandy Station was a small battle. The Federals lost 900 killed and wounded and the Confederates 500. But the battle's significance was large. Stuart came under heavy criticism from other officers, politicians, and even once-admiring ladies for allowing his headquarters to be surprised while his commanding general was visiting. Had Jones's men not gathered themselves in time to resist at Beverly Ford, the attack on Fleetwood Hill might have been a complete surprise. Stuart and Lee might have been killed or captured by what was hardly more than a harassment raid by the Federals.

What Stuart and Lee might have thought but did not say out loud was even more disturbing. The Federals who had attacked them were good—very good. Until that point in the war, Stuart and virtually every other Confederate cavalry commander had run rings around the Federal cavalry. That was natural, since the early Union cavalrymen were not trained horsemen. Rather, they were city boys ordered onto horses, while the Confederates were men who had been raised riding horses. But now, two years into the war, the city slickers had caught up with the help of officers like General Alfred Pleasonton, who had whipped the Yankee cavalry into shape with constant training and procurement of better horses.

Lee did not have much time to dwell on his close call. Within a few days, he would put the army on the road to Gettysburg.

Retrace your route toward U.S. 15, slowing to get another look at the house in the distance where Lee watched the battle. This battlefield was once threatened with development either as an industrial park or a racetrack, but most of it has been purchased by preservationists, so it will remain pristine.

Get back on U.S. 15/U.S. 29 and drive 2.1 miles north to Elkwood. Turn right on C.R. 674. It is about 4.6 miles to Kelly's Ford on the Rappahannock River. This ford was used by both sides during the war and played a role in numerous actions, including Brandy Station.

Kelly's Ford

Retrace your route back toward U.S. 15 for 0.8 mile, then turn right into a gravel parking lot. If you're in the mood for a stroll, walk about 0.5 mile northeast along the gravel path through a field and into the woods. To the right, you'll see traces of the stone wall the Federals used for protection while firing at Confederates in the open field to the left.

As the trail curves to the right, you'll see a stone marker on the left beside the path. This is the spot where Major John Pelham of Alabama—"the Gallant Pelham," as Lee called him—was mortally wounded on March 17, 1863.

Pelham was the beau ideal of the Confederate soldier. The son of a planter, he entered West Point in 1856 but resigned just weeks short of graduation when Alabama seceded from the Union. He was a master of artillery while in school, and his talents were soon recognized by the Confederacy. The 22-year-old showed how good he was at First Manassas. Stuart then heard about him and gave him an eight-gun battery of horse artillery, a special unit of guns that traveled with the cavalry to give it extra punch.

Pelham's contribution to the use of artillery was to go to a spot on the field, unlimber, drop several shells on his target, then limber up again and move to another part of the battlefield before the Federals had time to find his range. This rapid movement was something new to artillery, which had previously stayed in one spot until forced to move by enemy action. At Fredericksburg in December 1862, Pelham took two guns out in front of the Confederate right and successfully held up the entire left-wing assault of the Federals, who thought they were being hit by an entire battery of guns, instead of the two pieces Pelham was moving every few minutes.

It was the kid in Pelham that got him killed. While riding along to check out some reported action at Kelly's Ford, he found more than he bargained for—a full-scale assault by General William Averell's 2,100-man Union cavalry division. For more than five hours, Averell's horsemen fought the cavalry of Fitz Lee. While sitting on his horse watching the action at this spot 0.8 mile from Kelly's Ford, Pelham was hit in the back of the head by a Federal shell fragment. When an aide turned to Pelham to say something, he saw the major lying on his back, his eyes wide open. No wound was apparent until the aide lifted Pelham and felt blood on his hand. Pelham never regained consciousness and died later that afternoon in the Culpeper home of a female friend.

The path continues to the Rappahannock River and Wheatley's Ford, which is the proper name of the place near which Pelham was killed, though historians have always called it Kelly's Ford.

Return to your vehicle and head again toward U.S. 15/U.S. 29. After about 0.6 mile, look to the left for a farmhouse with a distinctive red roof. This is the Brannin House, built in 1780. This area was the scene of a Confederate charge leading from the house across the road into the woods on the right. One story says that the staircase inside the Brannin House has a bloody footprint on every other step, which suggests that it was used as a hospital during the war.

After another 1.4 miles, slow your car as the road crosses a creek. This area saw first a charge, than countercharges by both sides.

Drive another 0.3 mile to the intersection with Newby's Shop Road (C.R. 673). This is as far as the Federals advanced. When Averell got back to Kelly's Ford, he left a sack of coffee with a note for his old friend Fitz Lee, who had once told Averell to bring some coffee with him if he ever decided to come across the river.

Continue on C.R. 674 to U.S. 15/U.S. 29 and turn north. After about 11 miles, take the exit for downtown Warrenton on to East Shirley Avenue. Watch for Culpeper Street at the light; turn right to head downtown. You'll see a simple, two-story white frame house on the left at 118 Culpeper. This was the home of John Q. Marr, the first Southerner killed in the war.

Look for a place to park near the junction of Culpeper and Main Streets. Walk two long blocks east on Main to Fourth Street. Here on the corner is the house that John Singleton Mosby and his family occupied after the war.

John Singleton Mosby House

TOURING VIRGINIA'S AND WEST VIRGINIA'S CIVIL WAR SITES

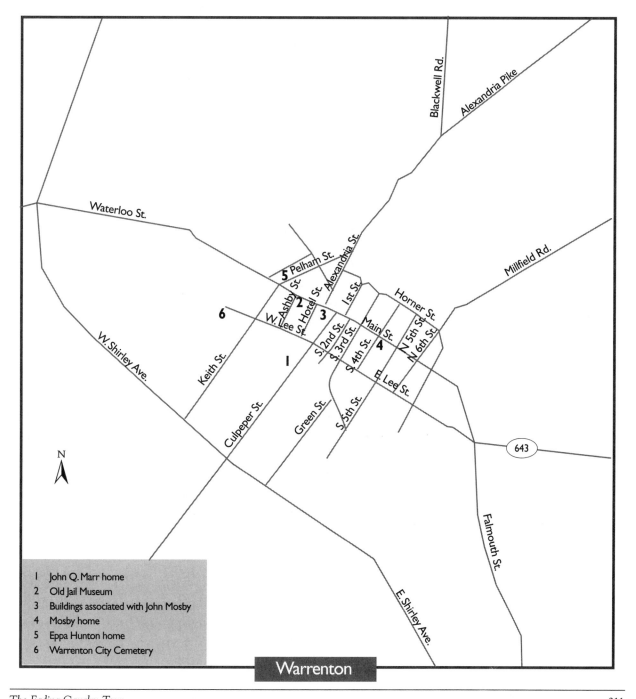

1 John Q. Marr home
2 Old Jail Museum
3 Buildings associated with John Mosby
4 Mosby home
5 Eppa Hunton home
6 Warrenton City Cemetery

Warrenton

Turn around and walk west on Main for four blocks to the Old Jail Museum, located on the western side of the courthouse at the corner of Main and Ashby Streets. Note the monument to Mosby on the lawn of the courthouse.

Inside the museum are several interesting displays, including one on John Quincy Marr, the leader of the Warrenton Rifles, a militia group formed out of fear following the slave uprising at Harpers Ferry in 1859. Marr, the local sheriff, became a member of the delegation that voted Virginia out of the Union, but it was his death that made him a footnote in history. At 3 A.M. on June 1, 1861, Marr was shot down by Union cavalrymen racing through Fairfax Court House. He was thus the first Southerner to fall in the war. Technically, he was a Virginia militiaman, as he had not been sworn in as a Confederate officer.

Also on display is the uniform of General William Fitzhugh Payne, a Confederate who had the misfortune of being wounded three times and captured three times. Payne, a graduate of V.M.I. and the law school at the University of Virginia, found early success in the war as captain of the Black Horse Cavalry, a unit formed primarily around Warrenton that helped drive the panicked Federal army back to Washington after First Manassas. Wounded in the face at Williamsburg, he was captured and later exchanged. He was then wounded by a saber in a fight near Hanover, Pennsylvania, and was again captured. After being exchanged, he was wounded at Five Forks. He made his way home to Warrenton and was resting there when Federal soldiers broke into his house on the night of April 14, 1865, and took him into custody.

The reason why the Federals bothered to arrest a wounded Confederate general five days after Lee surrendered is murky. The explanation may lie in the timing. President Lincoln was shot that same night. One report in the *Official Records* says that General Payne was taken into custody in accordance with an order to arrest all suspicious persons. One of the Lincoln conspirators was Lewis Powell, who tried to kill Secretary of State William H. Seward. Powell had once rented a house from a family named Payne in a town not far from Warrenton. Powell also adopted the alias Lewis Paine. Perhaps this tenuous connection was enough for the Federal government to take General Payne into custody again. He was not released until

June. He returned to practicing law and lived until 1904.

Though no display at the museum mentions it, the Lincoln assassination almost touched Mosby. Powell had been one of Mosby's Rangers for a brief time before deserting to join John Wilkes Booth's conspiracy. But the Federal government could make no connection to Mosby, so he was not arrested.

In one display case are some fascinating artifacts related to Colonel Mosby, the "Gray Ghost." Hotheaded, crafty, deadly, brilliant—Mosby was all those things, just what the outgunned and undermanned Confederacy needed. He was twenty-seven when the war started. His career began simply enough, as a cavalryman in a unit formed in southwestern Virginia, near where he had been practicing law at Bristol. Within months, he was a scout for Stuart's cavalry. By the end of 1862, he was leading his own command under the controversial Partisan Ranger Act, passed by a reluctant Confederate Congress.

Rangers operated behind enemy lines essentially at the whim of their commanders, rather than in ranks under layers of command bureaucracy, like troops in the regular army. Their job was to raid wagon trains, tear up railroads, gather intelligence, and make as big a nuisance of themselves as possible, so the Federal army would have to send large numbers of troops away from the front lines to chase them down.

Mosby was the absolute best at this type of warfare. Though most of his raids included fewer than 50 men, and though he never had more than 800 in his entire command, he gave Grant and his generals fits as they tried to maintain order in the upper counties of Virginia. Even the Federals called the area "Mosby's Confederacy."

His tactics were simple—hit and then run. His men carried no sabers and had no horse artillery following them, as regular cavalry units did. What they did have were several pistols draped around them and their horses—enough firepower that they could decimate a Federal unit.

The best-known exploits of Mosby's Rangers came early and late in the war. They once captured a Union general in his bed. And near Harpers Ferry on October 12, 1864, they robbed a train carrying a $173,000 Union payroll. They split the proceeds among themselves.

Confederate generals tired of hearing about such exploits and complained that the rangers should be in the regular army like everyone else, rather than sleeping in their own beds at night. The Confederate Congress retracted the Partisan Ranger Act, though the secretary of war allowed Mosby's and Hanse McNeill's men to continue their operations.

Mosby survived numerous gun battles that left him with seven wounds and a long list of men he had personally killed in combat. He made a mistake after the war by becoming friends with General Grant, who had once ordered Mosby hunted down and killed, no matter what the cost. Mosby's conversion into a Republican so angered Virginians that one of them took a potshot at him one night as he stepped down from a train a few blocks from this museum.

Mosby lived to the age of 83, finally dying in 1916—one of the last and most famous Confederate warriors.

In the display dedicated to Mosby is the window through which he was shot by Union soldiers late in the war (see The Mosby's Confederacy Tour, page 38). The display also contains a woman's bonnet soaked in Mosby's blood. When he was shot, the woman of the house where Mosby was staying handed him her bonnet to try to stop the flow of blood. Mosby wiped his mouth with blood to make it look like he had been shot fatally in the lungs. He shoved his colonel's coat out of sight under a piece of furniture. The Federals believed him when he said he was a lieutenant. They saw the blood on his mouth and left him to die. Though Mosby recovered, the war ended soon after he was back in fighting shape.

Also in the display case is a pistol that once belonged to a ranger. It was a deadly tool. One historian has counted 18 Federals who were killed by that Colt revolver.

When you are ready to leave the museum, walk behind the courthouse to the Warren Green Hotel, built in 1876 to replace the original hotel of that name, which burned in 1874. General George McClellan stood on the second-floor balcony of the old Warren Green Hotel to bid his men farewell when he was fired by Lincoln in November 1862.

Turn around and look at the building on the corners of Hotel, Lee, and Culpeper Streets. This is the California Building, built in 1850 by future Confederate general William "Extra Billy" Smith after his return from the 1849 California gold rush. After the war, Mosby had his law office in this building.

Warren Green Hotel

Also note the building on the eastern side of Culpeper Street at the junction with Lee and Hotel Streets. During the war, this was a barbershop. One day, Mosby came in for a shave and a haircut. Soon afterward, a Federal officer and two soldiers entered the shop to question the barber about Mosby. The man being shaved lay flat on his back in the chair, thick lather dripping from his face. When questioned, he identified himself as Lieutenant Johnson, paroled by the Federals. The barber vouched for the man, saying he was a hog butcher. Satisfied, the Federals left. Not long thereafter, Mosby wiped the lather from his face, paid for his close shave, and returned to his command.

The building just south of the barbershop on Culpeper now serves as the Fauquier Club. It was a private residence during the war. Mosby brought Union general Stoughton here after capturing him at Fairfax Court House.

Walk north on Culpeper to Main Street, turn left, and curve around Courthouse Square to where Main becomes Waterloo. Continue two blocks to the corner of Waterloo and Pelham Streets, where you'll see the home of Confederate general Eppa Hunton.

A self-educated man, Hunton learned law on his own and was named commonwealth attorney before the war. Though he performed well at First Manassas, it is evident from reading his medical records why Hunton never became a famous general. He was one sick man, suffering the whole war from a variety of ailments ranging from vertigo to chronic diarrhea to fistulas erupting on his backside. He did manage to ride a horse across the field on the third day at Gettysburg and not get killed, but he was wounded in the knee. After the war, he returned to law and politics, eventually serving in both the United States House and Senate. He was the only Southern member of the commission that resolved the electoral college dispute between Samuel Tilden and Rutherford B. Hayes in 1876. The election of Hayes meant the end of the occupation of the South by Federal troops.

Turn left on Pelham Street and walk to the second entrance to Warrenton City Cemetery. Inside the cemetery, follow the hard-surfaced road to the top of the hill, then go left to reach the Confederate Monument to unknown soldiers.

Behind the monument is the grave of General Payne, whose marker is inscribed, "His love of his state was the absorbing passion of his life, the

Confederate monument in Warrenton City Cemetery

motive of every action, the inspiration of every feeling. He loved Virginia with a love far brought out of the historic past. There was no pulse in his ambition whose beauties were not measured from her heart. In war and peace, a soldier in Virginia's honor." That inscription captures the feeling of many Southerners—particularly Virginians, since they were the first to feel the hand of war. Their state was being invaded, and they would fight to the death to protect it.

Mosby is buried to the right of the Confederate Monument. It is a surprisingly simple stone for such a flamboyant man.

After leaving Mosby's grave, walk down the hard-surfaced road that curves back to the right. Follow it until you see a wall of boxwoods around a grave. Here lie the remains of General Lundsford Lindsay Lomax, a fine Confederate cavalry commander.

Lomax was a slow starter in the war. That was mainly because he fought out west under less-than-outstanding commanders. He transferred east at the urging of his friend Fitz Lee and took over command of the regiment headed by Turner Ashby before his death. Lomax gained the trust of his men during several raids and the come-from-behind victory at Brandy Station.

Instead of surrendering with Lee, Lomax tried to cut his way through to Joseph Johnston's army in North Carolina. Once he got there, he found that Johnston, too, was ready to surrender.

After the war, Lomax was elected president of Virginia Polytechnic Institute. He resigned from that position to help collect and edit the 128-volume *Official Records of the War of the Rebellion*, still considered the primary source for details on battles. One other service he rendered was serving as a commissioner for Gettysburg National Battlefield Park from 1905 to 1913.

Despite his status as a general, a congressman, and a senator, Lomax lived such a low-key existence that the tombstone cutter transposed his middle and first names. The error has never been corrected.

Walk toward town from Lomax's grave. Look east to where Lee Street would enter if it ran directly into the cemetery. Here, in line with the street and about 50 yards in from the edge of the cemetery, is the grave of Captain John Quincy Marr, the first Southerner to die in the war. The inscription is nearly worn away.

Return to Waterloo Street. Walk east on Waterloo and Main to get back to your vehicle. Drive west on Main for half a block to pick up U.S. 15 Business heading north, which soon runs into U.S. 15/U.S. 29 North. After driving about 2.5 miles, you will pass a hill called Chestnut Hill during the war.

In another 5.9 miles, you will drive over Broad Run at a place called Buckland Mills during the war for a grist mill that no longer stands. There is not much to see here. Your attention will be occupied anyway, thanks to the four lanes of traffic rushing back and forth to Washington, D.C.

On October 19, 1863, Stuart found himself defending the southern side of Broad Run against Union cavalry led by Custer and Judson Kilpatrick, who were trying to harass Lee's fallback after the disaster at nearby Bristoe Station. Stuart's second-in-command, Fitz Lee, was several miles away leading a second column south—a column that Custer and Kilpatrick didn't know about. Lee sent Stuart a note saying that he would set a trap at Chestnut Hill if Stuart would lure the Federals there.

Stuart's men made a big show of being panicked as they jumped on their horses and rode toward Warrenton on what is now U.S. 15. The Yankees should have been suspicious that Stuart didn't try to set fire to the wooden bridge over the creek. Stuart didn't want the bridge burned. That would have slowed the Federal advance.

As the pursuing Yankees reached Chestnut Hill, Lee's men fired on them from the woods. Dozens of Federals were cut down in the road. Others leaped into a nearby stream; some of them drowned. As quickly as they had ridden down the road, the Federals wheeled and rode in the opposite direction. Now, it was the Confederates' turn to take up the pursuit.

Instead of shooting their enemies, they turned the chase into a game. As they passed each Federal, they grabbed him by his coat and jerked him out of the saddle on to the ground. More than 250 Federals were captured that way.

Known as the "Buckland Races," this incident provided plenty of humorous fireside stories for months to come. But it was also one of the last times that the Confederate cavalry soundly whipped the Federals. Too many Federals mounted on too many fresh horses were coming south.

About 3 miles after crossing Broad Run, turn right on C.R. 619 (Linton Hall Road) at a gas station. Drive 5.6 miles to the light at Va. 28. Cross Va.

28 and continue to a railroad track. The area stretching several hundred yards westward and northward to where Va. 28 crosses Broad Run was a killing ground during the Civil War.

General A. P. Hill's Third Corps chased the retreating Federal army of George Meade for several days in October 1863. On October 14, Hill himself rode ahead to find the Federals. From a hill near Bristoe Station, he saw them moving north along the Orange & Alexandria Railroad. Anxious to fight, Hill ordered two brigades under John R. Cooke and William Kirkland to attack the Yankees. Hill did not scout the ground in front of him and did not send out skirmishers. More importantly, he didn't look to see what was on the other side of the railroad track. He just ordered his men forward.

Had skirmishers been thrown out, they would have found what Hill could not see. More than 3,000 Federals under General G. K. Warren were hiding on the eastern side of the railroad embankment. Without warning, the Federals stood and fired into the flanks of the Confederates marching northward. The range to the closest Confederates was 40 yards.

The battle was over in 40 minutes. The two brigades, made up mostly of North Carolinians, lost more than 1,400 men in that time. Warren's Federals lost only 500.

When Lee rode up to view the disaster, the Tar Heels were still lying where they had fallen. Hill and Lee paused looking at the dead until Lee finally said, "Well, General, bury those poor men and let us say nothing more about it."

Lee likely felt some responsibility for the disaster. He had promoted Hill to lieutenant general, a position Hill didn't like. Hill fancied himself a fighting general, a man who led his troops into battle, not one who stayed behind the lines to plot strategy. A proper corps commander would never have ordered his men into battle without scouting the ground, but Hill never thought about the big picture. He saw only what was immediately in front of him.

Turn around and return to Va. 28. Turn left and drive south on Va. 28 for 8.3 miles. Turn left on Elk Run Road, then immediately right on Old Catlett Road. Pull into the parking lot at the historical marker. The tour ends here.

This is Catlett Station. On August 22, 1862, Stuart and more than 1,500 cavalrymen descended on this place, which served as a Union supply depot and the command post of General John Pope. Stuart's men totally surprised the camp. They cut the telegraph lines, set fire to goods, and discovered Pope's tent. They took his dispatch book and his best dress uniform. One of Stuart's officers tried to take a buffalo robe, but a large dog guarding his master's gear refused to let the Confederate have it without a fight. Rather than kill the dog, the officer let it keep the robe.

One of the Federals captured was a woman posing as a man. She figured she could plead her case and win her release when she revealed herself to be a woman, but Stuart told her that if she wanted to play the role of a male soldier, she could also play the role of a captured soldier.

At first, Lee was disappointed at Stuart's inability to burn a nearby railroad bridge because it was too wet. Then he read Pope's dispatch book and realized that Pope was expecting to be reinforced by McClellan. It was then that Lee launched the campaign that would result in Second Manassas in order to destroy Pope before McClellan could arrive. Stuart sent a note through the lines to Pope offering to trade the coat for Stuart's hat, which had been captured several months earlier at Verdiersville. Pope was not amused, and Stuart's hat was not returned. The coat was sent to Richmond, where it was displayed in the State Capitol.

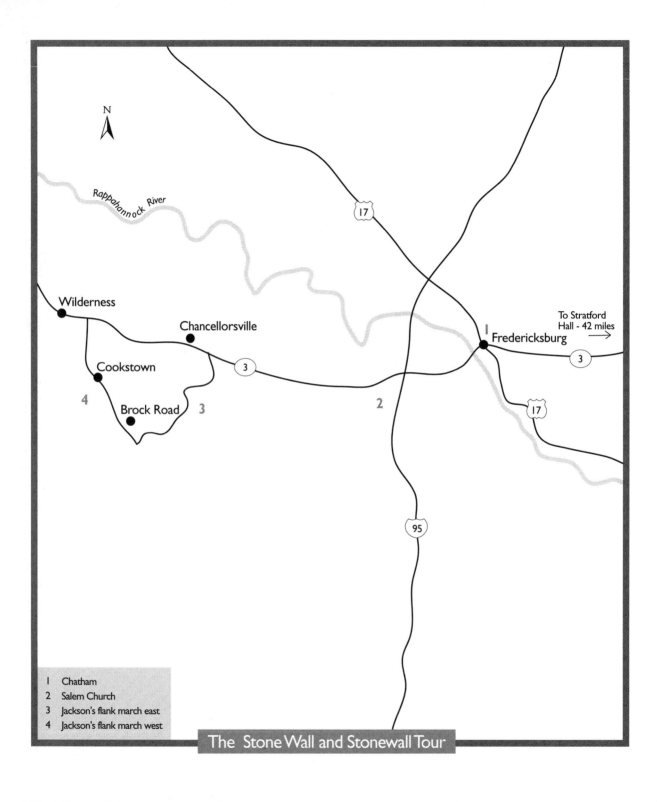

N

Rappahannock River

Wilderness

Chancellorsville

Cookstown

③

4

Brock Road

3

③

②

⑰

①Fredericksburg

To Stratford
Hall - 42 miles
→

③

⑰

㊄95

1   Chatham
2   Salem Church
3   Jackson's flank march east
4   Jackson's flank march west

The Stone Wall and Stonewall Tour

The Stone Wall and Stonewall Tour

This tour starts in the river town of Fredericksburg and ends in the woods around a town that never was, Chancellorsville. These were the sites of Lee's two greatest victories.

At Fredericksburg, the tour takes in both the Union artillery positions at the beautiful mansion called Chatham Manor and the target of that artillery, the town on the southern side of the Rappahannock. It traces the deadly route that Union soldiers had to take in attacking Marye's Heights. From downtown, it moves along the Confederate right flank, where the Union attack almost succeeded. After leaving Fredericksburg, the tour stops at Salem Church, then moves on to Chancellorsville, where you can drive over the same road that Stonewall Jackson's corps took to surprise the Union right flank.

The tour is only about 37 miles long but will likely take all day, as it visits three National Park Service museums and involves a walking tour of downtown Fredericksburg.

THE TOUR OFFICIALLY STARTS at Chatham, located on Va. 3 on the northern side of the Rappahannock River, across from Fredericksburg. But Robert E. Lee historians might like to begin with a long side trip to Stratford Hall, Lee's birthplace.

Stratford Hall is located 42 miles southeast of Fredericksburg; follow Va. 3, then turn on to C.R. 214. Robert was born here to Richard "Lighthorse Harry" Lee and Ann Carter Lee on January 19, 1807, in the room called "The Chamber," where his crib is preserved. In the adjoining nursery where Robert slept, visitors can see some fireplace irons stamped with the images of angels. Stratford Hall tradition says that the last thing four-year-old Robert did before leaving Stratford Hall for the family's new home in Arlington was to crawl into the fireplace to say good-bye to the angels who had kept him company.

Though he never lived here as an adult, Lee kept alive the hope that he would one day return to Stratford Hall. At Christmas 1861, he comforted his wife on the loss of Arlington to Federal occupation by writing, "I wish I could purchase Stratford. It is the only other place I could go to now acceptable to us, that would inspire me with pleasure and local love."

Retrace your route to Chatham to complete the side trip.

Chatham was built over a three-year period ending in 1771 on land that was first viewed in 1608 by Jamestown colonist John Smith. By the start of the Civil War, it was owned by James Horace Lacy and was known as the

Lacy House. When the Federals started filtering down toward Richmond in 1862, it was occupied first by Irvin McDowell and then by a host of other generals, who valued it not so much for its beauty as for the view out its southern entrance.

The Lacy House was built on Stafford Heights, which rises a couple of hundred feet above the Rappahannock—not much by mountain standards, but more than enough to make it valuable ground for placing more than 100 Union cannons. By December 11, 1862, those cannons covered the yard of the house. The steeples of the town's churches were to be used as aiming points. The cannons on the grounds today show what an easy target the Federals had.

Inside Chatham Manor are displays on the history of the house. The far western room is where both Clara Barton, the founder of the American Red Cross, and poet Walt Whitman practiced their nursing skills. All nine rooms of the house were used as operating rooms or hospital space. Barton dutifully recorded the names and burial locations of the 130 men she could not save, so they could be dug up later and given a more proper service. Whitman came to the hospital looking for his wounded brother. Finding

Chatham

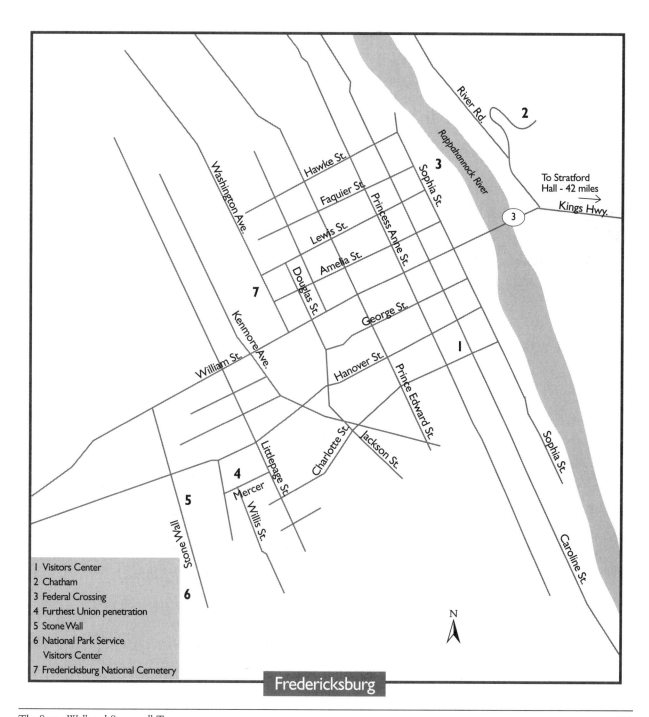

1 Visitors Center
2 Chatham
3 Federal Crossing
4 Furthest Union penetration
5 Stone Wall
6 National Park Service
   Visitors Center
7 Fredericksburg National Cemetery

Fredericksburg

him only slightly injured, the poet, already well known, stayed to nurse the men as best he could. The thoughts he wrote down on notepaper were later published in books of his poetry.

A newspaper reporter's description of the house after the battle is vivid: "Every floor and wall was saturated in blood. All that is elegant is wretched and all that is noble is shabby and all that was once civilized elegance now speaks of ruthless barbarism."

Looking at Fredericksburg from Chatham

When you are ready to leave Chatham, drive across the Rappahannock on Va. 3. Follow the signs to the Fredericksburg Visitors Center, located at 706 Caroline Street at the junction with Charlotte Street. (This is not the National Park Service visitor center.) A walking tour of the downtown area will help you get an idea of what the Federals felt as they climbed from the river toward Marye's Heights, where the National Park Service visitor center is located.

The modern town has grown into the battlefield area. During the war, Fredericksburg hugged the river and extended outward for only four blocks. Beyond that, the outskirts consisted of open fields and a few scattered houses—ideal ground for a defending army but terrible ground for an attacking army needing woods, swales, and fences to hide behind.

When Virginia seceded from the Union on April 17, 1861, the 4,500 citizens of Fredericksburg, a colonial town founded in the 1720s, must have worried that they might be in the middle of a battlefield one day. The town lies just 50 miles south of Washington and 50 miles north of Richmond. When the Confederate Congress voted on May 20, 1861, to move the capital from Montgomery, Alabama, to Richmond, Fredericksburg's citizens likely started growing even more nervous, as their town was now an obvious military target for the Union. By the time Federal troops starting chanting "On to Richmond!" before First Manassas in July 1861, the townspeople may have known that the opposing armies would one day clash on the banks of the Rappahannock.

After the Federals were defeated at First Manassas and went streaming back into Washington, the townspeople may have breathed a sigh of relief. Like many Southerners, they figured the Yankees would give up the idea of bringing the South back into the Union after the bloody nose they got on the banks of Bull Run. That did not happen. Instead, the Union issued calls for more volunteers to fight the South's insurrection.

Richmond became the North's major target in May 1862, when General George McClellan decided it would be practical to attack the Confederate capital by moving his Army of the Potomac by sea, then up the Peninsula between the York and James Rivers. At the same time, an army corps under General Irvin McDowell stood poised to move virtually unmolested through Fredericksburg toward Richmond. However, President Lincoln held McDowell back to protect Washington from General Thomas J. "Stonewall" Jackson, who was whipping one Union army after another in the Shenandoah Valley. For a while, Fredericksburg escaped destruction.

Had McClellan succeeded in taking Richmond from the Peninsula, Fredericksburg would have been spared its taste of war. But the emergence of General Robert E. Lee as the new leader of the Army of Northern Virginia during the Seven Days Campaign forced McClellan to back away while he was within earshot of the church bells of the capital city.

By the summer of 1862, President Lincoln was right back where he had started a year earlier. The Confederate army remained intact, and Richmond, just 100 miles south of the White House, was still the Confederate capital. Lincoln tried another general, John Pope, for a few months, but Pope was badly defeated at Second Manassas in August. When Lee started marching through Maryland on his way to Pennsylvania in September, Lincoln decided to fire Pope and give McClellan one more chance to defeat Lee. The two sides fought to a standstill at Sharpsburg, after which Lee withdrew back across the Potomac to await an attack on Southern soil that never came, as McClellan let his army rest.

In Lincoln's mind, it rested too long. He fired McClellan for a second time. The president then turned the command of the Army of the Potomac over to General Ambrose Burnside, a man who was well liked by his fellow officers but whose judgment had already been called into question at Sharpsburg. During that battle, Burnside had tried repeatedly to march his Ninth Corps across a small bridge over Antietam Creek. Two hundred Georgia riflemen held up Burnside's corps all day, while the general ignored the fact that the creek could have been forded, as it was only waist deep. Burnside's delay allowed Lee to receive reinforcements, which saved the Southern army.

Burnside's plan for his new command was simple. He would march the Union army, camped around Warrenton, overland toward Richmond before Lee's army, which had scattered in an attempt to keep watch over all the Federal forces, could react. The focus of the Union march would be Fredericksburg.

Burnside left Warrenton on November 15, 1862, after sending a request to General Henry Halleck in Washington to have several dozen pontoon wagons rushed to Fredericksburg. The army would use the pontoons to ford the Rappahannock, since the Confederates had destroyed the bridges over the river.

General Burnside moved his entire army to Falmouth, a small town on the northern side of the Rappahannock, in just two days, a march so fast that Lee lost track of where the Federals were. Burnside's leading units found that the river was low—low enough that they could have forded it and taken the city from the handful of Confederate troops present. But Burnside refused to allow that, fearful that rains would raise the river and leave the smaller part of his army at the mercy of the Confederates, who were now rushing toward the southern side of the Rappahannock.

Even after the rest of his army arrived at Falmouth, Burnside insisted on waiting for the pontoons, though his men still could have waded the river— just as they could have waded Antietam Creek. That wait allowed Lee's entire army to reach Fredericksburg by November 21. The pontoons finally arrived on November 24. By that time, Lee's army occupied the 7-mile-long ridge behind the town. The 90,000 Confederates dug in and positioned their 307 cannons so they could sweep the entire slope from the river all the way up the heights. The head of the Confederate artillery confidently predicted that "a chicken couldn't live on that field."

It was obvious to Burnside's subordinate generals and to the 120,000 men in the ranks that their advantage had been lost because of the delay in getting the pontoons. There was no way the Union army could move from the river up those slopes against the dug-in Confederates. The Federals would have to figure out something to do other than attack at Fredericksburg.

To everyone's amazement, Burnside informed his commanders that he would fool Lee. Instead of wasting time looking for an unprotected crossing, the Federals would attack Fredericksburg, the strongest part of the Confederate line. His generals tried in vain to get Burnside to reconsider. Their reluctance to plan the details of the attack bordered on insubordination.

Lee himself was amazed at the Federals' preparations. It went against every military principle to attack an enemy that had such a strong defensive position. It was a disaster waiting to happen. Lee reasoned that if the Federals really wanted to attack him, he would let them.

In the predawn darkness on December 11, 1862, Federal engineers started trying to bridge the Rappahannock. It was dangerous work. The engineers had to run out a pontoon, position it lengthwise down the river, lay some planks over it, then pull up another pontoon and lash it to the first. A brigade of Mississippians reinforced by several companies from the Eighth Florida Regiment started shooting the engineers. Federal artillery massed at Stafford Heights on the northern side of the river then started firing into the town in an attempt to kill the Confederate riflemen.

Watching the Federal cannons destroy the village that prided itself on being the hometown of George Washington, Lee commented, "Those people delight to destroy the weak and those who can make no defense. It just suits them."

Finally realizing that the engineers could not complete their mission under fire, a few boatloads of Federal infantrymen rowed across the river and landed on the southern bank. They pushed the Confederates hard, moving from street to street, one of the few instances of such combat during the war.

Finally, Lee ordered the Mississippians and Floridians back to the safety of the heights, abandoning the town without much of a fight. What everyone but Burnside must have figured out was that Lee wanted the Federals in Fredericksburg. They would be easy to shoot from the ridge the Confederates held. The Federals thus trudged across the pontoon bridges unmolested.

All day on December 12, Fredericksburg was ravaged by the Union army, perhaps out of irritation that the houses had been used as sniper positions by the Confederates, or perhaps out of a sense of foreboding among the Federals that many of them would be killed when they tried to attack the Confederate position. Plaster walls were smashed. Furniture was piled in the streets and set afire. Pianos were chopped into pieces. The seething Confederates watched in silence, knowing that the Federals would soon pay for their vandalism.

On the morning of December 13, the Federals on the left flank began moving across the mostly open fields against Stonewall Jackson's men, who were waiting in the wooded part of the battlefield.

On the right flank, the Federals massed in the narrow streets of Fredericksburg and slowly, reluctantly started up the slope toward the house called Brompton on Marye's Heights, held by General James Longstreet's men. The Union's famed, proud Irish Brigade was without its distinctive green regimental flag, which had been shipped back north for repairs after being shredded at Sharpsburg. The men of the Irish Brigade clipped sprigs of boxwood to their caps to demonstrate their solidarity—and to help identify their bodies later.

All day long, more than 40,000 Federals from 15 states took turns attacking Marye's Heights, which was protected at its base by a stone wall bordering the farm road where the Confederates stood. Three Federals made it to within 25 yards of the wall before dying. Nine thousand others never made it that far. By contrast, fewer than 2,000 Confederates fell on this end of the line.

The Federals initially met with better success on the left. Unhampered by the narrow streets in town, they could mass and attack where they wanted. At one spot, they moved so swiftly through a gap in the Confederate line that they caught some South Carolinians with their arms stacked, unprepared to meet a Union charge. Only a spirited counterattack saved the Confederate line.

By the end of the day, just over 5,000 Confederates had been killed or wounded, while more than 12,600 Federals had suffered the same fate, most of them on the bare ground before the stone wall on the right flank. Many of the Union wounded froze to death that night. Others survived by pulling the bodies of their comrades around them into human breastworks to block the shots of nervous Confederates fearful of a Union night attack.

Two days later, the Federals pulled back across the river. Burnside rested his army for a month before trying to attack Lee again. On January 19, 1863, he launched a march westward along the riverbank. The plan was to cross at Bank's Ford and then turn east to hit Lee's flank. But as soon as the march started, the Federals fell victim to a two-day torrential downpour of freezing rain. The roads became bottomless mudholes. Cannons and wagons sank up to their hubs. A march that should have taken no more than six hours became a four-day out-and-back ordeal that became known as "Burnside's Mud March." Hundreds of men died or became incapacitated from sheer exhaustion without the Confederates firing a shot. The notation "Died at Falmouth, Va.," became a catchall for Union bookkeepers, who had no idea why men had simply keeled over on the march or in camp. Hundreds deserted and headed north, tired of and frightened by what they perceived as Burnside's incompetence.

Lincoln had seen all he needed to. Two days after Burnside returned to camp, he was relieved of command in favor of one of his corps commanders, General Joseph Hooker, who would prove no better a leader in the woods around a house called Chancellorsville.

From the Fredericksburg Visitors Center, walk north on Caroline Street for four blocks to Amelia Street and turn east, toward the river. Go one block to Sophia Street and turn north. Across the river is the Lacy House, the main Union artillery position.

Walk three blocks on Sophia Street. Just before Hawke Street, you'll see some historical markers describing this as the area where "Barksdale's Mississippi Brigade" shot at the engineers building the pontoon bridge. There is no mention of the contribution of the 150 Floridians who were in "point blank range of the enemy," according to one official report. The Mississippians sniped at the Federals from inside houses fronting the river, while the Floridians had to fight in the open.

The third Union regiment to row over the river into town was the 20th Massachusetts. At the head of one of its companies was a young Harvard dropout, Captain Oliver Wendell Holmes, Jr., who would survive the war, go back to law school, and eventually serve 30 years as a United States Supreme Court justice.

Turn left on Hawke Street and walk one block; nearly 100 Federals fell in this block.

Turn left on Caroline Street. For a while, Federals in the houses on the eastern side of Caroline fought with Confederates in the houses on the western side of the street. Local history says that the Mississippians were under orders to start falling back, having successfully tricked the Federals into thinking the Confederates were desperate to keep them out of the city. Somehow, a captain of the Mississippians learned that an old Harvard classmate—perhaps Holmes—was opposite him. The proud Southerner was not about to let his old classmate beat him, so he ordered his men to make a stand. The Mississippi captain had to be placed under arrest by another officer so his men could withdraw as ordered.

Walk two blocks on Caroline to Lewis Street, turn right, go one block to Princess Anne Street, turn left, and proceed two blocks to the Old Market House, located at 907 Princess Anne. Built in 1816, the Old Market House is now the home of the Fredericksburg Area Museum, which you may want to visit before marching up toward the heavy fighting site.

The Confederate troops defending the river moved southwestward from this point to the safety of Marye's Heights. The fighting of December 11, 1862, ended here. The next day, December 12, the Federals looted while the Confederates seethed.

Continue one more block on Princess Anne to Hanover Street. It was on the morning of December 13 that the reluctant Federals started up Hanover Street. Walk toward Marye's Heights. Turn right on to Hanover.

Walk toward Marye's Heights on Hanover. After two blocks, you reach Prince Edward Street, which marked the end of the town and the beginning of the killing ground. Continue another long two blocks on Hanover. When you reach the intersection with Kenmore Avenue, imagine yourself walking down into a slippery drainage ditch filled with freezing water; Kenmore now covers that ditch. The ditch proved a welcome natural defense for the Confederates, as the Federals had to slow their march to cross it. When planning their attack, Burnside's generals insisted that the ditch would hamper their assault. Burnside, on the other hand, maintained that the ditch didn't even exist. He said he had been in Fredericksburg just a few months earlier and remembered no such ditch.

As soon as the brigades re-formed after crossing the ditch, they began their series of fruitless charges up the slope. From this point forward, the men moved at double-quick, a fast walk.

Continue on Hanover for two blocks to Littlepage Street. Scores of Federals sought refuge behind the house on the right at 801 Hanover.

Turn left on Littlepage and walk one block to Mercer Street. At 700 Littlepage is another house that stood during the fighting.

Turn right on Mercer and march straight ahead to the stone wall. Lieutenant Colonel Joshua Lawrence Chamberlain, the second-in-command of the 20th Maine, spent the night somewhere near where Mercer and Willis

Streets meet today. He dragged bodies all around him to form a human fort and pulled the dead men's coats over him, as he had left his own in town. Once during the night, Chamberlain crawled along what he thought was his battle line to urge his men to dig themselves shallow trenches for protection. When he came upon a man throwing soil down the slope, rather than up it, Chamberlain chided him for not paying attention to the correct way to build a protective earthwork. The man replied in a thick Southern accent that he knew where the Yankees were—down the slope. Chamberlain had crawled away from his own line and into the forward rifle pits of the Confederates.

Chamberlain survived the attack on the wall and seven months later became the Union hero of Gettysburg for holding on to Little Round Top.

On the right near the stone wall is a statue honoring Sergeant Richard Kirkland of the Second South Carolina, the "Angel of Marye's Heights." Following the Union attack on the wall, the 19-year-old Kirkland could not stand to hear the cries of the wounded Federals in front of his position. Disobeying direct orders, he jumped over the wall and took water to the wounded. The Federals did not shoot at him as he went about his mission of mercy.

Stone wall at Marye's Heights

Nine months later, Kirkland was killed at Chickamauga, Georgia.

Pass through the stone wall, most of which was reconstructed in the 1930s, and turn left, heading toward the National Park Service visitor center. Towering above this point is Brompton, the large house atop Marye's Heights. The small white home is the Innis House, still pockmarked with Federal bullet holes. Farther along is what remains of the foundation of the Martha Stephens House. Mrs. Stephens refused to leave her home during the battle. Instead, she made frequent trips to the well to relieve the thirsty Confederates.

It was in this area that a fragment from an artillery shell cut the femoral artery of General T. R. Cobb, who bled to death. A former Confederate congressman, Cobb had resigned from that position to take field command.

Innis House

Continue to the museum at the National Park Service visitor center. The Fredericksburg National Cemetery rises above it.

After touring the museum, walk north on the Sunken Road to William Street and turn right, heading back toward town. After three long blocks, you will reach the Confederate Cemetery. Turn left on to Washington and enter the cemetery from Washington Avenue. Turn immediately to the right and walk about 30 yards along the wall, looking for the obelisk honoring W. E. and J. R. Cunliffe.

This obelisk shows why walking in old cemeteries can be so rewarding. The whole wartime history of the brothers is told on the monument. One of them, W. E., died famously. The monument details how he "was struck down by the same volley that struck the immortal Jackson. He survived only 30 hours, breathing while life lasted an earnest prayer for the salvation of his beloved country." His brother, J. R., was killed the next year just a few miles away at the Wilderness. The inscription reveals that the monument was "erected by their fond, afflicted mother who is left childless."

Next to the Cunliffe brothers is the grave of General Abner Perrin, a South Carolinian known mostly for his reckless ambition. Perrin told his aides he would emerge from the Battle of Spotsylvania Court House "a live major general or a dead brigadier." While leading reinforcements into a breach in the line at Spotsylvania, Perrin was shot from his easily targeted horse by seven different riflemen. Perrin is one of the few generals who was not returned to his home state after his death.

Walk along the wall past Perrin's grave until you reach the monument to General Dabney Maury, who led an unremarkable military career in Mississippi and Alabama. It was after the conflict ended that Maury made his greatest contribution to the war. In 1868, he founded the Southern Historical Society, which preserved Southern recollections of the war and helped make Robert E. Lee a Confederate icon.

Near Maury are the graves of General Carter Stevenson, who served out west, and General Henry Sibley, who tried to capture New Mexico for the Confederacy. Never much good to the Confederacy, Sibley was hired by the Egyptian army after the war to teach artillery. He is most noted for inventing the Sibley tent, a tepee-style tent that had a stove in the center.

Walk toward the Confederate statue, which stands over the graves of more than 3,000 Confederate soldiers. To the right of the statue at the end of the civilian section is the grave of General Daniel Ruggles. Ruggles is a bit of a puzzle. An 1833 West Point graduate, he fought in both the Seminole War in Florida and the Mexican War before resigning from the United

States Army as a captain in 1861. He quickly moved up the Confederate ranks to become a general. In his first major battle, at Shiloh in April 1862, he garnered criticism from his superiors for being slow to come on to the field. But when he did arrive, he gathered a number of cannons and blasted the Federals from their stronghold in the Hornet's Nest, a crucial action in the battle. Still, his superiors criticized him, and he never received another field command.

Just down from Ruggles, at the end of the military burial sites, is the grave of Captain Keith Boswell. Jackson's chief of engineering, Boswell was killed in the same volley that killed the general. Originally buried in the same family cemetery that still holds Jackson's arm, Boswell was later moved here.

Turn left at Boswell's grave and walk pass the Confederate statue, heading to the first iron fence. Inside the fence is the grave of General Seth Barton, a man who never seemed to find his place in the command structure and was blamed for several defeats.

When you are ready to leave the cemetery, continue down William Street to Caroline Street. Turn right on Caroline to return to your car at the visitor center parking lot.

Depending on where you found parking and how you negotiated the one-way streets, you have to drive three blocks south of the visitors center to get on U.S. 1 Business (Lafayette Boulevard). Then head west toward the National Park Service visitors center. Continue past the visitors center and cross over Va. 3 (Blue-Gray Parkway). Following the brown signs, immediately turn left on Lee Drive. Park in the lot and walk up the hill.

This was the site of Lee's headquarters. It was from here that he watched the Federal attack disappear into the woods on his right, then reappear with Confederates in pursuit. Pleased at what he saw, Lee said, "It is well that war is so terrible, lest we would grow too fond of it." On display at the site is a 30-pounder Parrott rifle. The Confederates had only two of these heavy guns at Fredericksburg, one of which exploded near Lee during the battle. He was not hurt.

Continue on Lee Drive. The Confederate trenches you'll see all along the left side of the road suggest how large the battlefield was.

After 3.8 miles, pull over at the site of the mortal wounding of General

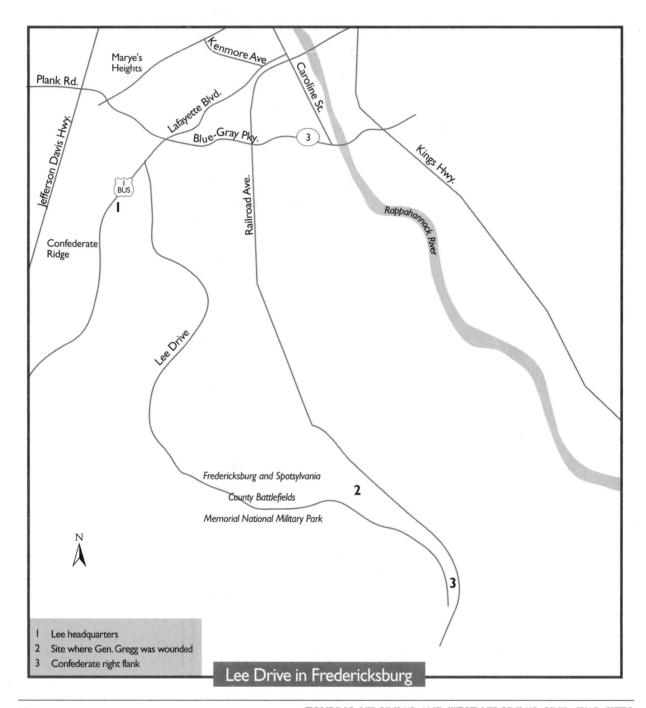

1 Lee headquarters
2 Site where Gen. Gregg was wounded
3 Confederate right flank

Lee Drive in Fredericksburg

Maxcy Gregg, which is depicted in a painting placed here. Gregg, one of three Confederate generals to sign South Carolina's Ordinance of Secession, was resting with his men in this section when several regiments of Pennsylvanians burst through the woods. Gregg was rallying his men when a rifle ball hit his spine. The Federals were eventually repulsed. It was this action that led Lee to make his famous "war is so terrible" remark.

Stonewall Jackson, who had quarreled with Gregg on several occasions, came to the South Carolinian's deathbed the next day to settle their disputes and to urge Gregg to look forward to the afterlife.

Continue 0.4 mile, then pull to the left to see the stone pyramid erected after the war to pinpoint the farthest penetration by the Federals.

Stone pyramid that pinpoints the farthest penetration by the Federals

Continue to the end of Lee Drive. This was the location of 14 Confederate cannons that did not fire on the Federal cannons, but rather remained hidden so they could open up on the Federal infantry.

It was about a mile in front of this position that a baby-faced, 24-year-old major from Alabama acquired the nickname "the Gallant Pelham" from Robert E. Lee. With just two cannons and a handful of brave men, John Pelham held up the entire Federal infantry assault. His technique was to fire the cannons a few times, then quickly move them to a different location before the Federal cannons could get their range. While the whole left half of the Federal artillery tried to kill Pelham, the Union infantry sat for more than two hours, convinced that it faced many more cannons. The Federals did in fact face the 14 hidden guns, but it was Pelham's two cannons that stopped them. It was only after he received a direct order from J. E. B. Stuart to retire that the boy major returned to his lines. His concept of constantly moving artillery was an innovation in warfare.

Retrace Lee Drive to U.S. 1 and turn right. After a short distance, get on Va. 3 heading west. Follow the busy Va. 3 past I-95 and get in the left lane as soon as practical. Just over 1 mile after I-95, turn left on Salem Church Road. Turn left again at the first light, located at an unnamed access road for a fire station. Turn left again to reach the parking lot of Salem Church.

This little brick structure, nestled here among some of the most garish overdevelopment found on any battlefield, was the central object of the Battle of Salem Church, fought on May 3, 1863. While most of the Union army was fighting at Chancellorsville, 6 miles to the west, the Federals left behind in Fredericksburg discovered that the Confederates had virtually abandoned Marye's Heights. After taking the Heights, the troops under General John Sedgwick were marching toward Chancellorsville thinking that they could hit Lee's flank when they ran into General Lafayette McLaws's Confederates, who were gathered around Salem Church. The Federals suffered nearly 5,000 casualties and never made it past the church, which still shows gouges where Federal bullets hit it.

Retrace your route to Va. 3 and continue west. It is about 6 miles from Salem Church to a traffic light located at the ruins of Chancellorsville. It was a house, rather than a town, that lent its name to the great battle that took place around it.

Continue 1 mile to the National Park Service Chancellorsville visitor center.

Salem Church

Chancellorsville has always been regarded as Robert E. Lee's boldest, brightest, and riskiest battle. So many things could have gone wrong. Had the 75,000 Federals made a frontal assault against what they thought was the whole Confederate army, they would have found fewer than 14,000 men in line, and Lee himself would likely have been killed or captured. Had Stonewall Jackson's men not broken the Union right flank, the Confederate army would have been split into two easily defeatable pieces.

The Federals started out with a reasonable plan—nearly the same one that Burnside had tried five months earlier during his ill-fated "Mud March." Burnside's replacement, General Joseph Hooker, took his army northwest and forded the Rappahannock with the intention of sweeping down on Lee, thinking Lee would be caught unaware in Fredericksburg.

But Lee, who had been keeping a watch on Hooker, quietly moved his men out of Fredericksburg to face the threat. He knew his army was in danger. He had fewer than 50,000 men to face 75,000 Federals in the open countryside. There was no high ground to give him the advantage he had enjoyed in Fredericksburg. Lee rushed Stonewall Jackson's men ahead to blunt Hooker's advance. To the Confederates' surprise, Hooker pulled back into defensive works when faced with the first wave of Confederates.

After that initial attack, J. E. B. Stuart's cavalry discovered something about Hooker's position. Hooker's right flank was "in the air," meaning that

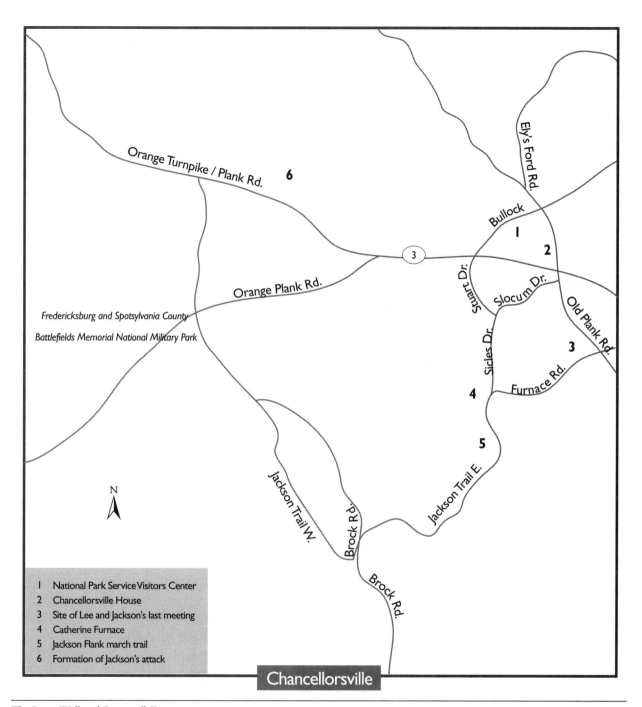

Orange Turnpike / Plank Rd. **6**

Ely's Ford Rd.

Bullock

1

2

Stuart Dr.

Slocum Dr.

Orange Plank Rd.

③

Fredericksburg and Spotsylvania County

Battlefields Memorial National Military Park

Sicles Dr.

Old Plank Rd.

3

Furnace Rd.

4

5

Jackson Trail E.

N

Jackson Trail W.

Brock Rd.

Brock Rd.

1	National Park Service Visitors Center
2	Chancellorsville House
3	Site of Lee and Jackson's last meeting
4	Catherine Furnace
5	Jackson Flank march trail
6	Formation of Jackson's attack

Chancellorsville

it was not anchored to anything defensible, such as a ridge line, a river, or deeply dug trenches. The soldiers on the far right side were vulnerable to attack because they were camping in the open.

That night, Lee and Jackson sat on two cracker boxes to discuss what they should do with Stuart's information. Lee proposed that Jackson follow a road out of sight of the Federals. That road eventually emptied on to the Orange Turnpike or Plank Road (what is now Va. 3) on the flank of the Federals.

Lee, who thought up the basic plan, asked Jackson how many troops he would take with him.

"My whole corps" was the reply. The departure of Jackson's 28,000 men would leave Lee with 14,000 to face the Federals, who had 75,000 troops.

Early the next morning, Jackson sat shivering around a fire waiting for the appropriate time to move his men. Just then, his sword, which had been leaning against a tree all night, fell to the ground. Nervous officers glanced at one another. Since the Crusades, an untouched sword that falls to the ground has been considered a bad omen.

Mounted at the head of his column, Jackson met again with Lee. No one was close enough to hear the words the two spoke, but Jackson's gesture was enough. He thrust his arm westward. Lee nodded, and the two generals parted for the last time.

Jackson's column was spotted almost immediately by Federal lookouts posted in the trees at Hazel Grove, a farm located about a mile toward the Union lines. The Federal cannons opened up, and the Confederates scurried out of the way. The sighting was actually good for the Confederates. When word of Jackson's movement reached Hooker, the Union general assumed it meant that the Confederates were retreating, rather than fighting. Oddly, he made no move to attack what he assumed was a beaten column.

Jackson's 6-mile-long column snaked through the woods all day long until it finally reached the Orange Turnpike or Plank Road again. Quietly, Jackson placed his men in a mile-long battle line facing east. At 5:15 P.M., the men started forward. Rabbits and deer ran ahead of them, bursting out of the tangled undergrowth into the camps of the Union's 11th Corps, whose men had stacked arms and were eating dinner.

It was Jackson's good luck that those men were likely the most inexperienced and unappreciated troops in the Federal army. The 11th Corps was made up mostly of German immigrants, many of whom had been taken off the boats in New York and put into blue uniforms before they even had a chance to learn English.

As soon as the Germans saw the onrushing Confederates, they ran—for a while. But then they began to organize themselves, and resistance became stiffer. On Jackson's far right, one of his more inexperienced generals halted his men in the belief that they were about to be attacked. Jackson's advance slowed at just the time when it needed to be gaining speed.

As darkness grew, the impatient Jackson rode beyond the safety of his own lines to determine if the attack could continue using the light of the full moon. He and his aides made an error. They did not inform the nervous Confederates on the front line that they would be on a scouting mission.

Jackson rode several hundred yards into no man's land despite the warning from his aides that he was vulnerable to Federal snipers. He stopped only when he heard the sound of Federal axes felling trees to be thrown up as breastworks. Convinced now that he had to relaunch the attack before the Federals dug in, Jackson wheeled his horse and started back toward his own lines.

The party was heading southwest along a little-used trail called the Mountain Road when a single shot from the Confederates rang out. Then a few more shots were fired. One of Jackson's men rode toward the firing, shouting that they were friends. However, just a few minutes earlier, a Union officer scouting the Confederate lines had shouted the same thing and escaped back to Federal lines. And now Jackson and his party were coming from the direction of the Federals.

After the first ragged shots came a full volley, ordered by the major of the 18th North Carolina. Ten of the 19 men in Jackson's party were hit. Four were killed instantly.

Jackson was wounded in the upper left arm and through his right hand. Aides eased him to the ground. Within minutes, a stretcher was brought forward to bear him to the rear. A Federal shell then hit one of the stretcher bearers, and Jackson was tossed heavily to the ground. Minutes later, he was again dropped when one of the litter bearers tripped over a root.

When Lee heard that Jackson was hurt, he ordered Stuart to take command of the corps. The fighting died down that night, despite Jackson's wish that matters be pressed. The next morning, Stuart resumed the attack, pushing Hooker back toward the Rappahannock. Lee split his army once again, rushing reinforcements to Salem Church to stop Sedgwick. By the end of the day, both Hooker and Sedgwick pulled back.

It was a costly battle for both sides. The Federals lost 17,000 men, killed and wounded, and the Confederates 13,000. At the time, it was thought that Jackson would be out of commission for a while. Though it seemed likely that his arm would have to be amputated, many men before him had lost their arms and returned to fight.

But Jackson would not come back.

Start your exploration inside the museum. If you are interested in continuing with The Overland Campaign Tour after you complete the present tour, ask at the desk for a parking pass for Ellwood, a plantation house visited in the Wilderness portion of the next chapter.

When you are ready to leave the museum, walk to the left around the back of the building, where you'll see a monument to Jackson at the spot where the general was first tended.

Continue around the back of the museum; the path will direct you to the spot where historians now believe Jackson was shot while coming down the Mountain Road, which has mostly disappeared. The 18th North Carolina was stationed across what is now Va. 3 opposite the visitor center.

Return to your car. Turn right out of the parking lot on to Bullock Road. Drive to the intersection with C.R. 610 (Ely's Ford Road) and turn right. Across the road is a marker showing Hooker's last line of defense.

Drive 0.7 mile on C.R. 610 and pull off before crossing Va. 3 to view the ruined foundation of the Chancellorsville House. Hooker was almost killed here when a Confederate shell struck a pillar on which he was leaning.

Cross Va. 3, drive 1 mile to Furnace Road, and turn right. This is the spot where Lee and Jackson, perched on cracker boxes, held their last council of war.

Drive 0.9 mile on Furnace Road and pull over. This is where Jackson's column was located when Federal scouts in the trees at Hazel Grove, a mile to the north, spotted it. The scouts thought it meant that the Confederates were retreating.

Continue on Furnace Road. Matthew Fontaine Maury, the man who charted the seas, was born in the middle of the woods near here.

Drive another 0.4 mile and turn left to visit Catherine Furnace. In the 1840s, this was a working furnace that processed iron for the manufacture of farm tools. It was operated by the Wellford family, whose son, Colonel Charles Wellford, later acted as a guide for Jackson on his march through the area.

It was here at the furnace that the 23rd Georgia fought a rear-guard action that saved Jackson's flank march from being discovered. What historians have not determined is why the captured Georgians did not reveal Jackson's march. Maybe they simply kept their mouths shut. Or maybe the Federals assumed the Confederates were retreating and didn't bother to ask.

You'll see Jackson Trail East across the parking lot at Catherine Furnace. Assuming the unpaved road is passable, drive southwest on Jackson Trail East, which is the same road Jackson's 28,000 men took. After about 2.7

Catherine Furnace

miles, turn left on the paved Brock Road (C.R. 613), go 0.25 mile, then turn on to the unpaved Jackson Trail West. Jackson intentionally turned left on Brock Road to confirm the Union scouts' suspicion that he was retreating south. But once the head of his column moved down a swale, he turned on to this trail.

Follow Jackson Trail West for 1.5 miles until it again intersects Brock Road. Turn left. After 0.8 mile, you will cross the Orange Plank Road (C.R. 621). Jackson intended to turn right on this road to come in on the Federals' flank, but when he rode ahead to where it intersected the Orange Turnpike or Plank Road (what is now Va. 3), he confirmed that the Federals were too close. He then returned to the column and continued marching his men on Brock Road.

Just after passing the intersection with the Orange Plank Road, you will pass an upturned cannon marking the spot where Union general Alexander Hays was killed on May 5, 1864, during the Battle of the Wilderness. It was Hays who stopped Lee's attack at the stone wall at Gettysburg. It is 1.5 miles to Va. 3. Turn right on to Va. 3.

After about 3.3 miles on Va. 3, you'll see a marker in the median. It was

Jackson Trail East

near this spot that Jackson's men burst out of the woods and into the Union camps. The land is mostly cleared pastures today, but it was heavily wooded at the time of the battle. The fighting took place from this point to where the visitor center stands today, 2 miles east. It was here that Jackson's men, giving the Rebel yell, had their finest moment.

For the sake of convenience, the tour ends back at the visitor center. If you plan to continue with The Overland Campaign Tour and have not yet picked up a parking pass for Ellwood, you should do so at this point.

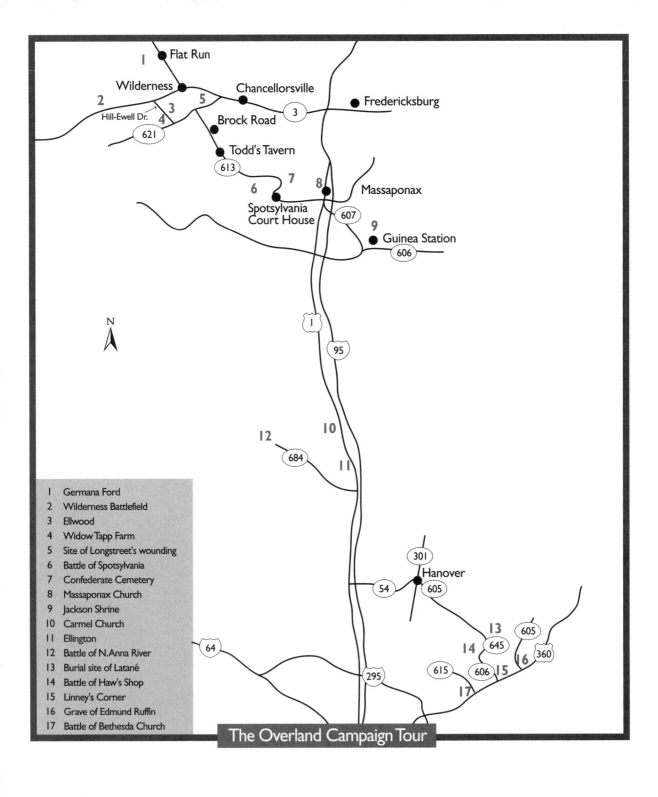

The Overland Campaign Tour

The Overland Campaign Tour

This tour starts near the Wilderness, just west of Chancellorsville. The Wilderness looks nothing like it did in 1864, but you can still visit some of the sites that brought terror to both sides, including a spot where Lee was in grave danger. Next, the tour visits Spotsylvania Court House, a battlefield that was contested for nearly two weeks and that saw some of the worst fighting of the war. From there, it follows the route of Jackson's ambulance to the Jackson Shrine, where the general died in bed. It then moves to the North Anna River, where some of the best surviving Civil War trenches are preserved. From there, it heads toward Richmond, stopping at several historical sites.

The tour is 90 miles long and will occupy a full day.

THE TOUR STARTS where the previous one ended—at the National Park Service visitor center for the Chancellorsville Battlefield, located off Va. 3 about 7 miles west of I-95. You will need to pick up a parking pass for Ellwood from the visitor center before beginning this tour.

From the visitor center, drive west on Va. 3 for 3.9 miles, where you'll see a historical marker detailing the amputation of Stonewall Jackson's arm. The amputation was performed on the southern side of the road in a hospital set up at the Wilderness Tavern. Jackson's physician, Hunter Holmes McGuire, did the surgery early in the morning on May 3, 1863. The arm was carefully wrapped by Jackson's chaplain, J. Tucker Lacy, and taken across the road and up the hill to the family cemetery at Ellwood, a house belonging to Lacy's brother. Ellwood was owned by the same man who owned Chatham, the home above Fredericksburg that was used by the Federals to shell the town.

Bear right at the traffic light to stay on Va. 3; you are now heading north. In about 4.5 miles, you will cross the Rapidan River. At the first opportunity, make a U-turn and head back south on Va. 3. Just after recrossing the river, turn right on to the unnamed gravel road and make your way down to the river.

This is Germana Ford, one of the principal crossings of the Rapidan since colonial times and one of the fords used by the Federals at Chancellorsville and the Wilderness. It was the crossing by the Federal Fifth

Germana Ford

and Sixth Corps on May 4, 1864, that opened the battle at the Wilderness and the Overland Campaign. The crossing was observed by Confederates on Clark's Mountain, to the west. The Federals laid two pontoon bridges on the river and poured across, confident that Lee would be caught unaware.

About the time that the Federals were crossing the river, the new commander of all the Union armies, General Ulysses S. Grant, was telling the commander of the Army of the Potomac, George Meade, that the objective was Lee's army. Wherever Lee went, the Union army would go. This was a drastic change in strategy in the Eastern theater. For the first three years of the war, the Union army had concentrated on geographical objectives, such as Manassas and Richmond, or had sought individual battles with Lee. When the Federals suffered losses such as those under McClellan and Pope, they had pulled back and thought of a new strategy. But now, Grant was informing Meade and Lincoln that under his command, there would be no more pulling back.

This new strategy amused some Union officers. When someone asked Lieutenant Colonel Horace Porter, a Grant aide, how long it would take to reach Richmond after crossing Germana Ford, Porter replied confidently, "Four days, but if General Lee objects, the trip could be prolonged."

General Lee did indeed object.

Return on Va. 3 to the traffic light at the intersection with Va. 20 and turn right on to Va. 20. Drive slowly. After 0.5 mile, turn left on to an unmarked drive leading into the woods; you'll see a small white sign on the edge of the culvert. The drive may be blocked by a cable. If so, park to one side and leave your Ellwood parking pass visible on the dashboard, so rangers can see it. This visit to the burial site of Jackson's arm may require a round-trip walk of about 1 mile. If the drive is not blocked, you may continue in your car to Ellwood.

The National Park Service is restoring the house located here. The grounds were a staging area for the Battle of the Wilderness. Grant made his headquarters about several hundred yards away from the house, across what is now Va. 20. Early in the battle, Confederate batteries began to find the range of Grant's headquarters. Someone quietly suggested that the general might think about moving to safety. Grant, who had no fear of death,

Ellwood

said, "It strikes me that we should order up our own artillery and make them move."

The Lacy family cemetery is about 100 yards southeast of the house down a path. The stone over Jackson's arm is the only monument in the cemetery. Since the stone was not erected until 1903 by one of Jackson's staff members, it is doubtful that the Federals knew what was buried here. Nor did they find the raincoat that Jackson wore the night he was shot. It was initially stored in a shed on the property, since its new owner had no idea of its historical significance.

Stone marking the burial site of Jackson's arm

Buried for a time in an unmarked grave beside the arm was Captain James Keith Boswell, Jackson's chief of engineers, who was killed at age 24 by the same volley that wounded Jackson.

It was Boswell upon whom Jackson depended to find the quickest and best routes for his army. And Jackson depended upon Boswell's best friend and tent mate, Jed Hotchkiss, when he wanted a map of the route Boswell had selected. Jackson had great trust in Boswell. For example, when he learned that Boswell had a girlfriend in Fauquier County, that was enough incentive for Jackson to send the young engineer into the county to find the roads that would place Jackson's corps at the rear of Pope's army in August 1862. Boswell thus helped position Jackson's corps for Second Manassas. He also helped lay out Jackson's flank march at Chancellorsville. After Lee and Jackson ordered him on a night reconnoitering mission of the Union front on May 1, 1863, Boswell reported back that the Yankee center and left were impregnable. That sewed up the strategy to attack the Union right.

After Boswell did not return the night Jackson was wounded, Hotchkiss went looking for him the next morning. He found his friend near where Jackson had been wounded, dead with two bullets in the heart, though "his look in death was peaceful and pleasant as in life," according to Hotchkiss. He took Boswell to the family cemetery at Ellwood, where Jackson's arm had been buried earlier in the day. As the moon rose, Hotchkiss wrapped his friend in his uniform and lowered him into a grave. Lacy, Jackson's chaplain, offered a prayer.

"I wept for him like a brother. He was kind and gentle and with as few faults as most men. Peace to his memory," wrote Hotchkiss in his journal.

Boswell's body was later moved to the Fredericksburg cemetery.

Return to your vehicle and continue west on Va. 20 for about 1.5 miles to the Wilderness Shelter Exhibit. The 2-mile trail that starts behind the shelter is one of two walking tours for the Battle of the Wilderness. This particular trail covers the ground where General John B. Gordon attacked the Union right flank.

Tactically, Grant could not have picked a worse place to start his war against Lee than the Wilderness, which was called that for very good reason. The region was one massive thicket heavy with low-lying, tangled vines and underbrush that farmers had never bothered to try to clear away. They simply farmed around it and let nature have its way. There were few roads and hardly any paths through the growth. It was not meant to be a battlefield.

But Grant knew that Lee's army was nearby, and Lee's army was the objective, no matter how poor the battlefield. On May 4, 1864, nearly 120,000 men, accompanied by horses, wagons, and artillery, pushed across Germana Ford on their way to find Lee.

Observing from Clark's Mountain, Lee could not believe his luck and Grant's audacity. The Union commander was going to try to push his way through the most untamed part of Virginia. Lee rushed two corps—one under Ewell along the Orange Turnpike (what is now Va. 20) and the other under A. P. Hill along the Orange Plank Road (what is now C.R. 621)—to meet the Federals. Coming along behind would be Longstreet's First Corps.

Though the Confederates were outnumbered two to one, Lee figured he would be able to use the Wilderness as a defensive position. In fact, because it was so difficult for either army to maneuver in the brush, the battle was fought along the two roads leading into the Wilderness, creating two entirely separate actions going on at the same time within 3 miles of each other.

The Federal Fifth Corps under General Gouverneur K. Warren found Ewell's men along Saunders Field, behind this shelter, early in the morning on May 5. The undergrowth worked against both sides, as the lines were easily broken and units were easily separated from their commands. Confederate general John Marshall Jones, an 1841 graduate of West Point who later served as an instructor there, was shot from his horse and instantly killed on the far side of the field during the afternoon.

The fighting continued until that night. Fires started by musket and cannon flashes raged over the battlefield, burning the wounded of both sides alive. The armies could do nothing to help their fallen comrades.

Near the end of the day, after lobbying Lee long and hard, General John B. Gordon received permission to launch an assault on Grant's right flank. That assault crushed the resistance. Had Lee agreed earlier, the Confederates might have rolled all the way to Grant's headquarters. But just as Jackson's flank assault at Chancellorsville had bogged down in the growing darkness, so did Gordon's attack.

At the same time that the northern part of the battle was being launched, Hill's men were 3 miles away marching north to try to seize the intersection at Brock Road (what is now C.R. 613). Jackson had used that road to surprise the Union right flank just a year earlier. If the Confederates could reach the intersection and entrench themselves along both roads, they would be able to choke off any Union advance.

Having figured out the same thing, Grant rushed a Union division to the crossroads first. Federal reinforcements came up from Winfield Scott Hancock. Slowly but surely, Hill's men were pushed south along the Orange Plank Road.

Then, in the nick of time, Longstreet's men came up to crash into the advancing Federals, much as had happened 18 months earlier when Hill's division showed up to save Longstreet at Sharpsburg.

Over the course of two days of fighting, Grant watched as first his right flank and then his left were pushed back in on him by a force half his size. He suffered 18,000 casualties, compared to 11,000 for the Confederates.

After walking the trail, return to your vehicle and continue west on Va. 20 for 0.2 mile. Turn left on Hill-Ewell Drive, a park road that did not exist during the war. It is easy to see that the Wilderness is not what it once was. Houses are scattered in the woods along the left side of the road.

After 0.7 mile, pull to the right at the Higgerson Farm, which was one of the three major clearings in the Wilderness. Federal troops trampled the garden of Mrs. Permelia Higgerson, who shouted at them and swore that they would regret what they had done to her farm. After battling Ewell's men, the Federals retreated past Mrs. Higgerson, who taunted them. One

Pennsylvania officer commented that the troops had not paid much attention to her on the way in, but that when they were on their way out, he found himself admitting that she was right.

What the Pennsylvanians encountered at the Higgerson Farm was "the champion mud hole of all mud holes," as one soldier put it. Once they got into the mudhole, the Confederates let them have it. The Federals were so shocked at the attack that one of their regiments poured fire into the regiment right in front of it; unfortunately, it turned out to be another Pennsylvania regiment.

The real blame for the retreat, one soldier said, lay in the fact that all the officers were too drunk to issue orders.

Continue 0.5 mile to the Chewning Farm, the high ground of the battle. This low plateau offered the Federals a clear view to the west (where fighting was going on at Parker's Store along the Orange Plank Road) and to the north (toward the crossroads). The division of Federals occupying this ground was not happy about it, as it was almost surrounded by Confederates. The Federals were eventually pushed off the high ground.

Continue 2 miles to C.R. 621 (Orange Plank Road) and turn right. After 0.5 mile, you will reach Widow Tapp Farm, the scene of one of the most dramatic moments of the war. Pull into the parking lot past the monuments. A walking trail takes in this part of the battlefield.

This was the location of Lee's headquarters during most of the battle, as it was one of the largest cleared areas in the forest, encompassing about 300 yards of open space. On the other hand, it was not a safe place. Early on May 5, Lee, Stuart, and Hill were conferring when they looked up and saw a line of Federal skirmishers emerging from the woods just yards away. Apparently not recognizing the important men they were seeing, the spooked Federals turned around and disappeared back into the woods.

On the morning of May 6, Lee was facing disaster. Hill's Third Corps was exhausted. As the men came down the road toward Lee's headquarters, their slow retreat became a run, almost a rout. If the whole corps collapsed, the Union forces would pour in behind it, and the Confederate army would be lost.

At just the right moment, Longstreet's First Corps came up the Orange Plank Road, holding its line of march despite the flood of retreating men rushing past it. As Lee looked to the north beyond his last-ditch line of artillery defending the road, the first regiment of Longstreet's men came into view to the south, behind Lee. Lee knew they must be Longstreet's troops, but he didn't recognize the general leading them. It was John Gregg, who had not before served with Lee.

Lee dashed up to Gregg. "General, what brigade is this?" he asked.

"It is the Texas Brigade," Gregg said proudly.

"The Texas Brigade has always driven the enemy, and I want them to do it now. Texans always move them!" Lee shouted, waving his hat at the men marching past him. "I want every man to know that I am here with them!"

It took a few moments for the Texans to realize that Lee was speaking literally. He rode his horse along with them, apparently intending to take part in the charge they would be spearheading.

"Go back, General Lee! Go back! Lee to the rear!" the column began to shout.

Lee seemed not to hear the men at first, his eyes fixed on the road to the north, looking for the Yankees he knew were coming.

Finally, General Gregg shook Lee out of his trance and pointed to the men around him, who stared up at Lee. One particularly large Texan grabbed Traveller's reins, making it clear without saying a word that Lee would ride no farther forward.

The dejected Lee turned his horse around after the Texan let go of the reins. Seeing Longstreet, Lee rode back to confer with his corps commander. The 800 Texans again started marching north on the Orange Plank Road. Within a half-hour, nearly 600 of them lay on the road killed or wounded. But their brigade had done its job. It stopped the Federal assault and bought time for the rest of Longstreet's men to come up.

Here on the northern edge of Widow Tapp Farm is a pink granite monument to the Texas Brigade and a small marker engraved "Lee To The Rear!" This marks the spot where Lee's men demonstrated their love for him. Though they did not hesitate to give their own lives, they refused to risk that of their commander.

Drive north on the Orange Plank Road. Just past the intersection with Hill-Ewell Drive is a monument to Union general James Wadsworth, a 56-year-old New York politician and lawyer. Wadsworth should never have

been on the field, since he had no experience leading men in combat. But thanks to his connections, here he was. It was near this spot that Wadsworth ordered a regiment forward to attack down the road. That regiment's colonel was incredulous that any general, experienced or not, would order men from behind a log fort and into the open to fight an advancing enemy. Wadsworth insisted. The colonel said aloud that his men were being led to their deaths.

Wadsworth was shot through the head during the battle. He later died in a Confederate field hospital. After the Federals abandoned their defensive position, the Confederates rolled over it and northward up the road, sending the Federals into a panic.

Continue north for 0.2 mile, where you'll see a large, wooden gray sign on the left. Pull well off the road. It was in this area, less than 5 miles from where Lieutenant General Stonewall Jackson was shot by his own men on May 2, 1863, that Lieutenant General James Longstreet was shot by his own men on May 6, 1864. The circumstances were remarkably similar, though Longstreet's wounding took place in the morning and Jackson's in the evening.

Having marched to the western side of the Orange Plank Road, the men of the 12th Virginia were nervous about being at the front of a column that would soon meet stiff resistance, as the Yankees were less than 0.5 mile north of their position. While the Virginians were pondering their line of march, Longstreet, South Carolina generals Micah Jenkins and Joe Kershaw, and several aides gathered a few hundred yards to the south to confer on how best to attack the crossroads. Longstreet sent a column of men to the southeast to find an unfinished railroad cut, which was to be used as a makeshift road. Then he and his aides formed a column and rode ahead, with Jenkins's men coming behind. Those troops were apparently dressed in dark gray uniforms.

An aide suggested to Longstreet that a lieutenant general—a corps commander in charge of a third of Lee's army—should not be riding at the head of his troops. That was the same warning that an aide had given to Jackson a year earlier. Both generals ignored the advice.

As the column moved forward, the men of the 12th Virginia found their way back on to the road. In their rear, they saw men approaching in dark-colored uniforms. Apparently without orders, the Virginians fired into the troops they believed were Federals who had worked in behind them. Jenkins's men instinctively returned the fire.

Caught in the crossfire was Longstreet and his staff. Jenkins was shot from his saddle, a bullet through his brain; he suffered fits of delirium for hours until his death. Longstreet was lifted from his saddle by the force of the bullet that tore through his throat and shoulder. Kershaw, who was not hit, dashed between the columns shouting "Friends!" until the firing stopped.

Aides lifted Longstreet from his horse and laid him on the ground until stretcher bearers arrived. As the general was carried off, someone laid his hat over his face to shield him from the sun. Still conscious, Longstreet could hear men speculating that he was already dead. To dispel the rumor before it got started, he grabbed the hat and waved it over his head to show that he was alive.

When Lee rode up to Longstreet's ambulance, Longstreet was in no shape to tell him the status of his still unfolding battle plan. Some historians believe Longstreet intended to surprise the Federal left by coming up the unfinished railroad. If the Federal left had been turned, the Confederates could then have pushed the left wing in on the center at the crossroads. Instead, after a long delay while the troops were realigned and new commands were issued, Lee ordered an attack on the Union center. That attack almost succeeded but was ultimately pushed back.

At the end of the two days of fighting, neither side could claim victory. Grant had not crushed the Confederate army. Neither had Lee's two attacks rolled back the Federals. The Wilderness was a draw.

Following the battle, Lee moved toward Spotsylvania Court House, several miles away.

The Union forces—generals and soldiers alike—looked to Grant for leadership. In one direction lay the fords across the Rappahannock River; after Chancellorsville the previous year, the Union army had headed back north to lick its wounds before going after Lee again. This time, Grant rode to the crossroads and waved his hand south. He was going to chase Lee. For the first time, a Union general who had fought Lee was going to follow him. It marked a turning point in the war.

Continue to the intersection with C.R. 613 (Brock Road), the center of Hancock's line and the focus of Lee's attack. Turn right on C.R. 613 and head south. This is the same route that Warren's Fifth Corps and Hancock's Second Corps took on their way to Spotsylvania Court House. It is also the route that Stonewall Jackson's ambulance followed in carrying him away from the battlefield in May 1863.

It is 4.4 miles to Todd's Tavern, the site of a cavalry clash the day after the Wilderness.

Continue about 3.75 miles to the Spotsylvania Battlefield. Turn left and stop at the shelter to view the exhibit. At the entrance to the battlefield is a monument to John Sedgwick, marking the spot where the Union general was killed.

It is hard to categorize Spotsylvania Court House as a battle. Most engagements during the war lasted anywhere from several hours to three days. The Seven Days Battles around Richmond lasted a full week. Spotsylvania Court House lasted twice that.

The battle began just two days after the Wilderness ended. The stubborn Grant, sore at fighting Lee to a draw though he had twice the men, tried to outmarch Lee toward Richmond. When Lee discovered what Grant was doing, he rushed his leading division toward Spotsylvania Court House and won the race. On May 8, the Confederates started fighting from entrenchments set up just northwest of the town.

It was vicious fighting for nearly two weeks. Early in the battle, a fire broke out in Spindle's Field, a no man's land between the two sides' trenches that was filled with Federal wounded. Some South Carolinians tried to rescue the Federals from the approaching flames, but when Northern sharpshooters started picking off the would-be rescuers, the South Carolinians were ordered back to their trenches. Both sides were forced to listen to the screams as the flames reached the helpless men.

On May 9, General John Sedgwick, commander of the Federal Sixth Corps, visited the front trenches, located near where Brock Road and today's National Park Service road intersect. When he and his aides arrived, they were warned about a particularly good Southern sharpshooter, who had wounded some men in a nearby Union artillery battery. Sedgwick's aide elicited a promise from his commander that he would not get near the cannons. In fact, Sedgwick joked about it, asking who was in charge of the corps—he, a major general, or the aide, a major.

That was just like Sedgwick, a 50-year-old West Point graduate who was fondly known by his men as "Uncle John." A fighting general, he had been hit three times when his brigade was attacked from three sides at Sharpsburg in September. Always a joker, he remarked that he hoped the next time he got a bullet, it would finish him, as he found this wounding business painful.

May 9 was intended as a day of rest for the men, but Sedgwick, always thinking of their safety, ordered some of them to dig deeper trenches to better shield themselves. After a while, he noticed that they were digging the trenches in front of the battery of cannons—a stupid position, since they would face the danger of Confederate fire directed at the cannons, as well as the danger associated with the concussion of their own guns.

Sedgwick strode forward, apparently forgetting that he had promised not to get near the artillery position. As he was talking to the infantrymen, a few Confederate bullets began to drop. The general, who had been hit in the stomach by a spent ball fired at long distance only the day before, laughed at the efforts of the infantrymen in ducking the minie balls. Chiding the men, he said, "They couldn't hit an elephant at this distance!" He had just finished making his comical observation a second time when the soldiers distinctly heard a dull thud, but no rifle boom.

Sedgwick slowly turned and faced his aide. As the puzzled aide looked at the general, blood began to spurt from a small hole under Sedgwick's left eye. He was dead before he hit the ground.

Sedgwick was right about the minie balls falling among his soldiers. Fired from a great distance, they were reaching the end of their trajectory. Just as he had experienced the day before, anyone hit with a standard minie ball from that distance would likely suffer no more than a hard jolt to the body.

But the general was wrong about the bullet that struck him. It came from a British Whitworth rifle, a specially made .45 caliber sniper's rife that fired a hexagonal bullet. Its effective range was over a mile.

Several men from South Carolina and at least one from Georgia claimed credit for shooting Sedgwick, one of the highest-ranking Federal generals killed during the war.

If you have the energy, you may want to walk the Spotsylvania History Trail, a 7-mile hiking trail that begins near the shelter.

In the interest of time, this tour will follow the driving route through the battlefield, which visits several of the important sites included on the hiking trail, most notably the famous Mule Shoe.

The Mule Shoe was part of the Confederate entrenchments constructed along the battlefield's natural ridges. Because of the lay of the land, the trenches had to be extended outward toward the Federal line in order to take control of the high ground. Thus, the line bulged out toward the Yankees in the shape of a mule shoe, with the open end toward the rear of the Confederate line.

When Lee saw the Mule Shoe, he was unsure about the safety of his lines. True, the Mule Shoe protected the high ground. But on the other hand, it stuck out from the rest of the trenches. It was also the narrowest point of the Confederate line. The Federals would therefore have an open invitation to attack it.

They did just that. The first time the Mule Shoe was attacked was on the evening of May 10. And the man who led the assault was as close to a military genius as the Union army had.

He was Colonel Emory Upton, a 24-year-old who had graduated from West Point in 1861. Upton was unbound by the traditional methods of fighting that the 40- and 50-year-old generals ahead of him practiced. He thought that the time-honored method of fighting—standing in a long ling and firing into the enemy, who also stood in a long line—was outdated.

Upton proposed a lightning-quick thrust, a punch-through at the Mule Shoe during which his men would try to do little actual fighting until they had broken the line. He was given 12 regiments—5,000 soldiers. He also received the promise that he would be made a general if his plan worked.

Upton arranged the men in an arrow shape, three regiments wide and four regiments deep. He ordered his officers to give only one command— "Forward!" He also ordered that no man was to stop to help any wounded.

When Upton's men poured out of the woods at a dead run, the Confederates were surprised. Charges weren't usually carried out until the final 20 yards or so. They never covered 200 yards.

By the time the Confederates fired one or two volleys, thousands of running Yankees were cutting into their lines. The punch plan had worked. The two sides thrust at each other with bayonets and knives, one of the few times during the entire war when bayonets were used extensively in battle.

But as the minutes dragged on, the generals who had been skeptical of Upton's plan let him down. His 12 regiments had punched through the line, but Grant did not immediately send enough supporting troops into the breach. The only soldiers who tried to help were repulsed. Upton thought he had ordered the last regiments in line to hold back in reserve, but he found them in the Confederate lines. When he looked back to the Union lines, he found that no one else was coming to help him.

More and more Confederates rushed to the breach. Men who had been captured by the Federals early in the attack now overpowered their guards and sprinted back to their lines.

Finally, Upton had no choice but to retreat. His temporary success in breaking the Confederate line had come at the cost of 1,000 men—20 percent of his force. When he looked at the Union generals who had watched him break the Confederate line, he must have been disgusted that they had not sent the entire army into the breach. But he kept his views private. He had motivation. The next day, his commander kept his promise and made him a general.

Upton survived the war. He served five years as the commandant at West Point, which allowed him the opportunity to teach the cadets his theories on warfare.

But he had little chance to enjoy his postwar life. Once, during a visit to the post dentist, the dentist heard an odd throbbing sound coming from Upton's head. Upton acknowledged that the sound sometimes kept him awake at night.

He suffered terrible migraine headaches that prevented him from sleeping. He also endured memory loss. In 1881, Upton killed himself with his service revolver while stationed in San Francisco. A doctor who knew him speculated that the headaches and the odd throbbing sound may have been caused by a brain tumor.

Two days after Upton's assault at Spotsylvania, Grant tried the same thing. This time, he used an entire corps—Hancock's Second. And he started at 4:30 A.M., rather than 6:00 P.M., as Upton had been ordered to do.

Monument at Bloody Angle

The Southerners were shocked to see nearly 30,000 men rushing at them across an open field. The resulting battle lasted almost 20 hours, much of it in a rainstorm. Eyewitness accounts agree that it was the most savage fighting of the war, man to man, bayonet to bayonet. The air was so thick with minie balls that a 20-inch-thick tree in the Confederate trenches was cut down by them; the trunk of that tree is on display in the Smithsonian Institution in Washington, D.C. A portion of the Mule Shoe was renamed "the Bloody Angle" in memory of the fighting that took place there.

Confederate general Abner Perrin was hit by seven minie balls and killed while leading his men in a counterattack. The general did something very foolish—he rode his horse and made himself an obvious target. Before the battle started, he had joked to a friend that it would leave him either a live major general or a dead brigadier. He thus predicted his own death.

When the Federals finally penetrated the Bloody Angle—thanks in part to the withdrawal of some supporting artillery at Lee's order—the Confederates went swarming back toward Lee's headquarters near the Harrison House. As General John Gordon was gathering his men to make a stand, he noticed Lee edging forward on Traveller. Finally, it struck Gordon what

Lee was doing. He was planning to personally lead the counterattack, just as he had tried to do less than two weeks earlier among the Texans on the Orange Plank Road.

Gordon rode up and grabbed Traveller's bridle. "You must not expose yourself," he told Lee. "Your life is too valuable to the army and to the Confederacy for you to risk it so wantonly. We are Georgians. We are Virginians, we need no such encouragement. These men will not fail you today, will you, boys?"

The regiments shouted no. Some of the men crowded in front of Traveller, intentionally blocking the horse from enemy fire with their bodies. Others physically turned Traveller away from the front.

Gordon led Lee's horse away and handed the reins to a soldier. By that time, the Federals were no more than 60 yards away. The men who had protected their general just moments ago now charged toward the enemy and disappeared into the smoke. That charge blunted the Federal attack, giving Lee time to form another line 400 yards south of the Bloody Angle.

On the morning of May 13, the Federals surveyed the ground they had won at the cost of 10,000 Confederates and 9,000 of their own men. The sights they recorded in print can still sicken a reader today. One Union soldier assigned to burial detail recalled that many of the bodies were unrecognizable as men because they had been hit so many times. They were "more like masses of jelly," he wrote. Another examined a dead friend and determined that the man had been hit so many times that he could not measure four inches in any direction on the body without finding a bullet hole.

After two weeks of fighting, the Confederates had retreated about 400 yards. They were waiting for a Federal attack in trenches just as strong as those they had occupied earlier. Both armies had lost about a third of their effective strength, but the Confederates still had great confidence in their leader.

On the other side, Grant's generals were unsure of their new commander. In three weeks, he had thrown his men into two of the most vicious battles of the war, and though he had outnumbered Lee better than two to one, he had not won either fight. They were not sure that Grant would last any longer than the generals before him. Sure, Grant would fight, but if he started many more battles like these two, his army would be destroyed.

Today, it is hard to imagine the frightful scenes that took place here. The battlefield in front of the Confederate trenches is open and dotted with a few Federal monuments. The Confederate trench line has almost disappeared, though there is a marker showing the location of the tree cut down by Federal rifle balls.

East of the Bloody Angle about 300 yards is the McCoull House, located near where Gordon stopped Lee from riding forward. A sign marks the spot.

Site of the McCoull house

Follow the park road to C.R. 208. Turn right and follow C.R. 208 toward the town of Spotsylvania Court House. After 0.5 mile, you'll reach a Confederate cemetery, located back off the road to the left. All of the Confederates here are buried by state.

Continue into town. Turn left at the light on to C.R. 608 and look for the Spotsylvania County Museum on the right. The museum offers some relics from the battle and a nice diorama of the action.

Continue south on C.R. 608 for 5.5 miles to Massaponax Church. A photographer climbed into the attic of this church and took a remarkable series of photographs of Grant and his staff sitting in the churchyard on pews that had been removed from inside. Most photographs of the day were carefully posed in studios because of the need for the subject to remain still for at least six seconds. By contrast, these appear to have captured a real staff meeting, with generals looking at maps, newspapers, and orders. What they depict is Grant planning his next try at Lee. Two oak trees that look to be the same size as the ones in the original photos stand in the churchyard today, giving the impression the churchyard is still in the 1860s. These photos of Grant and his staff can be found in any good photographic history covering the Overland Campaign.

Massaponax Church

Just past the church, turn right on U.S. 1 South. Get into the left lane and turn left on C.R. 607 (Guinea Station Road) after 0.3 mile; you'll see a brown sign indicating that this is the Stonewall Jackson Ambulance Route. Follow C.R. 607 for 5.3 miles until it ends at C.R. 606. Turn left, drive across a railroad track, and turn immediately left into the Stonewall Jackson Shrine.

Jackson arrived here on May 4, 1864, after riding 27 miles from Wilderness Tavern in an ambulance. His doctors intended for him to convalesce here before going aboard the train to Richmond. Instead of putting him in the plantation house owned by Thomas C. Chandler, they placed Jackson in a small, white office building, as it would be easier to control visitors there and would also be more quiet. When Jackson arrived, he apologized to Mr. Chandler for not being able to shake hands with him, as he had been shot in the palm of that hand.

For the first few days, Jackson seemed to be on the road to recovery, which cheered his friend and doctor, Hunter Holmes McGuire, and his black servant, Jim Lewis, both of whom stayed by his side constantly. Then, on Thursday, May 7, five days after his wounding, Jackson awoke to pain in his side. McGuire listened to his chest and felt his pulse. He suspected the onset of pneumonia, as Jackson had complained of a cold before he was shot. The pain from the gunshots and from being dropped several times while he was being rushed to the rear on a stretcher had probably strained his immune system.

McGuire gave Jackson a mixture of opium and whiskey to keep him sedated while he sent for other doctors. He worried that there was nothing anyone could do for the general. That evening, Jackson's wife and daughter

Guinea Station, where Jackson died

arrived from Richmond. When Anna saw her husband, she knew he would never recover.

Over the next two days, several doctors came to see Jackson. All of them agreed that pneumonia was taking over his lungs and that nothing could stop it. Anna finally told her husband on Saturday that the doctors agreed his case was hopeless. Jackson asked Dr. McGuire's opinion, and he told Jackson the truth. That night, Jackson asked that Anna and her brother, an aide to the general, sing him a hymn.

On Sunday morning, May 10, Anna and the doctors told Jackson that he would die that day. When he realized it was Sunday, he said that he "preferred" to die on the Lord's day. Anna asked him where he would like to be buried, and he said Lexington. Finally, they brought baby Julia in to see her father for the last time. He managed to stroke her head and call her "Little Comforter."

Late that morning, Jackson said aloud to the people in the room, "It is the Lord's day. My wish is fulfilled. I always wished to die on Sunday."

As word spread across the plantation, men gathered around the little house. As Jackson began to slip into unconsciousness, he called out orders to various generals and aides. He called for his old Confederate antagonist, A. P. Hill, whom he had often criticized: "He must come up!"

At 3:15 P.M. on May 10, 1863, Jackson seemed to relax. According to McGuire, he looked up, appeared to see something, smiled, and then said, "Let us cross over the river and rest under the shade of the trees." Moments later, he died.

The house is frequently open for touring, but if you find it closed, walk to the side and peer in the window, where you'll see the bed in which Jackson died. On the mantel is the clock McGuire looked at to record the exact time of Jackson's death. Everything in the room is just as it was when Jackson was here.

When you are ready to leave, turn left on Va. 606 and drive 0.5 mile, then turn right into the parking lot at the country store.

Across the road is the Motley House. In 1864, Grant, chasing Lee after Spotsylvania Court House, stopped at this house and absently put his cigar down on a bench. As the cigar began to burn into the wood, Mr. Motley, a very brave or very foolhardy man, berated Grant for damaging his property.

Grant took up his cigar and did not burn down Mr. Motley's house.

Turn around and stay on C.R. 606, heading west. After about 5 miles, you will cross I-95. Just beyond the interstate is U.S. 1. Turn left to head south on U.S. 1. It is 13.7 miles to C.R. 658. Turn right, then immediately left into Carmel Baptist Church. On May 23, 1864, Grant's scattered corps used this church as a gathering spot before attacking Lee, who had set up a defensive line on the North Anna River, just south of here.

Return to U.S. 1 and continue south. After 2.5 miles, turn right on C.R. 689 (Ox Ford Road). Slow down at the house located on the left 0.4 mile down C.R. 689. Just past the house, you'll see the remnants of a road heading down the slope. This road led to the Chesterfield Bridge over the North Anna.

Get back on U.S. 1 and cross the North Anna. If traffic permits, slow down and look at the brick house to the right. This is Ellington, a home where several generals on opposing sides were almost killed. A Union artillery shell slammed into the front section of the house, narrowly missing Lee when he stopped here. A few days later, Burnside and Hancock were at the house when a Confederate artillery shell exploded in the front yard, narrowly missing them.

In 0.2 mile, you'll reach some historical markers describing the action here.

Continue south on U.S. 1 for 2 miles, then turn right on C.R. 684 and follow the signs for North Anna Battlefield Park, which is maintained by Hanover County. It is 2.6 miles to the park, located next to a quarry.

Do not despair at the closeness of the quarry, which is actually hidden from view by tall berms, or believe that the noise of the heavy equipment is an intrusion on yet another piece of history. This park may be the best-preserved Civil War battlefield in the country. If you have to pick just one battlefield walking tour to take, choose this one, particularly if your traveling companions like to complain that they have no interest in or understanding of Civil War battles. The people who preserved this battlefield, The Blue-Gray Education Society, installed detailed signs at 10 stops. The signs explain the battle as seen from each vantage point. The Confederate earthworks here are so well preserved that they still have the traverses— mounds of dirt for the Confederates to duck behind if they were flanked.

The Battle of North Anna River, fought from May 23 to May 26, 1864, was part of Grant's slow push toward Richmond and his pursuit of Lee. Grant could never move his army as fast as Lee's, so Lee was able to get south of the river and dig in, putting the natural defense of the river in front of him. What Lee did not count on was the speed at which Grant pursued him. Grant's army came up so quickly that Lee was unable to burn the Chesterfield Bridge behind him. Hancock's men took the bridge and poured across the river toward Lee's southern side.

But the river also worked to Lee's advantage, since Grant had to break up his army into three pieces. And the river's winding course meant that those pieces could not easily rejoin into one.

Lee formed his army into an inverted **V** shape, the tip of the **V** pointing at an obvious place to cross, Ox Ford. One Yankee general took the bait. That was James H. Ledlie, a New York civil engineer who bore the distinction of being a coward, an alcoholic, and the worst general in the Union army. Ledlie sent his brigade right at the point of Lee's **V**. As the soldiers, who hated the drunken Ledlie, reluctantly advanced, Confederates swept out from either side of the **V** and smashed them. Ledlie was not there to

Confederate trenches at North Anna River

share their fate. He was behind the lines drinking.

Upriver at Jericho Mills, A. P. Hill tried to force Warren's Federals back to the northern side of the river, but he failed. Lee confronted Hill. Though it was uncharacteristic of him to become publicly angry with one of his generals, he openly asked Hill, "Why can't you be like Jackson?"

Hill, who had no answer to a question like that, was forced to fall back to the left leg of the **V**.

Downriver, the Federals made no further headway, though they did reach the southern side of the river.

Even though his army was outnumbered, Lee had the Federals where he wanted them, in three pieces and unable to communicate easily with each other. But then nature took over. Lee became violently ill with diarrhea and was confined to his tent. Hill, who had failed to throw back the Yankees on the left flank, was also sick. Longstreet's wounds would keep him down for weeks.

For some reason, Lee did not turn over the task of crushing Hancock to the Confederate general who faced him, Richard Anderson, who had taken over Longstreet's corps. All Lee did was lie on his cot muttering, "We must strike him [Grant] a blow; we must not let him pass us again!"

Grant finally recognized the trap Lee had laid for him and took the opportunity presented by the strange lull in the action to pull his forces back from the North Anna.

The battle, which cost each side about 2,600 men, was relatively small, but its significance was great in Lee's mind. He believed he had missed his one great opportunity to defeat Grant's army piece by piece.

When you are ready to leave the battlefield, return to U.S. 1, which was Telegraph Road during the war. Turn right, drive 7.2 miles, and turn left on Va. 54 at a traffic light in Ashland. After 5.8 miles, you will reach Hanover Court House. This community was an important rail connection to Richmond and the scene of a small battle in May 1862.

Turn right and drive south on U.S. 301. After 1.5 miles, turn left on C.R. 605 (River Road). Go 6.4 miles and slow down when you see a large white house under some trees on the left. This is Summer Hill Plantation; note that it is private property. Buried on the grounds is Captain William Latané, the only member of Stuart's command to die during the ride around McClellan's army in the summer of 1862. After his death, a painting was commissioned showing his body being lowered into the grave by women and slaves. The mournful scene was published as a print that was sold throughout the South as a fund-raiser for the war effort.

Just past the house, turn right on C.R. 644. It is about 2.5 miles to C.R. 606. A historical marker is located in the churchyard to the right of the intersection.

Today, this area is called Studley. In 1864, it was known as Haw's Shop, after a blacksmith's shop. A dismounted cavalry battle was fought here on May 28, 1864, between the Federals under Generals David Gregg and Alfred Torbert and the Confederates of Fitzhugh Lee and Wade Hampton. The Federals won control of the crossroads during the relatively small fight, but the Confederates exacted a tiny measure of revenge, though they didn't know it at the time. One of the Federals killed at Haw's Shop was John Huff, a 45-year-old member of the Fifth Michigan Cavalry. Seventeen days earlier at Yellow Tavern, just north of Richmond, Huff had put a pistol ball into the side of J. E. B. Stuart. Stuart had died the next day.

Turn left on C.R. 606 (Stutley Road), which is one of the roads Stuart took on his 1862 ride. Drive 3.4 miles to Linney's Corner. This is where Latané was mortally wounded.

In 0.5 mile, you will reach U.S. 360. Turn left and drive 1.2 miles on U.S. 360, then turn left on C.R. 628. To the right near the intersection is Malbourne, now a private home. Malbourne was the wartime estate of Edmund Ruffin.

If the South had a symbolic leader in the decades before the war, Ruffin was he. A self-taught agriculturist, he virtually invented the idea of bringing science to farming. By the 1840s, he was famous for his experiments and his articles on how to replenish soil that had been ruined by mineral-hungry cotton.

As he grew more famous, Ruffin became an outspoken critic of the North, which he felt was trying to free the slaves, whom he believed were essential to the Southern farm economy. When careful Virginia refused to secede with the firebrands of South Carolina, Ruffin moved to the latter state. According to legend, on the night of April 12, 1861, someone handed him the lanyard of a mortar at Fort Johnson, and he fired the first shot at Fort Sumter. He was 67 years old. Pictures taken at the time show him as an old man with below-the-shoulder white hair. He may have been old and un-fashionable, but the fiery look in his eyes was evidence of his unyielding commitment to the South.

Ruffin was really nothing more than a symbol. He never held any office in the Confederate government. All the same, Northerners knew who he was. When the Federals came up the James River in 1862, they made sure they burned his plantation to the ground.

The end of the war found Ruffin at his estate in Amelia County. On June 17, 1865, he wrote a final entry in his diary, discussing how he did not want to live under the domination of "the vile Yankee race." He then wrapped a Confederate flag around his body and shot himself. His body was sent here for burial in his family's cemetery.

Return to U.S. 360 West and turn right to head toward Richmond. After you pass Studley Road, it is about 3.5 miles to C.R. 615. Turn left and follow the signs to Bethesda Church.

It was here on May 30, 1864, that Confederate colonel James B. Terrill was killed in fighting leading up to the Battle of Cold Harbor. Terrill's body was left on the field, where it was buried by the Federals. This was one of the few times in the war that a general officer's body was not returned through the lines. The body was later exhumed and reburied in a family cemetery in Mechanicsville, though the exact site of the general's remains is unknown. It is indeed proper to say *general*. Colonel Terrill's staff later got word that on May 31, the day after he was killed, Terrill had been confirmed as a brigadier general by the Confederate Congress.

His brother, a Union general, had been killed in October 1862 in Kentucky. The Terrills' father, torn by the loss of both sons, supposedly erected a monument to them on or near the family homestead. It was marked, "Only God Knows Who Was Right." That legendary monument has never been found by historians.

The tour ends here.

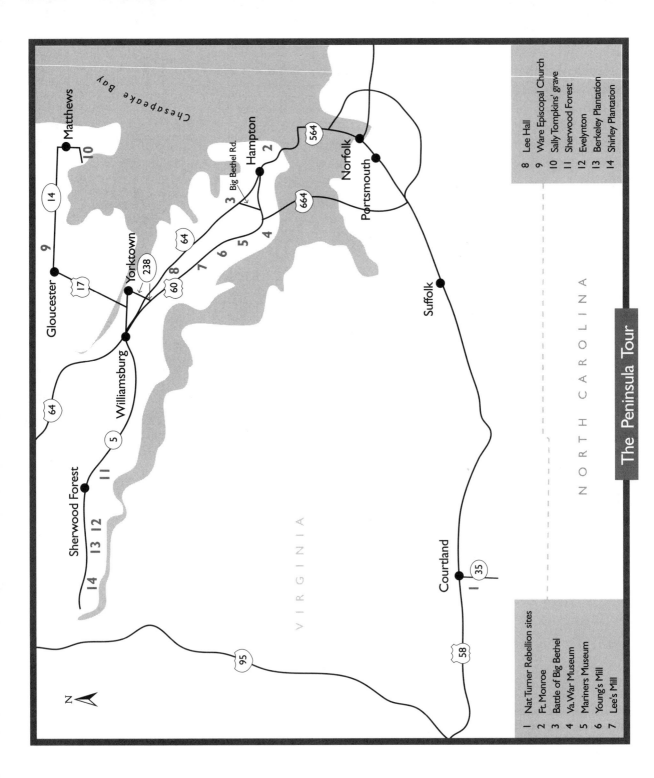

The Peninsula Tour

Chesapeake Bay

Matthews
10
14
9
Gloucester
17
Yorktown
238
60
64
Big Bethel Rd.
Hampton
2
3
564
Norfolk
4
5
6
7
8
664
Portsmouth
Williamsburg
5
64
Sherwood Forest
11
13 12
14
Suffolk
VIRGINIA
95
Courtland
35
1
58
NORTH CAROLINA

N

1   Nat Turner Rebellion sites
2   Ft. Monroe
3   Battle of Big Bethel
4   Va. War Museum
5   Mariners Museum
6   Young's Mill
7   Lee's Mill

8   Lee Hall
9   Ware Episcopal Church
10   Sally Tompkins' grave
11   Sherwood Forest
12   Evelynton
13   Berkeley Plantation
14   Shirley Plantation

The Peninsula Tour

This tour starts at the scene of the worst slave uprising in history, the Nat Turner Revolt, which took place 30 years before the war but was still fresh in the minds of Southerners. It then moves to the coast to visit several museums dedicated to the war's naval history, then traces McClellan's trek up the Peninsula. The tour makes a short side trip to the grave of one of the few true angels of the war, then visits Colonial Williamsburg and the James River plantations.

The tour is approximately 215 miles long and may require three days, due to its length and the number of sites it visits, some of which played minor roles during the Civil War but major roles during the American Revolution.

THE TOUR BEGINS near a town that never experienced the horrors of combat. Rather, horrors occurred here 30 years before the war. The incident that took place in Southampton County created deep-seated fears among whites around the South about what would happen if 4.5 million slaves were suddenly set free.

Start at the historical marker on Va. 35 at Cross Keys, about 10 miles south of Courtland (known as Jerusalem in the 1830s). After reading the marker, head north on Va. 35 to Cross Keys Road (C.R. 665) and turn left. Drive 1.3 miles to a stop sign, then turn right on Clarksbury Road (C.R. 668) and go 2.1 miles. To the left is Cabin Pond Lane. It was down this road at Cabin Pond (not accessible from the road) that Nat Turner hatched his famous plot and found his first victims.

According to the 1830 census, there were 520,000 slaves and 710,000 white people living in Virginia. In many counties dominated by large cotton plantations, blacks outnumbered whites. Whites, who tended to view blacks as inferior thinkers prone to reverting to the savagery of "darkest Africa," were uncomfortable with this reality. On one hand, plantation owners needed—or thought they needed—large numbers of slaves to run their operations. On the other hand, they also realized that they and their families were greatly outnumbered, should the slaves try to organize themselves and strike back.

It had happened earlier in Southern history.

In 1739, near Charleston, South Carolina, several dozen slaves managed to kill a number of whites during the Stono Rebellion.

In 1800, a slave named Gabriel planned an insurrection during which slaves would march on and burn Richmond. One of the slaves told his master, and 35 of the ringleaders, including Gabriel, were subsequently hanged. Governor James Monroe, the future president, reported to the Virginia General Assembly that slave owners "could no longer count with certainty the tranquil submission of their slaves."

In 1811, more than 200 slaves near New Orleans killed a number of whites before their rebellion was put down by an armed force of plantation owners.

In 1822, Denmark Vessey, a black man who had bought his way out of slavery and learned to read, studied Gabriel's sophisticated plan for his insurrection and tried to duplicate it in Charleston, South Carolina. But before the plot was put into motion, one of Vessey's followers turned him in to his master. Vessey and 35 other ringleaders were executed.

There was another slave revolt in 1831. While this one also failed, it lasted far longer than any of the others, was much more bloody, and united the white population in fear of the blacks.

In 1831, Southampton County had a little over 16,000 people, 6,600 of them white and 9,500 of them black. Some 1,700 of the blacks lived free, while the rest were slaves. One of the latter was Nat Turner, a trained carpenter whose life as a slave was relatively easy, as he was an artisan whose skills were bought by plantation owners around the county. He did not have to work in the fields or perform any of the other chores common to slaves.

One additional thing set Turner apart from other slaves—he could read and write, something that was supposed to be illegal. He had apparently been taught by one of his owners. When Turner started studying the Bible, he learned about signs from God that were sent to believers.

In 1828, when Turner was 28, he heard a voice saying to him that the time would soon come "when the first shall be last and the last shall be first." Pondering the meaning of that, he slowly started developing the idea that it would soon be time for another slave rebellion.

On February 12, 1831, there was an eclipse of the sun, which Turner interpreted as the sign for which he had been waiting. He started telling a few slaves about his plans.

On August 13, there was another strange sight in the sky, a day-long atmospheric condition that kept the sun shrouded in a greenish haze, which frightened both the uneducated slaves and their supposedly sophisticated white owners as well. Turner took this as a sign that God was instructing him to start something soon. He began solidifying his plan, which was simple—kill every white person in the county without consideration of age or sex.

At 2 A.M. on August 22, 1831, the Nat Turner Revolt began on the Travis Farm near Cabin Pond when Turner climbed in a second-story window of the house, then opened the front door. Turner's men killed Mr. and Mrs. Travis with axes. They also killed Turner's nine-year-old owner, who had inherited Nat, and dashed the Travises' newborn baby against the fireplace.

Before dawn, the small knot of violent slaves killed 20 men, women, and children on six farms. At each farm, Turner's men took the horses and firearms.

What surprised the insurgents was that few slaves willingly joined them. Many were repelled at the violence of the attacks on their masters and fled into the woods themselves. Some of those who stayed were forced at gunpoint to join the band.

By 9 A.M., the band reached the home of Captain Thomas Barrow, a veteran of the War of 1812 who had built his own road eastward from his farm. Before he was killed, Barrow held off the marauders long enough for his wife to escape.

Next, the band started marching down Barrow Road toward the road that would take it to Jerusalem, the county seat. By that time, it had grown to about 50 people, though speculation is that most of the killing was done by a hard-core group of fewer than a dozen. Some accounts say that Turner himself killed only one person, a young girl. The rest he delegated to his most trusted followers.

The greatest number killed at any one place was 11 at Levi Waller's house, which sat off Barrow Road. Most were children who attended a school Waller ran.

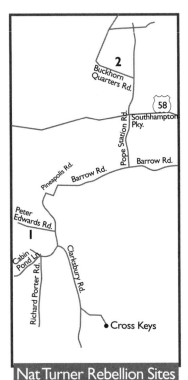

Nat Turner Rebellion Sites

1 Peter Edwards house
2 Dr. Simon Blunt house

The last victim, number 60, was killed around noon near the intersection of Barrow Road and the road to Jerusalem.

When the slaves reached the intersection, they turned north toward town. By then, warnings had swept the county, and most of the white women and children were rushing toward the county seat, while the white men organized themselves into a militia.

In a field near the crossroads, the militia caught up with the band. Shots were exchanged, but few wounds were suffered by either side. Finding their path toward Jerusalem blocked, Turner's men turned north. They started marching up a long lane toward a plantation, where they hoped to obtain more arms. Instead, they came under heavy attack from the owners of the house, who fired on them from the upstairs windows. Then more slaves came on the scene. Turner was surprised that they were not rushing to join him, but rather to help their master fight him.

Turner pulled back and fled southward. His band began to fall apart as the slaves who had been forced to join him broke for what they hoped was the safety of their own plantations. Once more, the militia caught up with Turner's band. Several of the slaves were killed along Barrow Road.

By that time, word had reached Richmond. Governor John Floyd rushed trained militiamen to the county. He refused to ask for help from the United States Army out of fear that what was happening in Southampton was the opening of a full-scale slave revolt. He might need to request those troops later.

Several of Turner's ringleaders were now dead. He finally fled alone back to where he had started near Cabin Pond. He went into hiding in a hole he had apparently dug in anticipation of trouble.

What he left behind was death. The rebellion, which historians count as lasting four days before it was finally stopped, left at least 60 white people dead. There has never been an accounting of blacks killed during the fighting with the militia and afterward, when angry owners confronted the slaves who had left the plantations either willingly or not. Revenge killings swept through the county and even dipped into North Carolina. Richmond newspaper editors wrote about "the slaughter of many Blacks, without trial, and under circumstances of great barbarity."

While his followers and the people he expected to free were being tried and executed or killed by their masters that August, Turner himself disappeared. Hundreds of militiamen scoured the county looking for him. Finally, on October 30, more than two months after the revolt, he was captured by a local farmer. At the time, Turner was carrying a sword he had apparently picked up from one of the houses of his victims.

On November 11, 1831, Turner was hanged, but not before his lawyer supposedly wrote down his "confessions." At least 40,000 copies of a pamphlet detailing his confessions were published. It was that pamphlet that became the basis for *The Confessions of Nat Turner*, the 1966 Pulitzer Prize–winning novel by William Styron.

Peter Edwards House, where Nat Turner was kept after his capture

The Nat Turner Revolt had far-reaching and long-lasting effects, both positive and negative. The Virginia legislature debated emancipation. A resolution to free the slaves narrowly failed after Governor Floyd decided that he would make it one of his goals to gradually free the slaves and remove them from the state. The abolition movement, horrified at the murder of whites and blacks alike, grew stronger in its call to abolish "the peculiar institution," as it was known at the time.

But while this debate was going on among intellectuals, both slave owners and whites who didn't hold slaves began to view blacks with deeper suspicion. If this race of people could kill women and children, the thinking went, what else was it capable of doing? And if blacks were freed, what would they do in revenge for the years they had been enslaved?

When John Brown staged his raid on Harpers Ferry in 1859 (see The Harpers Ferry Tour, page 62), he brought rifles and pikes that he intended to use to arm the slaves. Brown hoped to accomplish what Turner had failed to do 28 years earlier—start a statewide, then a region-wide, slave revolt.

After Brown's raid, the South looked on the North with even greater suspicion. Turner's rebellion had been a grass-roots movement started by a charismatic man who held sway over other blacks. By contrast, Brown's raid was planned and financed by wealthy white Northerners. In the minds of Southerners, Brown's raid was an organized attempt by white Northerners to murder white Southerners in their sleep. And when Lincoln won the presidential election of 1860 after years of making speeches about freeing the slaves, the South took it as a further signal that the North was ready to stage more raids such as Brown's. Though 30 years had passed since the Nat

Turner Revolt, stories of women and babies chopped to death by axes were still fresh in the minds of Southerners.

The South was thus caught between a rock and a hard place. It knew that slavery was a national issue that wasn't going to go away, yet it feared freeing 4.5 million blacks from bondage. After Lincoln's election, the South felt that there would be no more compromises over slavery and that it was about to be dictated to by a North that had no economic investment in slavery and nothing to fear from freed slaves. The South dug in its heels and told the North that it would deal with slaves on its own terms.

By 1865, the defeated South had to deal with slavery on the North's terms.

There is little on Cabin Pond Lane today to call forth the memory of the Nat Turner Revolt. No houses belonging to the victims still stand on the lane.

The first road to the left off Cabin Pond Lane is Richard Porter Road. A slave girl belonging to the Porters gave the alarm to the family about the killings. The Porters then escaped and started spreading the word to the rest of the county.

Continue on Clarksbury Road past Clarksbury Baptist Church. About 0.1 mile beyond the church, turn left on Peter Edwards Road (C.R. 724). After 0.5 mile, look to the left. The unpainted two-story home at the end of the lane is the Peter Edwards House.

When the insurgents reached this house, they found that the white people had already been warned by Old Jeff, their black overseer, who had sent them into the woods. Five slaves joined Turner's band as it moved on in search of more victims. After the revolt, Old Jeff pointed out those slaves, who were then executed.

Turner was captured near this house and spent some time under guard here before being sent to Jerusalem.

Return to Clarksbury Road and turn left. After 1 mile, turn right on Pineapolis Road (C.R. 653). Drive 0.8 mile, then turn right on Barrow Road (C.R. 658). In 1831, this was one of the few roads in this part of the county. It was along Barrow Road that many of the killings took place. Most of Turner's men marched down this road, peeling off when they came to lanes leading to family farms.

It is about 3.3 miles to the next road, Pope Station Road (C.R. 609). If you care to make a short side trip, continue 3 miles on Barrow Road to Va. 35. It was in the field on the right just north of the intersection that the militia met and fired on Turner's band, driving it back west. Return to Pope Station Road to complete the side trip.

Drive north on Pope Station Road for 0.4 mile to U.S. 58. Carefully cross the four lanes of traffic to stay on C.R. 609. After crossing the railroad tracks, turn left on Buckhorn Quarters Road (C.R. 652). Drive 0.4 mile and look to the right to see the house at the end of the long dirt lane.

During Turner's rampage, Dr. Simon Blunt, the owner of the house, assembled his slaves and told them about the revolt. He said they had two choices—they could help him defend the house or they could join the revolt. All of them agreed to defend the property.

As Turner and his band walked up this long dirt lane, they were fired on by the whites in the house and the black overseer on the porch. Dr. Blunt's loyal slaves then rushed from behind the house with hoes, rakes, and clubs and waded into the insurgents. Shocked that blacks were fighting him instead of joining the revolt, Turner retreated.

Lane where the Nat Turner Revolt ended

The rest of the blacks in Turner's gang saw what he had seen. If slaves were fighting slaves, it meant that the revolt was falling apart. They promptly melted into the countryside, hoping to make it back to their farms before their masters discovered they had been part of the revolt. Most of the masters were not fooled. Some historians estimate that more than 100 blacks—guilty and innocent alike—were formally executed or informally murdered in retaliation for Turner's killing of whites.

Retrace your route to U.S. 58 and head east. The sword that Turner carried is sometimes displayed at the courthouse in Courtland. The jail where he was kept is no longer standing.

It is about 34 miles on U.S. 58 to U.S. 58 Business in Suffolk. Follow the business route to the downtown area, then turn north on Main Street and proceed to 510 North Main to visit Riddick's Folly. Now a house museum, Riddick's Folly was the headquarters of Union general James Peck when Suffolk came under siege during the spring of 1863. Unable to retake the town, the Confederates soon abandoned the effort and started moving north toward Gettysburg.

Sailor at the Confederate Monument

Ben Butler's headquarters

Continue north on Main until it intersects U.S. 58; head east on U.S. 58 again. As you near Portsmouth in about 18 miles, follow the signs directing you east toward Portsmouth to get on I-264. Take Exit 7 off I-264—the last exit before the tunnel under the Elizabeth River—and drive four blocks to High Street. Turn right on High. Located on the river at 2 High Street is the Portsmouth Naval Shipyard Museum, which contains some relics from the CSS *Virginia*.

Drive away from the river on High Street for three blocks to Court Street, where you'll see the large Confederate Monument, erected in 1881. Each branch of the Confederate service is represented, and all of the figures are very lifelike. The sailor has a large handlebar mustache.

Turn right on Court and go two blocks to London Street. Near the intersection at 420 London is a house that was used as a hospital during the war.

At 412 London is the house used by the Union provost marshal.

Continue north on Court Street to the large house on the right at 315 Court. This is the home that Union general Ben Butler used as his headquarters when he occupied the city. It may have been here that Butler picked up his nickname of "Spoons" for stealing some family silverware.

Turn around and return on Court Street to London Street. Turn right on London, drive two blocks to Washington Street, and turn right again. Drive two blocks to see the three-story home at 408 Washington. During the war, this house was owned by a man who hid medicine for the Confederates underneath the hearthstone of his fireplace.

Turn around and drive back to London Street. Turn right on London, go three blocks to Fort Lane, and turn right. Watch for the entrance to Cedar Grove Cemetery.

Near the entrance is a monument to Confederate soldiers. The monument is made of rock taken from the dry dock at the Gosport Naval Shipyard, where the CSS *Virginia* was built.

Continue driving the main cemetery road. On the right 50 yards from the end of the road is the grave of Commodore James Wallace Cooke, the Confederacy's most successful ironclad commander.

Cooke had been in the United States Navy for more than 30 years when the war started. A North Carolina native who lived in Portsmouth, he cast

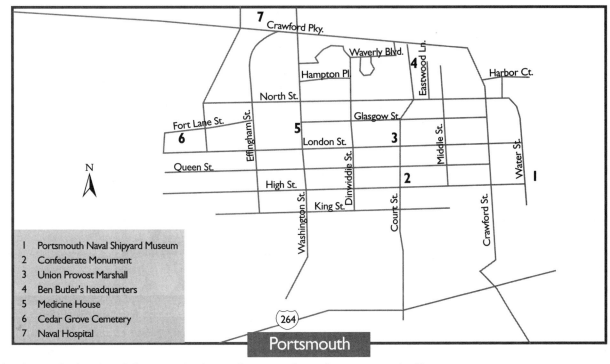

Portsmouth

1. Portsmouth Naval Shipyard Museum
2. Confederate Monument
3. Union Provost Marshall
4. Ben Butler's headquarters
5. Medicine House
6. Cedar Grove Cemetery
7. Naval Hospital

his lot with the Confederacy, which was happy to have him, as naval officers were in extremely short supply. Put in command of a small steamer in the North Carolina sounds, Cooke was wounded and captured but was soon exchanged.

When he returned to duty, he was placed in charge of the construction of the CSS *Albemarle*, which was being built in a North Carolina cornfield far up the Roanoke River. A smaller ironclad than the *Virginia*, she would have just two cannons, but they would be 8-inch rifled Brookes—the best cannons yet designed. Each of those guns, mounted facing forward and rearward, could be aimed out of any of three gunports, whereas the *Virginia*'s guns were fixed. One other advantage the *Albemarle* held was that she could operate in much shallower water than the *Virginia*.

Cooke poured his energy into finishing the 152-foot-long ship, confident that if she worked as well as it appeared she would on paper, the Confederates would have a ship capable of breaking the Union blockade of Southern ports.

In early March 1864, Cooke was ordered to use the *Albemarle* to help a Confederate land force retake the town of Plymouth, North Carolina, from the Federals. She wasn't finished, but it was time to prove her value. The ship started downriver as mechanics were still bolting her armor down. On March 19, the *Albemarle* went into action at Plymouth, immediately sinking one wooden gunboat and driving off another.

On May 5, Cooke and the *Albemarle* attacked the entire Union fleet blockading the mouth of the Roanoke River. He took on seven ships and drove them away, but his ironclad suffered some damage in the process. The smokestack was so riddled by shells that the engine could hardly get up the steam to limp back home. The ship's furniture and the cook's supply of bacon were thrown into the firebox to generate heat.

That was Cooke's last action aboard the ship. A sickly man, he had to be relieved of command of the *Albemarle*, which was later sunk in Plymouth by a Union raiding party. Cooke died in 1869, one of the South's greatest naval heroes.

On the opposite side of the main road is the grave of Captain John Julian Guthrie. First appointed to West Point, Guthrie later transferred to the Naval Academy at Annapolis, Maryland. On April 21, 1861, nine days after the firing on Fort Sumter, he was serving as executive officer of the USS *Saratoga* when he led a boarding party on to a slave ship, the *Nightingale*, on the Congo River in Africa. Guthrie freed more than 900 potential slaves, then arrested the ship's captain and impounded the *Nightingale*, which was owned by a wealthy Boston man.

When Guthrie returned from that duty, he found that his native Virginia had seceded, so he resigned from the United States Navy and joined the Confederate navy.

Guthrie survived the war, only to drown while trying to save some victims of a shipwreck off the North Carolina coast in 1875. His career demonstrates the rich ironies found throughout the war. Guthrie, a Southerner from slave-holding Virginia, arrested the last slaver, a Northerner from abolitionist Massachusetts.

When you are ready to leave the cemetery, retrace Fort Lane and London Streets to where London intersects Effingham Street. Turn left on Effingham and follow it to where it ends at the United States Naval Hospital at the intersection with Crawford Parkway. The hospital may or may not allow visitors, depending upon the terrorism threat, as determined by the Department of Defense.

In the naval cemetery here is a monument to the 200 sailors from the USS *Cumberland* who died at their guns as the ship sank after being rammed by the CSS *Virginia* in March 1862.

At another location on this vast naval base is the dry dock where the *Virginia* was constructed. Still an active dry dock, it is not open to visitors.

From the naval hospital, turn east onto Crawford Parkway and follow it to the Portsmouth Visitors Center, next to the Holiday Inn. If you have the time, you might enjoy the trolley tour of the base that leaves from the Portsmouth Visitors Center. The tour stops at Norfolk Trophy Park, where some pieces of the *Virginia*'s armor plating are on display. If you wish to take this tour, make sure you have photo identification, such as a driver's license.

Two other important war artifacts at the Norfolk Naval Base are not on any tour. The two Brooke cannons from the *Albemarle* rest in front of the old NATO headquarters. North Carolina historians have been lobbying for the historic cannons to be turned over to them for a more prominent display at a museum in Plymouth. But the United States Navy still refuses to part with the cannons it captured from the Confederate navy.

From the visitors center, drive south on Crawford Parkway, following the signs to the I-264 exit. Go east on I-264, heading into the tunnel under the Elizabeth River. Take the exit for the Nauticus museum in downtown Norfolk. Turn right off Waterside Drive on to Commercial Place and drive one block to East Main Street. You'll see the large Confederate Monument at Commercial and Main. Find a place to park nearby.

Walk one block east on Main, then turn right on City Hall Avenue and go one block north to the General Douglas MacArthur Memorial, located at 421 East City Hall. The World War II general and his wife are buried beneath this building, which served as Norfolk's city hall in 1861. The mayor surrendered to Union forces on the front steps of city hall on May 10, 1862. MacArthur's father was a Union soldier.

Walk back to Main Street. At 101 East Main is the old United States Customs House, used as a dungeon by Federal forces during their occupation of the city.

Return to your car and drive all the way to the end of Main into the

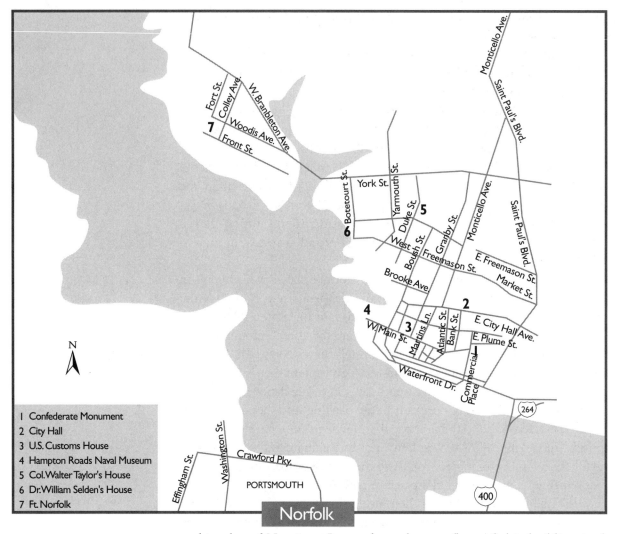

Norfolk

1 Confederate Monument
2 City Hall
3 U.S. Customs House
4 Hampton Roads Naval Museum
5 Col. Walter Taylor's House
6 Dr. William Selden's House
7 Ft. Norfolk

parking lot of Nauticus. Located on the top floor of this building is the Hampton Roads Naval Museum, which is open even on days when Nauticus is closed.

One of the most interesting exhibits here is a full-scale replica of the USS *Monitor*'s turret, complete with eight layers of inch-thick iron plating. Among the other exhibits are pieces of the *Virginia*'s iron plating and the ship's bell from the USS *Cumberland*, which was sunk by the *Virginia*. You'll also see artifacts from the CSS *Florida*, a Confederate sea raider. The *Florida* was captured in a South American port and towed back to the United States. It then sank mysteriously in Norfolk's harbor.

When you are ready to leave Nauticus, turn left on to Boush Street. Drive to West Freemason and turn left again. Located at 227 West Freemason at the intersection with Duke Street is the boyhood home of Colonel Walter Taylor, one of Lee's most trusted aides. Taylor chafed at being a staff officer responsible for distributing orders—so much so that he sometimes snuck away to do some fighting. He refused to go with Lee to the meeting with Grant at Appomattox Court House.

Drive another three blocks on Freemason. On the southwestern corner of Freemason and Botetourt Streets is the home of Dr. William B. Selden, who served as surgeon general of the Confederate army.

Fort Norfolk

Turn right on Botetourt, drive two blocks to Brambleton, and turn left. After you cross the bridge, look for the sign for Colley Avenue. Drive two blocks on Colley to Front Street, then turn right to reach Fort Norfolk. This old, unrestored fort, built in 1810, lies just in front of the Corps of Engineers building. Its magazine provided many of the shells that armed the CSS *Virginia*. It is usually open for a self-guided tour.

Retrace your route to Brambleton and turn right. After 1 mile, turn left on Monticello Avenue. Monticello runs into St. Paul's Boulevard, which eventually intersects I-64. Go west on I-64 through the tunnel under the James River. Take Exit 268 and turn left on to Va. 169 East or Mallory Street, watching for the signs to the Casemate Museum. Follow Mallory to the first light or Mellen Street, also listed as Va. 143. Turn right and follow the Casemate Museum signs. Since this is an active military base, have your photo identification ready; tell the guards you are going to the Casemate Museum. You'll drive over a one-way road controlled by a traffic signal that goes over the moat around the fort. Get your bearings once inside the fort. This is the same way you will leave.

Outside the museum, on the other side of the line of houses facing it, is the "Lincoln Gun," a 15-inch Rodman cannon that was the largest gun cast during the war. It had a range of 4 miles and was named after Lincoln as a sign of respect.

Fort Monroe took 15 years to build. One of its principal engineers was a young lieutenant named Robert E. Lee, who lived in a house here from 1831 to 1834. That house, located in front of the Casemate Museum, has recently been restored.

Lee's house at Fort Monroe

The fort figured prominently in several campaigns. The Union troops going to the first real land battle of the war, Big Bethel, left from here. General Butler accepted the first runaway slaves at this fort, dubbing them "contraband" of war, a nickname that stuck. McClellan used the fort as a base to kick off the Peninsula Campaign. Lincoln visited here in 1862 to urge the army and navy commanders to start cooperating with each other. The attack on Fort Fisher, North Carolina, which led to the fall of Wilmington, was launched from here. And in early 1865, the Confederate vice president secretly met here with Union officers to discuss ending the war.

The first exhibit you'll see inside the fort is a 32-pounder cannon with a good explanation of how naval cannons were fired. The museum also contains the casemate where Jefferson Davis was kept in chains for more than four months after his capture in May 1865. Davis was never allowed to snuff out the light in his room the whole time he was imprisoned here. He was watched 24 hours a day. Finally, in October 1865, a Union doctor took pity on him and asked that he be moved to more comfortable quarters.

Walk to the top of the museum to get a glimpse of the James River. To the far right was the area where the *Monitor* and the *Virginia* fought on March 9, 1862.

The *Virginia* serves as an example of how inventive a country without resources can be when forced to fight a superior nation. When the war started, the Confederacy had no navy. What it did have was the Gosport Naval Yard, once the most sophisticated naval base in the United States but now part of the Confederacy.

It also had the hulk of the USS *Merrimack*, a steam frigate that had arrived at Gosport for engine repairs weeks before the war started. When the war came, the Union commander at Gosport waited too long to take the *Merrimack* out of the port. The vessel was then set afire in the hope that she would explode and be of no use to the Confederates.

The *Merrimack* did burn to the water line, but she didn't blow up. The Confederates had a perfectly good hull on which to put something, though they were not sure what.

TOURING VIRGINIA'S AND WEST VIRGINIA'S CIVIL WAR SITES

It was at that point that the Confederate naval secretary, Stephen R. Mallory, got the idea of using the *Merrimack*'s hull to construct an ironclad, a new type of ship that was being experimented upon in Europe. The idea was simple and bold—build a vessel that could withstand the shells fired by the Union's wooden ships. If the vessel could accomplish that, then the planned Union blockade could not be enforced.

On July 11, 1861, the *Merrimack* went into dry dock and the *Virginia* started taking form on the Union frigate's hull. The design was nothing spectacular. The ship would be 262 feet long and 51 feet wide. She would have four inches of iron plating over two feet of wooden boards—more than enough armor to repel the biggest shells that ships could throw at her. She would be armed with 10 cannons—six 9-inch Dahlgren smoothbores, two 6.4-inch Brooke rifles, and two 7-inch Brooke rifles, one at each end of the vessel. That mixture of cannons came about because the Confederates had to make what they could of the cannons saved from destruction when Gosport was captured from the Federals. It would take a crew of 320 men to operate the *Virginia*. On the negative side, she had one gigantic design flaw—she drew 22 feet of water, which meant that she could not go up most rivers and would have to be careful not to hang herself up on sand bars.

The Confederates did not make much of an effort to conceal their work on the *Virginia*. They might have been engaging in psychological warfare in an effort to frighten the Federals about what would be coming down the Elizabeth River.

That plan backfired when the North decided to build its own ironclad. It went with an innovative design consisting of a hull that sat mostly below water, topped by an armored turret containing two 11-inch Dahlgren smooth-bores. The ship, under construction in Brooklyn, New York, was much smaller than the *Virginia*—172 feet in length and 34 feet in width. She was christened the *Monitor* after her designer, John Ericsson, read an article about how the Confederacy needed a monitor to keep it in check.

All summer and fall, it was a race toward completion. The *Virginia* was finished on February 17, 1862, and the *Monitor* on February 25. Within a week, the *Monitor* was on her way south. Her crew knew what the target was to be.

The *Virginia* did not even bother with sea trials. She went into action on March 8, attacking the USS *Cumberland*, a sloop-of-war. As the men of the *Cumberland* had feared, their solid shots bounced harmlessly off the iron sides of the Confederate ship. The captain of the *Virginia*, Franklin Buchanan, formerly the first superintendent of the United States Naval Academy, decided to test one of his major weapons on the *Cumberland*—he rammed the wooden ship with the iron-tipped prow that rested below the ironclad's water line. The *Cumberland* went down, and more than 200 Union sailors went with her.

The *Virginia* then turned her attention to the USS *Congress*, setting the frigate afire.

As the day wound to a close, the *Virginia* chased the USS *Minnesota* into shallow water, where she ran aground. The *Virginia* finally broke off, figuring she would come back the next day to finish the job.

When the *Virginia* steamed toward the *Minnesota* the following morning, the Confederates were surprised to see a little "cheesebox on a raft" appear from behind the wooden ship. The *Monitor* had arrived the previous night and was ready for combat.

For the next four hours, the two ships cruised around laying shots into each other, with little effect. The *Virginia* had more firepower, but she was slower and harder to maneuver. The *Monitor* was a more difficult target, but the muzzle velocity of her guns was not quite enough to crack the Confederate ship's armor.

When the two ships finally broke off their battle, both sides declared the contest a draw. The two vessels would never fight each other again. The *Virginia* was blown up by her crew in May when the Federals captured Norfolk. And the *Monitor* never again enjoyed as much fame as she did that one day. She was used as a blockading ship, and she also steamed up the James River almost to Richmond, but her effectiveness was never fully realized. She sank off Cape Hatteras, North Carolina, on December 30, 1862, while being towed south to be used in the blockade off South Carolina. Sixteen men went down with her.

Leave Fort Monroe the way you came in. Get back on I-64 and head west to Exit 263. Drive about 1.5 miles west on U.S. 258, then turn right on Big Bethel Road. It is about 4.3 miles to a little bridge; slow down when you see a reservoir on the left. Located behind a locked chain-link fence are some monuments commemorating the battle that took place here on land that is now underwater.

The Battle of Big Bethel was fought on June 10, 1861. Though it was hardly even a skirmish when measured against the actions that came after it, it was nonetheless the first real land engagement of the war. This discounts the Philippi Races, which took place in western Virginia on June 3; that action was more of a running retreat than a battle.

The Union strategy that brought about Bethel was sound. Having heard about a Confederate encampment at Bethel Church, the Federals wanted to advance in the middle of the night and capture the enemy before dawn. They left in two columns from Fort Monroe.

The Confederates did not start the firing near Bethel. In fact, they were not even involved in it initially. When one Union column grew suspicious of the sounds of another column moving nearby, its men started calling out a password, "Boston." The second column's commander had not been given any password, so "Boston" meant nothing to him, and he did not respond. The first column then started firing on the second, since it did not know the password.

The Confederates woke up and wondered who was doing all the firing. By the time the Federals figured out that they were shooting at each other, they had killed and wounded a number of men.

The Confederates defended themselves admirably at Bethel, proving for the first time in the Civil War that fighting from trenches was much preferable to fighting in the open, as the Federals were forced to do. After an hour, the Federals retreated. They suffered 18 killed and 53 wounded. The Confederates lost one killed, Private Henry Wyatt of North Carolina, the first Confederate soldier to die in the war. His body was taken to Richmond, where he was treated as a hero.

Since the Confederates were outnumbered two to one at Bethel, they got the false idea that they would always be able to defeat a force at least twice their size. But the Federals learned from this first battle.

Return to U.S. 258 and turn right. After 1.9 miles, exit at Warwick Boulevard (U.S. 60). Turn immediately left into the Virginia War Museum. This museum offers displays on all the wars our nation has fought, as you might guess from the World War I Renault tank sitting in the lobby. The Civil War section is located to the right. The museum has a good collection of uniforms, swords, muskets, and pistols, including a copy of the type of single-shot pistol that killed President Lincoln.

Get back on Warwick Boulevard and drive north for 4.4 miles to the Mariners Museum. The collection here contains articles salvaged from the *Monitor*, including her propeller (which is presently undergoing restoration) and a signal lamp with red lenses. According to eyewitnesses on the towing vessel, this signal lamp was the last thing visible before the ironclad slipped beneath the waves. A continuously running videotape at the museum shows the condition of the ship today. The *Monitor* lies upside down, her thin iron hull disintegrating. Soon, the only part of the ship left will be the heavy turret and its two cannons. It is believed that the only skeleton that might be recovered after more than 137 years underwater lies inside one of those cannons. According to survivors, the ship's cat was placed in one of the cannons, after which a waterproof wooden stopper was capped over the end. This was to keep the cat out of the way while his shipmates tried to save the ironclad from sinking in the rough seas. In the rush to abandon ship, he was forgotten.

Drive another 2.7 miles north to the preserved Young's Mill. The first line set up by the Confederates to defend the Peninsula from McClellan's march stood beside this mill. The Confederate trenches extended 3 miles eastward from this point. No fighting was done here, as General John Magruder pulled his forces back.

The mill may be visited, but doing so requires a U-turn into traffic, then another U-turn in the right direction. There is little to see here.

Go another 2.3 miles north on U.S. 60, then turn left at the traffic light, then right on to Old Courthouse Way, then left into Warwick Courthouse. The small building was the headquarters of Union general Erasmus Keyes during part of the Peninsula Campaign.

This was also the site of the launching of Professor Thaddeus Lowe's balloon, the *Constitution*, which the Union army used to keep watch on the Confederates. The nation's foremost aeronaut in the 1850s, Lowe was known around the country for his balloon flights, one of which had taken him more than 900 miles from Ohio to near Charleston, South Carolina, just after the firing on Fort Sumter, a feat that got him briefly imprisoned for spying.

Lowe joined the Union army early in the war. He went aloft frequently to observe Confederate positions. Though his balloon was always tethered to the ground, it was sent aloft several hundred feet. On occasion, the Confederates tried to shoot it down; they never succeeded. But even geniuses can be unappreciated. While McClellan saw the value of aerial observation, the generals who followed him did not. Lowe eventually resigned from the army in disgust.

George Custer once went aloft from this site.

Return to U.S. 60 by turning left on to Old Courthouse Way and driving 0.6 mile to U.S. 60. Turn left and drive another 2.8 miles, then turn left on Lee's Mill Drive. Take the first left into Rivers Ridge Circle, a housing development. Here in the woods among the houses are some trenches left over from Magruder's second line. This line came under fire on April 5, 1862. The action here has drawn little attention from historians, since the Battle of Shiloh in Tennessee—the two-day bloodbath that shocked both North and South—began the following day.

Get back on U.S. 60. Drive 1.8 miles, then turn right on Va. 238. Within 0.6 mile, turn left into Lee Hall, a preserved house that was the headquarters of Confederate generals Joseph Johnston and John Magruder early in the campaign.

Turn left and continue east on Va. 238 for another 1.4 miles, then pull to the right to see Endview Plantation. Built before 1720, this house was a resting spot for George Washington's troops on their way to Yorktown. It was also the Civil War home of a Dr. Curtis, who organized a company of Confederates. The Federals occupied Endview after the Confederates pulled back to Yorktown.

After another 2.7 miles, turn right on Crawford Road (C.R. 637) and follow the brown signs to Yorktown National Battlefield Park; en route, you will cross U.S. 17.

Though the park is interpreted as a Revolutionary War site, the Confederates and the Federals occupied the same trenches that had been dug 80 years earlier. The siege of Yorktown lasted a month, from April 5 through May 3, 1862. Though Magruder, the Confederate commander, would later fall apart under pressure, he was brilliant in this campaign. He had only 10,000 men to face 105,000 Federals, but for a month, those Federals did not attack Yorktown out of fear that a superior force was hiding in the trenches. Every day, Magruder made a show of moving his men from one

Yorktown Confederate entrenchments

---

part of the field to another, knowing that Union observers would report to McClellan that new troops were arriving. Magruder also ran trains at all hours of the night. Men shouted orders to regiments that did not exist, making it appear that reinforcements were arriving from Richmond. To show the strength of his defenses, Magruder had thick oak trees cut down, stripped of their branches, and painted black. From a distance, they looked like huge siege cannons. The elaborate ruse kept the Federals at bay.

All that April, McClellan built up his artillery and made ready to shell the trenches. There was one brief battle on April 16 at Dam Number 1, located a few miles south of here. Believing it would be only the first of many such actions, McClellan remained timid, which was exactly what the Confederates needed to strengthen Richmond's defenses.

The entire Confederate army stole away in the middle of the night on May 3.

From the park, look for the signs to U.S. 17 and head north over the York River. A small star fort was located on the northern side of the bridge in Gloucester. The fort was designed so that if any Union ships tried to run the gauntlet, they would be caught in a crossfire.

About 10.8 miles after crossing the river, turn right on Va. 14 at a traffic light. Drive 2.3 miles east, then turn right into Ware Episcopal Church. About 20 yards inside the walled cemetery, you'll see a gravestone with a cross on top. Here lies General William Booth Taliaferro.

An aristocrat who studied at the College of William and Mary and Harvard, Taliaferro was a Virginia legislator, a presidential elector, and a militia commander. He was also a man who did not think things through to their conclusion. In 1861, he was placed under the command of Stonewall Jackson, who ordered the men under General William Loring—including Taliaferro—to spend the winter in Romney, Virginia. Feeling that their position was too exposed to Union attack, Loring and Taliaferro lobbied the politicians back in Richmond to let them return to the Shenandoah Valley. This enraged Jackson, who never forgave officers who went over his head.

For reasons unclear, Taliaferro continued to serve under Jackson's command long after the two should have been separated for their own good. When he finally transferred, he fought in Georgia and South Carolina and at the last major battle of the war, at Bentonville, North Carolina. He out-lived Jackson by 35 years. "Statesman, Jurist, Scholar, Grand Master Mason," his tombstone reads.

Continue east on Va. 14. After 11.5 miles, turn right on C.R. 611 (Courthouse Road). Drive 2.3 miles, then turn right at the stop sign in downtown Matthews back on to Va. 14. Go 1.8 miles, turn right on C.R. 614, drive 0.3 mile, and pull into the lot at Christ Episcopal Church. Buried under a large stone in front of the church is Captain Sally Louisa Tompkins, the only woman made an official Confederate officer during the war.

She was a real captain, though she was not a fighter. Rather, she was a healer who never thought of herself as long as there was a wounded or sick man to tend. Twenty-seven years old when the war started, Sally responded to the government's call to care for the wounded at First Manassas by opening her own private hospital in Richmond, where she was living. It was a small hospital set up in a house owned by Judge John Robertson, but it saw many soldiers come and go. Records show that 1,333 Confederates were treated there over the course of the war, only 45 of whom died under her care. Stories say that Sally was a stickler for cleanliness and fresh air, two commodities that were decidedly lacking in most Civil War hospitals.

Her remarkable record of saving lives did not impress the bureaucrats in the Confederate government, who passed regulations trying to shut down private hospitals. It was President Davis himself who made Sally an official captain in the cavalry, so she could draw military supplies to keep her hospital open.

Captain Sally survived all the fevers that swept through her hospital and became a noted Richmond citizen after the war. She never married and slowly used up her inheritance on charity work in the city. She eventually moved into a home for Confederate women and died at the age of 83. She was given a full military funeral and sent back to her home county for burial. She lies beside her beloved sister Elizabeth, who raised money to build this church. Sally requested in her will that she be buried next to her sister, who had died more than 50 years earlier.

In all the North and South during the war, there was probably no more selfless a person than the modest, loving woman who lies under this stone. Her marker is engraved with a verse from the 25th chapter of Matthew: "I was hungry and you gave me meat. I was thirsty and you gave me a drink. I was sick and you visited me."

In 1980, Sally Tompkins briefly became famous again when John Lennon and Yoko Ono bought Poplar Grove, the house where she was born. The locals say that John and Yoko stayed in the house only once, as they could not stand the quiet of rural Virginia. They moved back to the hustle and bustle of New York City, where Lennon was murdered that same year.

Retrace your route west on Va. 14 and south on U.S. 17 all the way to the York River. Just after crossing the bridge, follow the brown signs to Colonial Parkway, which will lead you to Colonial Williamsburg, located about 13 miles away. From the Colonial Williamsburg Visitors Center, pick up U.S. 60 heading east. Drive 1.7 miles, then turn right on Quarterpath Road. After about 0.2 mile, look for an interpretive sign in a parking lot. Though there is little to see here today, this was an important area during the war. Quarterpath Road ran roughly in an east-west line across the Peninsula, linking 13 Confederate redoubts, or small dirt forts, constructed to protect Williamsburg from the approaching Federal army.

Return to U.S. 60 and turn right. Drive 0.1 mile to the Fort Magruder Inn—which is misnamed, since Fort Magruder lies to the east. This was actually the site of Redoubt Number 3. Park and walk through the lobby into the courtyard. This may be the only Civil War fortification in the country located next to a hotel swimming pool. The lobby of the hotel has a small display on the Battle of Williamsburg, fought on May 5, 1862.

Fort Magruder

Drive back toward Williamsburg on U.S. 60, which turns to the right. Immediately after crossing a railroad overpass, turn right on Penniman Road. Drive 1.6 miles, passing through the traffic light at Va. 143. Located on the right behind a chain-link fence is Fort Magruder, part of the Warwick River Line east of Williamsburg.

This was the center of the Confederate line. It was here that the Confederates under James Longstreet beat back an attack by Joe Hooker but were then outflanked by General Winfield Hancock. The Confederates left their fort and attacked Hancock, but that attack was so uncoordinated that Hancock did not suffer greatly. The whole battle was fought in a driving rainstorm, which made orders difficult to follow.

Both sides claimed victory after the battle, the Federals because they were in possession of the field and the Confederates because they considered it a holding action, so the rest of their army could retreat toward Richmond to prepare for the coming Union attack.

Though it was called the Battle of Williamsburg, no fighting took place in the streets of the old colonial capital. Several local houses were used as hospitals.

Return to U.S. 60 and turn left. After crossing the railroad overpass, turn immediately right on to Va. 5. Drive west on Va. 5 past the College of William and Mary on the edge of Colonial Williamsburg. The Wren Building, today's administration building, served as a hospital after the battle. The Confederates marched east from the Wren Building up Duke of Gloucester Street toward the fighting.

About 18 miles outside Williamsburg, you'll see a historical marker for Fort Pocahontas, a Union fort built in the spring of 1864 to guard Wilson's Bluff. On May 24, 1864, the fort was attacked by Confederate cavalry in one of the few battles of the war in which all the attackers were white and all the defenders black. The Confederate cavalry ultimately withdrew. The battle produced a total of about 150 casualties on both sides.

After another 1.8 miles, pull into Sherwood Forest, the prewar home of John Tyler, the president of the United States from 1841 to 1845. Tyler died early in 1862, before he could take office as a member of the Confederate Congress.

A lover of states' rights and a hater of national banks, Tyler may have been the loneliest president ever. He took office just one month after the man elected president, William Henry Harrison, died in office. Historians speculate that the politicians who pushed for Tyler as a vice presidential candidate never dreamed he would become president and were shocked when it happened. Even Tyler's own party, the Whigs, disowned him. Virtually his entire cabinet resigned when he vetoed a bill that would have created a national bank. Tyler's major achievement came in extending United States foreign policy, including opening up trade and extending the Monroe Doctrine to Hawaii.

Tyler wanted to annex slaveholding Texas into the country but was thwarted in that bid. He chose not to run for president in 1844. He would not have been elected anyway, since the Whigs had disowned him. He retired to this plantation in 1845 and did not emerge again on the political scene until 1861, when he won a seat in the Confederate Congress. His remains lie in Hollywood Cemetery in Richmond because his family feared the Federals would dig him up if he were buried on his plantation. The only cemetery on the property is for the pets of Sherwood Forest. The graves there date back to the dogs and cats owned by Tyler himself.

The Union army did try to burn Sherwood Forest, but a Federal sailor who felt guilty about setting fire to the home of a United States president snuffed the flames.

Turn left back on to Va. 5 and continue 5.4 miles to C.R. 618 (Wilcox Wharf Road). Turn left on C.R. 618 and drive 1 mile to the James River. It was here that steamboats ferried two Union corps across the James to begin the attack on Petersburg in June 1864. Three miles downstream, a 700-yard-long pontoon bridge was laid across the river over the course of three days. The rest of the army crossed there.

Return to Va. 5, turn left, and drive 2.5 miles. To the left is the site of Evelynton, the home of Edmund Ruffin, the staunch secessionist who may have fired the first shot at Fort Sumter in April 1861. The original house was burned by the Federals, but a reconstructed home is open for tours.

Continue on Va. 5 for 2 miles. Turn left on C.R. 640 to reach Berkeley Plantation, established in 1619. This plantation was owned for a time by the Harrison family, whose members included Benjamin Harrison V, a signer of the Declaration of Independence. This was also the birthplace of President William Henry Harrison.

For about a month starting on July 2, 1862, this house served as the headquarters of General George McClellan as he made his way back from the Peninsula Campaign after failing to capture Richmond. Scattered around the house were nearly 100,000 demoralized men, who could not understand why they were retreating after having defeated Lee's army in most of the Seven Days Battles, including the last one, which was fought at Malvern Hill, just 7 miles away.

There was some action here, as Confederate cavalry under J. E. B. Stuart threw a few shells at the Federals. One is still lodged in a house beside the main home. But that was the only attack on the Union base, which was also called Harrison's Landing. Following the disaster at Malvern Hill, Lee decided that his men were too exhausted to push the Federals into the James River.

James River where Grant's army crossed

Berkeley Plantation

Detail of Berkeley Plantation showing the cannon ball from the attack by J. E. B. Stuart's cavalry

President Lincoln visited here on July 8 in the hope of prodding McClellan back into action, but his trip from Washington was wasted. McClellan had been insisting for weeks that he needed reinforcements, which never came. He was not about to attack again without them.

It was in this plantation house that McClellan wrote the "Harrison's Landing Letter," in which he, a general, instructed the president of the United States on how the war should be conducted. The letter made it clear that McClellan was fighting only to restore the Union and was not interested in freeing the slaves or waging war on the civilian population of the South—a course of action already being tried by some Union generals.

It was near the end of July at Harrison's Landing that Union general Dan Butterfield and his regimental bugler experimented on the last few bars of the 25-year-old "Tatoo," a bugle call that traditionally ended the day in military camps. When they finished, they had a new song, "Taps," which has since been played at the funerals of fallen soldiers.

On August 8, the Federal army left Harrison's Landing after a six-week stay, never having made an offensive movement, as McClellan had hinted he would do and Lincoln had demanded. A few weeks after leaving here, McClellan sat back and watched General John Pope go down to defeat at Lee's hands at Second Manassas. Then, in September, the smug McClellan, reluctantly restored to command by Lincoln, followed Lee into Maryland, where the two armies fought to a standstill at Sharpsburg.

As for McClellan's demands in his letter to Lincoln, nothing he asked for was granted. Within weeks of receiving the letter, the president issued an order for the confiscation of Southern property, approved Pope's plan to attack civilians in retaliation for guerrilla activity, and drafted the Emancipation Proclamation.

Return to Va. 5 and turn left. After 4 miles, you will reach Shirley Plantation, the last of the James River plantations that may be visited. Shirley Plantation was the birthplace of Robert E. Lee's wife, Mary.

The tour ends here.

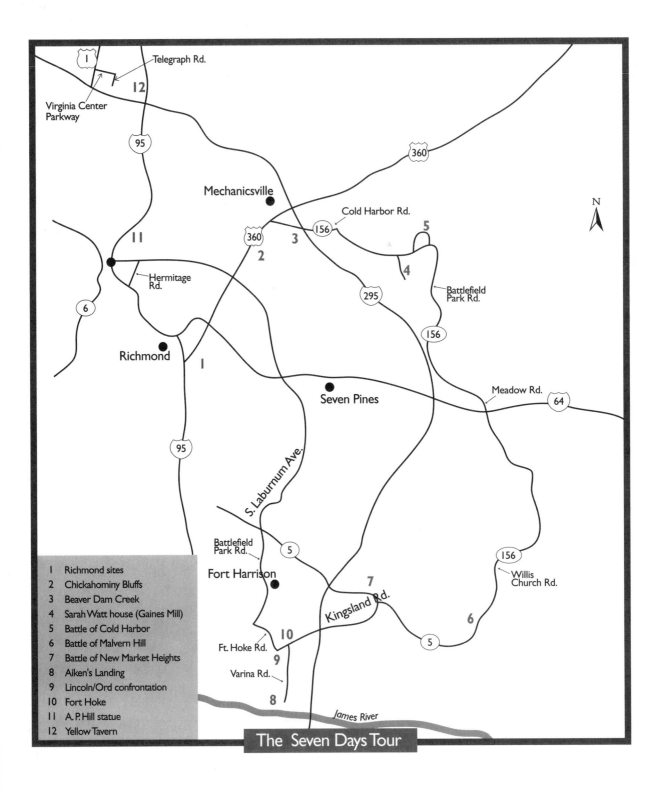

The Seven Days Tour

1 Richmond sites
2 Chickahominy Bluffs
3 Beaver Dam Creek
4 Sarah Watt house (Gaines Mill)
5 Battle of Cold Harbor
6 Battle of Malvern Hill
7 Battle of New Market Heights
8 Aiken's Landing
9 Lincoln/Ord confrontation
10 Fort Hoke
11 A. P. Hill statue
12 Yellow Tavern

The Seven Days Tour

This tour starts in eastern downtown Richmond, visiting sites where thousands of Confederates were nursed and where thousands of Union prisoners were kept. It then moves eastward to the sites of the Seven Days Battles, where Robert E. Lee became famous. It also stops at a battlefield where black soldiers bravely won the day, at several dirt forts that defended Richmond, and at the place where Mary Todd Lincoln first showed her creeping insanity. Next, the tour curves back into Richmond, where it stops at the statue of A. P. Hill before ending at the site where J. E. B. Stuart was mortally wounded.

The tour measures just 65 miles but will likely take all day, as it stops at several National Park Service sites.

THE TOUR STARTS at Chimborazo Hill, located at Broad Street and East 32nd Street in the eastern part of Richmond; if you are arriving from I-95, get off at Exit 74. Park your car nearby to enjoy a brief walk.

There is nothing left of the Chimborazo Hospital complex today. But starting in the fall of 1861, this hill was filled with 150 buildings covering 40 acres. In effect, the complex was a city on the outskirts of Richmond. It had its own herd of cattle and a herd of 500 goats to provide milk for the never-ending supply of wounded soldiers. More than 76,000 men were treated here for their wounds or diseases.

Chimborazo was the most famous of the hospitals in the city, but there were dozens of others as well, including ones founded by the individual Confederate states to try to take care of their own soldiers. The Alabama hospital was run by Juliet Hopkins, a young widow who spent $200,000 of her own money on it. She was wounded twice while serving as a battlefield nurse at the Battle of Seven Pines outside Richmond.

Walk west on Broad Street to 29th Street. Turn left on 29th and go south to Libby Hill Park, which overlooks the James River. The park boasts a tall column with a bronze Confederate soldier on top. Below here were Rocketts Landing and the Confederate Naval Yard. The most famous person to step ashore at Rocketts Landing was President Abraham Lincoln.

In a move that still confounds historians and that must have terrified his wife and staff at the time, President Lincoln landed here on April 4, 1865, just one day after Richmond officially fell to Federal forces. Lincoln, saying that "the nightmare is over and I want to see Richmond," took a boat from Washington to this point. Traveling with him was his son Tad.

Without much fanfare—and more importantly, without much military support other than a small squad of nervous sailors—the party came ashore at Rocketts and started up the slope toward the center of the city. As the president walked, word spread. Scores of former slaves rushed to see the man who had freed them. Some tried to kneel to him, but Lincoln urged them to stand like the men they were, telling them that they would never have to kneel to another human being.

Lincoln walked all the way to the Confederate White House, more than a dozen blocks away. Once there, he sat behind what he thought was President Davis's desk and gazed out the window. He then jumped up, grabbed Tad by the hand, and toured the house.

Lincoln spent the rest of the day riding around in an open carriage, as the Union commander scrambled after him trying to provide security for a president who insisted on touring the enemy's capital so soon after the Confederate president had vacated it. No one in Richmond tried to shoot Lincoln, though everyone recognized him. Ironically, someone in Washington had shot a hole in Lincoln's hat while the president was on a late-night ride some months earlier. And it was in Washington just 10 days after his visit to Richmond that Lincoln fell to John Wilkes Booth.

Return to your car at Chimborazo. Turn left on Broad, heading toward downtown.

The southeastern corner of Broad and 28th Streets was the site of the house, no longer standing, where General Joseph E. Johnston was taken after being wounded at the Battle of Seven Pines. He was replaced by Robert E. Lee.

To the right several blocks up 28th Street is Oakwood Cemetery; note that this is not a suggested stop, as the neighborhood is rough looking. Oakwood Cemetery is the final resting place of more than 17,000 Confederates, most of whom died during the Seven Days Campaign or in local hospitals afterward. It also contains the graves of many Union soldiers who died in nearby prisons.

Oakwood was the site of a temporary burial in March 1864. Colonel

Ulric Dahlgren was a one-legged Union cavalryman who was killed while leading a controversial raid on Richmond; the raid failed when Confederate militia caught up with his lost and overwhelmed command. When Dahlgren's body was searched, the colonel was found to be carrying papers that outlined the objective of the raid—killing President Davis and the Confederate cabinet. The papers' authenticity has been debated for years. Recent scholarship suggests that they contain an accurate description of what Dahlgren intended to do, even if the murders were not expressly ordered by higher Union authorities.

The citizens of Richmond were incensed when they learned of the assassination plan. Lee even wrote a letter to Union general George Meade asking him what he knew of the plot. Meade expressed ignorance and asked down the chain of command in an attempt to find out who had ordered the murders. Even Dahlgren's commanding general, Judson Kilpatrick, claimed not to know of any plot, although he was supposed to have linked up with Dahlgren once both bodies of Union cavalrymen penetrated Richmond's defenses.

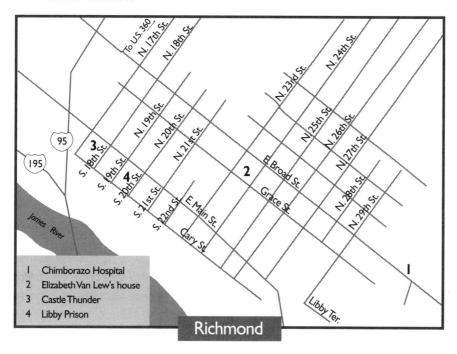

1 Chimborazo Hospital
2 Elizabeth Van Lew's house
3 Castle Thunder
4 Libby Prison

Richmond

Davis ordered Dahlgren buried in Oakwood, rather than having the body returned through the lines, as would likely have been done under normal circumstances, particularly since Dahlgren was the son of Admiral John Dahlgren of the Union navy.

Just over a month after the burial, Elizabeth Van Lew, a Richmond woman who was a valuable Union spy, went to the cemetery with some helpers. She dug up the coffin and opened it to look at the Union colonel's body. She mentioned how his features still had a "look of firmness or energy stamped upon them," though she also noted that mold was starting to grow on the remains. She had Dahlgren's body spirited out of the cemetery and reburied on a farm outside the city. After the war, she alerted Union authorities to its location. Dahlgren was subsequently dug up and taken to Philadelphia, where he was reburied more than a year after his death.

Turn left off Broad on to 24th Street. Drive one block to Grace Street and turn right. The house occupied by Elizabeth Van Lew stood on the site now occupied by the Belle Vue School.

Van Lew loved being called "Crazy Bet" by her neighbors, who looked down their noses at the New York City–born abolitionist who walked the streets in tattered, out-of-fashion clothes talking to herself. In fact, she felt that if people thought she was crazy, they would be unlikely to figure out that she was one of the craftiest spies in the Union network.

There is no doubt that Crazy Bet was effective in collecting and passing along details on conditions inside the Confederate capital. Grant himself said so. And he showed his appreciation by making her postmistress of Richmond after the war. According to some stories, she grew bold enough late in the conflict to send Grant fresh flowers from her garden, which he displayed on a table outside his tent.

Van Lew may have flaunted her Unionist leanings too much for her own good. During McClellan's Peninsula Campaign, she made up a room for him in her house, so he could make his headquarters there once he captured the city. That did not win her any friends among her neighbors. Later, she openly took gifts and food to Union officers in a prison just a few blocks from her house. What the prison officials never knew—or at least could not prove—was that she also took them military information and returned with whatever the prisoners could tell her.

In 1864, there was a large breakout from Libby Prison, during which more than 100 officers escaped. It has been speculated that Van Lew supplied the men with maps and lists of safe houses to help them get back north. Historians have long wondered about the thickness of the ceiling on her front porch. It looks tall and wide enough to hold men in hiding.

No one will ever know. When Van Lew died in 1900, not a single Richmond neighbor went to her funeral. And when her grand, old house fell into disrepair, no one volunteered to save it. It was demolished instead.

Turn left off Grace Street on to 23rd Street, drive two blocks and then turn right on Main Street. Follow Main to 18th Street, turn left, drive one block to Cary Street, and turn left again. Two famous prisons were located near here.

Castle Thunder stood at Cary and 18th Streets. One of the persons imprisoned here may or may not have been a woman named Loreta Janeta Velesquez, a half-Spanish, half-French 24-year-old born in Cuba. Velesquez claimed great adventures during the war while posing as Lieutenant Harry T. Buford and later as a spy for the Confederacy. The title of her 1878 book was *The Woman in Battle: A Narrative of the Exploits and Adventures of a Woman Officer in the Confederate Army*. She claimed to have met both presidents and fought in both theaters of the war. Historians know that she did exist and that she at least worked as a spy in Washington, but they have no idea how much of what she wrote ever really happened.

Drive two blocks on Cary to 20th Street and turn right into the parking lot. This was the site of Libby Prison, named after the unfortunate Mr. Libby, who simply meant to advertise his tobacco warehouse when he painted his name on the side of the building. Nothing of the prison remains today, though a historical marker stands at the site.

A three-floor warehouse divided into eight rooms, Libby housed hundreds of officers starting in 1863. It developed a bad reputation because it was so crowded that men had to sleep in shifts. Anyone venturing near a window stood a chance of being shot.

Continue on Cary to 21st Street, turn left, go to Main Street, turn left again, and get into the right lane. Turn right on 17th Street at the sign for U.S. 360 East. Drive 1.1 miles and turn right on to Fairfield Street, still following U.S. 360 East. Follow Fairfield for 0.5 mile, then turn left on to

Sign for Chickahominy Bluffs

Mechanicsville Turnpike or U.S. 360 East. Drive for 2.8 miles and turn right at the National Park Service sign for Chickahominy Bluffs.

The raised platform located here today does not reveal much, but in late May 1862, there was a lot to see just to the north, near Mechanicsville. It was from this vantage point that Lee watched the opening movements of the Seven Days Battles.

The Seven Days Battles did not constitute Lee's debut for the Confederacy. That had come nine months earlier, when he demonstrated that he was unable to control his own generals—much less the enemy—while trying to push the Federals out of western Virginia using troops under John Floyd and Henry Wise. On that occasion, Lee spent most of his time settling disputes between the two vain former Virginia governors now serving as generals. It was then that he was given the unflattering nickname "Granny" Lee, which suggested that he was an aging officer who had seen better days on the battlefield. An embarrassed Jefferson Davis sent Lee south to inspect the defenses in Florida, Georgia, and South Carolina—busywork for a general who had failed. The president later brought Lee back as a personal adviser.

Then, on May 31, 1862, Joseph Johnston was hit in the arm by a minie ball and in the chest by a shell fragment while riding through the woods at Seven Pines, east of Richmond. Johnston suffered a broken shoulder blade and two broken ribs, injuries that would prevent him from leading the defense of Richmond against the 110,000-man Union army marching up the Peninsula.

Davis had a limited choice of generals and little time in which to make it. Beauregard was out west, and Davis hated him anyway. Magruder had performed well in slowing McClellan on the Peninsula, but Johnston did not like the pomposity of the man and had hinted to Davis that Magruder's skills were lacking. The only general available on short notice was Lee. The day after Johnston was wounded, Lee took command of what would become known as the Army of Northern Virginia.

Luckily for him, McClellan did not immediately launch an attack on Richmond. Had he done so, he might have won, as the Confederates were in disarray after Johnston's wounding. Instead, McClellan did what he did best. He waited. That gave Lee time to reorganize the army, appoint new brigadiers, and dig more earthworks around the city. That did not make him popular with the average soldier. In fact, he acquired a new nickname that did little to improve his image—the "King of Spades."

As the infantrymen were digging, Lee sent J. E. B. Stuart and his cavalry on a scouting mission. On June 12, 1862, Stuart and 1,200 men left Richmond with orders to find out if McClellan's right flank was "anchored" on the Chickahominy River or if it was "in the air." The distinction was important. If McClellan was using the river as a defensive position, Lee would have to avoid that flank. If not, the flank could become a target. What Stuart found was that the Union right flank, consisting of about 30,000 men, was on the northern side of the Chickahominy and that the other 80,000 Federals were on the southern side some distance away. McClellan had left his right flank vulnerable to attack.

Instead of returning the way he had come, Stuart, worried that Federals might be pursuing him, decided to ride completely around McClellan's army. The giant circle took four days to complete. When Stuart got back to the Confederate lines, he had a new reputation as a cavalryman willing and daring enough to do just about anything.

When Stuart reported what he had learned, Lee immediately saw his advantage. If he could crush the Federal right flank with overwhelming numbers, he could start rolling up the Union line toward the James River.

He put the plan into motion by secretly ordering Jackson, whom he barely knew, from the Shenandoah Valley to reinforce him. On June 23, 1862, Lee, Jackson, D. H. Hill, A. P. Hill, and James Longstreet met at the Dabb House north of Richmond to discuss the plan of attack. The five men had never before been in a strategy session together. Their unfamiliarity with each other would hurt.

Though the attack was to start on June 26, a small engagement at Oak Grove on the 25th actually opened the Seven Days Battles, which took place from June 25 to July 1. The plan was for virtually the entire Confederate army to descend on the Federals. But Lee, a man given to writing vague orders, never quite made it clear to Jackson that the army would wait for him to arrive before commencing the attack. All day long, the other Confederate divisions waited for Jackson, who, not knowing he had a time-table to meet, was hours late in arriving. Finally, in the late afternoon on

June 26, and without specific orders to do so, A. P. Hill threw his men into the Federals, who were entrenched at Beaver Dam Creek just east of Chickahominy Bluffs.

When you are ready to leave the bluffs, return to U.S. 360 East, turn right and drive 1.4 miles to Va. 156, and turn right. After 0.3 mile, turn right into the National Park Service site for Beaver Dam. This area was visible to Lee during the battle.

Across this swampy land were 30,000 dug-in Federals under the command of General Fitz John Porter, a 39-year-old New Hampshire native. Porter must have been dumbfounded by the determined attack across the swamp by Hill's outnumbered division. With little fanfare, he smashed Hill flat. Hill lost 1,500 men to Porter's 360. It was an inauspicious start to Lee's command of the army.

Historians have pondered why Jackson did not arrive for a battle in which he was supposed to be the key player. One writer has even speculated that he accidentally drugged himself with too much laudanum—an opium-and-alcohol mixture—and didn't even know what was happening. Most historians suspect that the general was simply exhausted from too many late nights—too many strategy sessions with himself that he kept to himself. Jackson had been fighting all up and down the Shenandoah Valley just weeks earlier. Then came the forced march from the Valley to Richmond. His body and mind simply gave out on him.

That night, General Porter sent a note to McClellan detailing the battle. Instead of rejoicing at the Union victory, McClellan panicked. He believed that Jackson's late appearance indicated a huge reinforcement of Confederates. McClellan pulled Porter back several miles to Gaines Mill.

Turn right on to Va. 156 leaving Beaver Dam Creek. After about 5 miles, watch on the left for a modern housing development called Gaines Mill. After passing it, slow down if traffic permits. On the left about 0.1 mile past the development is the small creek on which the original Gaines Mill stood. The third day of the Seven Days Battles opened here when Hill encountered the rear guard of Porter's army on June 27, 1862.

Follow Va. 156 until it makes a sharp turn to the left; at that point, follow the brown signs and go straight ahead to another National Park Service site, the Sarah Watt House. Some historians have said that the battle at Gaines Mill should be called the Battle of Watt House Hill, as most of the heavy fighting occurred around this house, rather than down by the mill.

Sarah Watt House

Just as they had done the day before, A. P. Hill's men rushed forward, leaving Cold Harbor Road (what is now Va. 156) and climbing up the hill toward the Sarah Watt House. Once again, Lee waited on Jackson to attack. Once again, Jackson was confused about where he was supposed to be and when he was supposed to be there. He took the wrong road, then gave a verbal order to an aide, who garbled it enough that the men receiving it had no idea what they were supposed to do. Once again, Jackson was hours late in arriving on the battlefield. And all during that time, Hill's men were being cut to pieces.

When Jackson finally arrived, he and Lee met in the road, and Lee pointedly said, "I had hoped to be with you before," a gibe that translated to "Where in the world have you been all day?"

Jackson's men finally did carry the position, the Texans of John Bell Hood leading the way. But it was a costly day for the Confederates, who suffered more than 9,000 killed and wounded, compared to nearly 7,000 for the entrenched Federals.

What Lee did not know at the time was that McClellan was still panicking. The Federals had won the previous day decisively and had inflicted more damage on the Confederates here, yet McClellan ordered his men in a full retreat to the James. He had twice as many men as Lee, had seriously bloodied Lee, and could have advanced on Richmond to draw off Lee. Still, he saw himself as having lost to Lee.

Once Lee understood that McClellan was already thinking of himself as the loser in the contest, he pressed even harder.

When you are ready to leave the Sarah Watt House, turn right on to Va. 156. After 0.2 mile, turn left to visit the Cold Harbor shelter. Follow the loop road through the National Park Service property.

Cold Harbor was not fought until 1864, two years after the Seven Days. By that point, the Union commander was Grant, rather than McClellan. But as fate would have it, it took place right in the middle of the Seven Days Battlefield.

The Battle of Cold Harbor, fought on the first three days of June 1864,

Union side of Cold Harbor

was Grant's darkest hour as commander of the Union armies. Had he told Lincoln the truth about it, he might have been fired.

After leaving the North Anna River, Grant moved toward Cold Harbor to line himself up for an attack on Richmond. He sent cavalry troops ahead to capture the crossroads, but those troops were pushed out by advancing Confederates. The crossroads changed hands a few times but finally settled into Confederate hands.

Grant was determined that he would own the Cold Harbor crossroads. When his generals and common soldiers looked out from the woods toward the crossroads, they could see Confederates throwing up dirt and digging themselves in deeper. To reach them, the Federals would have to march across open, flat land. Grant didn't care. He wanted that road. When they learned that a frontal assault across open land was to be ordered—much like Lee had tried the summer before at Gettysburg—the Federals resigned themselves to death. Many of them pinned their names on pieces of paper and put them underneath their uniforms, so their bodies could be identified after the charge.

At 4:30 A.M. on June 3, more than 40,000 Federals attacked. In less than half an hour, more than 7,000 of them lay killed or wounded on the field. Most of them were shot down during the 10 minutes they rushed the massed cannons and muskets of the Confederates, which easily covered the ground. Fighting from their trenches, fewer than 1,500 Confederates were killed or wounded.

Grant had made a terrible mistake in ordering the frontal assault, just as his men predicted. When he first cabled news of the battle back to Washington, he intentionally downplayed the number of casualties. He later claimed he didn't have time to do a full accounting before sending the telegram. He must not have been looking at the acres of men lying dead in front of him.

The scene of most of the heavy fighting is not in National Park Service hands, but lies east and south, where time and farming have wiped out signs of the trenches. Nonetheless, the drive though the National Park Service land shows how close the lines were to each other—within earshot, in fact.

After completing the loop road, turn left back on to Va. 156, then take an immediate right to see the Garthwait House, used as hospital during

Cold Harbor. One story describes how blood ran through the boards of the first floor and fell like rain on the civilians hiding in the basement.

Return to Va. 156 and continue in your original direction. It is 2.5 miles to Grapevine Bridge. Pull over to read the historical markers. On June 29, 1862, Jackson had to pause just west of where the modern-day bridge over Boatswain's Creek stands in order to rebuild the bridge the Federals had destroyed. It was near here that Jackson received a poorly worded order drafted by one of Lee's staff members. The order should have commanded Jackson to cross the Chickahominy River and advance on the Federals. Instead, the way Jackson read it, he was supposed to stay near the Chickahominy and prevent any Federals from crossing the river. Once again, Lee would be expecting Jackson on the battlefield, and Jackson would not be coming in time.

Leaving Grapevine Bridge, turn immediately left on to Old Hanover Road, then turn left on Grapevine Road. After 1.9 miles, turn left on Meadow Road. This was the vicinity where the Battle of Savage Station was fought on June 29—without Jackson, who never arrived. Instead, Magruder attacked without Jackson. He did little damage to the Federals but great damage to his own mental well-being and reputation. Observers of the battle talked about how strangely Magruder acted. Modern-day historians speculate that he may have had a nervous breakdown, brought on by Lee's order for him to attack. Up to that point in the war, Magruder had always been a defender of trenches, not an attacker.

Drive southeast on Meadow Road. You will cross I-64, then reach U.S. 60 (Williamsburg Road). About 2 miles west of this intersection is Seven Pines, just outside today's Richmond National Airport. Seven Pines was where Johnston was wounded on May 31, 1862. Another mile past that is Oak Grove, the site of the first small battle of the Seven Days.

Continue straight across U.S. 60; you are now on Va. 156 again. Drive about 4 miles to White Oak Swamp and look for a spot to pull over. It was just west of here that Jackson's artillery set up on a hill and fired at the Federals across the swamp. And that is about all that happened. The exhausted Jackson spent much of the day napping as his frustrated subordinates waited for orders. He never gave any. Fought on June 30, this was the sixth of the Seven Days battles.

About 2 miles away, Longstreet was engaging the Federals at Frayser's

Farm—also called Glendale and about half a dozen other names.

Stay on Va. 156 to Glendale. Pull over at Glendale National Cemetery.

The brigades of Longstreet and the already-mauled A. P. Hill went into battle here at 4 P.M. on June 30. At first, the Confederates were successful, even capturing the Union general in charge of this part of the battlefield. Unfortunately for them, the area was very close to most of McClellan's army. When Union reinforcements rushed forward, the Confederates fell back in the darkness. Jackson never even saw the battlefield until marching over it the next day.

During the night, the Federals fell back to Malvern Hill.

Drive another 2 miles, then slow down at the ruins of the Willis Creek Church parsonage, located on the right. This is where the Confederates formed on July 1 for the charge up the open ground of Malvern Hill—right into the muzzles of dozens of Union cannons.

Proceed to the National Park Service shelter on the top of Malvern Hill, which is only a slight elevation. A few cannons point down the hill toward the parsonage. It is easy to see this place as a killing ground. It was up this hill that the troops of Lewis Armistead, John Magruder, and D. H. Hill charged with no more thought or purpose than to do just that—charge.

The plan was to knock the Federal cannons out with a massed artillery barrage, but the Confederates couldn't manage to put their guns into place. As soon as some would unlimber, the Federal cannons would find their range and knock them out. Jackson ordered some guns into an open space on the field. They were smashed before they could do any good. From the Federal point of view, it was a magnificent gunnery exhibition, thanks to Colonel Henry Hunt, a Michigan native who knew as much about artillery as anyone in either army.

Though the Confederate cannons had accomplished nothing against the Federal artillery, three of Armistead's regiments, without any clear orders to do so, attacked the Federal lines. Other Confederate units joined in and pushed for the crest of the hill.

D. H. Hill later commented, "This was not war. This was murder."

Hunt's Union artillerymen put away the solid shot and explosive shells that had so successfully knocked out the Confederate cannons and switched to canister. Canister was nothing more than a can filled with minie balls. When the cannon fired, it thus became a giant shotgun. On this day, the

Federals had more than 100 giant shotguns, while the Confederates had lost almost all of theirs. The Battle of Malvern Hill was thus fought by Union cannons against Confederate muskets.

The cannons won, making this one of the few instances during the war when artillery fire was so well placed that it turned the tide of combat. By the time the battle was over, more than 5,500 Confederates had fallen, compared to only 3,200 Federals.

Though he had won the battle, McClellan still retreated toward the James River. Lee's army, having suffered more than 20,000 casualties versus McClellan's 16,000, did not pursue. The Seven Days was over. Richmond was safe.

The Seven Days was a strange campaign. McClellan won virtually every battle, yet he continued to leave the fields to the Confederates. Lee's army fought on its own ground, yet his commanders could not seem to find the right roads to the right battlefields. Nor could any of them read a watch and arrive at the right time. Lee prepared vague orders, which were often ignored even when his commanders understood them. Under normal circumstances, Lee might have been relieved of command for failing to coordinate his army.

But he wasn't. Despite all the mistakes made by Lee and his sleepy new lieutenant, Jackson, they had pushed McClellan back from the gates of Richmond. To the citizens of the South, that was all that mattered. The Seven Days Battles solidified support for Lee, which would only grow stronger when he reorganized the army into two corps, one under Longstreet and one under Jackson.

As for Jackson, it was only following the Seven Days that he seemed to come awake. The day after Malvern Hill, he had his army clear the bodies off the battlefield. It was grim work, as most of the dead had been horribly mangled by cannon shells. When someone asked him why he was being so meticulous, he replied that he was going to attack over this field soon, and that it did not do men any good to attack over ground still occupied by the bodies of their comrades.

Jackson pushed Lee to attack McClellan at his base on the James, believing that the Confederates could crush the Union forces with their backs to the river. Lee gently refused. His army was badly hurt. And he may have also figured that if the smallness of the Confederate army was finally revealed to McClellan, the Union general might turn bold enough to launch a full-scale assault. Up to that point, McClellan had been operating under faulty intelligence that Lee's army was at least as large as, if not larger than, his own. McClellan had not seen Lee's entire army himself, and Lee probably figured that was a good thing.

What was wrong with Jackson during the last week of June 1862? All the evidence suggests that he was just mentally and physically exhausted. Once he found time to rest, he fought just as hard and as brilliantly as he ever had. He never repeated the strange episodes of aimlessness during the 10 months he had left to live.

Return to Va. 156 and continue south one mile, then turn right on Va. 5. You will pass the junction with Kingsland Road after 1.8 miles; continue 0.5 mile on Va. 5 to the historical marker for the Battle of New Market Heights. Drive up the gravel road just before the marker. You'll see the remnants of trenches on the left as you proceed up the slight hill.

This is one of the most historic battlefields of the war for black Americans. On September 29, 1864, six regiments of United States Colored Troops took New Market Heights, a strong Confederate position that had been successfully defended against two white Union assaults. The battle was so fierce that 14 of the 16 Medals of Honor awarded to black soldiers during the war came from this one fight.

The man who ordered the attack was General Ben Butler, a Massachusetts politician who had served on every front from Fort Monroe on the Peninsula to New Orleans. He was not well respected by other Union officers, and his commanders tried to shuffle him away from the high-profile fighting. Since Butler was an abolitionist, they gave him black troops to put in his Army of the James.

While other Union commanders thought black soldiers were unreliable at worst and unproven at best, Butler had a different opinion. As he put it, "The Negro had not had sufficient opportunity to demonstrate his valor and his staying qualities as a soldier. I determined to put them in position, to demonstrate the fact of the value of the Negro as a soldier and that the experiment should be one of which no man should doubt, if it attained success."

Butler was right about the way his fellow generals viewed blacks. The first time blacks had been given the chance to fight a real battle was in July

1863, when Union generals threw them against Battery Wagner at the mouth of Charleston Harbor in South Carolina. It was a poorly planned assault doomed to failure from the start, but the black soldiers of the 54th Massachusetts Regiment went in anyway. More than half of them did not return. The embarrassed white generals muttered something about it being the blacks' fault that the fort was not taken.

Now, a year later, despite the proof in blood of the bravery of black troops in general and the 54th in particular, Union generals were still unwilling to put them on a par with white troops. Even if the blacks could fight, the generals did not believe they had the intelligence to lead. The highest rank a black man could achieve at this stage of the war was sergeant. All officers were white.

Butler decided to prove everyone wrong. Though he had white regiments under his command, he picked the black regiments to lead the attack.

At 3 A.M. on September 29, five regiments made ready to advance on the hill. From where Va. 5 stands today, the attack came from left to right, south to north. As the men prepared their weapons, Butler himself rode up to them. He told them that when they took the trenches, they should cry, "Remember Fort Pillow!" Five months earlier, a large number of black troops had been killed at Fort Pillow in Tennessee. Rumors in the North said that they had been murdered after surrendering. What actually happened remains unclear to this day. Some historians believe that many of the blacks killed at Fort Pillow were battlefield deaths at the hands of Confederates who were angry that the fort's white commander had refused several chances to surrender.

As the black regiments advanced on the entrenched Confederates on New Market Heights, they must have wondered about their commander. General Charles Paine was a Harvard-educated lawyer. A close friend to Butler, he had boasted the same military experience as Butler when the war started—exactly none. Having been shuffled from command to command until ending up with Butler, he had no business planning or leading such an attack—and he proved it early. Paine strung his men out in a long line, did not provide support troops should any of his regiments break through, and started his attack before getting word that the white units on his right were in position.

The black troops pushed through an open field and up a ravine, then ran into something Paine had not prepared for—obstructions such as cut brush and abatis (sharpened sticks). They were stopped in their tracks, right within range of the Confederate muskets. The first two regiments that got close to the Confederate line were cut to pieces. Several Medals of Honor were later awarded to the color guards for saving their regimental flags.

Another black regiment got the call the next time. Instead of putting his men in a long line, that regiment's colonel lined them up six companies wide and 10 ranks deep, much like Emory Upton had done at the Mule Shoe at Spotsylvania Court House just a few months earlier (see The Overland Campaign Tour, page 257).

What the Federals did not know was that the Confederates were thinning their lines on New Market Heights. At the same time the black brigade was advancing on the heights, Butler was also attacking Fort Harrison to the south. Since the Confederates considered Fort Harrison more important than New Market Heights, they were moving out.

With fewer Confederates to fight, the blacks moved into the trenches. One subsequently won the Medal of Honor for continuing to fire his musket after his left hand had been mangled. Five sergeants were given the medal for taking command of their companies after all the white officers were killed or wounded. Though casualties were heavy—almost 40 percent of those engaged—the men proved that they were as good as any white soldiers.

After the battle, one of the surviving white lieutenants found his color sergeant, the man assigned to carry the regimental flag, lying on the field with both his legs shattered by a cannonball. The lieutenant broke the sad news to the man that he would not survive. The sergeant replied, "Well, I carried my colors up to the works and I did my duty, didn't I?"

Butler described the battle's aftermath this way: "When I reached the scene of their exploit, their ranks broke, but it was to gather around their general. I felt in my heart that the capacity of the Negro race for soldiers had then and there been fully settled forever."

Though Butler believed in his men, he was never able to overcome the racism of Grant and Sherman, both of whom refused to accept blacks under their direct command. And after the war, the 180,000 United States Colored Troops who had fought on all fronts from Virginia to Texas received a final insult when the black soldiers in the Army of the James were denied permission to march in the grand review down Washington's Pennsylvania Avenue, while Grant's and Sherman's all-white armies were treated as heroes. The victory parade of the war that freed the black man from slavery was thus a whites-only affair.

It is ironic to look back at the way black soldiers were treated by both sides. Though it was officially against Confederate law to arm slaves, black musicians, cooks, body servants, and soldiers drew the same pay and duties as whites and were sprinkled throughout the Southern regiments. Meanwhile, the Union's black soldiers were segregated into all-black regiments. The Confederates integrated their army in 1861, a feat not accomplished by the United States Army until 1950.

Retrace your route to the junction with Kingsland Road and turn right. After about 3 miles on Kingsland Road, turn left on Varina Road. Follow Varina Road to where it dead-ends near the James River.

During the war, this was Aiken's Landing. President and Mrs. Lincoln arrived here to review the Army of the James on March 26, 1865. When Lincoln's ship landed, one of the first men to come aboard was General Phil Sheridan, the cavalryman whose command had burned out the Shenandoah Valley and killed J. E. B. Stuart. The tall president gazed down at the diminutive cavalryman and said, "General Sheridan, when this peculiar war began I thought a cavalryman should be at least six feet four inches high, but I have changed my mind. Five feet four inches will do in a pinch."

Turn around at the river. As you head back up Varina Road, imagine this to be a corduroy road, a road paved with logs laid across it to give wagons traction. Lincoln mounted a horse and rode off with Sheridan to review the troops, who were assembled in a field near the intersection with Kingsland. Bouncing over the logs in an ambulance wagon behind the generals were Mrs. Lincoln and Mrs. Grant. Since Mrs. Lincoln's head was hitting the ceiling of the ambulance, she was not starting her day in a good mood. That mood grew more dark when she arrived at the parade ground.

Lincoln did not impress everyone who saw him that day on the parade ground. A colonel on General Meade's staff wrote to his wife that the president was "the ugliest man I ever saw. I never wish to see him again."

Mrs. Lincoln and Mrs. Grant pulled up just in time to see the president riding down the reviewing line. Mrs. Ord, the wife of General Edward Ord, was riding at his side. When Mrs. Ord saw the ambulance, she excused herself and rode toward the first lady and the commanding general's wife. She was about to encounter a tornado.

As soon as Mrs. Ord reached the ambulance, Mrs. Lincoln exploded. "What does this woman mean by riding by the side of the president and ahead of me? Does she suppose that he wants her by the side of him?" she asked.

The officers standing around had no idea what to do. How do you restrain a woman who happens to be the wife of the president of the United States? When Mrs. Grant tried to defuse the situation, Mrs. Lincoln turned on her.

"I suppose you think you'll get to the White House yourself, don't you?" she screamed.

Mrs. Grant replied, "I am quite satisfied with my present position."

An aide to Ord tried to calm the situation by claiming that the president's horse was merely being gallant and wanted to ride beside the horse of Mrs. Ord.

"What do you mean by that?" screamed the first lady.

The tirade went on for some time. Embarrassed officers and soldiers tried to turn away. Mrs. Ord took the abuse out of fear of further angering Mrs. Lincoln but finally burst into tears.

It is unclear if the president noticed the exchange

The next night, Lincoln hosted a dinner for the Grants on board a ship at City Point, located several miles south of here. Mrs. Lincoln was not through with Mrs. Ord. She demanded that her husband remove General Ord because of the actions of his wife. General Grant gently told Mrs. Lincoln that Ord was a good officer.

Later that night, the aide who had been riding with Mrs. Ord was awakened and told to report to the president's stateroom aboard the ship. There, Mrs. Lincoln tried to get him to agree that Mrs. Ord was being forward with the president. The president merely looked tired and disgusted with his wife.

The aide later wrote this of Mrs. Lincoln during the trip: "She was at no time well; the mental strain upon her was great, betrayed by some nervousness approaching hysteria, causing misapprehensions, extreme sensitiveness as to slights or want of politeness or consideration."

Turn left back on to Kingsland Road. Drive about 1 mile to Fort Hoke/Brady Road and turn right; you'll see trenches on the left. It is 1.8 miles to Fort Hoke and Fort Harrison. There is an interesting trail through Fort Harrison, which was renamed Fort Burnham after Union general Hiram Burnham was killed near here.

Fighting took place here on September 29, 1864, the same day New Market Heights was attacked. The familiar name of this action is the Battle of Chaffin's Farm. It was a battle of opportunity. When Grant learned that Lee had detached some of his meager forces from Petersburg and sent them to the Shenandoah Valley, he figured he would strike Lee while he was at his weakest and where his lines were the thinnest. Grant sent 18,000 men from the Petersburg side of the James over a pontoon bridge to attack Fort Harrison and New Market Heights.

General Ord's white troops were successful in storming Fort Harrison, since it was so thinly manned, but General Burnham fell in the assault and Ord himself was hit in the leg.

The next day, Lee tried to retake the fort, which he considered key to the long-term defense of Richmond. His three assaults failed at least partly because of the Federals' repeating rifles, which provided much more firepower than the Confederates could muster with their single-shot muskets.

When you are ready to leave Fort Harrison, continue 0.5 mile north to Fort Johnson, which the Confederates built after losing Fort Harrison. Fearing that the Federals would try digging a tunnel underneath their trenches, as they had done the previous month at Petersburg, the Confederates dug a 27-foot ditch in front of the fort.

Just beyond Fort Johnson is Fort Gilmer. After the black troops took New Market Heights, they were to attack Fort Gilmer after an exhausted white division made no headway on the northern face. Black regiments made all the attacks from the east. A mixed-up order sent four companies of one regiment in a skirmish line to attack the fort. Barely half of those black troops made it to the ditch in front of the fort, as several hundred Confederates were able to concentrate their fire on fewer than 200 Union soldiers. Those blacks who reached the wall of the fort discovered that it, too, was protected by a steep ditch. As soon as they tried to climb the dirt wall, they were shot down. Their captain finally surrendered what was left of his command. All four companies of the Seventh United States Colored Troops mistakenly sent as a skirmish line thus simply disappeared from the rolls, dead or captured.

After the battle, Butler had a special medal struck for the black soldiers who took part in the action at New Market Heights and Fort Gilmer. One side was inscribed, "Freedom will be theirs by the sword." Butler later wrote that for years afterward, black men who had served under him would stop him in the streets to display their prized medals.

When you are ready to leave Fort Gilmer, continue a short distance to the junction with Va. 5 and turn left. After about 0.9 miles, turn right at the light on to Laburnum Avenue. Drive 12.5 miles through heavy urban traffic to Hermitage Road.

The remains of Ambrose Powell Hill lie beneath a bronze statue of the general at the center of this intersection. Hill's body was dug up from Hollywood Cemetery and moved here in 1892 by a former soldier and local developer who claimed he wanted to honor the general, but who may have been using Hill to promote his new suburban residential development.

Grave of A. P. Hill

The general's statue is a traffic hazard, to be sure. Drive past the statue, then turn around at the first opportunity, as you will next be heading south toward the city on Hermitage Road. Park to get a good look at the statue.

A. P. Hill was unique in that he was on the mind of both Jackson and Lee in their last conscious moments. Both of Hill's superiors gave orders to him in their dying delirium. It was not that Hill was highly trusted or even well liked by either man. It may have been that he was exasperating.

Thirty-nine years old when he was killed south of Petersburg in April 1865, Hill was born a rich boy in Culpeper, Virginia. He graduated in the middle of West Point's class of 1847, a year behind Jackson. He served in the Mexican War and had more than 20 years in the service when he resigned to join the Confederacy. He rose quickly, making major general in May 1862.

Hill became prominent during the Seven Days Battles by demonstrating what would prove both his strength and his weakness. He was bold and impatient, two traits that have good and bad sides. Being bold in attacking can surprise and defeat an enemy. On the other hand, being so bold as to attack by yourself without waiting for help can get your men killed. Hill often did just that, as at Beaver Dam Creek and Gaines Mill in the Seven Days, and later at Bristoe Station.

Assigned to Jackson's corps, Hill distinguished himself in many actions, though Jackson developed a deep dislike for the man because he was not pious. Indeed, Jackson may have learned all he cared to about Hill back at West Point. Hill apparently contracted gonorrhea in his days at the academy, and the disease was beginning to ravage his body by the time of the war.

Though Jackson had Hill arrested once for disobeying a minor order about resting his men, Hill never let his anger keep him from fighting. It was Hill's men who saved Lee's army at Sharpsburg when they marched the 22 miles from Harpers Ferry and went straight into battle. Wearing blue overcoats they had captured at Harpers Ferry, they got close enough to the Federals to smash them to pieces with a few volleys, ending the Yankees' best chance at winning the battle.

Lee appointed Hill to lieutenant general in May 1863, after Jackson's death. That may have been Lee's greatest mistake. Hill was a fighting general who liked to lead his men into battle. He was not suited to be a lieutenant general, who would be expected to stay behind the lines and plan the movement of divisions. Time after time, he displayed that. His worst mistake came at Bristoe Station, where he ordered brigades into an attack without checking the ground in front of him. A whole Union division rose up from behind a stone wall and massacred 1,300 of his men in just a few minutes.

On April 2, 1865, Hill and a staff member were riding south of Petersburg when they stumbled upon two Federals. Hill, a commanding general of Lee's army, should have turned around and ridden to safety. Instead, he drew his pistol, rode right up to the Federals, and demanded that they surrender. They responded by shooting him through the heart. Historians have speculated that Hill may have realized his venereal disease was in its final stages, and that he boldly challenged the Federals with the intention of dying a military hero, rather than a man driven insane by an illness resulting from the indiscretions of youth. At the time, his wife was just a few miles away at his headquarters. She was seven months pregnant.

The staff member survived the encounter. When he reported to Lee that Hill had been killed instantly, Lee responded, "He is at rest now. We who are left are the ones to suffer."

After viewing Hill's statue, drive south toward Richmond on Hermitage Road. Get on I-95 North after a few blocks. Drive 6.4 miles, then get on I-295 North at Exit 84-B. After just 0.25 mile on I-295, take the exit for U.S. 1 North. Turn left on Virginia Center Parkway at the first light. Drive to the second road and turn right on Telegraph Road. Go 0.2 mile and pull to the right in front of the monument to Lieutenant General James Ewell Brown Stuart, commander of the Confederate cavalry. The tour ends here.

This is Yellow Tavern, named after a nearby stagecoach stop. Yellow Tavern was the site of the last battle of the lovable, glory-seeking Stuart. The action here took place on May 11, 1864, at the same time Lee and the infantry were fighting at Spotsylvania Court House.

The battle was really a trap set by General Sheridan, who sent four brigades of Union horsemen toward Richmond knowing that Stuart's two brigades would have to stand and fight. What Stuart didn't know was that Sheridan's real goal was not to attack Richmond. It was to attack Stuart himself.

For more than two hours, the opposing sides charged and countercharged. At one point, Stuart rode up to a line held by one of his companies just as the Federals charged through it, both on foot and on horseback. Stuart pulled out his LeMat, a huge, .40 caliber, nine-shot revolver with a shotgun barrel for good measure. He fired at the Federals running past him. One of those Federals snapped off a shot from his .44 caliber revolver at the officer with the plumed hat. Stuart was hit in the side, the ball penetrating his intestines.

As he was being led away in an ambulance, Stuart spied some of his men leaving the field. "Go back! Go back! Do your duty as I have done and our country will be safe! I would rather die than be whipped!" he shouted.

Later, he told friends that if he should die, he was ready.

The ambulance took him to his brother-in-law's house in Richmond. Stuart knew he would die, though no doctor told him. It was common knowledge that a wound in the intestines would lead to peritonitis. He gave instructions about the disposition of his horses, his spurs, and his sword. Told of his condition, his wife, Flora, set out from north of Richmond to try to reach his side.

As he lay dying, Stuart heard a commotion outside. It was an ambulance carrying one of his top cavalry generals, James B. Gordon of North Carolina. Gordon had been wounded less than 24 hours after Stuart while fighting Sheridan near Meadow Bridge over the Chickahominy River. Stuart's aides did not tell him who was in the ambulance.

Stuart died at 7:38 P.M. on May 12, not long after requesting that those officers present sing his favorite hymn, "Rock of Ages." Stuart tried to sing along, then turned to his doctor and said, "I am going fast now. I am resigned. God's will be done."

Hampered by torn-up railroads and bridges, his wife did not arrive for another five hours.

When word was sent to Lee at Spotsylvania, he said, "Stuart never brought me a piece of false information. I can hardly think of him without weeping."

General Gordon died of blood poisoning six days after his wounding.

Erected in 1888, the monument stands 30 feet from where Stuart was shot while sitting astride his horse behind a split-rail fence. The monument is flanked by two 10-pounder cannons. While this seems like odd symbolism for a cavalryman, Stuart did have horse artillery with him some of the time. The monument is inscribed, "Fearless and faithful, pure and powerful, tender and true. He saved Richmond, but gave his life. This stone was erected by his comrades."

The site of the mortal wounding of one of the South's greatest heroes is now in a housing development.

J. E. B. Stuart's wounding site

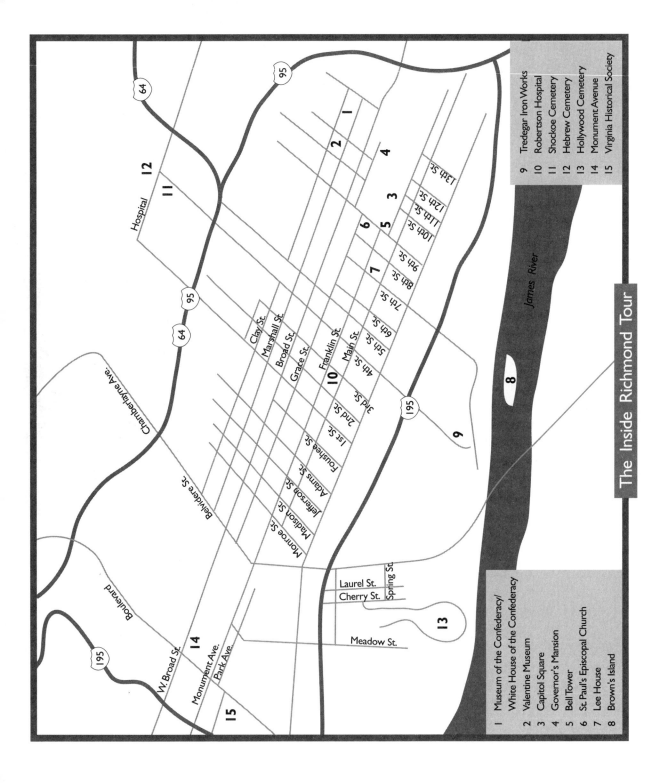

The Inside Richmond Tour

1 Museum of the Confederacy/
  White House of the Confederacy
2 Valentine Museum
3 Capitol Square
4 Governor's Mansion
5 Bell Tower
6 St. Paul's Episcopal Church
7 Lee House
8 Brown's Island

9 Tredegar Iron Works
10 Robertson Hospital
11 Shockoe Cemetery
12 Hebrew Cemetery
13 Hollywood Cemetery
14 Monument Avenue
15 Virginia Historical Society

James River

Hospital

Clay St.
Marshall St.
Broad St.
Grace St.
Franklin St.
Main St.

5th St.
6th St.
7th St.
8th St.
9th St.
10th St.
11th St.
12th St.
13th St.

4th St.
3rd St.
2nd St.
1st St.
Foushee St.
Adams St.
Jefferson St.
Madison St.
Monroe St.

Chamberlayne Ave.
Belvidere St.

Laurel St.
Cherry St.
Spring St.
Meadow St.

W. Broad St.
Monument Ave.
Park Ave.
Boulevard

64
95
195

The Inside Richmond Tour

This tour starts with a walk among some of Richmond's most historic sites. It begins at the Museum of the Confederacy and the Confederate White House, two must-see stops for anyone studying the war. It then visits the Virginia Capitol, the church where Jefferson Davis was worshiping when he heard that he had to evacuate the city, the Lee House, where the most famous photographs of the general were made, and the Tredegar Iron Works, the factory that kept the South alive. From there, it proceeds to a hospital site and the area where Richmond's women rioted for want of bread. Next, the tour moves by vehicle to the graves of a Union spy and some Jewish soldiers, then to Hollywood Cemetery and the graves of many Confederate heroes. It ends with a visit to the Virginia Historical Society and a drive down Richmond's famous Monument Avenue.

Though the tour is only 8 miles long, it will take a full day, as it visits two extensive museums and covers about 3.3 miles on foot.

THE TOUR STARTS at the Museum of the Confederacy and the White House of the Confederacy, located at Clay and 12th Streets in downtown Richmond; if you are coming from I-95, take Exit 74 and follow the signs directing you to the museum. Parking is at a premium in this area. Use the parking deck next to the museum.

The Museum of the Confederacy started more than 100 years ago in what is now the Confederate White House, the wartime home of Jefferson Davis and his family. In the 1970s, a larger, modern structure was built next to the White House, and the Davis home was restored to the way it looked in 1861.

Before you enter the museum, you'll see the anchor and the drive shaft of the CSS *Virginia* and the anchor chain of her first victim, the USS *Cumberland*, a steam frigate that was rammed and sunk by the Confederate ironclad. More than 200 Union sailors went down with the *Cumberland* off Norfolk in 1862.

One floor of the museum tells the story of the war from the Confederate side.

You'll note that some displays show a sense of humor. The huge saber of Prussian adventurer Heros Von Borcke, a six-foot-seven, 250-pound aide to J. E. B. Stuart, is displayed next to the delicate sword of Prince Camille Polignac, a much smaller French adventurer who was made a major general in the Confederate army. Polignac sometimes confused his men by issuing orders in French. Unable to pronounce his name, they called him "General Polecat."

Also on display are two telescopes of note. One was used by General P. G. T. Beauregard to observe the Union army at First Manassas. The other was used by Admiral Raphael Semmes to find Union ships when he commanded the CSS *Alabama*.

Among the flags on display is the prototype of the Confederate battle flag. That flag was designed by sisters at Beauregard's request in the wake of the confusion at First Manassas, when it was difficult to tell which side was which. The sisters designed a flag based on the blue cross of St. Andrew, placed on a background of red to reflect the Celtic heritage of most white Southerners. Thirteen stars were added to represent the 11 states of the Confederacy, plus Kentucky and Maryland, which sent many men to serve the South. Two versions of the flag were used—square for regiments in the East and rectangular for regiments in the West. Each regiment (ideally, 10 companies of 100 men each) was issued a flag either sewed by the women of their communities or manufactured and purchased. The men would then paint the names of their major engagements on the flag.

In another display case is Thomas J. "Stonewall" Jackson's sword, a United States–issue weapon that he carried the entire war. It may have been this sword that rusted in its scabbard from disuse and that fell after being leaned against a tree the night before Jackson was wounded. Celtic tradition says that a sword that falls of its own accord is a sign that its owner will soon die.

The sword and pistol of General Joseph Johnston are in one case. The sword is surprisingly simple for a weapon belonging to one of the top generals in the army, but it had sentimental value—Johnston's father had worn it during the American Revolution. When Johnston was wounded at the Battle of Seven Pines east of Richmond, his aides took his sword and his pistol belt off him to check his wounds. They left both on the field. When Johnston discovered they were gone, he asked an aide to ride back to the battlefield to see if they could be recovered. The aide found them and returned them to the greatly relieved Johnston.

You'll also see the headquarters flag of General Lee, a modification of the first national flag of the Confederacy with the stars arranged in an **A** shape. Nearby is a tent set up to show how Lee slept on the field. On a table are his broad-brimmed hat, his gloves, his eating utensils, and other artifacts.

A very sober display contains the amputation kit that Jackson's surgeon used to cut off the general's left arm during the Battle of Chancellorsville.

In the same case is a sketchbook belonging to Captain Keith Boswell, Jackson's chief engineer, the man the general trusted to find him roads on which to march. The last entry is a sketch of the fords around Chancellorsville. You'll note that the book has been ruined by a bullet hole. Boswell was carrying it in the pocket over his heart when he was hit in the same volley that wounded Jackson. A minie ball pierced both the book and his heart, killing him.

Nearby is a sentimental display containing the sword of General Lewis Armistead. Armistead crossed the wall at Gettysburg during the third-day charge but was struck down by a bullet as he touched a Union cannon. A Mason among the Federals noticed the sign of distress given by Armistead and comforted the mortally wounded Confederate general. Someone took the general's sword, but it was returned to Armistead's family in 1906 at a reunion of Union and Confederate veterans.

In the same display are the telescope of General Richard Garnett, who was killed in the same charge, and the coat of General James Kemper, who was severely wounded.

The racial diversity of the Confederate leadership is treated in a display on General Stand Watie, a Cherokee chief who was the only Indian to make general in either army. You'll see the flag of his unit, the Cherokee Mounted Rifles. Watie's command was the last to surrender in the war.

A display on General Ambrose Powell Hill contains the cape, sword, and hat he was wearing on the day he was shot and killed near Petersburg.

The tragic failure of another commander, John Bell Hood, is also covered. Like A. P. Hill, Hood was a good fighting general who turned out to be a poor thinking general. A quote from a common soldier when Hill was given command of the Army of the Tennessee shows the troops' opinion of him: "Thousands of men cried at the news." Hood ordered an attack at Franklin, Tennessee, in November 1864 that shattered the army, as the smashed pocket watch of General John Adams in the display demonstrates.

Adams was one of six Confederate generals who died in the charge.

Another display case contains the new uniform coat and the dress sword that Lee wore to the surrender meeting with Grant. Grant did not ask for Lee's sword, a symbolic gesture of surrender dating back hundreds of years.

In another case is the frock coat worn by Jefferson Davis on the day in May 1865 when he was captured in Georgia. That morning, Mrs. Davis threw a shawl around her husband's shoulders as he walked outside the tent. Within minutes, a Union patrol surrounded the camp, and a false story started that Davis had tried to escape disguised as a woman. The Federal government promoted the story in an attempt to discredit Davis, but even the Union soldiers who captured the Confederate president agreed that there was no truth to the story.

The other two floors of the museum contain rotating displays.

After you have enjoyed the museum, walk next door to the White House of the Confederacy, which is open for guided tours. Built in 1818, it was used by the Confederate government as a home for Jefferson Davis and his family for more than four years. The social and political center of Richmond and the Confederacy, it was used much like the White House in Washington, both as a home and as a working office for the president.

The house has been restored to look the way it did when the Davis family lived here. About 60 percent of the furnishings are original, recovered by the museum over the years from the families that bought them when they were auctioned by the city after the war to pay debts. The wall coverings and carpets appear gaudy by today's standards but were the height of fashion during the 1860s. The parlor has been furnished as it was when Davis met there with generals and political leaders.

There is a library on the first floor that the museum staff believes the Federals may have mistaken for Davis's office. President Lincoln visited the Confederate White House just one day after Davis fled the city. Federal sources recorded that Lincoln sat in Davis's chair, but they did not record that he visited the second floor of the house. Lincoln stayed in the house only a few minutes and may have believed the small library was Davis's office.

On the second floor are the bedrooms of the Davis family. Davis frequently worked in his second-floor office instead of walking to his downtown office.

In recent years, the staff here has collected some evidence that may dispute a long-told story that the Federal government had a spy inside the Confederate White House who stole secrets from Davis's second-floor office. For many years, it was believed that a black maid named Mary Elizabeth Bowser collected intelligence while working in the White House, which she then passed along to her spymaster, Elizabeth Van Lew, the Unionist woman who had placed Bowser in the job. According to a diary kept by another spy, Bowser could read and write and had a photographic memory. She would clean up President Davis's desk and look at the papers on it. Every morning, she would walk out to meet the man delivering bread and verbally report what she had seen. That man, also a spy, would pass the information to Van Lew, who would write it down and smuggle it out of the city to Union lines.

There are problems with that story, however. Van Lew was well known in Richmond as a woman brazen enough to prepare a room for General George McClellan in anticipation of his capturing Richmond during the Peninsula Campaign. It would not have made sense for the wife of the Confederate president to hire a maid on the recommendation of a Union sympathizer. Of course, the hiring might be explained by an entry in Van Lew's diary that says she got Bowser into the Davises' employ by going through a friend, so they would not know her connection. Still, it seems unusual that the Confederate White House would not know the few friends the Unionist Van Lew had in Richmond.

The evidence that the staff has in its possession is a letter written by Mrs. Davis after the war explaining to a friend that she never employed anyone named Bowser in the White House. It appears that Mrs. Davis was either covering up an embarrassing lapse in security or that a false story has been told for more than 135 years. There is also the possibility that Bowser used an assumed name.

The third floor is not open to visitors. It is believed that some of the family's servants had bedrooms there.

One of the people who may have slept on the third floor was Jim Limber. Jim was a little black boy of about six or seven when Mrs. Davis spotted him being whipped by a black man on the streets of Richmond. After grabbing the whip from the man and determining that Jim was either an orphan or an abused child, she took him home to the Confederate White

House. He lived there with the Davises and was a playmate of their children. The society of the day would never have approved anything like a formal adoption of a black boy by a white family, so it seems likely that the Davises treated Jim like a ward—someone they felt a responsibility toward.

Jim Limber accompanied the Davises on their flight from Richmond and was with them when they were captured in Georgia. The Federal soldiers took the boy—who was screaming "Mama!"—from Mrs. Davis. She never saw him again. Mrs. Davis made inquiries about him, but Federal officials saw a political danger in humanizing the Davis family's concern for a black child and never attempted to reunite them. Jim Limber thus disappeared into history.

As you leave the White House, you'll pass a wooden railing that serves as a reminder that even powerful men experience tragedy. Five-year-old Joe Davis was his father's pride and joy. The president was always willing to take time out from meetings to hear the young boy's prayers. On April 30, 1864, Joe fell from the railing while walking along it, probably in imitation of his older brother. He fell more than 15 feet and struck his head on the pavement below. He died in the children's bedroom. Davis spent all night mourning the death of his son, even ignoring a message from Lee that Grant was about to launch his spring assault on the Confederacy. Among the notes of condolence that arrived was one from President Abraham Lincoln, who was returning the favor Davis had done when Lincoln's son Willie died in 1862.

Walk one block west on Clay Street to the Valentine Museum at 1015 East Clay Street. Displayed inside is a death mask of Stonewall Jackson. It is so detailed that you can see the faint scratches on the general's face left by the branches that struck him as his frightened horse wheeled after his wounding. Also at the Valentine Museum is the early model for the statue of the sleeping Lee that is now on display at the Lee Chapel in Lexington.

Continue a half block on Clay Street to 10th Street, turn left, and proceed one block to Capitol Square. The large statue of George Washington was carved in England and placed on this site in 1858. The South was so enamored of Virginia's native son that this statue was used as the model for the Confederate seal.

Nearby are statues of Stonewall Jackson and Dr. Hunter Holmes McGuire,

Jackson's surgeon, who founded the college of medicine at Virginia Commonwealth University.

On the southeastern end of Capitol Square is the Governor's Mansion, built in 1814. It was home to two wartime governors, John Letcher and William Smith. Stonewall Jackson's body lay in state at the Governor's Mansion on the night of May 11, 1863, before his funeral the next day in the Capitol.

Walk inside the Capitol to visit the legislative chamber, where the Confederate Congress met throughout the war. Lee did not think much of the politicians who occupied this room. He once described them to an aide as men who were unwilling to do more than "chew tobacco and eat peanuts."

A statue of Lee stands on the spot where he accepted command of Virginia's troops on April 21, 1861. Nearby is a bust of Joseph E. Johnston.

It was in this same room that Jackson's casket was placed in front of the Speaker's chair. It was draped with the second national flag of the Confederacy—the first time the "Stainless Banner" was ever used. The rectangular flag was white with a square Confederate battle flag in the upper corner. The original is on display at the Museum of the Confederacy.

When you are ready to leave the Capitol, walk west to the bell tower, built in 1824. This tower signaled Richmond for all major events, from fires to military emergencies. During the war, its bells rang almost continually. The most important ringing came in April 1865, when the occupying Federals summoned citizens to help fight the fire that had started when retreating Confederates blew up the city's remaining war supplies.

Cross Ninth Street, turn right, and walk to St. Paul's Episcopal Church, located at the corner of Ninth and Grace Streets. This was the spiritual center for many of the city's leaders, including Davis and Lee, who often attended services here. Davis was in church on Sunday, April 2, 1865, when he received a note from Lee telling him that Petersburg had fallen and that it was time for the cabinet to evacuate Richmond. Davis's pew is marked.

It was in February 1865 that the church experienced its saddest moment. On January 19, General John Pegram married Hetty Cary, one of the prettiest belles of the city. Pegram was one of the best hopes the Confederacy had left. Active in the war since the first battles in western Virginia, he had fought out west before returning to Virginia to join Lee. Less than three weeks after presiding over the marriage at St. Paul's, the same priest performed a funeral for Pegram, who had been shot through the heart at the Battle of Hatcher's Run south of Petersburg.

Turn around and walk south on Ninth Street to Franklin Street. Turn right on Franklin. Located at 707 East Franklin is a private business. Though the lower floor of this house can't be viewed from the street, it contains what must be the most famous back door in the South.

Door of the Lee House

This is the home where Mrs. Robert E. Lee lived from 1864 through 1865, and it was to this house that the general came after surrendering at Appomattox Court House. A few days after the surrender, noted photographer Mathew Brady knocked on the door. Lee, one of his sons, and aide Walter H. Taylor agreed to pose for a remarkable series of photographs showing a defeated general. It was with this series of photographs that the legend of Robert E. Lee as a Southern icon started. The door is the very same, down to the vertical cracks that can be seen in some of the photographs.

What made the photographs special was the door itself and Brady's placement of Lee in relation to it. The panels of the door form a perfect cross, and whether by chance or by purpose, Brady placed Lee's head in the center of the cross, with the cross above him, or with the cross over his shoulder. Those images inspired Southerners to think of Lee as a weary Christian soldier who did his duty for his country and his state.

Turn around and walk back to Seventh Street, turn right, and head toward the James River. Located in the river is Brown's Island, the site of a facility that manufactured musket cartridges. In March 1863, that facility blew up, killing 10 women instantly and mangling their bodies so badly that identification was impossible. Thirty other women later died of their wounds, and another 20 were left with serious burns. Making ammunition was women's work, as most of the men were in the army. The cause of the explosion was never established, but it likely was a spark that landed in a container of black powder.

Continue south to where Seventh Street ends at Tredegar Street at the river. Turn right and walk about 0.3 mile to visit the Tredegar Iron Works, a facility that was in the process of being converted into a National Park Service visitor center at the time of this writing. Tredegar was built in 1837. Most of it was torn down after the war, but some of the more important buildings—such as the cannon foundry—have been saved.

The Confederacy could not have survived as long as it did without this ironworks. More than 1,000 cannons were manufactured here. The iron plating for the CSS *Virginia* and several other ironclads was rolled here. Even experimental weapons such as "torpedoes"—more accurately, mines— were built at this facility.

The boss of the factory was General Joseph Reid Anderson, a brilliant 1836 West Point graduate who spent little time in the military before going to work for the Tredegar Iron Works in 1841. By 1860, Anderson had used his engineering skills to make Tredegar one of the leading iron foundries in the nation—a rarity in the South, where agriculture was king.

Tredegar Iron Works

Anderson joined the Confederate army and fought in the Seven Days Battles before he resigned and put his mind to better use by running the iron foundry again. Overcoming a constant shortage of raw material, Anderson kept the foundry working for the entire war. When Richmond caught on fire, he forced his men to stay at their posts and keep his buildings from burning.

After the war, Anderson continued running Tredegar, turning out rails to rebuild the Southern railroads.

Retrace your route to the corner of Seventh and Main Streets. If you would like a short side trip, turn left on Main and walk to Third Street. This corner was the site of the Robertson Hospital. A commercial building now stands on the site.

The Robertson Hospital was the most successful hospital in Richmond. It was also one of the smallest, being little more than a private house. Named after the judge who owned it, the hospital was really the creation of Sally Tompkins, a 27-year-old single woman who opened it to treat soldiers after First Manassas.

When professionally trained male doctors saw that the untrained Tompkins was having greater success in saving patients than they were, they did what came naturally. They demanded that the government shut her down, pointing out that the law stated that all military hospitals had to be run by military personnel. President Davis then did something unconventional. He appointed Tompkins a captain in the cavalry, giving her a rank that would allow her to continue drawing military supplies.

Records show that 1,333 Confederates were admitted to Tompkins's hospital and that only 45 died. The key to her success was apparently cleanliness, an idea that had not yet caught on with many in the medical establishment.

If you take the side trip, walk back on Main all the way to 13th Street. If not on the side trip, turn right at 7th and go to 13th and Main. This is the general area where the Bread Riots raged.

On April 2, 1863, some 400 hungry women rallied on the Capitol lawn to draw attention to the fact that the poor of the city were starving. The crowd grew restless and moved south through this area, breaking into shops and stealing food and other goods. The situation grew so bad that the militia was called out to confront the rioters at Main and 15th Streets.

Jefferson Davis himself rushed to the scene, pleading with the crowd of women to disperse. He even emptied his pockets of a few coins to show them that he was no richer than they. In the end, he ordered the militia to fire on the women if they didn't disperse. The women finally did leave. The newspapers never reported the incident out of fear that the North would learn how desperate things were in the capital city.

The riot did have a positive effect, in that the city subsequently established a more efficient system of collecting food and distributing it to the poor.

Turn north on 13th, walk through the capitol grounds and retrieve your car at the Museum of the Confederacy. Because of constant construction to the hospital, it is difficult to give precise directions. Find the best way west to 4th Street. Turn right on Fourth and go about 0.3 mile to Hospital Street. Turn left on Hospital Street. To the left is Shockoe Cemetery. Drive to the second entrance, turn in, and go about 50 yards, looking for a black arrow pointing to the right toward the grave of Elizabeth Van Lew.

As you might expect of an infamous Union spy, Van Lew's grave is different from every other one in the cemetery. It is marked with a boulder sent from Massachusetts by a Union soldier she helped escape. On it is the inscription, "She risked everything that was dear to her—friends, fortune, comfort, health, even life itself—all for one absorbing desire of her heart— that slavery might be abolished and the Union preserved."

When she died in 1900 at the age of 82, not a soul from Richmond came to her funeral. No one had forgiven her for working for the Union.

Across the street is the City Alms House, built before the war and used as General Hospital Number 1.

Walk across Hospital Street into Hebrew Cemetery. The military cemetery for the Jews of Richmond is surrounded by ornate ironwork designed to look like stacked muskets, furled flags, and crossed sabers. A monument inside the ironwork reads, "To the glory of God and the memory of the Hebrew Confederate soldiers who rest in this hallowed spot." Erected in 1866 by the Hebrew Ladies Memorial Association, it was one of the first postwar monuments in the South. The Jews buried here were from Virginia, Texas, Louisiana, Mississippi, South Carolina, North Carolina, and Georgia. Conscious of anti-Semitism when raising money for the monument, the ladies ended one appeal with these words: "In time to come, when our grief shall have become, in a measure, silenced, and when the malicious tongue of slander, ever so ready to assail Israel, shall be raised against us, then, with a feeling of mournful pride, we will point to this monument and say, 'There is our reply.' "

In 1860, the Jewish population of the United States was under 150,000— less than one-half of 1 percent of the country's 30 million people. By contrast, there were more than 4.5 million slaves in the country at the start of the war. Many of the Jews had arrived barely 30 or 40 years before the war. Jews were therefore still considered newcomers to the country.

Though the Jews were scattered among both Northern and Southern states, they more readily ascended into the higher classes in the South, perhaps in part because the South was settled primarily by independent-minded Scots and Irish, who brought few continental prejudices with them, compared to settlers in the North.

At the start of the war, there were two Jewish United States senators, David Levy (later changed to Yulee) of Florida and Judah P. Benjamin of Louisiana. Both resigned their seats to serve the South, Yulee in the Confederate Congress and Benjamin as a cabinet member. But while neither man tried to hide the fact that he was Jewish, neither embraced or openly practiced his religion. Both men married outside the Jewish faith.

No accurate records exist on how many Jews joined the Confederate army, but their number probably at least equaled the 6,000 said to have served in the Union army. Many rose high in the ranks. Abraham C. Myers was the army's first quartermaster general, a position he lost when his Christian wife called Mrs. Jefferson Davis "an old squaw." David De Leon became the Confederacy's first surgeon general. Major Raphael J. Moses served as a commissary officer for General James Longstreet's corps and proved so valuable that Lee once refused to grant him a furlough to go back to Georgia to implore the farmers to grow more food. It was Major Moses who carried out the last official order given by the Confederacy—taking the remaining $30,000 in gold coins in the treasury to Augusta, where it was to be used to pay for the care of the wounded. He turned the money over to a Federal officer only after eliciting a promise that it would go for that purpose. The Federal officer kept his word.

When the war started, there were two Jewish congregations in Richmond, Beth Ahabah and Beth Shalome. Both contributed young men to the fighting. Many of the Jewish soldiers signed up with a unit called the Richmond Blues.

Because there were so few Jews, the Confederacy did not recruit any rabbis to serve their religious needs. Early in the war, the Reverend Maximilian J. Michelbacher of Beth Ahabah wrote a prayer, had it printed, and mailed it to all the Jewish soldiers he could find. He hoped it might help them keep in touch with their religion.

Michelbacher did what he could for the Jews in the army. On at least three occasions, he wrote Robert E. Lee asking that the general give leaves to Jews so they could return home for religious observations.

"I will gladly do all in my power to facilitate the observance of the duties of their religion by the Israelites in the army and will allow them every indulgence consistent with safety and discipline. If their applications be forwarded to me in the usual way, and it appears that they can be spared, I will be glad to approve as many of them as circumstances will permit," Lee replied on September 20, 1864. Unfortunately, by that time, Richmond and Petersburg were surrounded, and the Jews could not be spared.

Michelbacher also did what he could to fight a rising tide of anti-Semitism. He gave a speech in Fredericksburg in 1863 in which he defended Jewish merchants wrongfully accused of gouging prices. As the war wore on, the stories persisted. The congregation of Beth Ahabah voted to start a fund for the poor in the hope that it would be a good public gesture, but the people of Beth Shalome rejected the idea in the belief that the poor were the responsibility of all religions, not just the Jews.

Of course, discrimination against Jews was just as prevalent in the North. Most Southerners seemed to treat the Jewish soldiers decently. One story tells of how Major Hart, a Jew from Louisiana, was wounded in the leg during a battle near Richmond. He was carried to a nearby house, where a surgeon prepared to saw off the leg. The lady of the house protested, saying that Hart was much too handsome to go through life without a limb. She offered to nurse him back to health. Hart kept the leg and became friends with the gentile family. One day after the war, he stopped at the family's home for a meal. When the lady of the house's daughter-in-law complained that there was no ham on the lunch table, the woman smiled and said, "No, there shall be no ham on my table when my Jewish son is here."

Return toward town on Fifth Street. Turn right on Broad Street and drive about 10 blocks. Look to the left when you pass Madison Street. One block over on Grace Street was the house where J. E. B. Stuart died in May 1864. That house was torn down long ago.

Drive three more blocks and turn left on South Belvidere Street

Grave of Henry Wyatt

Confederate pyramid monument

Grave of J. E. B. Stuart

(U.S. 1/U.S. 301). Just before I-195, turn right on Cumberland. Drive one block, then turn left on Laurel Street, following the signs for Hollywood Cemetery. You can stop at the office between 8:30 A.M. and 4:30 P.M. to pick up a free map showing the graves of dozens of famous people in this cemetery. The office also sells a book containing photographs of Confederate generals' graves.

Leaving the office, turn right on Confederate Avenue, following the blue line on the road. Start the drive up the hill. Look for a cast-iron dog on the left. Stop and walk across the road to the right. Behind two bushes is the grave of Private Henry Wyatt, the first Confederate soldier killed in the war. Wyatt, a North Carolinian, died at Big Bethel on June 10, 1861, when he and several other soldiers were ordered to set fire to a house that could be used as cover by Federal sharpshooters. He was the only Confederate to lose his life in the battle.

Continue on the road until you reach a large pyramid made of boulders, dedicated to the Confederate unknowns buried in the cemetery. The capstone was placed by a prisoner, who was granted his freedom for climbing the rough-cut stones.

Drive to the top of the next hill, near a street. Here is the grave of General George Pickett. Pickett's monument is unique in that each face gives a history of the brigades that fought under his command. At his feet rests his wife, LaSalle, who outlived her husband by decades and who dedicated her life to remaking Pickett from a middling general into a Southern hero. She was moved to his side a few years ago.

Continue following the blue line down Western Avenue, then left on to Ellis Avenue. On the right at the bottom of a curve is the obelisk of J. E. B. Stuart.

Continue following the blue line up Hillside Avenue to the Presidents Circle. Here rest President James Monroe, President John Tyler, Matthew Maury, and General Joseph R. Anderson.

Tyler died before he could take office in the Confederate Congress.

Though Maury was born far from the sea—actually on the Chancellorsville Battlefield—he wanted to sail. Injured in an accident, he was confined to a desk, where he spent his time studying how the winds and the currents affected the ocean. His studies proved valuable to all navigators. During the war, he clashed with the secretary of the Confederate navy over what types of ships the South should be building, so he spent most of his time in England buying supplies.

Anderson was the man behind Tredegar Iron Works.

Continue following the blue line. Stop just before curving left on to Monroe Avenue. Walk to the left. Two graves in, you'll find the small tombstone of General Philip St. George Cocke. Cocke, an 1832 graduate of West Point, was more a farmer than a soldier, resigning after two years of service to study agriculture. He served on the board of military advisers at V.M.I. for nine years and was president of that board when Thomas J. Jackson was offered a job as professor. Cocke fought in only two minor engagements before committing suicide in December 1861. Judging from the stories told by his family, he seems to have suffered a nervous breakdown.

Grave of George Pickett

Follow the blue line up Jeter Avenue until it intersects a road leading to a circle on the right. Park and walk to the right front portion of the circle to find the grave of Henry Heth. Supposedly the only general Lee ever called by his first name, Heth gets mixed reviews from most historians. He was a fighter, but he often made mistakes and never owned up to them. It was Heth who sent his entire division into battle on July 1, 1863, at Gettysburg, ignoring Lee's express order not to bring on a general engagement until all the army was ready. Because Heth started fighting before he could be reinforced, his division was held up, which gave Federal reinforcements time to arrive. Those reinforcements kept the Confederates from occupying the high ground behind Gettysburg—ground they would continue to attack for two fruitless days.

Grave of Henry Heth

Follow the blue line down the hill to Davis Circle. The entire Davis family is buried here.

Park to admire the statue of Jefferson Davis. Davis died in 1889 while visiting New Orleans and was originally buried there. Years later, his body was moved to Hollywood Cemetery.

Walk to the edge of the circle to find the small tombstone of Joe Davis, which was erected with the help of money raised from his little playmates around Richmond.

Just southwest of Davis Circle is the grave of Fitzhugh Lee, the general's nephew. Fitzhugh Lee started the war as a Confederate staff officer. Severely wounded, then captured while recuperating, he did not return to service until late in the war, at which time he ended up in command of cavalry.

Grave of Jefferson Davis

The Inside Richmond Tour

Grave of Fitz Lee

A view of the James River from Hollywood Cemetery

His reputation was tarnished at the end of the war when he went off with Pickett for a shad bake at Five Forks while his men were being smashed 2 miles away.

Drive along the James River. The island on the other side that has a pedestrian bridge running to it is Belle Isle, formerly a prison camp for Federal soldiers.

After passing Tyler Circle, keep watch on the left for graves with an iron fence around them. Here lie the remains of the Pegram family, including John Pegram, the young general who was killed three weeks after his wedding, and his younger brother, 24-year-old colonel William "Willie" Pegram. Though he looked more like a bespectacled schoolboy than a soldier, Willie Pegram was one of the best gunners in the Confederate army. He was killed on April 2, 1865, at Five Forks, just a few days after his brother's death and a week before Lee's surrender.

Continue on the road through the cemetery. When you are just about to leave the property, slow down and look to the right for a tombstone with a Confederate flag carved into it. This is the grave of John Imboden, who never seemed to hit his stride as a general. Imboden made news early in the war by capturing the Federal arsenal at Harpers Ferry. After being ordered to disband his partisan rangers, he was given another command, but he subsequently angered Lee on several occasions by acting independently of orders. He ended the war guarding prisoners.

Next to Imboden is evidence of a family tragedy. In January 1862, General James Longstreet got to spend a week in Richmond with his wife, Louise, and their four children. Almost as soon as he returned to his duties with the army, Longstreet received a telegram informing him that all four children had been stricken with scarlet fever. He hurried back to Richmond in time to watch his one-year-old daughter die on January 25. The next day, his four-year-old son died. Five days later, his six-year-old son died. The Longstreets were so saddened that neither attended the children's common funeral, which was planned by the general's old friend George Pickett. All three children are buried here under a triple stone. The oldest son of the family survived.

When you leave the cemetery, retrace your route to Broad Street. Turn left on Broad and follow it past Boulevard Street. Continue at least four

TOURING VIRGINIA'S AND WEST VIRGINIA'S CIVIL WAR SITES

blocks, watching for an opportunity to turn left before reaching I-195. After making the left turn, go one block, then turn left on Monument Avenue and drive east.

Located at Monument Avenue and Belmont Avenue is a statue of Matthew Fontaine Maury, unveiled in 1926.

At Monument Avenue and Boulevard Street is a statue of Stonewall Jackson, unveiled in 1919. It was sculpted by the local man who also did the Virginia Monument at Gettysburg. The horse Jackson is riding was based on a local racehorse, rather than on Little Sorrel.

Turn right on Boulevard and drive one block to the Virginia Historical Society. Inside this building are a number of Civil War exhibits, including an example of every firearm and sword manufactured in the South, four large murals depicting the "Four Seasons of the Confederacy," Mrs. Lee's wheelchair, and J. E. B. Stuart's uniform. An exhibit on slavery describes how some of the slaves who were freed in this country emigrated to a new African nation, Liberia, and created a successful business for themselves—slave trading.

Virginia Historical Society

Return to Monument Avenue, turn right, and continue east. At Stafford Street, you will see a statue of Jefferson Davis, erected in 1907.

Next comes Strawberry Street and the largest statue of all, that of Robert E. Lee, erected in 1890.

The last statue, at Lombardy Street, is that of J. E. B. Stuart, erected in 1907.

Park nearby if you can find a spot. There are two places of interest here, where Monument Avenue becomes Franklin Street.

At 1205 West Franklin is St. James Episcopal Church, which has a stained-glass window dedicated to the memory of Sally Tompkins.

Just down the block at 1109 West Franklin is the Beth Ahabah Museum and Archives, which has some items that belonged to Judah P. Benjamin, as well as some old letters regarding Jewish Confederate soldiers. The original temple was located near where the Museum of the Confederacy stands today.

The tour ends here.

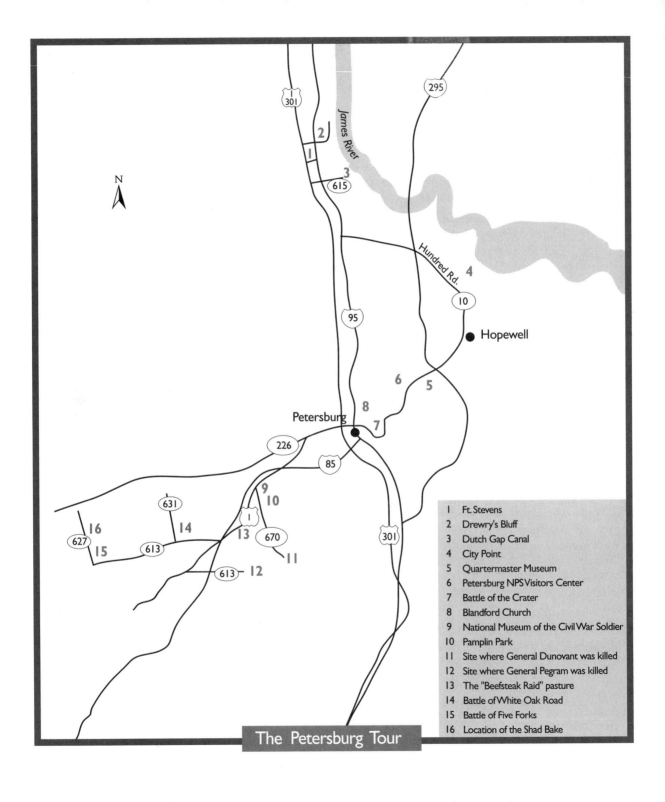

N

301

James River

2

1

3

615

295

Hundred Rd.

4

10

95

Hopewell

6

5

8

7

Petersburg

226

85

9

10

631

1

14

13

670

16

627

15

613

11

613

12

301

1	Ft. Stevens
2	Drewry's Bluff
3	Dutch Gap Canal
4	City Point
5	Quartermaster Museum
6	Petersburg NPS Visitors Center
7	Battle of the Crater
8	Blandford Church
9	National Museum of the Civil War Soldier
10	Pamplin Park
11	Site where General Dunovant was killed
12	Site where General Pegram was killed
13	The "Beefsteak Raid" pasture
14	Battle of White Oak Road
15	Battle of Five Forks
16	Location of the Shad Bake

The Petersburg Tour

The Petersburg Tour

This tour starts on the southern side of Richmond at Drewry's Bluff, a tiny fort that saved the city from attack by river. It then moves to City Point, a logistical center for the Union army, where Grant brought in thousands of tons of supplies to defeat the Confederates. From there, it moves to the Petersburg Battlefield, visiting the Crater as well as Blandford Church, one of the most beautiful war memorials ever built. The tour then visits several downtown Petersburg museums before heading to the southern side of town, where the Union finally penetrated the city's defenses. It ends at Five Forks, the site of the battle that sealed the city's fate.

The tour is 60 miles long but will take at least a day, depending on how long you care to linger at the several battlefields and museums.

THIS TOUR of the Petersburg area starts on the southern side of Richmond at Fort Stevens. If you are approaching from I-95, take Exit 64 between Petersburg and Richmond, head west on Willis Road for a short distance, then turn north on Pams Avenue. The preserved dirt fort is on the left.

Fort Stevens was part of a defensive line designed to protect Richmond from Federal advance from the south. In May 1864, it came under attack when General Ben Butler tried to make a move on Richmond. The line held.

Return to Willis Road and turn right. Proceed 0.5 mile to U.S. 301/U.S. 1, turn right, and drive about 0.5 mile to C.R. 656 (Bellwood Road), following the brown signs for Fort Darling, better known as Drewry's Bluff. The road passes under I-95. Turn left on to Fort Darling Road, which looks at first like an entrance ramp to the interstate. It parallels the interstate before making its way to Fort Darling.

In May 1862, this little dirt fort on the James River was much more important than it looks today. Early that month, the Confederate army withdrew from Yorktown and Williamsburg and the CSS *Virginia* was blown up, since it no longer had the port of Norfolk to call home. With the *Virginia* gone, the way up the James River to Richmond appeared to be open to Union gunboats, which meant that the Union navy would be free to shell the Confederate capital.

The only place the Confederates believed they might stop such an action was here at Drewry's Bluff, where the James narrows just 7 miles below

Richmond. What made this an ideal position was that the bluff was more than 100 feet above the water. That meant that the Confederate guns could be aimed well down the river, then depressed toward the water should a gunboat draw close. But the guns on board the Union ships could not be elevated high enough to fire at the bluff.

To further protect the river, the Confederates sank some old ships in the channel, which would make it that much more difficult for Union ships to maneuver. The *Virginia*'s former crew was assigned to man the heavy naval guns, creating the unlikely scenario of seamen manning shore batteries to fight enemy seamen.

On May 15, the USS *Monitor*, the same ship the *Virginia* had battled back in March, and the USS *Galena*, a wooden ship with iron sheathing, sailed up the James. For four hours, the land-based Confederate seamen poured shots down on the Federals. The *Galena* was hit numerous times and was eventually crippled. The *Monitor*, which had been so effective against another ironclad, proved useless against the shore battery on the bluff, as it could not raise its guns high enough to hit the Confederate batteries. In time, the Union ships withdrew, and Richmond was saved.

In 1864, the fort was the site of a land battle at which the Federals were again defeated.

Before you leave the well-preserved fort, look down on the James to see how good a position this was for the Confederates.

Retrace your route to U.S. 301 and head south. After 1.6 miles, look to the left for a restaurant called The Halfway House. General Ben Butler used this building as his headquarters.

You will then go under an overpass after 2.4 miles. The ridge ahead was where the Federals massed for their 1864 attack on Fort Darling.

After about 3 miles on U.S. 301, turn left on Osborne Road (C.R. 616) and follow the signs for Henricus Historical Park. After about 0.2 mile on Osborne, bear left on Coxendale Road (C.R. 615). In 1.6 more miles, you will cross a railroad track and pass a power station before reaching the park.

The small museum at the park concentrates on the 1611 settlement located in this area.

Follow the trail to the James River. At the end of the trail is Dutch Gap Canal, a project that seemed like a good idea at the time but that proved to be deadly busywork for hundreds of United States Colored Troops.

In 1865, the James River ran straight up to Drewry's Bluff and those deadly Confederate guns. Butler looked at a map of the river and decided he could bypass the guns and move on Richmond if he could do one simple thing—divert the river.

Dutch Gap Canal

It was not a wild idea. Here at Dutch Gap, the river made a tight bend—so tight that it seemed possible to create a canal deep enough to float Union gunboats and leave the Confederate fort high and dry, without any river below it.

Butler started digging the canal in August 1864, using thousands of black soldiers from the Army of the James. His men worked through the heat of summer. Some of them dropped dead at their shovels. The work was further hampered by Confederate snipers who took aim at the digging men. By November, nearly 70,000 cubic yards of dirt had been removed, all by hand. In January 1865, Butler decided he would speed matters by blowing up large portions of the canal using tons of black powder. When an explosion was set off, it moved the dirt just fine. On the other hand, it moved much of it back into the canal that had already been dug.

Grant and his Army of the Potomac watched all this digging with detached interest. To Butler's face, Grant expressed interest in the project. Behind Butler's back, Grant grinned. He did not value the help of the Massachusetts political general. He was satisfied to keep Butler's black men digging while he squeezed Lee at Petersburg.

In the end, the Dutch Gap Canal was never finished, and Richmond was never attacked from the lower James River. By April 2, 1865, Grant's men broke the lines around Petersburg, and Richmond fell anyway. All those months of digging and the lives of the black soldiers had been for nothing.

Mother Nature had the last laugh. Not long after the war, all the work Butler's men had put into the canal finally paid off. Heavy rainstorms collapsed the remaining walls of dirt, and the James River finally cut its own canal through Dutch Gap. Today, it is the main channel of the James, though water still flows beneath Drewry's Bluff.

Retrace your route to U.S. 301. Drive about 1 mile south on U.S. 301 to Va. 10 (Hundred Road) and turn left. Go about 9 miles on Va. 10 into

Hopewell, following the brown signs to City Point. Confederate and Union forts and trench lines were located along and just off this road.

Pull into the parking lot at City Point. This spot was settled in 1613. Remarkably, the land remained in the same family until being sold to the National Park Service.

The Eppes House at City Point served as the headquarters of Grant's quartermaster. The general himself, the commander of all Union forces, ignored the warm, comfortable bedrooms of the house and spent most of his time at City Point in a rough cabin, which has since been reconstructed on its original site. In fact, Grant told his officers that they would all sleep in tents, just as his men in the field were doing. But while he was away at a meeting, his officers rushed to construct cabins. When Grant returned, he moved into a cabin, ignoring the fact that his subordinates had disobeyed a direct order. Grant refused to move into the Eppes House mainly because he realized how important the quartermaster's job was.

If any site other than a battlefield can be considered crucial to the Union victory, it is City Point. For 10 months, this port on the James and Appomattox Rivers served as a gigantic supply base. At any one time, there might be 125 supply ships tied up at its eight wharves. Sometimes, there were more than 200 ships in the natural harbor. Everything Grant needed to supply—and oversupply—the 100,000 men and 60,000 animals besieging Petersburg passed through this port. City Point had everything, including a railroad that ran from the port toward Petersburg. The rail line was so close to the city that Grant had a large mortar mounted on a railroad car so it could shell the town.

Across the river in Hopewell was a large hospital capable of caring for 10,000 men. Not far beyond that hospital was another one, located on the Appomattox River at Butler's headquarters. This latter hospital, at Point of Rocks, had a very special nurse named Clara Barton.

It was not a large facility. Assigned to the 10th Corps under Butler, it rarely held more than 100 patients. But they were enough to keep Barton busy. She took particular concern in feeding the men decent meals, something that had not occurred to the doctors running the hospital. Later, Barton moved with the hospital when it was relocated closer to the fighting. Some histories call her the superintendent of nurses at the hospital, but that title was never officially granted. The wily Butler may have told her she held it, though he didn't have the power to award it.

All the knowledge she had gained on the battlefields of Virginia came in handy when Barton formed the American Red Cross in 1881. She headed that organization until 1904.

Abraham Lincoln visited City Point on two occasions—once in June 1864, when he accompanied Grant to the front lines in Petersburg, and again in late March 1865, when the war was nearly over. On that second trip, his wife, Mary, accompanied him and made his life hell. Once, when they traveled up the James to review the troops besieging Richmond, she lost control of herself and ended up shouting at a woman whom she believed was trying to steal the president away from her. On another occasion, Lincoln was at the telegraph office next to the Eppes House when his son kept telling him that "Mother" wanted to see him right away. A Union officer heard the president mutter under his breath, "Will that woman ever leave me alone?" Lincoln then walked down to his ship to see what his wife wanted.

The president visited the large hospital at City Point on April 8, 1865, and set some sort of record by shaking hands with more than 6,000 men in one day. His secretary later wrote that Lincoln's hand was severely cramped afterward. He would be dead just over a week later.

Such a large target as City Point could not be ignored by the Confederates. On August 9, 1864, a Confederate secret agent named John Maxwell successfully exploded an ammunition barge at one of the wharves, blowing more than 40 soldiers and sailors to oblivion. Grant himself was showered by body parts at least 200 yards away but was unhurt.

Maxwell did not have to swim underwater or sneak on to the base at night to get his bomb aboard the barge. He simply had a Union soldier carry it. After fashioning the bomb, the Confederate wired it to a simple timing device, put it in a box, walked up to a sentry, and told him that the captain of the barge wanted the box carried below. The sentry did what he was told. For years, the truth about how the bomb was placed was unknown. Finally, the spy, convinced he would not be arrested and hanged for murder, went public with the tale. A model of the timing device is on display inside the Eppes House.

City Point was the scene of an interesting meeting among Lincoln, Grant, and Sherman on March 28, 1865.

The two generals asked Lincoln what he expected of them once they cornered the two largest Confederate armies—Lee's in Petersburg and Johnston's in North Carolina.

"Let them all go, officers and all. Let them have their horses to plow with and their guns to shoot crows with. Treat them liberally, I say. Give them the most liberal and honorable terms," Lincoln responded.

When word of this got back to the radical Republicans in Washington, what few friends Lincoln had among them quickly dropped him. They could see the handwriting on the wall. They knew it was only a matter of time before the South was defeated, and they wanted the rebels to suffer a harsh penalty for the war. They wanted nothing to do with Lincoln's plan for a mild and easy reunion.

Some historians suggest that Lincoln's subsequent assassination might have been orchestrated by those same radical Republicans. According to that view, Lincoln's sudden, violent removal from office gave them a martyr. It also gave them free rein to move forward with their own ideas on how to punish the South. Still, most evidence points to southern sympathizer John Wilkes Booth.

After visiting the wharves, leave City Point. On your way out, you'll see a Union dirt fort built by Grant, who finally realized how vulnerable the port was after Confederate cavalry was sighted 6 miles away.

Turn right on Randolph Road. You'll pass Randolph Hospital, the site of the large Union hospital. Look for the signs for Va. 36.

Turn left on Va. 36, heading west toward Hopewell and Petersburg. You'll reach the Hopewell Visitor Center in 3.4 miles just before I-295. In 1864, this spot was the site of the Battle of Baylor's Farm, a small fight involving black soldiers.

You'll reach Fort Lee and the United States Army Quartermaster Museum on the left less than 2 miles after passing under I-295. Though most of the displays are not related to the Civil War, the museum does have Grant's favorite horse saddle and a display of other saddles used by the cavalry.

On the right just past the entrance to Fort Lee is the visitor center for

Petersburg National Battlefield Park. The visitor center tells the history of the Signal Corps, a Confederate innovation attributed to artilleryman Edward Porter Alexander. You'll also see pieces of the fuse that was used to blow up the Crater in August 1864. One interesting display contains two minie balls fired so in line with each other that they met in midair and were mashed together.

Walk around the outside of the visitor center to see Battery Number 5, where the fighting began in June 1864. Along the way, you'll pass 20 different artillery pieces.

The Union forces had an opportunity to end the fighting at Battery Number 5, but confusion over orders stopped them, as it had many other times during the war. On June 15, 1864, more than 30,000 Federals from the 18th Corps and the Second Corps rushed this fort, overpowering the 2,300 Confederates and capturing more than 1.5 miles of the Confederate line. But the Federals under William Smith and Winfield Hancock apparently could not believe what they had done. They milled around for more than 24 hours instead of rolling up the Confederate line.

General P. G. T. Beauregard rushed his few thousand Confederates from one section of the line to another while sending frantic messages to Lee in Richmond. Lee, who had been expecting Grant to attack the capital city, was unsure if Beauregard was being fooled, so he was slow to send reinforcements. Luckily for Lee, Grant's officers were slow, too. By the time they finally tried to move, Lee had realized the attack was real and had shifted his men down from Richmond. What had been a wide-open breach in the Confederate line was now closed up tightly. A victory that could have been won in days—if not hours—would not be achieved for nearly 10 months.

Walk the trail past Battery Number 5 to see "the Dictator," a 17,000-pound, 13-inch Federal seacoast mortar that was first operated from a rail car, then unloaded here. "The Dictator" fired a 220-pound shell loaded with 20 pounds of black powder. It could shell the city from more than 2.5 miles away. The shells were set to explode at treetop level, so they would spread their shrapnel. During the siege, the mortar lobbed more than 200 shells into Petersburg. While the gun looked fearsome, the civilians at whom it was aimed were entertained by it more often than not. They would watch the shells arc high over the city and speculate on where they would land.

Cannons displayed near Battery Number 5 at Petersburg.

The problem for the Union gunners was that they couldn't tell where the shells were landing and so could not redirect their fire.

Coming a year after the civilians of Vicksburg had been shelled, the shelling of Petersburg's citizens marked a continuing escalation in the type of warfare proposed by Sherman and Grant. They wanted to take the war right to the home front. By destroying private homes and businesses and creating civilian casualties, the Union hoped to create unrest in the Confederate armies. But the shelling, looting, burning, and violence unleashed upon women and children in the cities and on farms seemed to have the opposite effect. The more the Union punished civilians, the more resolute they became. Petersburg's citizens never demanded the surrender of their city. And the Southern soldiers did not desert to defend their homes.

Return to your vehicle and begin the driving tour of the battlefield.

Along the way is a stop at a winter quarters, where you'll see how both armies set up crude huts with tents for roofs.

Winter quarters at Petersburg

Stop at Harrison's Creek. This is the point to which the Confederates fell back in June 1864, during the first Union assault. It is also as far as the Confederates got in March 1865, when they poured over Fort Stedman in an attempt to break the Union siege line around the city.

Continue to Fort Stedman. This was the scene of Lee's last attempt to break out of Petersburg. What set the stage for the battle on the morning of March 25, 1865, actually occurred more than 100 miles away in the Shenandoah Valley. General Phil Sheridan had defeated the last Confederate force in the Valley earlier in the month and was now free to move toward Petersburg. Lee knew that Sheridan's forces would strengthen Grant so much that the Federals might try a new offensive to break his lines. Lee felt that his only choice lay in making an offensive move before Sheridan arrived.

The plan was to strike Fort Stedman, the Union outpost closest to the strongest part of the Confederate line, then move toward City Point. While Lee did not believe it was possible to capture the rich supply dump, he did think Grant would have to shorten his lines to face the attack. That would allow some of the Confederates to escape through the resulting gap. Those Confederates could then link up with Joe Johnston's army in North Carolina.

Fort Stedman

Before dawn, several thousand Confederates under General John B. Gordon quietly rushed Fort Stedman, a small facility armed with six cannons and just 300 Union soldiers. The attack showed promise of success until a quick-thinking Union division commander, not waiting for orders from higher up, threw his men into the breach and fought the Confederates to a standstill. Within minutes, other Federal units poured in from either side and surrounded nearly 2,000 Confederates, who decided to surrender rather than die trying to get back to their lines. Altogether, Lee lost the services of more than 4,000 men he had been counting on to continue the fight. It must have been at this point that he started contemplating that the end was very near.

The next stop is Fort Haskell, a neighboring Union fort that sent men to help at Fort Stedman.

The next stop is the Taylor Farm, where the Union army massed more than 200 cannons and thousands of men for an attack on the Confederate line in August 1864.

All that summer, the two armies faced each other, separated in spots by less than 200 yards. They were so close that they could shout insults at each other. Frustrated Union officers could not figure out how to dislodge the Confederates. One of them mentioned almost in jest that they should tunnel underneath the Confederates and come up on the other side.

Someone who did not take the suggestion in jest was Lieutenant Colonel Henry Pleasants, a civil engineer who had coal miners in his regiment, the 48th Pennsylvania. Pleasants went to his miners and asked them if digging a tunnel was possible. They dug into the dirt, studied how the ground would react, and said yes—and that they were just the miners to do it.

Pleasants sold the idea to his boss, Ninth Corps commander Ambrose Burnside, who sold it to Grant. Other engineers scoffed at the plan, claiming that the Confederates would hear and see the digging, that the air inside the tunnel would be too foul, that it would take too long—all kinds of reasons.

The miners paid them no attention. They just started digging. They used some tricks they had learned from coal mining, such as digging an air shaft halfway across the field and then building a fire underneath the opening, so fresh air would be drawn into the mine to replace the warm, stale air rising from the shaft.

The men dug around the clock for more than a month, finally finishing their work on July 23, 1864, at a point they estimated to be right under the Confederate lines. It took four days to place more than four tons of gunpowder in 320 kegs in a chamber hollowed out along the Confederate lines. By the time the miners finished, the tunnel was nearly 600 feet long and 75 feet wide at its far end, resembling a **T**. Gunpowder filled the top of the **T**.

While the engineers put the final touches on the shaft, four divisions of troops began to train for what to do once a hole was blown in the Confederate lines. The division selected to go in first was made up of black troops under General Edward Ferrero, a New Yorker whose sole military experience before the war had been teaching West Point cadets how to dance. Someone—probably not Ferrero—wisely instructed the soldiers to march around the giant hole that would be formed when the gunpowder blew up. The idea was that the Confederates would be so stunned by the explosion that they would be easily swept from the field by well-trained Union divisions rushing around the hole and then breaking away in opposite directions.

Just hours before the powder was set to explode, Grant and his second-in-command, Meade, met to discuss a political issue. What if the explosion did not come off as planned? Sending a division of black troops into the face of the Confederates might appear a racist act to the members of the abolitionist press, who already knew Grant didn't like United States Colored Troops. Grant began to imagine headlines charging that he intentionally sent blacks to their deaths in a hopeless attack.

Grant and Meade agreed to switch the order of attack, over the objection of Burnside. The blacks who had been training for the shock assault would be the fourth division into the breach, instead of the first. The frustrated Burnside told the commanders of the white divisions to draw straws to decide whose men would be first.

Looking back today, it seems incredible that such a momentous decision was left to chance. Even worse was the fact that the white divisions had not trained as hard as the black division. The whites had not been told to march around the hole. That failure in training came to haunt Grant's decision about which troops to send into the Crater.

Perhaps the biggest mistake of all was Grant's failure to relieve a totally incompetent general. The winner—or loser—of the draw, the man chosen to lead the attack on the Confederate line, was General James Hewett Ledlie, a New York civil engineer with no military service before the war. Ledlie's war career to that point had been less than stellar. In his first action, at Kinston, North Carolina, in 1862, he had commanded several batteries of artillery and had accidentally fired into a Union regiment, killing and wounding many men. The next day, a few miles away, he ordered the shells he was using to be short-fused, so they would explode on a Confederate ironclad under construction. The fuses were too short. The shells exploded over Union troops, killing many of them. Then, in 1864, the drunken Ledlie ordered a frontal assault on a strong Confederate position at the North Anna River. His men were cut down or captured. Ledlie had thus proven himself to be the worst general ever to put on a uniform. But Grant failed to drum him out of the army, apparently fearful of what New York politicians would do to him for firing one of their friends.

For a while, it looked like the whole idea of blowing up the Confederate line had been stupid to begin with. The scheduled 3:30 A.M. explosion never came. Two nervous miners volunteered to crawl into the shaft to find out what had happened. They discovered that the fuse had burned out at a splice. They made repairs, lit the fuse, and scrambled for the exit. At 4:44, the explosion came.

The sight and sound must have made men on both sides think the end of the world was at hand. One Federal described a scene that sounds a bit like an atomic explosion: "Without form or shape, full of red flames and carried on a bed of lightning flashes, it [the explosion's dust cloud] mounted toward heaven with a detonation of thunder and spread out like an immense mushroom whose stem seemed to be of fire and its head of smoke."

Two South Carolina regiments and a battery of artillery ceased to exist, blown to tiny bits. Ground that had been solid was now a hole 150 feet long, 60 feet wide, and 25 feet deep. A rim of dirt had been blown 12 feet above the rest of the land.

For at least five minutes, both sides just stared at the hole. Some surviving Confederates fled from their trenches on either side of the Crater, just as the Federals had hoped. The opportunity was at hand. Finally jarred into action by screaming officers, Ledlie's division started forward. Since no one

had told the men to march around the hole, they marched right down into it.

Marveling at the steaming earth, some of the Federals stopped to stare. Others forgot whom they were fighting and stopped to pull at what few survivors could be found buried in the dirt. Some Union soldiers started trying to climb back out of the hole. They found it hard to get their footing on the slippery earth. Behind them, more Federal units poured into the Crater, blindly following the men in front of them, rather than moving to either side.

Finally, the shocked Confederates recovered. The regiments under General William Mahone began to press in on the Crater. Coehorn mortars—small mortars carried by four men—were brought forward to lob shells into the Federals milling at the bottom of the hole. Trenches abandoned after the explosion now began to refill with Confederates.

Finally, the black division of Ferrero moved forward. Just as they had been trained to do, the soldiers moved to either side of the hole. But by that time, the Confederates' fire was growing fierce. The black soldiers were forced into the same hole with the white Federals.

What the Federals could not have known was that most of Mahone's Confederates—the men closest to the Crater—were from Petersburg and the counties to the south and east. That area included Southampton County, where Nat Turner had staged his bloody slave revolt in 1831, in which dozens of white women and children had been hacked to death. When Mahone's men advanced on the Crater, they wanted one thing—revenge for the shelling of their homes and for the slave revolt that was still fresh in the minds of Southerners, though it had occurred 33 years earlier. The Confederates gave little quarter to the Federals at the bottom of the Crater. Some Southerners lay on the rim and fired down into the Federals at point-blank range. Others loaded muskets and handed them forward. There were no calls for the surrounded Federals to surrender.

Around noon, the Confederates tried a successful ploy. They put their hats on their ramrods and lifted them over the rim of the Crater. The waiting Federals at the bottom fired a volley at what they thought were the exposed heads of the Confederates. Knowing that the Federals' rifles were now empty, the Confederates leaped over the rim and rushed into the hole with knives, bayonets, and pistols. Again, no quarter was given to whites or blacks wearing blue uniforms. This was a personal fight. The only Federals to escape were those who ran the fastest.

By early afternoon, the fighting was over. Nearly 4,000 Federals had been killed or wounded. Few prisoners were taken. The Confederates lost just 1,500, almost a quarter of them killed in the explosion.

Not among the casualties were Union generals Ledlie and Ferrero. You can't be shot when you're hiding. After ordering their men forward, Ledlie and Ferrero went into a bombproof shelter several hundred yards in the rear, where they spent the battle sharing a bottle of rum. Incredibly, when their officers finally found the cowards and requested permission to retire from the Crater, Ledlie and Ferrero refused to give the order. Instead, they instructed their men to stay in the hole and fight, while they served themselves another drink.

Months after the battle, Ledlie was finally forced out of the army. But for reasons still unclear, Ferrero was promoted, though he was not given any other combat commands. After the war, Ledlie returned to civil engineering and Ferrero to dancing.

When you are ready to leave the Taylor Farm, proceed to the last stop on the battlefield tour. A walk leads from the parking lot past the opening of the shaft and then past a ventilation shaft before reaching the remains of the Crater. It does not look very impressive today, after more than 135 years of erosion.

Behind the Crater is a monument to the South Carolinians who died in the explosion. In one of those strange wartime occurrences, the South Carolinians were commanded by General Stephen Elliott, Jr. It was Elliott's grandfather who had developed sea-island cotton, the fine strain of cotton that revolutionized the entire industry along the South Carolina coast. Sea-island cotton was in such demand in the North and around the world that it greatly increased the need for slaves to grow and harvest it. So, in a sense, the black and white Federals who attacked the Crater were fighting a symbol of the Old South—a descendant of the man who had created the need to expand slavery.

General Elliott survived the severe wounds he received here, only to die from complications in 1866.

Leaving the park, turn right on U.S. 301. Drive 0.5 mile, then turn into the parking lot at Blandford Church.

Blandford Church

Inside this church are 15 windows designed and crafted by Louis Tiffany of New York City. They serve as a shrine to dead Confederate soldiers. Each Confederate state and border state that sent soldiers to the war has a window, with the exception of Kentucky, which did not raise the minimum $300 that Tiffany needed to craft the windows. The windows depict saints; the respective states are identified at the bottom. You will be astonished at how bright the windows are, even if it's a cloudy day. The windows are not lit artificially. This project was Tiffany's effort at bringing North and South together.

The adjoining cemetery holds the remains of thousands of Confederate soldiers, including General William Mahone, who is buried in a tomb. Though he fought hard the entire war and even survived a bullet to the chest, Mahone considered himself sickly. Some reports say he consumed only tea, crackers, eggs, and milk. One indulgence he granted himself in the field was to keep a milk cow and laying chickens at his headquarters.

Turn right on to U.S. 301 and continue 0.5 mile to East Washington

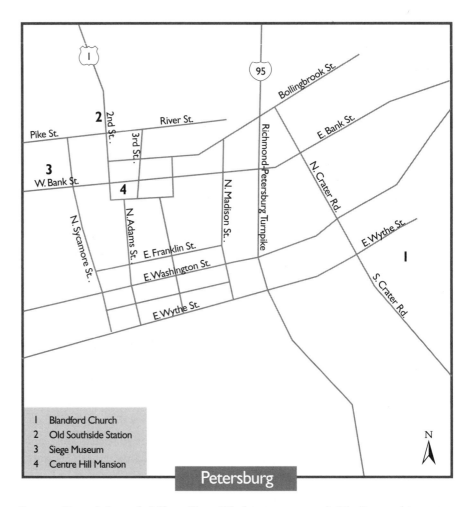

Map legend:

1 Blandford Church
2 Old Southside Station
3 Siege Museum
4 Centre Hill Mansion

Petersburg

N

Southside Station

Street. Turn left and follow East Washington over I-95. From this point westward, the town of Petersburg was in range of the Union cannons. More than 800 houses were struck by shells during the 10-month siege.

At the third traffic light after I-95 about 1 mile after leaving the church, turn right on Sycamore Street. Follow the signs to the Petersburg Visitors Center. Leave your car here.

The old Southside Station, located on River Street behind the visitor center, was the object of many shellings during the war. The Union army wanted to knock out the railroads leading into Petersburg and thus cut off the flow of supplies into the city.

Walk back up Sycamore two blocks to Bank Street and turn right. The Siege Museum is located in the middle of the block. Among the displays here are a wagon that the Federals converted into a traveling field office, a doll whose porcelain head was decapitated by a Federal shell without being shattered, and an interesting five-shot revolving cannon prototype. Since another prototype of this same cannon exploded while being tested, no one had the nerve to experiment with this model, so it has been preserved. Also on display are some printed price lists for goods. By the end of the war, chickens cost $50 each and barrels of flour $1,500 in highly inflated Confederate dollars. A Union soldier observing Petersburg after its occupation commented that "it will take a generation for the city to recover."

From the Siege Museum, walk east on Bank Street for two blocks to Adams Street and turn right. In the middle of the block is Centre Hill Mansion. Built in 1823, the house survived the shelling and was visited by leading war figures on both sides.

Retrace your route to your vehicle and start driving back up Sycamore. Turn left on Wythe Street and prepare to get on to I-85 South. Since the junction with I-95 is also close by, be careful to get on the correct interstate.

Drive about 5 miles on I-85. Just before reaching Exit 63-A, look to the left to see Fort Gregg. When this fort was about to fall to the Federals on April 2, 1865, Lee sent a message to Davis in Richmond that Petersburg would soon need to be evacuated and that Richmond would follow. The 500 Confederates who held Fort Gregg fought the Federals hand to hand, buying time for Lee and the rest of his army to set up a defensive line, which they later abandoned under cover of darkness to begin the slow march to Appomattox Court House.

Spot where A. P. Hill was killed

Take Exit 63-A and head south on U.S. 1 toward Pamplin Park. For now, ignore the signs for Pamplin Park. After about 0.75 mile on U.S. 1, look for A. P. Hill Drive on the right. Follow A. P. Hill Drive as it loops to the right. At the rear of the loop, line yourself up with the house on the southwestern end of the loop. Walk into the woods about 75 yards. A marker stands at the spot where Lieutenant General Ambrose Powell Hill, the commander of Lee's Third Corps, was killed on April 2, 1865. The marker was placed in 1912 by some of Hill's veterans.

No one is sure what Hill was thinking on the day he died. He had just

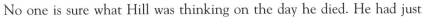

learned of a break in the lines and was on his way to his headquarters when he and an aide stumbled upon two Union soldiers. The two Confederates could have—should have—ridden away from the danger, just as Lee had ordered Hill to do just minutes earlier. Instead, Hill drew his pistol and rode right at the two Federals, demanding their surrender. They responded by shooting him in the heart. Hill was dead before he hit the ground.

Most of his friends considered Hill close to death months before he was shot. The general was gravely ill, probably from the venereal disease he had contracted many years earlier at West Point. Friends and subordinates had noticed a steady decline in his health. At times, Hill was too sick to follow the simplest orders. Historians have long speculated that his insistence on riding toward the Federals may have fulfilled some kind of wish to be killed in the line of duty, rather than to be consumed by an unseen disease while lying in bed.

Return to U.S. 1 and turn left. After less than 100 yards, turn right on Duncan Road. Located on the right within 0.5 mile is the National Museum of the Civil War Soldier, a private museum owned by the Pamplin Foundation. The first phase of the museum opened in the summer of 1999. The remaining three phases are planned to open over the next 12 years. The first phase will feature more than 9,000 square feet of exhibition space. Among the attractions will be sculptures, indoor murals, and audio guided tours that will trace a soldier's life from joining the army to living in camp, being on the march, and fighting a battle.

Turn to the right back on to Duncan Road, then turn immediately left into Pamplin Park, which is part of the same museum complex. Inside the museum here are various displays on the action at this site, as well as a large photograph showing Confederates captured at nearby Five Forks. Of interest to historians are the various uniforms worn by the men in the photograph, including one young man's "wheel hat," which might have belonged to his father or grandfather, as such hats were last worn in the Mexican War, which ended in 1848.

Behind the museum building are Confederate earthworks that were manned until April 2, 1865, when the Federals made their breakthrough. Also on the site are reconstructed winter quarters, which demonstrate how the Confederates spent the winter of 1864–65. You can also see a cannon emplacement overrun by the Federals that April 2.

A long trail at the northeastern end of the property leads to some well-preserved rifle pits once occupied by Confederate pickets and snipers. Looking at these holes in the ground and then looking back at the main Confederate line some 200 or more yards in the rear will give you an idea of how lonely picket duty must have been.

Across Duncan Road is Tudor Hall, the headquarters of Samuel McGowan, a very good general from South Carolina who was wounded four times in the war.

When you are ready to leave Pamplin Park, turn left on Duncan Road. Drive 2.1 miles, then turn left on Wheaton Road (C.R. 674). After 1.9 miles on Wheaton Road, turn left on C. R. 613 (Squirrel Level Road). Drive 0.2 mile, then turn right on C.R. 742 (Plantation Road). It was on this short road that a man charged into certain death just to prove his bravery to his president.

General John Dunovant of South Carolina was a self-made soldier who had started as a sergeant in a volunteer regiment during the Mexican War. He was apparently such a good soldier that 10 years later, he was appointed captain in the 10th United States Infantry, even though he was a civilian at the time.

When the Civil War started, he resigned his commission and joined South Carolina's forces. In 1862, Dunovant was cashiered out of the army for drunkenness, supposedly at the order of Jefferson Davis himself. Dunovant used his family connections to get back into the service. He made his way to Virginia, where he apparently kept his drinking in check, if not hidden.

On September 30, 1864, his men were driven back by a brigade of Union cavalry near this spot. The next day, Dunovant found himself again facing the Union cavalrymen, who were behind the swamp at the bottom of this road.

The senior Confederate officer, General Matthew Butler, asked his commanders if there was a way to flank the Federals on the far side of the swamp. Dunovant suggested that the Confederates simply charge them. Butler ignored him. It seemed like suicide to come down off the high ground they held into the guns of waiting Federals. But Dunovant kept insisting that he be allowed to charge the Federals. Finally, Butler, exasperated by his subordinate, said, "Charge them, sir, if you must!"

Dunovant went to his men and told them that they had the honor of

Winter quarters at Pamplin Park

charging the Federals. His men were not enthused. Finally, Dunovant demanded that they follow him, which they reluctantly did. Dunovant was on his horse leading men on foot. He got as far as the bridge over the creek before he fell with a bullet to the heart. The regiment's medical director rushed on to the field to see if he could retrieve the general. He, too, was killed.

When Dunovant's body was finally recovered, some of his men grumbled that they had known he was drinking again.

Retrace your route to U.S. 1 and turn left. After about 4 miles, turn left on Dabney Mill Road (C.R. 613). Drive 1.9 miles, then pull to the right. On February 6, 1865, this was the site of the Battle of Hatcher's Run, a fight to control the Boydton Plank Road (what is now U.S. 1), which helped supply Lee's army in Petersburg. This is where Confederate general John Pegram was killed. The Confederates actually won the battle on February 6 but lost the same ground the next day. Every fight outside the trenches was now costing them more and more men, who could not be replaced.

Return to U.S. 1 and turn right. After 0.3 mile, turn left on C.R. 613 (White Oak Road). Pull to the side, get out, and look back to the pasture on the other side of U.S. 1. In 1864, this pasture was used to keep about 3,000 cattle the Confederates had rustled from the Federals on what is remembered today as the "Beefsteak Raid."

That September, General Wade Hampton, the South Carolinian who had inherited command of the Confederate cavalry after the death of J. E. B. Stuart, was looking for some way to harm the Federals strangling Petersburg. One of his scouts sent to spy on City Point came back with some interesting information. The Federals had a herd of cattle at Coggins Point, about 6 miles from City Point.

On September 14, more than 3,000 cavalrymen left this area on a roundabout trip that took them 50 miles to Coggins Point on the James River. The Confederates swooped down on the Federal herders and gave them a choice—herd the cattle to Petersburg or be shot down right there. They chose to herd.

Within four days, Hampton returned with 2,468 steers, 304 captured soldiers, and 11 captured wagons. He lost only 10 killed and 47 wounded. An admiring Union newspaper called it a "perfect piece of raiding rascality." A chuckling Lincoln called it "the slickest piece of cattle stealing I ever heard of."

A few days later, Grant was having dinner with his aides when one of them asked how long it would take to starve Lee out of Petersburg. "Forever if you keep feeding him our beef," he replied.

It was a caper the fun-loving Stuart would have appreciated.

Drive about 1.5 miles on White Oak Road, then pull into the parking lot at the intersection with C.R. 631. This area was the site of the Battle of White Oak Road, fought on March 31, 1865.

Control of the Boydton Plank Road seemed to obsess Grant in the early spring of 1865. He knew that by capturing that road, he could cut off the last supply route to Petersburg.

The Confederates who were dug in along White Oak Road knew the importance of their position and were determined to keep the Federals from getting the road. At first, they were successful. They attacked the Federals with a vengeance, sending them running backward.

It was embarrassing for the Union that two understrength, underarmed, underfed Confederate brigades could rout an equal number of Federal troops. General Gouverneur K. Warren, the commander of the Fifth Corps, rode up to General Joshua L. Chamberlain, the hero of Little Round Top at Gettysburg, and pointedly asked him, "Will you save the honor of the Fifth Corps?"

Chamberlain then led his men in three counterattacks, each of which was beaten back by the Confederates. Finally, Federal reinforcements came up and forced the Confederates back to their defensive position along this portion of the preserved battlefield.

The Federals held the road that night. Portions of Warren's corps were subsequently ordered to support General Phil Sheridan's cavalry, which was set to attack General Pickett at Five Forks.

Get back on White Oak Road and drive 2 more miles to Five Forks. The small National Park Service office here is frequently unmanned, but information for a self-guided tour should be available outside the office.

On April 1, 1865, the Federals attacked the hastily organized lines at Five Forks, so named because five country roads converged at one point. The Confederates had arrived there only the night before, after retreating from Dinwiddie Court House a few miles away, much to the disgust of Robert E. Lee, who felt that Pickett had given up Dinwiddie too easily. He now ordered Pickett to "hold Five Forks at all costs."

Pickett received these orders yet seemed strangely unimpressed by them. Instead of throwing himself into defending his position, he lolled around. When a friend of his, cavalry general Tom Rosser, sent a note that he was planning to bake some shad he had caught in a nearby river, Pickett invited another friend, General Fitzhugh Lee, along for lunch. The two top generals on the field rode away without leaving anyone in direct command.

Just after noon, Sheridan's cavalrymen opened the attack. They fought dismounted while waiting for reinforcements from Warren's Fifth Corps. When Warren's men showed up, they charged in the wrong direction and found themselves caught in a Confederate crossfire. The enraged Sheridan realigned the men in the right direction.

Five Forks was not much of a battle, as the Confederates were outnumbered at least five to one. Of the 12,000 Confederates there, nearly half surrendered when surrounded.

It was a faulty map made by Sheridan's staff that had caused Warren's men to arrive late. Ignoring the fact that it was indirectly his fault that Warren had been behind schedule, Sheridan relieved Warren of command of the Fifth Corps, then refused to tell him why.

It was a strange but typical example of politics on the field. Warren, the only man in the Union army who had recognized the significance of Little Round Top at Gettysburg less than two years earlier, now found himself relieved of command because he was being called incompetent. At the same time, James Hewett Ledlie, who had done nothing but kill his own Union soldiers throughout his service in the army, had been promoted on several occasions and been given increased responsibility. The difference was that Warren happened to be a career military man with few friends outside the army, while Ledlie had highly placed political friends who could damage Grant's and Sheridan's future careers.

As for Pickett, he had no idea that Five Forks was under attack until he saw Federal soldiers approaching his picnic. He then rushed past the advancing soldiers, leaning on the opposite side of his horse to avoid their shots. But by the time he got to Five Forks, it was too late. The battle was over.

While Pickett cannot be excused for leaving his command in the face of the enemy, he may have had a valid reason for not knowing the Federals were attacking. He may have been the victim of an acoustical shadow, an occurrence sometimes experienced during the war when thick stands of trees and temperature inversions sent the sounds of battle up into the air, instead of in a horizontal direction. Some generals reported watching silent battles being fought just a few miles distant. In Pickett's case, he could not hear the sounds of shooting less than 2 miles away.

Pickett, never considered a great general anyway, lost whatever respect Lee may have had left for him. First, he had retreated from Dinwiddie Court House. Then nearly half his men had surrendered when he lost Five Forks.

One of those who died at Five Forks was young Willie Pegram, Lee's last great artillerist, who fell at his guns just before they were captured. Both Willie Pegram and his brother, General John Pegram, had fought the entire war and contributed greatly to the Confederate cause, only to be lost in the last days before the surrender.

Turn north off White Oak Road on to C.R. 627 and drive 1.2 miles. After crossing Hatcher's Run, you'll reach a road that some local with a sense of humor named Shad Bake Lane. The tour ends here, where Pickett filled his stomach while his men were being filled with bullets.

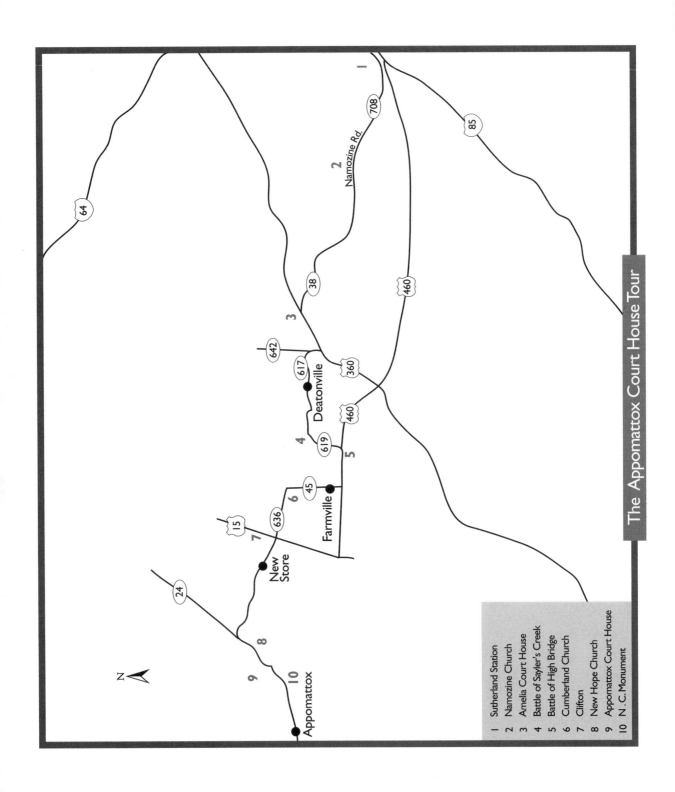

The Appomattox Court House Tour

N

64

85

708

Namozine Rd.

1

2

38

460

3

642

617

Deatonville

360

460

4

619

5

45

6

Farmville

636

15

7

New Store

24

8

9

10

Appomattox

1 Sutherland Station
2 Namozine Church
3 Amelia Court House
4 Battle of Sayler's Creek
5 Battle of High Bridge
6 Cumberland Church
7 Clifton
8 New Hope Church
9 Appomattox Court House
10 N. C. Monument

The Appomattox
Court House Tour

This tour starts at the site of the battle that cut the rail line into Petersburg. It continues along a winding road Lee hoped would lead him to supplies that would sustain his army as it made its way either west to safety or south to link with Joseph Johnston. The tour stops at points where Lee hoped to get supplies, at the site of the last major battle he fought, and at camping spots along the way. It ends at Appomattox Court House, which is as far as the Army of Northern Virginia traveled before Grant got in front of it, cutting off its only route to safety.

The tour is 105 miles long and can be completed in a day, but make sure you leave plenty of time to linger at Appomattox Court House, one of the quietest and most somber of our nation's parks.

THE TOUR STARTS south of Petersburg at the intersection of C.R. 708 and U.S. 460, about 4.5 miles west of I-85. It follows the state of Virginia's Civil War Trails Tour.

This is the site of the Fork Inn, a tavern and inn built in 1803. The Battle of Sutherland Station—considered the last battle of the Petersburg siege—was fought here on April 2, 1865.

After A. P. Hill's death, Lee appointed Henry Heth to command the Third Corps. Heth sent four brigades here to protect the Southside Railroad. During the three-hour battle, about 4,600 Federals attacked 4,000 tired Confederates, crushed their lines, and captured the railroad. The retreat route south was now cut off. Lee would have to move west along this road.

The inn is now a small museum.

Drive west on C.R. 708 (Namozine Road) for about 10 miles, then pull left into the parking lot of Namozine Church, which dates to 1847.

After the crushing Confederate defeat at Five Forks and the loss of the railroad at Sutherland Station, Union forces scrambled to pursue Lee's army and get in front of it. On April 3, two days after Five Forks and one day after Sutherland Station, General George Custer's cavalry caught up with some rear-guard Confederate cavalry under General Rufus Barringer. Namozine Church was a tiny engagement, hardly mentioned in most Civil War histories. Custer suffered 81 casualties here. Confederate losses are unknown.

Namozine Church where Barringer was captured

One Confederate who was lost was Barringer himself, captured by the Federals and taken to City Point. It turned out to be his lucky day. Barringer expected to be shipped immediately to a harsh prison camp, but as he was sitting in a tent, he heard a voice outside ask, "Mr. President, have you ever seen a live Confederate general?"

Into the tent walked Abraham Lincoln. In chatting with Barringer, Lincoln asked him if he knew a Barringer from North Carolina who had served in the United States House of Representatives. Barringer replied that the man in question was his brother. Lincoln then wrote a letter to Secretary of War Edwin Stanton telling him to give Barringer every consideration as a military prisoner.

Barringer did spend some time in prison. But he remained so appreciative of Lincoln's gesture that he became a Republican upon his return to Charlotte, North Carolina, which effectively killed his political career in a state occupied by soldiers ordered there by the Republicans.

Continue on C.R. 708 for 9.4 miles, then turn left on Va. 38 at Scott's Fork. It is 5 miles on Va. 38 to Amelia Court House. Follow the Civil War Trail signs through town to the railway station; en route, you will cross U.S. 360 Business.

When Lee arrived here on April 4, 1865, it must have broken his heart. He had ordered trains loaded with the army's last emergency reserve of rations to be sent here. When the railroad cars were opened, they were found to contain hundreds of artillery shells but no food. Novelist John Esten Cooke was watching Lee as the general looked inside the rail cars. Cooke later wrote, "No face wore a heavier shadow than that of General Lee. The failure of the supply of rations completely paralyzed him. An anxious and haggard expression came to his face."

Lee took the unusual measure of writing a plea to the people in the surrounding countryside. He asked them to send whatever food they could spare to the town to feed what remained of the Army of Northern Virginia. But the people had little food to share.

Lee rode to the western edge of the village when he heard gunfire. His cavalry was skirmishing with Federal troopers who had already caught up to the Confederate army. One Federal rode right at the Confederates. The Southerners cocked their revolvers, but Lee himself shouted, "Don't shoot!"

When the Federal got close, the Confederates saw that he was already wounded and unable to control his horse. Lee couldn't see any use in killing a wounded man.

It was outside Amelia Court House that a wagon train being driven and guarded by black Confederate soldiers was attacked by Union cavalry. The blacks opened fire on the surprised Union troopers, who broke off their assault for a few minutes before attacking again and finally capturing the wagons and the blacks.

Lee waited until midday on Wednesday, April 5, for the wagons to come back with food or for other rations to arrive by train. None came. He ordered the extra ammunition destroyed in the village, then hurried the army toward Jetersville. He had to turn northwest when he learned that the town was already occupied by Federals.

When you are ready to leave Amelia Court House, return to U.S. 360 Business, turn right, and follow it to U.S. 360. Drive west on U.S. 360 for 5.2 miles, then turn left on C.R. 671 in Jetersville. Follow C.R. 671 for 0.7 mile to C.R. 642, then drive 3.8 miles north on C.R. 642 to Amelia Springs.

Before the war, this was a nationally famous sulphur springs resort encompassing more than 1,300 acres and 20 buildings. The wealthy came here to relax in the soothing waters. Lee spent the night of April 5, 1865, at a private house nearby. As he ate dinner, the residents of the home kept everyone from coming near him. One young woman refused to let an aide enter until he draped a Confederate flag around her.

The next morning, Lee saw signs that his army was disintegrating around him. Companies that had slept in nearby fields the previous night had now disappeared. All that was left of them were muskets stuck muzzle down in the mud.

On Thursday, April 6, two Union spies were captured wearing Confederate uniforms. General Gordon asked Lee for permission to execute them. Lee refused, telling Gordon to keep the prisoners with him until he heard more from Lee. Lee saw no need for useless bloodshed.

The general got some good news at the resort. A train loaded with 80,000 rations was waiting for him at Farmville. Lee pondered whether to order the rations brought to him or to have them guarded where they sat. Farmville was 18 miles away. He decided to go to the rations.

At Amelia Springs, turn left on C.R. 617 (St. James Road). Drive 3.2 miles to Deatonville. This is where the Federals started to catch up to the main part of Lee's army.

Drive another 3 miles to the intersection with C.R. 618. At this crossroads, the Confederate wagon train turned right, while the main body continued straight ahead. The Federal Second Corps continued chasing the wagons, while the Sixth Corps pursued the main body of the army.

One Confederate colonel later wrote about how he passed Generals Dick Ewell, Custis Lee (Robert's son), and Seth Barton, who seemed deep in conversation. Then the colonel overheard Ewell remark, "Tomatoes are very good. I wish I had some." So much for deep-thinking generals figuring a way out of a bad predicament.

Around this time, a gap opened in the lines of the retreating army. The Federals took advantage of it, launching an attack and cutting off the division of General Richard Anderson from the rest of the Confederate army. Ewell's men turned back to try to help. The Confederates were now cut into four parts—the bulk of the men were with Lee and Longstreet heading toward Farmville; Ewell was on the southern side of Sayler's Creek; Gordon was to the west with the wagons; and Anderson was to the southwest.

Ewell's 5,000 men faced General Horatio Wright's 10,000, who set up artillery on the Hillsman Farm to fire on the Confederates on the ridge to the southwest. After a few charges and countercharges, the Federals swept Ewell's men away, thanks in part to the Union regiments being armed with Henry repeating rifles, the forerunner of the Winchester rifle, which would prove so valuable in the westward expansion of the country. More than 3,000 Confederates were captured here.

Hillsman Farm

On Gordon's end of the battlefield, things didn't go much better. Fighting started around the Lockett Farm. As the wagons reached the twin branches of the creek, they bogged down. Gordon's men were forced to abandon more than 200 wagons to the Federals.

Anderson was fighting cavalry. He, too, was overwhelmed, and another two Confederate generals were captured.

Altogether, eight general officers and more than 8,000 Confederates were captured at Sayler's Creek. In one day and one battle, Lee thus lost almost a fourth of the men he had left. As he viewed the remainder of his army streaming toward him in confusion, he remarked, "My God! Has the army been dissolved?"

General William Mahone answered, "No, General. Here are troops ready to do their duty."

"There are some true men left," Lee agreed. "Will you please keep those people back?" he then asked, pointing to the Federals advancing on him.

That night, a courier from Davis reached Lee and asked him what his plans were. Lee informed the courier that he could tell Davis that his objective was Lynchburg. Then Lee said something else: "A few more Sayler's Creeks and it will be all over—ended—just as I have expected it would end from the first." He seemed to be saying he had always known that the South could not win.

Continue on C.R. 617 to the Hillsman Farm. Built in the late 1770s, the house here is now preserved as part of the battlefield park. It was used as a hospital by the Federals.

Continue on C.R. 617 across Sayler's Creek. On the right at the top of the hill is a monument to both sides; visiting the monument requires a short walk from the road. The Confederates under Ewell fought their last battle at this site.

Looking toward Sayler's Creek

House with bullet holes at Lockett Farm

Turn around and retrace C.R. 617 to C.R. 618. Turn left on C.R. 618 to follow the route of Gordon and the wagon train. The road curves to the left and becomes C.R. 619. Stop at the house at the Lockett Farm. Bullet holes are still visible in the wooden siding of the home, which dates to 1858.

Continue down to the creek. Part of the double bridges are still visible. This is where the Confederate wagon train bogged down in the flooded bottom land of the creek.

Continue on C.R. 619 until it runs into U.S. 460 at Rice's Depot. Turn right on U.S. 460 and go about 1.75 miles to the bridge over the Appomattox River. Pull to the side at the historical marker.

The High Bridge, which carried the Southside Railroad over the Appomattox River, was located about 2 miles north of here. The site is not visible from any of today's public roads. Built in 1852, the bridge was 2,400 feet long and 126 feet high—an impressive structure for its time. One writer of the day noted, "There have been higher bridges not so long and longer bridges not so high, but taking the height and length together, this is, per-

Double bridges over Sayler's Creek

haps, the largest bridge in the world." Below the High Bridge was a much simpler wagon bridge.

On April 6, a raiding party of Federal cavalrymen attempted to capture the High Bridge intact. Leading them was Brevet General Theodore Read, the chief of staff for General Ord. Facing the Federals was a small force of cavalry led by General James Dearing.

Dearing's cavalry and Read's cavalry soon found themselves in a running fight. Reports differ on whether the men battled with sabers or pistols. Whichever the case, Dearing and Read squared off in a personal duel while still mounted on their horses. Dearing had the advantage, as Read had lost an arm earlier in the war. Just as he either shot or sabered Read, killing him, Dearing himself was shot, either by Read or one of Read's aides. Dearing fell to the ground within feet of Read.

Dearing was taken to a nearby farmhouse. While he was there, he pointed to the brigadier general's stars on his collar and then to Colonel Elijah White, the leader of a rough-riding band of cavalry nicknamed "the Comanches." "These belong on his collar," Dearing said. He knew that White had never risen higher in command because of his unwillingness to impose military discipline on his men. Even as he lay dying, Dearing wanted to acknowledge someone else's contribution to the war effort.

Dearing succumbed to his wound two weeks later, the last Confederate general to die in the field.

At the time of his death, Read was a lieutenant colonel acting in the appointed role of general while awaiting the approval of his commission. He is considered the last Union general to die in combat.

The day after the fight between Dearing and Read, the Confederates under Mahone and Gordon crossed here, blowing up the forts guarding the river and destroying 10 cannons that they felt were slowing their march. The soldiers set fire to both bridges, but pursuing Federals arrived in time to save the wagon bridge. The Federals of the Second Corps now had a short-cut they could use to try to get ahead of Lee.

Drive about 2 more miles, taking U.S. 460 Business into Farmville. In town, turn right at the light on to Va. 45 North. On the right at the second traffic light is a marker for the Prince Edward Hotel. Lee and Grant stayed in the same room at the Prince Edward on successive nights, which demonstrates how close Grant was getting. It was in the Prince Edward Hotel that Grant wrote his first letter to Lee suggesting that he surrender the Army of Northern Virginia.

The hotel fell down in the 1960s during an attempt to restore it.

After you cross the railroad tracks, pull to the left into a parking lot. It was here that Lee was able to collect some rations for his men.

It was also in Farmville that he received a friendly note from Grant informing him that Custis Lee, General Lee's son, was a prisoner but was unhurt.

It was less welcome news when the general's bad penny turned up. Who should attach himself to Lee in Farmville but General Henry Wise. The irascible former governor of Virginia had almost spoiled Lee's career before it got started by keeping up a constant feud with another bad general, John Floyd. Try as Lee might, he could never get the two old political enemies to cooperate with each other. It was because of those two that the Confederacy lost western Virginia to the Federals in November 1861.

Wise followed Lee around Farmville, harping about what he perceived to be the misconduct of Bushrod Rust Johnson, a fine general who had fought in dozens of battles out west and in Virginia. Lee finally threatened Wise with court-martial for talking out of turn about Johnson.

On the morning of Friday, April 7, just as Longstreet's men poured into Farmville to draw their rations, Lee learned that the wagon bridge under the High Bridge had not been burned. The Federals were now using it to draw closer. Longstreet's men threw their rations into wagons and started marching north. The Confederates set fire to the bridges over the river at Farmville to try to slow the Federals.

Drive 3 miles north on Va. 45 to Cumberland Church, located on the left. It was here that General William Mahone fought off two attacks by the Federals.

At 9 P.M. on April 7, Federal general Seth Williams rode to Cumberland Church under a flag of truce. He handed over a letter from Grant to Lee. Lee opened the letter, which Grant had written four hours earlier in Farmville. It read:

General Lee: The results of the last week must convince you of the hopelessness of further resistance on the part of the Army of Northern Virginia in this struggle. I feel that it is so, and regard it my duty to shift from myself the responsibility of any further effusion of blood, by asking of you the surrender of that portion of the C.S. Army known as the Army of Northern Virginia. Gen. U. S. Grant.

Without saying a word, Lee handed the note to Longstreet. Longstreet read it and said just two words in reply: "Not yet."

Lee wrote a note back to Grant that said:

General, I have read your note of this date. Though not entertaining the opinion you express of the hopelessness of further resistance on the part of the Army of Northern Virginia—I reciprocate your desire to avoid useless effusion of blood and therefore before considering your proposition, ask the terms you will offer on condition of surrender.

Not knowing of Lee's note back to Grant, at least half a dozen generals met among themselves that night and voted to ask Lee to surrender the army.

The man selected to convey their opinion, General W. N. Pendleton, an old Lee friend, could not find Lee on the night march from Cumberland Church. The next morning, Saturday, April 8, he rode up and down the line of march trying to garner the generals' support. Most of them, even hard fighters like Edward Porter Alexander and John Gordon, agreed that continuing the struggle was useless.

Then Pendleton approached Longstreet.

"Don't you know that the articles of war provide that officers or soldiers asking commanders to surrender should be shot?" was Longstreet's hot reply.

Pendleton finally found Lee resting under a tree. He presented his case to Lee, who replied, "I trust it has not come to that. We certainly have too many brave men to think of laying down our arms. They shall fight with great spirit, whereas the enemy do not. And besides, if I were to intimate to General Grant that I would listen to terms, he would regard it such an evidence of weakness that he would demand unconditional surrender, and sooner than that I am resolved to die. We must all determine to die at our posts."

Pendleton then replied, "We're perfectly willing for you to decide. Every man will cheerfully die with you."

Around noon, Lee reached a place called New Store, where he formally relieved Pickett, Bushrod Johnson, and Richard Anderson of their commands, as most of their troops had been captured at Sayler's Creek. He ordered them to go to their homes and await further orders—which they knew would never come. For reasons perhaps related to the debacle at Sayler's Creek—in which Pickett, Johnson, and Anderson had all played a part—Lee didn't want them around him in the final battles.

Early that evening, the head of the column reached Appomattox Court House, where it stopped to set up camp.

More and more men were leaving the ranks. A North Carolina captain observed, "One fact, a strange one too, it appears to me that our higher officers did not try to prevent this straggling. They seemed to shut their eyes of the hourly reduction of their commands, and rode in advance of their brigades in dogged indifference."

Lee set up camp on top of a small hill about 2 miles northeast of Appomattox Court House. That evening, some Federals rode near the Confederate lines. One was shot dead before the others shouted that they were carrying white flags. The flags were little more than handkerchiefs. The Confederates apologized for the man's death.

In time, General Seth Williams of Grant's staff appeared—under a larger, more easily seen flag of truce—and delivered a second letter from Grant. The letter was received by Lee at his hilltop headquarters. It read:

> General Lee—Your note of last evening in reply to mine of same date, asking the condition on which I will accept the surrender of the Army of Northern Virginia is received. In reply I would say that, peace being my greatest desire, there is but one condition that I would insist upon, namely: that the men and officers surrendered shall be disqualified from taking up arms again against the Government of the United States until properly exchanged. I will meet you, or will designate officers to meet any officers you may name for the same purpose, at any point agreeable to you, for the purpose of arranging definitely the terms upon which the surrender of the Army of Northern Virginia will be received.—U. S. Grant.

Lee immediately wrote a reply. He did not consult Longstreet this time.

> General Grant—I received at a late hour your note of today. In mine of yesterday, I did not intend to propose the surrender of the Army of Northern Virginia, but to ask the terms of your proposition. To be frank, I do not think the emergency has arisen to call for the surrender of this army, but as the restoration of peace should be the sole object of all, I desired to know whether your proposals would lead to that and I cannot therefore meet you with a view to surrender the Army of Northern Virginia but as far as your proposal may affect the C.S. forces under my command and tend to the restoration of peace, I shall be pleased to meet you at 10:00 A.M. tomorrow on the old stage road to Richmond between the picket lines of the two armies— R. E. Lee.

Leaving Cumberland Church, turn left to continue on Va. 45. Drive about 1.5 miles to C.R. 636 and turn left at Raines Tavern. In about 6.5 miles, you will cross U.S. 15. Look to the left just beyond U.S. 15. The white two-story house is Clifton. It was here just before midnight on Saturday, April 8, that Grant received the above letter from Lee. He read it but went to bed without replying. He understood that the end was just hours away.

Cumberland Church where Lee received the first letter from Grant

Continue on C.R. 636 about 4.5 miles through New Store. This is where Lee relieved the generals he no longer needed.

After another 8.1 miles, turn left on Va. 24. Drive south for 5.8 miles to New Hope Church. In the woods across from the church are trenches dug by Longstreet's men.

Drive 2 more miles, then turn into the parking lot on the left just inside Appomattox Court House National Park. Walk up the hill to Lee's last headquarters.

Just after writing his reply to Grant, Lee called a council of war at this site. All of his generals attended. Most of them sat on the ground.

"We knew by our own aching hearts that his was breaking. Yet he commanded himself, and he stood calmly facing and discussing the long-dreaded inevitable," General John B. Gordon later wrote.

Site of Lee's last headquarters

Though the end was obviously at hand, the generals agreed to make one last attempt to break through the slowing circling Union forces and head for Lynchburg. Fitz Lee's cavalry would lead the way, followed by Gordon's 4,000 infantrymen, then by Longstreet. Fitz Lee asked his uncle for permission to try to break out with his cavalry and head to North Carolina if Lee himself decided to surrender the infantry. Lee agreed.

After the meeting, Gordon sent a staff officer back to ask Lee where he should halt his men the next night, assuming they were able to get past the Federals.

Lee smiled when he replied. "Tell General Gordon I would be glad for him to halt just beyond the Tennessee line." Despite everything, Lee still had a sense of humor.

Before Lee retired, he noticed Pickett walking by. Lee remarked, "I thought that man was no longer with this army." Lee never forgave Pickett for failing at Five Forks. For his part, Pickett never forgave Lee for ordering his division to attack on the third day at Gettysburg.

The next morning, Palm Sunday, April 9, 1865, Lee arose and put on a brand-new uniform coat. His friend Pendleton looked at him with a quizzical expression.

"I'll probably be General Grant's prisoner, and I thought I must make my best appearance," Lee said in response to the unasked question. During the night, he must have made up his mind to surrender if his men could not break out of Appomattox Court House.

Early that morning, a Confederate doctor was captured west of the village. Unfortunately, that was the direction Lee needed to go. He commented that the Federal infantry "seemed to come out of the ground," meaning that there were a great number of them.

By dawn, Gordon's Confederates were in the village preparing to move westward to test the Federal lines. In the lead were North Carolinians under General Bryan Grimes. Grimes's men, under the direct command of another Tar Heel, General William Ruffin Cox, pushed the Federals from the road and waited for reinforcements, who did not come. Gordon then saw more Federals moving in.

Lee sent a note asking Gordon if he could make it through the Federals. Gordon replied, "I have fought my corps to a frazzle."

When Lee got Gordon's message that there were too many Federals, he said, "There is nothing left for me to do but go and see General Grant. I would rather die a thousand deaths."

Gordon learned that Lee was ready to surrender and sent orders to Grimes to withdraw—which Grimes declined to do until ordered by Lee. He was reluctant to give up the ground he had just won.

Grimes rode back and found Gordon. "Where shall I form my new line?" he asked.

"Anywhere you choose. We are to be surrendered," Gordon replied.

Grimes was enraged. He had just pushed forward and lost some men. "Why didn't you tell me? I could have got away! I'll take my men with me!" he shouted.

Gordon took Grimes by the shoulder and told him that Lee had already made the decision to surrender. If Grimes ignored that order, he would disgrace Lee. Grimes reluctantly agreed and told his men to retreat to the village.

As he prepared to meet Grant, Lee briefly considered suicide. "How easily I could be rid of this, and be at rest! I have only to ride along the line and all will be over. But it is our duty to live. What will become of the women and children of the South if we are not there to protect them?" he asked his staff.

Lee asked Longstreet twice if they should surrender. Longstreet nodded. Edward Porter Alexander suggested that the army scatter into the woods and try to link up with Johnston in North Carolina. Lee countered that the men would no longer be under any discipline and would take to plundering the countryside for food.

Lee made the decision then to go looking for Grant. He rode up the old stage road (what is now Va. 24). He was near the picket line at New Hope Church when his aides found a Federal officer on his way to see Lee with a letter from Grant. The Union commander's latest message read:

> General Lee, Your note of yesterday is received. As I have no authority to treat on the subject of peace the meeting proposed for 10:00 A.M. today could lead to no good. I will state, however, General, that I am equally desirous for peace with yourself, and the whole North entertains the same feeling. The terms upon which peace can be had are well understood. By the South laying down their arms

they will hasten that most desirable event, save thousands of human lives, and hundreds of millions of property not yet destroyed. Sincerely hoping that all our difficulties may be settled without the loss of another life. Gen. Grant.

Lee read the letter, then turned to Colonel Charles Marshall, an aide, and said, "Write a letter to General Grant and ask him to meet me to deal with the question of surrender of my army, in reply to the letter he wrote me at Farmville."

Lee then dictated the following:

> General Grant: I received your note this morning on the picket line, wither I had come to meet you and ascertain definitely what terms were embraced in your proposition of yesterday with reference to the surrender of this army. I now request an interview in accordance with the offer contained in your letter of yesterday for that purpose.—Gen. Lee.

Before Lee finished the letter, a rider rushed up to say that Fitz Lee's cavalry had found a way out. Lee ignored the supposed good news. He was ready to end the fighting.

In time, a Federal officer came forward to tell Lee and his aide that an attack was planned. Lee then wrote out a second note that read:

> Gen. Grant—I ask a suspension of hostilities pending the adjustment of the terms of the surrender of this army, in the interview requested in my former communication today.—Gen. Lee.

Lee saw Federals advancing toward him, so he left the picket line just as a message arrived from Fitz Lee saying that the earlier rumor that he had found a way out was untrue. Every road was covered by the Federals.

Worried that the Federals would attack before Grant made a decision on the surrender, Lee then sent a third note before the first two had been answered:

> General Grant—I therefore request an interview at such time and place as you may designate, to discuss the terms of the surrender of

this army in accord with your offer to have such an interview contained in your letter of yesterday.—Gen. Lee.

Lee waited for a reply in the shade of an apple tree beside a creek running below Appomattox Court House. Longstreet joined him. Longstreet, an old friend of Grant's, told Lee that Grant was an honorable man but that "if he won't give you honorable terms, break it off, and tell him to do his worst."

At that moment, a Federal officer arrived with a reply from Grant:

Gen. Lee—Your note of this date is but this moment [11:50 A.M.] received. In consequence of my having passed from the Richmond and Lynchburg Road to the Farmville and Lynchburg road, I am writing this about four miles west of Walker's church and will push forward to the front for the purpose of meeting you. . . .—Gen. Grant.

The detail of Grant's location was striking. Now, Grant himself was standing in the direction Lee had hoped to escape.

Lee and Marshall started riding toward the village. Colonel Walter Taylor, another aide, could not bear to make the trip. Marshall went ahead to find a suitable house. The first person he met was a merchant named Wilmer McLean, who showed him a vacant brick building that was unfurnished. When Marshall refused that place, McLean led him to his own house, a fine brick home with a wide porch.

When you are ready to leave Lee's headquarters, continue on Va. 24 toward Appomattox Court House. Just before crossing the river, look to the left. This was the location of the apple orchard where Lee rested and met with Longstreet.

On the opposite side of the road is the cemetery of the Sweeneys, the family who developed the five-string banjo into a popular instrument. Sam Sweeney played in Stuart's camp.

Continue on Va. 24. For the time being, ignore the signs for the visitor center at Appomattox Court House. About 0.5 mile past the visitor center, you will reach the parking lot for the North Carolina Monument. Leave your vehicle here and walk across the road to the small cemetery, which contains the graves of 18 Confederates and one Federal unlucky enough to die during the last days of the war.

Walk into the woods to see the North Carolina Monument. The inscription reads, "At this place North Carolina troops under Brig. Gen. Cox of Grimes' division fired the last volley April 9, 1865. Major Gen. Grimes planned the last battle fought by the Army of Northern Virginia." The stone thus bears out North Carolina's motto that its men were "First at Bethel, furthest to the front at Gettysburg and Chickamauga, and last at Appomattox."

Return on Va. 24 to Appomattox Court House and park your car at the visitor center. The tour ends here.

Walk into the park and turn left to view the reconstructed McLean House.

When Colonel Charles Marshall rode back for Lee, he led him to Wilmer McLean's home. Lee entered and sat at a small table in the parlor. As he waited, he fingered the fine white-handled sword given to him by a Maryland resident in 1863.

Meanwhile, Gordon and his men were still fending off the Federals west of the village. Gordon had pulled his men back from their advance, but the Federals were continuing to press him. Until he heard differently, he had to fight them.

McLean House

It was at that moment that Gordon received a note from Lee about the impending surrender. Gordon told an aide to ride forward with a white flag to tell the Federals that Grant would soon meet with Lee. It took the man several minutes to find anything white to use.

When the aide returned from the Federal line, he brought with him the gaudiest character Gordon had ever seen—a man with shoulder-length hair wearing a red bandanna around his neck. He introduced himself as General Custer and said he represented General Sheridan, who was demanding "a complete and unconditional surrender of all the troops under your command." If Gordon did not reply immediately, Sheridan would "annihilate" him, Custer said.

An irritated Gordon replied that he was not about to surrender his command without orders from his general. "If General Sheridan decides to continue fighting in the face of a flag of truce, the responsibility for the blood shed will be his, not mine," he said to Custer.

Custer rode away without that last big shot of glory that would be due the man who single-handedly accepted the surrender of the Army of Northern Virginia.

Minutes later, he was back, looking for someone—anyone—who would surrender to him. He found Longstreet and demanded that the Confederate general surrender.

Longstreet replied, "I am not in command. General Lee is, and he's gone back to meet General Grant in regard to our surrender."

Then Custer did something that could have gotten him court-martialed or even shot. He claimed to be in charge of an army that he did not lead. "No matter about General Grant. We demand the surrender be made to us. If you do not do so, we will renew hostilities, and any blood shed will be upon your head," he said.

Longstreet turned to his staff and ordered two divisions forward to the front lines. He was bluffing. He called one of those divisions "Pickett's division" and the other "Johnson's division." Both Pickett and Johnson had been relieved by Lee because their divisions no longer existed.

Custer fell for it. "General Longstreet, we had better wait until we hear from Grant and Lee. I will speak to General Sheridan about it; don't move your troops yet," he said. Custer was perhaps imagining how he would explain to Grant that he had restarted a war that had just ended. He wheeled his horse and left.

When Custer was out of earshot, Longstreet burst into laughter, commenting that the Union general had never learned to play "Brag," a poker game at which Longstreet excelled.

When Grant rode into the yard of the McLean House, he suddenly realized that he was not dressed for the occasion. He wore a common soldier's jacket adorned with the shoulder bars of a lieutenant general. He was spattered with mud and had no sword.

When Grant walked into the house, he mentioned to Lee that they had met on one other occasion, in Mexico. Grant said he would have recognized Lee anywhere. Lee acknowledged that they had met but said he could not remember what Grant had looked like.

It was 1:30 P.M. on Sunday, April 9, 1865.

The generals engaged in small talk. It was Lee who reminded Grant to get to the business at hand, the surrender.

Grant finally wrote out the following letter:

> General R. E. Lee Commanding C.S.A., Appomattox Court House, Va., April 9, 1865. General: In accordance with the substance of my letter to you of the 8th, I propose to receive the surrender of the Army of Northern Virginia on the following terms, to wit: Rolls of all officers and men to be made in duplicate, one copy to be given to an officer designated by me, the other to be retained by such officer or officers as you may designate. The officers to give their individual paroles not to take up arms against the Government of the United States until properly, and each company or regimental commander to sign a like parole for the men of their commands. The arms, artillery, and public property to be parked, and stacked, and turned over to the officers appointed by me to receive them. This will not embrace the side arms of the officers, nor their private horses or baggage. This done, each officer and man will be allowed to return to his home, not to be disturbed by the United States authorities so long as they observe their parole, and the laws in force where they may reside, Very respectfully, U. S. Grant, Lieutenant-General.

Lee read the letter and noted that Grant had left out the word *exchanged,* which should have come after *properly*. He penciled it in and read the document again. Lee asked if his cavalry could keep their horses. In the Confederate army, the men owned their horses, while in the Union army, the horses were government-issue. Grant refused that request but then changed his mind, saying that he would not put it in writing but would order his officers to let any man who said he owned the horse he was riding to keep it.

"That will have the best possible effect on my men," Lee said. "It will be very gratifying and will do much toward conciliating our people."

Before he left, Lee asked if the Federals could spare some rations, as his men had not eaten for several days. Grant ordered that 25,000 rations be given to the Confederates.

The surrender over, Lee mounted Traveller and headed northeast, back toward the apple orchard. As he rode, some of his men began to cheer. Lee took off his hat. Tears flowed down his face.

Behind him, the McLean House was stripped of its furniture by Federals fighting each other for souvenirs of the momentous occasion.

It was a much more somber day for the Confederates. One officer cut open the lining of his coat and took out two five-dollar gold pieces. He handed one to his black body servant and told him that he was free to go wherever he wanted, but that he, the officer, would likely go to a prisoner-of-war camp. The black looked at the gold piece and told his former master that they would go to prison together. He had promised his mother—the officer's childhood mammy—that he would bring the officer home safely, and he meant to keep that promise.

When Lee got back to his headquarters on the hill, he made a short speech: "Boys, I have done the best I could for you. Go home now, and if you make as good citizens as you have soldiers, you will do well, and I shall always be proud of you. Good-bye and God bless you all."

Not all of Lee's men surrendered. Several elements of cavalry were able to slip away, including Fitz Lee's troops. During his escape, Robert E. Lee's nephew saw a Confederate infantryman hurrying toward Appomattox Court House. Fitz Lee told the soldier it was no use, that Lee had surrendered. The man replied, "No, Uncle Robert would never do that. It must have been that dammed Fitz Lee!"

Several sites of interest are located within about 100 yards of the McLean House.

Walk to the museum. Among the displays here is one that mentions the 36 black men who surrendered with Lee. Most of them were teamsters, cooks, blacksmiths, or musicians. One of the last people killed in the war was Hannah, a black civilian who was mortally wounded when an errant Union artillery round crashed through her home—which was located nearby—and tore off her arm.

Near the museum is the tavern where the Federals set up a printing press to produce the paroles that all the Confederates were issued.

Walk past the tavern toward the Surrender Triangle, the open patch of land where the Confederate army marched on April 12 for the formal stacking of arms. Lee was not present on that sad occasion.

Surrender Triangle

The stacking ceremony was dramatic. The Confederates were led up the road four abreast by General John Gordon. Though Grant had accepted Lee's surrender, the men were unsure what would happen to them. Some feared they would be executed on the spot. Most expected some form of humiliation.

As the first Confederates neared the first Federals in line, the general commanding the Federals, Joshua L. Chamberlain of Maine, had his men "present arms," an arms movement in which the soldiers put their muskets in front of their chests. It was meant as a show of respect. No soldier made a sound—no jeers, no sneers. Chamberlain's command for the Federals to salute the Confederates they had been fighting for four years was the first gesture of conciliation of the postwar period.

Gordon, shocked and pleased, spurred his horse on to its hind legs. He then drew his saber and swept it from in front of his face down to the ground with a flourish—an officer's salute.

Near the Surrender Triangle is a house with a cannon in the front yard. One of the last shots of the Appomattox campaign was fired from this house. The Confederate cannon crew had not yet gotten word that a truce was in place. The shell killed at least two Federals.

Just beyond the house is the spot where Grant and Lee met one more time, the morning after the surrender. Grant gently asked Lee if he would write a letter to the other Confederate commanders in the field around the South, asking them to surrender as he had done. Lee refused, saying he was the general of only one army, not the leader of the Confederate government.

Though Lee did not watch or participate in the surrender ceremony, he wanted his men to know he was with them in spirit. Before he left for Richmond on April 12, he wrote out the following, the last order he issued:

> Headquarters Army of Northern Virginia, April 10, 1865, General Orders No. 9: After four years of arduous service marked by unsurpassed courage and fortitude, the Army of Northern Virginia has been compelled to yield to overwhelming numbers and resources.
>
> I need not tell the brave survivors of so many hard fought battles, who have remained steadfast to the last, that I have consented to this result from no distrust of them. But feeling that valor and devotion could accomplish nothing that could compensate for the loss that must have attended the continuance of the contest, I determined to avoid the useless slaughter of those whose past services have endeared them to their countrymen.
>
> By the terms of the agreement, officers and men can return to their homes and remain until exchanged. You will take with you the satisfaction that proceeds from the consciousness of duty faithfully performed, and I earnestly pray that a merciful God will extend to you His blessing and protection.
>
> With an unceasing admiration of your constancy and devotion to your Country, and a grateful remembrance of your kind and generous consideration for myself, I bid you all an affectionate farewell. R. E. Lee, General.

Take time to walk around Appomattox Court House. This is a quiet, reverent place, the spot where one country died and another was reborn.

Appendix

Museums and Other Historical Attractions

Virginia

Appomattox Court House
Box 218
Appomattox, Va. 24522
804-352-8987

Arlington National Cemetery
Arlington, Va. 22211-5003
703-695-3250

Belle Boyd Cottage
101 Chester Street
Front Royal, Va. 22630
540-636-1446

Belle Grove Plantation/
Cedar Creek Battlefield
336 Belle Grove Road
Middletown, Va. 22645
540-869-2028

Berkeley Plantation
12602 Harrison Landing
Charles City, Va. 23030
804-829-6018

Beth Ahabah Museum and Archives
1109 West Franklin Street
Richmond, Va. 23220
804-353-2668

Blandford Church
319 South Crater Road
Petersburg, Va. 23803
800-368-3595

Boyhood Home of Robert E. Lee
607 Oronoco Street
Alexandria, Va. 22314
703-548-8454

Brandy Station Foundation
P.O. Box 165
Brandy Station, Va. 22714
540-825-0433

Casemate Museum
P.O. Box 341
Fort Monroe, Va. 23651
804-727-3391

Christ Church
118 North Washington Street
Alexandria, Va. 22314
703-549-1450

City Point Unit of
Petersburg National Battlefield
1539 Hickory Hill Road
Petersburg, Va. 23804
804-458-9504

Cumberland Gap National Historical
Park
   Box 1848
   Middlesboro, Ky. 40965
   606-248-2817

Danville Museum
   975 Main Street
   Danville, Va. 24543
   804-793-5644

Evelynton Plantation
   6701 John Tyler Highway
   Charles City, Va. 23030
   800-473-5075

Exchange Hotel
   P.O. Box 542
   Gordonsville, Va. 22942
   540-832-2944

Fort Norfolk
   P.O. Box 6367
   Norfolk, Va. 23508
   757-625-1720

Fort Ward
   4301 West Braddock Road
   Alexandria, Va. 22304
   703-838-4848

Frank Sanders Memorial Park
   P.O. Box 730
   Saltville, Va. 24370
   540-496-5342

Fredericksburg and Spotsylvania
Court House National Military Park
   120 Chatham Lane
   Fredericksburg, Va. 22405
   540-373-6122

Fredericksburg Area Museum
   907 Princess Anne Street
   Fredericksburg, Va. 22401
   540-371-3037

Hampton Roads Naval Museum
   1 Waterside Drive, Suite 248
   Norfolk, Va. 23510
   757-444-8971

Historic Fork Inn
   19621 Namozine Road
   Sutherland, Va. 23885
   804-265-8591

Historic Staunton Foundation
   120 South Augusta Street
   Staunton, Va. 24401
   540-885-7676

Hollywood Cemetery
   412 South Cherry Street
   Richmond, Va. 23220
   804-648-8501

Lee Chapel
   Washington and Lee University
   Lexington, Va. 24450
   540-463-8768

Loudon County Museum
16 Loudon Street SW
Leesburg, Va. 22075
703-777-8331

The Lyceum
201 South Washington Street
Alexandria, Va. 22314
703-838-4994

Lynchburg Museum
901 Court Street
Lynchburg, Va. 24504
804-847-1459

Manassas Museum
P.O. Box 560
Manassas, Va. 20108
703-368-1873

Manassas National Battlefield Park
12521 Lee Highway
Manassas, Va. 22110
703-754-1861

Mariners Museum
100 Museum Drive
Newport News, Va. 23606
800-581-7245

Museum of the Confederacy/
White House of the Confederacy
1201 East Clay Street
Richmond, Va. 23219
804-649-1861

Natural Bridge Inn
P.O. Box 57
Natural Bridge, Va. 24578
540-291-2121

Natural Bridge Wax Museum
P.O. Box 85
Natural Bridge, Va. 24578
540-291-2426

New Market Battlefield Historical
Park/Hall of Valor Museum
P.O. Box 1864
New Market, Va. 22844
540-740-3101

Old Jail Museum
P.O. Box 675
Warrenton, Va. 20188
540-347-5525

Pamplin Park Civil War Site
6523 Duncan Road
Petersburg, Va. 23803
804-861-2408

Pest House Medical Museum/
Old City Cemetery
401 Taylor Street
Lynchburg, Va. 24501
804-847-1465

Petersburg National Battlefield
1539 Hickory Hill Road
Petersburg, Va. 23803
804-732-3531

Portsmouth Naval Shipyard Museum
420 High Street
Portsmouth, Va. 23704
804-393-8983

Richmond National Battlefield Park
(Tredegar Iron Works, Chimborazo,
Cold Harbor, Fort Harrison)
3215 East Broad Street
Richmond, Va. 23223
804-226-1981

Shenandoah Valley Folk Art
and Heritage Center
382 High Street
Dayton, Va. 22821
540-879-2681

Sherwood Forest Plantation
P.O. Box 8
Charles City, Va. 23030
804-829-5377

Siege Museum
15 West Bank Street
Petersburg, Va. 23803
804-733-2404

Society of Port Republic
Preservationists
P.O. Box 62
Port Republic, Va. 24471
540-249-5689

Spotsylvania County Museum
8956 Courthouse Road
Spotsylvania, Va. 22553
703-582-7167

Spotsylvania Court House Battlefield
120 Chatham Lane
Fredericksburg, Va. 22405
540-371-0802

St. Paul's Church
815 East Grace Street
Richmond, Va. 23219
804-643-3589

Stonewall Jackson House
8 East Washington Street
Lexington, Va. 24450
540-463-2552

Stonewall Jackson Museum
at Hupp's Hill
33229 Old Valley Pike
Strasburg, Va. 22657
540-465-5884

Stonewall Jackson's Headquarters
415 Braddock Street
Winchester, Va. 22601
540-667-3242

Stratford Hall Plantation
Stratford, Va. 22558
804-493-8038

United States Army
Quartermaster Museum
1201 22nd Street
Fort Lee, Va. 23801-1601
804-734-4203

Valentine Museum
   1015 East Clay Street
   Richmond, Va. 23219
   804-649-0711

Virginia Historical Society
   428 North Boulevard Street
   Richmond, Va. 23221
   804-358-4901

Virginia Military Institute Museum
   Jackson Memorial Hall
   Lexington, Va. 24450
   540-464-7232

Virginia War Museum
   9285 Warwick Road
   Newport News, Va. 23607
   757-247-8523

Warren Rifles Museum
   95 Chester Street
   Front Royal, Va. 22630
   540-636-6982

Yorktown National Battlefield Park
   Box 210
   Yorktown, Va. 23690
   757-898-3400

West Virginia

Barbour County Historical Society
   146 North Main Street
   Philippi, W.V. 26416
   304-457-4846

Belle Boyd House
   126 East Race Street
   Martinsburg, W.V. 25401
   304-267-4713

Carnifax Ferry Battlefield
   Route 2, Box 435
   Summersville, W.V. 26651
   304-872-0825

Craik-Patton House
   2809 Kanawha Boulevard
   Charleston, W.V. 25301
   304-925-5341

Droop Mountain Battlefield
State Park
   H.C. 64, Box 189
   Hillsboro, W.V. 24946
   304-653-4254

Greenbriar Hotel
   300 West Main Street
   White Sulphur Springs, W.V. 24986
   304-536-1110

Harpers Ferry National
Historical Park
   P.O. Box 65
   Harpers Ferry, W.V. 25425
   304-535-6223

Jackson's Mill Historic Area
   Route 1, Box 210-D
   Weston, W.V. 26452
   304-269-5100

Jefferson County Courthouse
    100 East Washington Street
    Charles Town, W.V. 25414
    304-728-3240

Jefferson County Museum
    200 East Washington Street
    Charles Town, W.V. 25414
    304-725-8628

North House Museum
    301 West Washington Street
    Lewisburg, W.V. 24901
    304-645-3398

Organ Cave
    417 Masters Road
    Ronceverte, W.V. 24970
    304-645-7600

Randolph County Historical Society
    P.O. Box 1164
    Elkins, W.V. 26241

Rich Mountain Battlefield
Foundation
    P.O. Box 227
    Beverly, W.V. 26253
    304-637-RICH

West Virginia Division of
Culture and History
    Cultural Center
    1900 Kanawha Boulevard East
    Charleston, W.V. 25305-0300
    304-558-0220

Chambers of Commerce and Information Centers

Virginia

Abingdon Convention
and Visitors Bureau
    335 Cummings Street
    Abingdon, Va. 24210
    800-435-3440

Alexandria Visitors Bureau/
Ramsey House Visitors Center
    221 King Street
    Alexandria, Va. 22314
    703-838-4200

Bath County Chamber of Commerce
    P.O. Box 718
    Hot Springs, Va. 24445
    540-839-5409

Charlottesville Visitors Center
    P.O. Box 178
    Charlottesville, Va. 22902
    804-977-1783

Culpeper Chamber of Commerce
    133 West Davis Street
    Culpeper, Va. 22701
    540-825-8628

Danville Visitors Center
    636 Main Street
    Danville, Va. 24543
    804-793-5422

Fredericksburg Visitors Center
706 Caroline Street
Fredericksburg, Va. 22401
800-678-4748

Greater Lynchburg Visitors Center
216 12th Street
Lynchburg, Va. 24504
804-847-1811

Hampton Visitor Center
710 Settlers Landing Road
Hampton, Va. 23669
800-800-2202

Harrisonburg Visitors Bureau
10 East Gay Street
Harrisonburg, Va. 22802
540-434-2319

Hopewell Visitor Center
201 Randolph Square, Suites C–E
Hopewell, Va. 23860
800-863-8687

Lexington Visitors Center
106 East Washington Street
Lexington, Va. 24450
540-463-3777

Loudoun Tourism Council
108-D South Street
Leesburg, Va. 20175
703-771-2170

Norfolk Visitors Center
232 East Main Street
Norfolk, Va. 23510
800-368-3097

Orange County Visitors Bureau
P.O. Box 133
Orange, Va. 22960
540-672-1653

Petersburg Visitors Center
425 Cockade Alley
Petersburg, Va. 23803
800-368-3595

Portsmouth Visitors Center
505 Crawford Street, Suite 2
Portsmouth, Va. 23704
800-767-8782

Spotsylvania County Visitors Center
4704 Southpoint Parkway
Fredericksburg, Va. 22407
800-654-4118

Warrenton/Fauquier County
Visitor Center
183-A Keith Street
Warrenton, Va. 20186
800-820-1021

Williamsburg Visitors Bureau
P.O. Box 3585
Williamsburg, Va. 23187
757-253-0192

Winchester/Frederick County
Visitor Bureau
    1360 South Pleasant Valley Road
    Winchester, Va. 22601
    540-662-4135

Wytheville Visitors Bureau
    150 East Monroe Street
    Wytheville, Va. 24382
    540-223-3355

West Virginia

Beckley/Southern West Virginia
Visitors Bureau
    P.O. Box 1799
    Beckley, W.V. 25802
    304-252-2244

Charles Town/Jefferson County
Chamber of Commerce
    P.O. Box 426
    Charles Town, W.V. 25414
    304-725-2055

Charleston Visitors Bureau
    200 Civic Center Drive
    Charleston, W.V. 25301
    304-344-5075

Grafton/Taylor County Visitors
Bureau
    214 West Main Street
    Grafton, W.V. 26354
    304-265-3938

Hurricane Visitors Bureau
    P.O. Box 1806
    Hurricane, W.V. 25526
    304-562-5896

Lewisburg Visitors Center
    105 Church Street
    Lewisburg, W.V. 24901
    304-645-1000

Martinsburg/Berkeley County
Visitors Bureau
    208 South Queen Street
    Martinsburg, W.V. 25401
    304-264-8801

Philippi/Barbour County
Chamber of Commerce
    P.O. Box 5000
    Philippi, W.V. 26416
    304-457-1958

Shepherdstown Visitors Center
    102 East German Street
    Shepherdstown, W.V. 25443
    304-876-2786

Weston/Lewis County Visitors Bureau
    P.O. Box 379
    Weston, W.V. 26452
    304-269-7328

White Sulphur Springs
Visitors Bureau
    34 West Main Street
    White Sulphur Springs, W.V. 24986
    304-536-9440

Bibliography

Adams, Charles. *The Civil War in the Shenandoah Valley: An Auto Tour Guide.* Shepherdstown, W.V.: Self-published, 1995.

———. *Roadside Markers in West Virginia.* Shepherdstown, W.V.: Self-published, 1995.

Allardice, Bruce S. *More Generals in Gray: A Companion Volume to* Generals in Gray. Baton Rouge: Louisiana State University Press, 1995.

Angle, L. C., Jr. "The Story of the Martha Washington Inn." *Historical Society of Washington County (Va.) Bulletin* (series 2, number 28, 1991).

Boyd, Belle. *Belle Boyd in Camp and Prison.* 1865. Reprint, Berkeley County Historical Society.

Bright, Simeon Miller. "The McNeill Rangers: A Study in Confederate Guerrilla Warfare." *West Virginia History* 12: 338–87.

Brookshire, William R., and David K. Snider. *Glory at a Gallop: Tales of the Confederate Cavalry.* McLean, Va.: Brassy's, 1993.

Calkins, Christopher M. *The Appomattox Campaign: March 29 to April 9, 1865.* Conshohocken, Pa.: Combined Books, 1997.

———. *From Petersburg to Appomattox.* Farmville, Va.: Farmville Herald, 1993.

———. *Thirty-six Hours before Appomattox.* Spotsylvania Court House, Va.: Self-published, 1980.

Cohen, Stan B. *The Civil War in West Virginia: A Pictorial History.* Charleston, W.V.: Pictorial Histories Publishing Company, 1976.

———. *A Pictorial Guide to West Virginia's Civil War Sites.* Charleston, W.V.: Pictorial Histories Publishing Company, 1990.

Coski, John M. *The Army of the Potomac at Berkeley Plantation: The Harrison's Landing Occupation of 1862.* Self-published, 1989.

Coulling, Mary Price. *The Lee Girls.* Winston-Salem, N.C.: John F. Blair, Publisher, 1987.

———. *Margaret Junkin Preston: A Biography.* Winston-Salem, N.C.: John F. Blair, Publisher, 1993.

Cromie, Alice Hamilton. *A Tour Guide to the Civil War.* Chicago: Quadrangle Books, 1964.

Cullen, Joseph. *Richmond Battlefields: A History and Guide to Richmond National Battlefield Park.* Washington: GPO, 1992.

Current, Richard N., ed. *Encyclopedia of the Confederacy.* 4 vols. New York: Simon & Schuster, 1993.

Davis, Burke. *J. E. B. Stuart: The Last Cavalier*. New York: Bonanza Books, 1957.

———. *They Called Him Stonewall: A Life of Lieutenant General T. J. Jackson, C.S.A.* New York: Wings Books, 1954.

———. *To Appomattox: Nine April Days, 1865*. New York: Rinehart & Company, 1959.

Davis, William. *Battle at Bull Run*. New York: Doubleday & Company, 1977.

Delauter, Roger U., Jr. *McNeill's Rangers*. Lynchburg, Va.: H. E. Howard, 1986.

Dickinson, Jack. *Jenkins of Greenbottom*. Charleston, W.V.: Pictorial Histories Publishing Company, 1988.

Dooley, Louise K. "Little Sorrel: A War Horse for Stonewall." *Army Magazine* (April 1975): 34–39.

Drewey, William Sidney. *The Southampton Insurrection*. Washington: Neal Company, 1900.

Evans, Thomas J., and James M. Moyer. *Mosby's Confederacy*. Shippensburg, Pa.: White Mane Publishing Company, 1991.

Everhart, William C., and Arthur L. Sullivan. *John Brown's Raid*. Washington: National Park Service, 1973.

Ezekiel, Herbert T., and Gaston Lichtenstein. *History of the Jews in Richmond, 1769–1917*. Richmond, Va.: Self-published, 1917.

Faust, Patricia L., ed. *Historical Times Illustrated Encyclopedia of the Civil War*. New York: Harper & Row, 1986.

Fleming, Martin K. "The Northwestern Virginia Campaign of 1861." *Blue & Gray* (August 1993): 10–63.

Forman, Stephen M. "A Glimpse of Wartime Washington." *Blue & Gray* (Spring 1996): 8–61.

Freeman, Douglas Southall. *Lee's Lieutenants*. 3 vols. New York: Charles Scribner's Sons, 1942.

———. *R. E. Lee*. 4 vols. New York: Charles Scribner's Sons, 1961.

Furgurson, Ernest B. *Chancellorsville 1863: The Souls of the Brave*. New York: Alfred A. Knopf, 1992.

Gallagher, Gary W. "Brandy Station: The Civil War's Bloodiest Arena of Mounted Combat." *Blue & Gray* (October 1990): 8–56.

Glatthaar, Joseph T. *Forged in Battle: The Civil War Alliance of Black Soldiers and White Officers*. New York: Free Press, 1990.

Hagerman, Keppel. *Dearest of Captains: A Biography of Sally Louisa Tompkins*. White Stone, Va.: Brandywine Publishers, 1996.

Haley, Megan. *The African-American Experience in Thomas Jonathan "Stonewall" Jackson's Lexington*. Lexington, Va.: Historic Lexington Foundation, 1994.

Hartley, Chris J. *Stuart's Tarheels: James B. Gordon and His North Carolina Cavalry.* Baltimore: Butternut & Blue, 1996.

Hastings, Earl C., Jr., and David Hastings. *A Pitiless Rain: The Battle of Williamsburg, 1862.* Shippensburg, Pa.: White Mane Publishing Company, 1997.

Heatwole, John L. *The Burning: Sheridan in the Shenandoah Valley.* Charlottesville, Va.: Rockbridge Publishing, 1998.

Hennessy, John J. *Return to Bull Run: The Campaign and Battle of Second Manassas.* New York: Simon & Schuster, 1993.

Holsworth, Jerry W. "The Story of Winchester, Virginia, in the Civil War." *Blue & Gray* (Winter 1997): 6–61.

Horn, John. *The Petersburg Campaign.* Conshohocken, Pa.: Combined Books, 1993.

Hotchkiss, Jedediah. *Make Me a Map of the Valley: The Civil War Journal of Stonewall Jackson's Topographer.* Dallas: Southern Methodist University Press, 1973.

Imboden, John D. "Jackson at Harpers Ferry in 1861." In *Battles and Leaders of the Civil War*, vol. 1, edited by Robert Underwood Johnson and Clarence Clough Buel. New York: Thomas Yoseloff, 1899.

In and around Culpeper: Walking and Driving Tours of a Virginia Piedmont Town. Culpeper, Va.: Museum of Culpeper History, 1998.

Jones, J. William. *Christ in the Camp.* B. F. Johnson & Company, 1887.

Jones, Terry L. *Lee's Tigers: The Louisiana Infantry in the Army of Northern Virginia.* Baton Rouge: Louisiana State University Press, 1987.

Jones, Virgil Carrington. *Ranger Mosby.* Chapel Hill: University of North Carolina Press, 1944.

Kennedy, Frances H., ed. *The Civil War Battlefield Guide.* 2nd ed. Boston: Houghton Mifflin, 1998.

Korn, Bertram. *American Jewry and the Civil War.* Marietta, Ga.: R. Bemis Publishing, 1995.

Lee, Richard M. *General Lee's City: An Illustrated Guide to the Historic Sites of Confederate Richmond.* McLean, Va.: EPM Publications, 1987.

Lesser, W. Hunter. *Battle at Corricks Ford: Confederate Disaster and Loss of a Leader.* Parsons, W.V.: McClain Printing Company, 1993.

Lowry, Terry. *The Battle of Scary Creek.* Charleston, W.V.: Pictorial Histories Publishing Company, 1982.

———. *Last Sleep: The Battle of Droop Mountain.* Charleston, W.V.: Pictorial Histories Publishing Company, 1996.

———. *September Blood.* Charleston, W.V.: Pictorial Histories Publishing Company, 1985.

Luvaas, Jay, and Joseph Cullen. *Appomattox Court House*. Washington: National Park Service, 1980.

Marvel, William. "The Battle of Saltville: Massacre or Myth?" *Blue & Gray* (August 1991): 10–60.

McKinney, Tim. *The Civil War in Fayette County, West Virginia*. Charleston, W.V.: Pictorial Histories Publishing Company, 1988.

Mewborn, Horace. "A Wonderful Exploit: J. E. B. Stuart's Ride around the Army of the Potomac." *Blue & Gray* (August 1998): 6–65.

Miller, O. R. "Skirmish at Hurricane Bridge." *Celebrating 110 Years in Hurricane, West Virginia* (1998): 24–28.

Moore, Samuel T., Jr. *Moore's Complete Civil War Guide to Richmond*. Richmond, Va.: Self-published, 1978.

Nesbitt, Mark. *Rebel Rivers: A Guide to Civil War Sites on the Potomac, Rappahannock, York, and James*. Mechanicsburg, Pa.: Stackpole Books, 1993.

Oates, Stephen B. *A Woman of Valor: Clara Barton and the Civil War*. New York: Free Press, 1994.

O'Neill, Robert F., Jr. "The Fight for the Loudoun Valley: Aldie, Middleburg, and Upperville, Virginia, Opening Battles of the Gettysburg Campaign." *Blue & Gray* (October 1993): 12–60.

Owen, Richard, and James Owen. *Generals at Rest: The Grave Sites of the 425 Official Confederate Generals*. Shippensburg, Pa.: White Mane Publishing Company, 1997.

Patrick, Rembert. *The Fall of Richmond*. Baton Rouge: Louisiana State University Press, 1960.

Peters, James Edward. *Arlington National Cemetery: Shrine to America's Heroes*. Kensington, Md.: Woodbine House, 1986.

Pryor, Elizabeth Brown. *Clara Barton: Professional Angel*. Philadelphia: University of Pennsylvania Press, 1987.

Read, Beverly. "The Painting of the Battle of New Market." Unpublished article available at the Virginia Military Institute Museum, 1988.

Rhea, Gordon C. *The Battle of the Wilderness, May 5–6, 1864*. Baton Rouge: Louisiana State University Press, 1994.

———. *The Battles for Spotsylvania Court House and the Road to Yellow Tavern, May 7–12, 1864*. Baton Rouge: Louisiana State University Press, 1997.

Riggs, David F. "Stonewall Jackson's Raincoat." *Civil War Times Illustrated* 16 (July 1977): 37–41.

Robertson, James I., Jr. *Civil War Sites in Virginia*. Charlottesville: University Press of Virginia, 1982.

————. *General A. P. Hill: The Story of a Confederate Warrior*. New York: Random House, 1987.

————. *Stonewall Jackson: The Man, the Soldier, the Legend*. New York: Macmillan, 1997.

Salmon, John. *A Guidebook to Virginia's Historical Markers*. Charlottesville: University Press of Virginia, 1994.

Sandburg, Carl. *Abraham Lincoln: The War Years*. New York: Harcourt Brace, 1939.

Sears, Stephen W. *To the Gates of Richmond: The Peninsula Campaign*. New York: Ticknor & Fields, 1992.

Sifakis, Stewart. *Who Was Who in the Civil War*. New York: Facts on File Publications, 1988.

Simonhoff, Harry. *Jewish Participants in the Civil War*. New York: Arco Publishing Company, 1963.

Snell, Charles W. "The Town of Harpers Ferry in 1859: A Physical History." Unpublished paper available at Harpers Ferry National Historical Park, 1959.

Sommers, Richard J. *Richmond Redeemed: The Siege at Petersburg*. Garden City, N.Y.: Doubleday & Company, 1981.

Stackpole, Edward J. *The Fredericksburg Campaign*. Harrisburg, Pa.: Stackpole Books, 1957.

Standing Ground: The Civil War in the Shenandoah Valley. Shenandoah Publishing House, 1996.

Stutler, Boyd. *West Virginia in the Civil War*. Charleston, W.V.: Education Foundation, 1963.

Tanner, Robert G. *Stonewall in the Valley: Thomas J. "Stonewall" Jackson's Shenandoah Valley Campaign, Spring 1862*. New York: Doubleday & Company, 1976.

Thomas, Emory M. *Bold Dragoon: The Life of J. E. B. Stuart*. New York: Harper & Row, 1986.

Tragle, Henry I. "Southampton Slave Revolt." *American History Illustrated* 6 (November 1971): 4–11.

Trudeau, Noah André. *Like Men of War: Black Troops in the Civil War, 1862–1865*. New York: Little, Brown & Company, 1998.

Tucker, Cary S. "Virginia Military Institute Cadet Battery Guns." *Military Collector & Historian* (Winter 1961).

Van Lew, Elizabeth. *A Yankee Spy in Richmond: The Civil War Diary of "Crazy Bet" Van Lew*. Edited by David D. Ryan. Mechanicsburg, Pa.: Stackpole Books, 1996.

Velazquez, Loreta. *A Woman in Battle: A Narrative of the Exploits and Adventures of a Woman Officer in the Confederate Army*. Santa Barbara, Calif.: Bellerophon Books, 1996.

Walker, Gary C. *The War in Southwest Virginia, 1861–1865*. Roanoke, Va.: A & W Enterprises, 1985.

Warner, Ezra, Jr. *Generals in Blue: Lives of the Union Commanders*. Baton Rouge: Louisiana State University Press, 1964.

———. *Generals in Gray: Lives of the Confederate Commanders*. Baton Rouge: Louisiana State University Press, 1959.

Welsh, Jack D. *Medical Histories of Confederate Generals*. Kent, Ohio: Kent State University Press, 1995.

———. *Medical Histories of Union Generals*. Kent, Ohio: Kent State University Press, 1996.

Wert, Jeffrey. *General James Longstreet: The Confederacy's Most Controversial Soldier*. New York: Simon & Schuster, 1993.

———. *Mosby's Rangers*. New York: Simon & Schuster, 1990.

Wertz, Jay, and Edwin Bearss. *Smithsonian's Great Battles and Battlefields of the Civil War*. New York: William Morrow & Company, 1997.

Whitehorne, Joseph W. A. *The Battle of Cedar Creek*. Strasburg, Va.: Wayside Museum of American History and Arts, 1987.

Zinn, Jack. *The Battle of Rich Mountain*. Parsons, W.V.: McClain Publishing Company, 1971.

Index

relationship with Traveller, 138; religion, 201; statue of, 192; tent of, 321; uniform of, 322
Lee, Robert E., Jr., 122, 133, 136-37
Lee, Sydney, 9
Lee, William Henry "Rooney," 133, 136
Lee Chapel, 134-38
Lee House (Lexington), 131-32
Lee House (Richmond), 326
Lee Jackson House, 133-34
Lee's Mill, 287
Leesburg, Va., 40
Lewis, Jim, 126-27, 261
Lewisburg, W.V., 88-90
Lewisburg Confederate Cemetery, 89-90
Lexington, Va., 121-43,
Lexington Presbyterian Church, 127
Libby Prision, 299
Lightburn, Joseph, 77, 78
Lilly, Robert, 149
Limber, Jim, 324
Lincoln, Abraham, 4, 18, 37, 41, 67, 83, 97, 225, 229, 273, 293, 295-296, 311-12, 341, 342, 362
Lincoln, Mary, 311, 312
Lincoln Museum, 109
Little Sorrel, 140, 143
Lockett Farm, 364, 365, 366
Logan House, 169-70
Long, Armistead, 194
Longstreet, James: at Clark's Mountain, 198; at Cumberland Church, 369; at Farmville, 368; at Fredericksburg, 228; at Second Manassas, 25, 27; at the Wilderness, 249, 252-54; children's deaths, 334; reaction to

surrender talk, 369, 373, 375; relationship with Custer, 377
Loring, William W., 52, 146, 171
Loudon County Museum, 40
Loudon Heights, 66
Lowe, Thaddeus, 286-87
Louisiana troops, 25, 153-54
Lyceum, The, 7
Lucy Long, 132, 139

McCampbell Inn, 127
McCausland, John, 47, 49, 101-2
McClellan, George: as battlefield leader, 41, 81, 225; at Harpers Ferry, 67; at Harrison's Landing, 292, 293; at Peninsula Campaign, 33, 287-88; at Rectortown, 37; at Rich Mountain, 82-83; at Seven Days, 300, 301, 303, 307, 308; replaces John Pope, 20
McCoull House, 260
McDowell, Va., 145-46
McDowell, Irvin, 12-13, 20-21, 83
McGuire, Hunter, 168, 245, 251
McLean, Wilmer, 10, 375
McLean House, 376-79
McMechen House, 46-47
McNeill, Jesse, 50-51, 52
McNeill, John Hanson, 48-49, 161-62
McNeill's Rangers (18th Va. Cavalry), 47-48, 51
Magruder, John, 287-88
Mahone, William, 349, 350, 351, 365
Malbourne, 266
Malvern Hill, 306-7
Manassas Museum, 27
Manassas National Battlefield, 20-27